DOROTHEA'S WAR

The Diary of a First World War Nurse

Edited by

RICHARD CREWDSON

Weidenfeld & Nicolson

LONDON

First published in Great Britain in 2013
by Weidenfeld & Nicolson

1 3 5 7 9 10 8 6 4 2

A CIP catalogue record for this book is available from the British Library.

ISBN: 978 0 297 86918 4

Designed by Bryony Clark
Printed and bound by CPI Group (UK) Ltd, Croydon, CR0 4YY

The Orion Publishing Group's policy is to use papers that are natural,
renewable and recyclable and made from wood grown in sustainable forests.
The logging and manufacturing processes are expected to conform
to environmental regulations of the country of origin.

Weidenfeld & Nicolson
Orion Publishing Group Ltd
Orion House
5 Upper Saint Martin's Lane
London, WC2H 9EA

An Hachette UK Company

www.orionbooks.co.uk

CONTENTS

ACKNOWLEDGEMENTS

The huge amount of encouragement I received from many of my friends and family in the lengthy task of transcribing and annotating this great diary is something for which I shall always be grateful. I have no hesitation in saying that it was worth the effort. In my research into many of the records of the First World War, the source that outshone all the others was the daily notebook kept up throughout the war by Dame Maud McCarthy, and transcribed on to the Scarlet Finders website (www.scarletfinders.co.uk) by Sue Light, to whom my special thanks are due for all her lively support and information. When it came to interpreting medical terms, the help I received in compiling the glossary from my very good friends Bob and Jane Jones (doctor and nurse respectively) was invaluable.

I would like to thank Peter Taylor, Publishing and Licensing Manager at the Imperial War Museum, for his interest and encouragement when I was first seeking a publisher, and to extend my warmest thanks to one of my oldest friends, Godfrey Hodgson, for arranging a memorable and productive meeting with Felicity Bryan, whose advice and enthusiasm opened a number of doors. The one I was happiest to pass through took me to Weidenfeld & Nicolson, where the wisdom and guidance I have constantly received from Bea Hemming has created the happiest of relationships. I would also like to thank Gillian Stern for all her enthusiasm and acute sense of *le mot juste*.

I am deeply grateful to my family for all their help and encouragement. Finally and pre-eminently, Geraldine my wife has given me so much support, not just in the daily round, but as adviser and computer consultant, and with the scanning and collating of all Dorothea's drawings. It has helped to make this book a labour of love.

RICHARD CREWDSON

INTRODUCTION

Dorothea was the aunt I never knew. But on reading her diary for the first time not long ago, I realized that I was now privileged to have a much better sense of what an exceptional person she was in the prime of her life than I could ever have had from getting to know her as a rather elderly relation. She was eleven years older than my father, and would have been in her mid-sixties before I was old enough to carry on any intelligent conversation with her, let alone ask about her reminiscences of the First World War. And would she ever have shown me her diaries? I doubt it.

The diaries remained in my father's possession for nearly seventy years. He kept them to himself; he never talked about them, or showed them to me or my sister. It was only after his death, when I received a letter from the Imperial War Museum to say that my father had expressed a wish to deposit the diaries there, that a search in his desk revealed the seven small notebooks. They were hard-bound and varied in size between 7 × 4½ inches and 3½ × 5½ inches. The scrawled, handwritten entries were obviously written at speed in an immediate, almost breathless style. There were no paragraphs; sentence followed sentence from the beginning to the end of each entry, with the word 'I' used only sparingly. Dorothea had no time for such trifles.

It did not take me long to realize that this was something special. In contrast to so much of the gloom and horror that has been written about the First World War, here was someone, a close relation, recording her experiences of nursing in military hospitals in France continuously for nearly four years with such vitality, wit and warmth. With her level-headed good humour and dedication Dorothea seemed able to cope with any crisis and record it, calmly and intelligently, always keeping a sense of proportion as well as her sense of humour. I was reminded of her Scottish cousins whom I knew well, and were always so full of fun. I felt that this masterpiece could not be kept in obscurity any longer. The diaries themselves are now safely in the permanent care of the Documents Department of the Imperial War Museum, whose patience I very much appreciate, and I am delighted that Dorothea's extraordinary story is finally published here for the first time.

Scattered through the diary at irregular intervals are more than eighty pen-and-ink illustrations, most of which have been reproduced in this book, not necessarily in the same place as they appear in the diary, as more often than not the surrounding text in the original seemed to bear little or no relationship to the drawing. This suggests that Dorothea usually did her drawing first, and then wrote up the diary afterwards (though there is one page in the diary where she clearly intended to do it the other way round, leaving an elegant but empty circular hole in the text!). The third notebook, beginning on 22 August 1916, was the first of the two smaller books, which must have acted as a disincentive to her drawing, as the book is devoid of any sketches. Fortunately Dorothea's artistic instinct revived after she began the next (equally small) book in February 1917 and some of her most amusing sketches appear at the end of that diary, as well as an interesting panorama of the hospitals at Wimereux, where by then she was stationed, with the top of the campanile of Boulogne Cathedral just visible on the horizon.

Like most diarists, Dorothea tried at first to keep up a regular routine of almost daily entries, but this soon evolved into two to four entries a week, which, despite an astonishing amount of letter-writing (to ex-patients as well as to family), she continued until July 1917. Then, without any word of explanation, there is a break of six weeks, and thereafter the entries become more irregular, although often individually longer. At the beginning of the long gap Dorothea had a period of leave, which would of course have broken the diary habit; but why did she not pick up her pen again when she returned to duty? The most likely reason is that at that moment the Third Battle of Ypres (Passchendaele) was raging, and continued throughout the dreadful August when it rained every day of the month, and the Flanders mud took almost as high a toll on the attacking troops as the German gunfire. The casualty rate was horrendous. Dorothea may, for the only time in the war, have been not only exhausted but also overcome by the terrible experiences and suffering of her patients, and unable to write rationally about them. The one letter to her parents and another to her sister Jean that do survive from these weeks say nothing beyond the fact that she is very busy – but, of course, all the nurses' letters would have been subject to censorship. It is interesting that when she did feel able to return to her diary we find her referring to the 'shell shocks' for the first time.

Dorothea spent nearly four years in France in total, working in three different hospitals. With no idea how long the war might last, each decision to 'sign on' for another six months' service could be an agonizing one. After sixteen months at No. 16 Stationary, on the windy clifftops at Le Tréport from June 1915 until October 1916, Dorothea was transferred, with only a day's notice, to No. 32 Stationary, Wimereux. In January 1918, she moved again, this time to No. 46 Stationary, Étaples. Life in the hospitals was hard and challenging, but it was seldom dull; things were constantly changing – busy one day, idle the next, Sisters here today, gone tomorrow, sudden orders to work in a different ward or to go on night duty, social occasions and entertainments, and opportunities to enjoy days off. This healthy mix is reflected throughout the pages of the diary.

When she arrived in France Dorothea was twenty-eight years old, having been born in Clifton, Bristol, in July 1886 and christened Dorothea Mary Lynette. Her father, Henry ('Harry'), after spending some time studying music in Leipzig, had become a solicitor with an office in Clifton. Soon afterwards he moved with the family to Nottingham, where he and Dorothea's mother spent the rest of their lives. She was a Fergusson from Glasgow, an expert watercolourist who for a time had had a close attachment with the painter James Paterson, who was on the fringe of the 'Glasgow Boys'. In Nottingham at weekends Harry, as organist and choirmaster of Holy Trinity Church, Lenton, was able to satisfy his love of music.

So Dorothea, with her sister Jean who was two years older, grew up in an arts-loving household.

The happiest moments of Dorothea's childhood were spent staying with her cousins in Scotland and the Lake District, and many photos survive from this time. The Crewdson family came from Westmorland, and had been established in Kendal for many generations. Many cousins still lived there and in Windermere, as Harry was the youngest of a large family. Dorothea's mother Peggy (Margaret) was one of three sisters, one of whom had married into the Tennant family and had six children, five girls and a boy. There were three boys in the other (Leeds) family. Dorothea's Fergusson grandfather, a prosperous industrialist, had bought a holiday retreat at Lochgoilhead in Argyll, and the photographs show that this was the place where the young cousins of the family had the greatest fun together.

Apart from some photos and a few sketches of happy holidays with her cousins in Scotland and the Lake District, virtually no records survive from Dorothea's childhood and adolescence. We know nothing about her education, though it seems likely that she would have had a governess. By the time she went to France in 1915 she had an enviable command of English, as well as good knowledge of French and German. But what did she do as a teenager and in her early twenties, and why did she not get married? We simply do not know. Such was her personality that she could not fail to have had admirers. Every now and again there is a mention in the diary of an 'old flame' – and in the course of her time in France she would attract plenty of new ones too – but for whatever reasons, she turned her back on them. Her sister Jean had married in 1908, so Dorothea would have been able to see her settling into the genteel domesticities of matrimony. Something must have been pulling her away from this.

Perhaps it was a social conscience. The Women's Social and Political Union (WSPU) was very active in Nottingham at this time. There is a possible clue. One of the best-known Suffragettes was Helen Kirkpatrick Watts, who served two prison sentences while she was a member of the movement. Not only did she live in Lenton, but she was the daughter of the Rev. A.H. Watts, Vicar of Holy Trinity Church, where Dorothea's father was the organist. Since she was about the same age as Dorothea, they must have known each other well. It seems likely that Helen's activities gave Dorothea the incentive to undertake some social work, and in the years before the war she acted as local branch Secretary of the Girls' Friendly Society (GFS), a Christian organization founded in 1875 to support lonely girls (mostly 'in service') who were cut off from home life. She also helped her mother with her work as the local Secretary of the Mothers' Union.

It was in 1911 that Dorothea took the decisive step that would determine her career path in the following years when she enrolled in the British Red Cross for training as a Voluntary Aid Detachment (VAD) nurse, and passed her examinations the next year. It is possible that she was persuaded by her great friend Cristabel ('Christie') Ellis, who lived in nearby Mansfield and travelled to France with Dorothea in 1915.

It is a typical piece of laziness in the use of the English language that individuals should have become known as VADs, when the initials actually stand for the whole 'Detachment'. The label, which was invented soon after the formation of the Territorial Army in 1908, was originally applied to the nursing units established in support of the Territorials, and similarly organized on a county basis. In this way Dorothea found herself enrolled in No. 36 South Notts Detachment, and a pre-war photograph survives of her standing in a single line of nurses, all in spotless Red Cross uniform, alongside a board with 'No. 36 South Nottingham' printed on it. Each of them would become known as a 'VAD'.

Although this is how the VAD nurses were originally enrolled, it was not how they were actually deployed after the Great War began in August 1914. There was no general mobilization whereby a whole detachment was sent off to serve together in a military hospital; it was left to individuals to volunteer. Fortunately in Dorothea's case an ordinary page-a-day diary survives for 1915, which she kept up

The South Notts Detachment in 1913. Dorothea is fourth from the left.

in minuscule writing until the day before she left London on 11th June. From this I have been able to follow the whole process (with its usual dramas of order and counter-order) whereby she and Christie found themselves en route for France.

During this six-month period in 1915, while she was still living at home, scarcely a day passed without Dorothea attending one hospital or another, or doing duty at one of the Nottingham railway stations serving tea and buns to the wounded soldiers on a hospital train. From 9 to 15 January and again from 6 to 12 February she was on duty every day at Nottingham General Hospital. Most of her time was spent cleaning and doing housework, but when free to do so she would follow the doctors around, watching operations and other medical procedures. Before long she was allowed to help with dressings and bandaging. In the intervening weeks she regularly visited hospitals and socialized with the nurses when they were off duty. On 5 March she and a 'lot of Red Cross' were asked by the hospital to come and help because there were many wounded soldiers coming in. She was on duty again at the hospital the following week. Then on 13 March, after several discussions on the subject, she and Christie both sent off their VAD papers offering their services in a military hospital. The following week Dorothea started a month's work at the

Nottingham Women's Hospital. This was real nursing and she was kept very busy, often helping with operations.

On 2 April Dorothea heard from the Red Cross, and although it was suggested that she should interview Matrons in nearby hospitals, she decided instead to go up to headquarters in London to get more information. She took the opportunity of also meeting with the Matron of the Chelsea Military Hospital, where she thought she might like to work. But a very different fate was in store for her and Christie. It was precisely at this time that the Matron-in-Chief and the Director-General of Medical Services (DGMS) at the War Office were coming under great pressure to relax the strict ruling that only fully trained military nurses were allowed to work in military hospitals in France. There were already more than forty British Military Hospitals and Casualty Clearing Stations in France by April 1915, and the need for still more hospitals was relentless. Casualties far exceeded estimates, and the military nursing services were working under extreme pressure. The head of military nursing in France, Miss McCarthy, had been favourably impressed by the VADs she had come across working in Red Cross and other non-military hospitals. Late in March she discussed with the DGMS the possible employment of VADs in the military hospitals. A letter was sent to the War Office recommending that the old ruling be relaxed. About this time too there was constant pressure from individual VADs working in France to be allowed to become military nurses.

The Matron-in-Chief finally accepted the inevitable and gave way. VADs could now be employed in military hospitals in France. By the second week in May, eighty VADs had arrived in France for assignment to these hospitals, and another lot followed shortly afterwards. To her complete surprise Dorothea received a letter on 22 May ordering her to France, and Christie got one the next day. It was a thrilling and unexpected prospect for both of them.

The following week was spent getting their 'trousseau' together. There was then a typical muddle at the Red Cross Headquarters when letters arrived instructing them both to go to Chelsea Military Hospital. This left the girls in great confusion and distress, but

Dorothea's father decided to intervene, and got a telephone message through to Mrs Furze, the Head of the VAD Selection Committee. Finally, on 10 June, having received fresh instructions the previous week, Dorothea and Christie left home for France. They were to report to Matron at No. 16 Stationary Hospital at Le Tréport, a small coastal town and port a few miles north of Dieppe. There were three hospitals at Le Tréport: No. 3 General, which had taken over a large hotel recently opened on top of the high cliffs above the town, No. 2 Canadian, a tented hospital nearby, and No. 16, which had been established in January 1915 and, as Miss McCarthy recorded on 2 April, was now ready to receive 1,000 patients.

According to Dorothea there were already eight VADs working at the hospital, so the professional military nurses there had had some experience of dealing with these keen but unproven volunteers. The core of the nursing services in the First World War military hospitals consisted of the 300 or so members of the Queen Alexandra's Imperial Military Nursing Service (QAIMNS), who had trained from the outset as military nurses, and mostly occupied senior or administrative positions, including the hospital Matrons. This

Dorothea and Christie's departure.
Christie is facing the camera; Dorothea is in the centre.

compared with nearly 11,000 professional nurses of the 'Reserve' (QAIMNSR), who had completed their three years' professional training, but mainly in civilian hospitals. As fully trained nurses they were naturally the senior members of the nursing staff, until the last months of the war, by which time senior VADs had acquired the same level of experience. Within the Reserve, there were actually two ranks, the Sisters and the nurses, and it was normal practice where there was no staff shortage (which there often was) for a Sister to be in charge of several wards with a nurse responsible to her for each. But so far as the VADs were concerned they addressed them all as 'Sister' and worked under their authority until they showed sufficient competence to take charge of a ward without supervision.

In the early years relations between the professionals and the 'amateur' VADs could be difficult. The Sisters had taken up nursing as a career, mostly because they had no alternative – they had to earn a living – and some of them felt resentful at the young lady volunteers who spoke and behaved differently from them. The tougher and more determined VADs had to prove themselves thoroughly capable and not afraid of hard work before this resentment disappeared. As her diary shows, Dorothea was not slow to express an opinion about each of the individual Sisters she got to know; some she loved working with, some she found rather trying, others almost impossible.

At No. 16 General in Le Tréport, her first posting, the divide between the Sisters and the VADs was perhaps accentuated by the Matron, Miss Drage, who was certainly the most formative influence on Dorothea during her first fourteen months. Miss Drage was an excellent, formidable and most efficient Matron, but she made no secret of the fact that when off duty she much preferred the company of the VADs. She seems to have had a real affection for Dorothea in particular. It was hardly surprising that in August 1916, on the day before Matron left for a new posting, Dorothea wrote: 'The Sisters seem to be hugging themselves with joy over her departure.' After she left, the class division, so far as it still existed at Le Tréport, evaporated; at Dorothea's next postings at Wimereux and Étaples it was imperceptible.

In addition to the nursing staff there were the Royal Army Medical Corps (RAMC) orderlies who played an essential part in the ward life of the military hospitals, with responsibility for all the heavy work routinely required in the wards, but also in many cases helping with the nursing care as well, especially at night. Dorothea writes a lot about the orderlies she worked with, whom she classified as excellent, difficult or hopeless. She made a point of cultivating the difficult ones (like Jones at Le Tréport) and really enjoyed establishing good relationships with them.

Given the terrible toll of casualties, so often the first thing we associate with the First World War, it would be natural to assume that throughout the war every ward in the military hospitals in France was continuously packed with wounded soldiers. In fact, except when a major battle was raging, this was not the case, due to the admirable policy adopted by the Army of getting their wounded men back to 'Blighty' (the slang word originally meant a wound bad enough to require the casualty to be sent home, but soon became a term for Britain itself) as soon as they were fit to travel, so that they could be treated and convalesce as near to home as possible. Most of the wounded brought by convoy to the hospitals in France were therefore 'in transit'. If they could be 'patched up' and had the strength to endure the journey, even on a stretcher, they would be sent home. Some, of course, were too badly wounded to travel and died in hospital, despite strenuous and special efforts to restore them to health.

The rapid 'throughput' of wounded men meant that the longer-term patients in the hospitals were those suffering from disease, of whom there were usually a great number. The wards in most hospitals were therefore separately classified as 'surgical' and 'medical' (Dorothea's last hospital in Étaples was an exception – until just before her arrival it had been an isolation hospital, for patients with infectious diseases, with no surgical facilities). As the diary shows, there were times when the medical wards were overrun by the wounded, and the tide could flow the other way too, with medical patients filling up the surgical wards if there was an epidemic of some sort.

Life in the trenches was one of the unhealthiest forms of existence ever experienced over a prolonged period of time, and no one can be surprised at the variety and severity of the illnesses that the hospital staff had to deal with. In addition, in the winter of 1918–19, staff in the medical wards were practically overwhelmed with the great flu epidemic, and the dreaded complication of pneumonia which often proved fatal.

The health of the nurses themselves was always a matter of concern: sick nurses were taken off duty as quickly as possible, and there were special convalescent homes (Hardelot, Mauritien and Villa Tino) where they could be sent to recover. While still at Le Tréport Dorothea was able to enjoy a few days' luxury at No. 3 General (next door to No. 16), one of the first of the British hospitals, which had been a grand hotel before the war, and where there was a ward for sick nurses. 'Here I am at No. 3, packed off all of a sudden for no earthly reason that I can see, to have my bally old finger doctored up,' she complained. In the days before antibiotics a septic finger was of course a good deal more serious than it would be now: as even Dorothea admitted, 'I am always rather nervous of septic fingers, you never know where the mischief will end quite.'

Some of Dorothea's happiest moments were the hours she was able to spend with the 'wee man', her little brother (and my father) Alastair – who by this time was well over six feet tall and a subaltern in the Coldstream Guards. His first appearance in the diary comes in September 1917, when he had been wounded (fortunately not seriously) in the Battle of Passchendaele, and turned up in the next-door hospital at Wimereux. Then in 1918 he was twice sent on training courses near Étaples, where Dorothea was working at the time. They would meet for meals and spend evenings together as often as they could arrange it.

When the war officially came to an end in November 1918 Dorothea had been nursing in France for three and a half years. For most military historians, the grand unintentional symbolism of 11 o'clock on 11/11 provides a backdrop against which they can compose summaries of the previous four years. Their story ends there. By contrast, the

Alastair and Dorothea at Paris-Plage, 2 July 1918

attention of political historians is focused six months or more ahead on the forthcoming Peace Conference. The immediate aftermath of the war has been a neglected subject, but Dorothea's work continued just as before, which makes her diary for this period of particular interest. There are only three entries between Armistice Day and the end of November, but they are long and evocative. Hospital life went on much the same, with very little in the way of celebration, and no sudden reduction in the number of patients, as the flu epidemic intensified. But for the first time in four years Dorothea was able to go home for Christmas, and shortly after her return she was singled out, as the most senior VAD nurse at No. 46 Hospital, to join a party on a three-day motor tour round the battlefields. Her description of this expedition, one of the highlights of her time in France (if only it had not been so icily cold!), is probably unique. February 1919 was notable for the ever-growing number of German soldiers who were being admitted as patients to the hospital, many of them half starving and in terrible condition. Dorothea thought it extraordinary that the British patients treated them with such sympathy and kindness.

There is only one diary entry in March 1919, on the 6th. It took Dorothea to the final page of the last of the notebooks that I discovered in my father's desk. She never started another. By this time all her old friends had departed and she admitted that there was no one now on the hospital staff that she was in the least bit interested in or cared to take up with. She was on night duty, tired, overworked and obviously longing to get home. 'There is a sort of feeling everywhere of just carrying on,' she wrote, 'with everyone rather stale and tired of work and tired of the state of things. But matters are not too bright at home with the flu and strikes and one thing and another. Let's hope that the country pulls itself together soon and emerges better and stronger in every way'. Yet she ends her entry, as so often, on a typically optimistic note: 'This finishes my volume. Next will come the "peace" number of the diary, and will see me home again I expect.'

She never did return to 'dear old Blighty'. Matron McCord's letter to Dorothea's mother written just a week later tells the sad end of the story, which was so sudden that it came as a terrible shock to the family. Dorothea's funeral had already taken place when Matron wrote; she was buried in the Military Cemetery at Étaples. Having been awarded the Military Medal for her bravery during an air raid in May 1918, she was posthumously honoured with the Associate Royal Red Cross Award (ARRC) for her devotion to duty and outstanding service. Dorothea's was a life not wasted, but complete and fulfilled, and the diary is her lasting legacy.

In the absence of any obituary or personal reminiscences there is little scope and really no need to add anything here about Dorothea as a person. The warmth of her personality, her quiet sense of humour, her love of fun (or 'frivoling', as she called it) and her delight in beauty and in nature radiate from the pages that follow. It will be for readers, assisted by her illustrations and her photograph, to recreate her image for themselves.

EDITOR'S NOTE

In editing the diary I have divided it into paragraphs for easier reading, and have added some footnotes where appropriate.

As regards the progress of the war, apart from being warned from time to time to be prepared for a 'big push', which meant that wards had to be cleared for a big intake of casualties, the nurses usually knew nothing more about the broader picture of what was actually going on at the battlefront than what they were able to read in the London daily papers. At the back of the book I have therefore added a few notes under the heading 'Chronology of the War', which may help towards putting Dorothea's comments into context. It is not intended in any way to be read as a comprehensive history of the war. A glossary of medical and military terms used in the diary can also be found on page xxiv.

Finally, as an appendix I have added a tribute to that amazing and indomitable Australian lady, Dame Maud McCarthy, GBE, upon whose energy and common sense the whole of the British Nursing Services in France throughout the war depended.

GLOSSARY OF MEDICAL AND MILITARY
TERMS AND ABBREVIATIONS

Military hospital services in France were broadly concentrated in three types of establishment: the General Hospital, Stationary Hospital and Casualty Clearing Station (CCS).

Blighty Originally Army slang for a wound requiring treatment in an English military hospital, the term quickly changed to mean Great Britain itself

blue-pus A highly contagious bacterial infection of an existing wound

Casualty Clearing Station (CCS) Evolved from the field hospitals of the South African War. Located as close to the battle zone as practicable, they were equipped to do urgent surgery, and it was the responsibility of the medical staff working there to decide whether patients should be sent back immediately to the UK or to a military hospital in France. It was dangerous work, often within enemy artillery range; VAD nurses were never deployed in a CCS.

cerebro-meningitis Inflammation of the brain membranes

clavicle The collar-bone

DGMS Director-General, Medical Services

DI Hospital shorthand for 'dangerously ill'. For all DI patients a nurse was detailed to 'special' the patient, usually on his own in a side ward, and she was not given any other duties.

diphtheria Highly infectious inflammation of mucous membranes

dysentery Inflammation of the large intestine; one of the 'enterics' diseases, usually causing severe diarrhoea

emphysema Breathing difficulties caused by a gas attack (or excessive smoking)

enterics Hospital department dealing with bowel diseases

erysipelas Streptococcal skin infection liable to lead to septicaemia (blood poisoning)

General Hospitals Intended to resemble as closely as possible the major hospitals in the UK, providing comprehensive medical and surgical treatment, with special emphasis on dealing with war wounds and diseases associated with trench warfare. Those opened in the early years of the war were mostly situated in a large hotel or château, well away from the front line, which had been commandeered for the purpose.

GSW Gunshot wounds

haemoptysis Coughing up blood from the lungs

haemorrhaging Reopening or rupture of a blood vessel resulting from wound or after amputation, causing bleeding

jaundice Raised bile level in the blood often caused by hepatitis

Lysol A disinfectant in common use

MO Medical Officer

nephritis Inflammation of the kidney

neurasthenics A diagnosis wrongly applied to shell shock cases

neuritis Inflammation of any nerve

orbit (of eye) The bony surround of the eye

pernicious anaemia A disease caused by low levels of iron in the blood

phlebitis Inflammation of veins (can be caused by standing for long periods)

pleurisy Inflammation of the chest membrane causing side pains

PUO 'Pyrexia [raised temperature] of Unknown Origin' (diagnosis required)

scabiosis Or scabies; a contagious skin disease

shell shock The term was initially discouraged by the authorities, and remained ill defined throughout the war, but came to refer a variety of nervous conditions resulting from exposure to battle

SI Hospital shorthand for 'seriously ill', one level down from DI; special attention still required, patients usually segregated if possible

skillets Medical slang term for physiology

spinal ambulance An ambulance specially adapted to carry patients with spinal injuries

Stationary Hospitals Originally smaller establishments with most of the accommodation under canvas, and intended to take the pressure off the General Hospitals, dealing with less serious cases. But it was not long before the distinction between the two types of hospital became blurred, and tents were routinely replaced with prefabricated huts. Most Stationary Hospitals acquired fully equipped operating theatres, but not all had an officers' wing or Sick Sisters' ward.

swelling of legs Or oedema; symptomatic of high blood pressure, heart failure or kidney disease

TB Tuberculosis: slow to develop, often a pre-war condition

tetanus Muscle spasm, lockjaw, sometimes following severe burns

tonsillitis Inflammation of the throat; can lead to septicaemia

trench fever The most common disease in trench warfare, caused by lice, rarely fatal, but requiring a recovery period of up to a month

trephine A surgical hole made to relieve pressure from bleeding, usually within the skull

X-rays Recently discovered, they provided huge benefits to surgery, but very few precautions were taken against the effects of radiation

PART ONE

No. 16 Stationary, Le Tréport

JUNE 1915 – OCTOBER 1916

584 LE TRÉPORT. — *Le Port et les Falaises d'aval.* — *The harbour and cliffs down the river.*

Seated here in the lounge of the Hôtel de Louvre in Boulogne – can hardly believe we have arrived after such a long time preparing for this great venture. All seems so unreal.

Boulogne is most military. Khaki everywhere – military motors, Red Cross ambulances and private cars speeding along the streets.

Christie and I are the sole remaining members of the VAD party we came over with this morning. At lunchtime the Matron in charge asked for two friends to go south to a hospital in Le Tréport and Christie and I spoke up. All the other nurses went off in two busloads to their hospitals in Étaples. There is a large contingent of Canadian nurses who also stayed behind.

We spent the afternoon wandering about Boulogne, vastly interested in the unusual aspect of the place. Now, after an exhausting day, Christie and I are waiting for supper feeling rather glad of rest.

The hotel here is full of officers coming and going. We're not allowed to tell our friends or relations anything about where we are going. We know it is Number 16 Military Hospital, but Le Tréport must not be mentioned.

SUNDAY, 13TH JUNE, 4 P.M.

In the train on our way to Le Tréport. Christie and I have certainly been seeing life since we landed. We didn't leave Boulogne until after two, so we had time this morning to wander along the quay to look at the hospital ships. Boulogne is under British occupation – the trains, ships, motors and men are all in army use and bent on business. Being Sunday we didn't neglect the good Kirk and went mid-morning to the English service held in a church not far from the hotel.

We are travelling now with the whole party of Canadian nurses who came over with us yesterday. We don't take to them greatly but converse with the ones in our compartment during the journey. They are all on their way to Rouen, but we get out before. As a group they are very active, waving to all the soldiers we pass on the way. We saw a large hut hospital in Étaples and thought this must be where the VADs were sent to yesterday. It looked very nice and fresh with white tents planted in neat rows. The whole life over here is intensely interesting, but a serious atmosphere prevails – much more the real business of war.

MONDAY, 14TH JUNE, 1 P.M.

Christie and I are sitting in the recreation tent after lunch, awaiting the coming of Matron, who I expect will give us orders about going on duty. We arrived yesterday at about six, after parting from our Canadian friends at Eu. One of them came on with us but not to the same hospital. When we got to Le Tréport, there was no one to meet us and we began to think there was something wrong and we were not expected. However, after a little while a motor ambulance tooled down the steep hill, took all our luggage and hustled us off back up the hill to the top of the cliffs.

The hospitals are right by the sea, up on the top of great white chalk cliffs – most airy and breezy. One hospital is in a hotel* and two others are under canvas. When Christie and I arrived, two very kind VADs duly showed us to our tent and helped us get our kit arranged. There are quite a lot of VADs here already, all came about a week ago except for six on night duty. A few of them are St John's Ambulance nurses.

We got more or less settled in after a while. Then, sitting up humble and attentive, we had an interview with Matron† in her sanctum. Supper was all together in the mess tent at about eight, and afterwards we went back to our tent to settle down for the night. It was rather a job but after a while we got things better organized

---

* The hotel, Le Trianon, had first opened just three years earlier, in 1912.
† Miss Drage, whom Dorothea would get to know well, was in charge of nursing at the hospital until August 1916.

8. British Camp On «Les Terrasses» - Camp Anglais sur «Les Terrasses»
Près le Tréport (Seine-Inférieure)

The cliff-top tented hospitals at Le Tréport.
Dorothea's hospital, No. 16, is furthest from the camera.

and tucked ourselves into bed between our blankets and rugs. I slept really very well considering the novelty of the situation.

Up at about 6.15. We dressed with slight difficulties, but managed to arrive at breakfast in fairly good time. We then went down to town by funicular railway and bought various things to add to the furnishings of our abode. We came back laden with parcels and spent the rest of the time until lunch disposing of our goods and getting tidied up.

Lovely bright weather today. Only hope it will last.

WEDNESDAY, 16TH JUNE, 8 P.M.

I forgot to write my diary yesterday and today have started rather late, in fact just now at suppertime. Getting more into the way of things after second whole day of work, though today was very slack, which has made me feel rather exhausted. It is very tiring looking for work.

Yesterday some new soldiers arrived.* They were in the wards when we came on duty and they looked very tired and sad and sore.

---

* The new arrivals were likely to have been soldiers wounded at the Second Battle of Ypres. See Chronology, p.349.

We spent nearly all morning getting them settled in. The doctor, a youthful physician evidently only just qualified, came to see the patients and after preliminary examination went round again to do their dressings. He is young but quite competent. Sister, Miss Jacobs and myself went with him to assist. It was very interesting seeing men fresh from the firing line. Not fresh – poor things – and some of their wounds were rather bad, though none serious.

One man, who had been shot in the chin and fingers, was wonderful while being dressed. The doctor fished about for a long time in his chin and finally got out a big piece of flattened-out bullet, and all the time the man never made a murmur. We were kept busy with this all morning, and there seemed a fair amount to do in the afternoon too before I went off duty from 2 until 6.

Today Christie and I were off duty at different times again so I went on my expedition with a round, rosy-faced VAD called Bownes. Quite jolly and friendly. We went down to town by the steps and had a most lovely view of the tremendously high cliffs, so white and steep. We came back laden with purchases and just managed to catch the funicular railway back up to the camp.

Another very easy day – nothing doing. Much too slack for my liking. Christie and I are now preparing for bed in our bell-tent domain. It's certainly a case of early to bed early to rise. Hope not to be so cold as last night. I bought an extra blanket in town today just in case.

FRIDAY, 18TH JUNE

Have just had hot bathe in my tent canvas bath. First experiment. Answered very well. Feel refreshed and having tidied up and boiled some water in my Etna, I can now write my diary in a quietness of mind till suppertime. Today passed quickly, though the work and the wards were very slack again this morning, especially so through the afternoon.

This morning we saw a large convoy of ambulances driving up to No. 2, the Canadian Hospital. Our turn will probably be next for taking in. Sister Garnett in our ward is quite nice and the

Sister-in-chief is nice too but we don't see so much of her. A man died in one of the wards at the other end of B line this afternoon. He had had an amputation and developed gangrene. He was a nice boy and everyone was sad about it. The very young doctor came round again this morning to do dressings. He is most quaintly youthful in many ways but seems to know what he is about.

Yesterday I found a little more to do but was not exactly busy. Had 2 till 5 off duty and went with a party of bathers to a little hamlet of summer villas nestling in a hollow of the steep white cliffs. Several of the visitors and VADs disported themselves in waves that were very big, almost too much so for comfort. I looked on with two others and wrote letters sitting on a wall in the hot sunshine. Then I walked back with a VAD leaving the bathers to follow after. Lovely air coming straight off the sea. Country here is delightful.

Don't seem to have much news of the war though we get daily papers. When the next convoy comes in perhaps we shall hear more details. C should be coming off duty any minute now. I see very little of her. I like all the VADs I have spoken to so far. Must try to get to know some of them better.

SUNDAY, 20TH JUNE

Sitting on the slopes above the cliffs in this lovely spot. Sea below us, sun shining on the cliffs above Tréport. A really beautiful view and so peaceful.

Yesterday C and I both got 5 till 8 off and went into town to do some shopping. We had various commissions from other people to fulfil and returned rather exhausted, laden with parcels. The weather was still bright and we climbed long steps up to our breezy upland. But it soon turned wild and windy and it was a very cold night.

Such lovely little blue and brown butterflies flit about in the grass round here in the sunlight. Fritillaries and blues, and larks sing early morning. A very delightful spot. Some more of our men went this morning so the wards are very empty now.

WEDNESDAY, 23RD JUNE

Ought to be having a bath this afternoon – just remembered! Too late now! Have been writing letters instead, one to Sheena to acquaint her with the fact that I have had a conversation with Allsopp, a man in Charlie's battalion – Seaforths – who happens, curiously enough, to be in C's wards.* He seems to know about Charlie and told me the story of his last charge. He spoke with admiration unbounded of his attractiveness. Allsopp himself rather resembles Charlie, which is odd. He spoke so nicely. I felt really more about it than I had ever done before. It brought it all home so keenly, speaking to this man over here and comparatively so near to the front. Poor Charlie! I hope and pray he didn't suffer much.

We had rain last night, the first since we came. Christie and I both woke up. Got out of bed, meditated on going out and loosening tent ropes, decided against it and went to sleep again. Nothing happened to our tent but it was difficult to get it to open this morning. Rather shrunk! It is lovely now, so bright and sunny.

Another convoy came in on Monday night. Made us very busy yesterday morning and our wards were nearly full. None of the men were very bad and nearly all are being packed off to base or England tomorrow, so not making long stay.

We are all awaiting a visit of inspection at the hospital here from Miss McCarthy, Matron-in-Chief of Hospitals in France. Seems

---

* Sheena and Charlie Tennant were Dorothea's first cousins. Charlie, the only boy in the family, was killed in action in 1915.

a very redoubtable person and not over-beloved, judging from remarks we hear.*

I enjoy life here very much indeed. Wonderfully healthy and free. Hospital part is sad but the men are very cheery considering and bear their wounds wonderfully well.

FRIDAY, 25TH JUNE

A little white and tabby cat is anxious to get on my knee as I sit here in the Mess tent. She is in fact established there now and gives me quite a feeling of being at home. Weather not very propitious. Woke up this morning to find everything damp and misty and our clothes and furniture and selves very clammy and uncomfortable. Rained while we were working in the wards so donned my mac and souwester to defy the weather and trotted up and down garbed thus. Talk of us moving into huts soon. One of the lines is already quartered there.

Yesterday there was great excitement: Hospital Day of concert and entertainments and in the evening, drinks at the Officers' Mess followed by a dinner party and attendance of only six members of the nursing staff. Lots were drawn by Miss Wall Jacobs on Wednesday evening at the suggestion of Matron. Miss Wall Jacobs won. I didn't get the chance of going to the evening concert and dinner.

The afternoon concert was for patients and the evening one for staff. We were entertained in the tent here. Great do. Delicious tea. Was so greedy and ate so much. The doctors came in too – quite a frivolous and animated scene. Miss W Jacobs seems to have enjoyed the dinner party last night very much. She was telling me about it this morning.

---

* See p. 356 for a brief biographical note on this very remarkable woman.

SUNDAY, 27TH JUNE

Have not had any time all day to write either letters or diary. Now, just scribbling a few words in the tent before preparing for bed. Time about 8.30. Just finished supper. There have been thunderstorms all day – not much thunder but a great deal of rain in heavy showers.

C is singing to an admiring audience in the tent. She has found quite a niche with her lovely voice and is often at the piano. Miss Huntley also gives us many selections. She is tremendously keen on her own singing, rather annoyingly so.

Feel a bit depressed tonight. I was off this morning and went to church with C. Nice little service and good sermon from the little portentous Padre.* Since, have been on duty all afternoon and evening and perhaps am rather tired. Sister Cowie has gone over to the new huts and C and Miss Huntley are working under her. They are not to have any patients until the next convoy comes in and then all the bad ones will go to them in the hut wards.

WEDNESDAY, 30TH JUNE

Just had a bath! Feel a different creature. It is a job though to get the deed done. Since I last wrote great changes have occurred. I am now installed in one of the huts under Sister Cowie and Sister Cavan. Christie and I lead changed lives now. We are so busy I hardly know what to do.

Yesterday morning I received my orders to transfer from B line. I had some regrets but not a broken heart. A convoy had come in during the night and when I got to work there was a mighty task before us – about seventeen patients in, not one of them yet bathed or dressed. Another Sister, Sister Cross, was on duty too and the three of us got to work, making beds and blanket-bathing every-body. Then Mr Cowper came round to do the dressings. There are twenty-four beds in the hut so we are not full up. Still, there was plenty of work with the men we had.

---

* This was none other than the later very celebrated T.B. ('Tubby') Clayton, the founder of the soldiers' rest centre Talbot House at Poperinghe, always known as 'Toc H'.

Things have changed since the first days here, when we VADs were looked down on. We seem to have fallen on our feet under Sister Cowie's regime. She is sweet and really makes no secret of considering us fairly capable. This afternoon I was on alone from 2 until 5 in the ward. I did a fomentation on a man's eye and washed everybody. I bustled round, tidied up, and had no end of a time. Sister Cowie came in occasionally. This evening C is on alone in her ward. Such great and wonderful responsibility is put upon us.

I had a short walk with Miss Arnold this afternoon. I like her very much. She suits me very well. Miss Awdry and Miss Fasker came with us but were rather given the cold shoulder.

Last night, at their invitation, C and I went to call on Miss Jacobs and Miss Haynes. We spent some time with them giggling and gossiping and feeding. I am disgracefully greedy in this place and find I am always eating or wanting to eat and the sight of nice cakes makes my mouth water.

The huts are very nice in some ways but rather stuffy after the tents. They require much more housework. If I had time I would do endless polishing and dusting and tidying.

FRIDAY, 2ND JULY

Nearly time to go back to the camp. Have just finished some correspondence and feel it is a relief to have got the letters written. I am sitting out here alone on the edge of a cliff, having a very peaceful time after a day of strenuous labour. Must say I got rather a surprise this morning to find another convoy in and the ward nearly full up again. No blanket-bathing had been done and we weren't quite finished when I came off duty at 5. We didn't start till Mr Cowper had been around to look at the men. Some are rather bad. One was operated on for a head wound when he came in, as was another man with a wound in his arm. The smell from the wounds was dreadful. Other cases are slighter. Sister Cavan and I worked away and Sister Cowie helped all day. Sister Cavan is very nice. I like her very much to work with. Sister Cowie is always a dear and it is a joy to do things for her. C came in during the morning from the next ward to help with the blanket-baths. I was on the go ceaselessly, no mistake.

Now I am enjoying the lovely peace and the scene and the evening light. The weather changed this morning and it is much finer but not very hot. It has been awfully damp the last two days and pouring part of the time.

Yesterday a lot of men went out of our ward. It was quite a job getting them into their kit. They are all going to England. Some were so pleased to go, smiling all over their faces.

Off duty from 2 till 5 yesterday. I went out with Arnold, Jobson, Alabaster and Fasker down into town and then by tram out to Mers and we walked up onto the cliffs to the far side. Had a blissful time then we came back to town and went into a hotel and gorged on strawberries and cream, fresh bread and butter and coffee and literally made pigs of ourselves. This is greediest place I have ever been in. We seem to be always eating and gullaravishing.

SUNDAY, 4TH JULY

Am just very tired tonight. Have worked frightfully hard all day and it has been so hot. The sun beat down on the tin roof of our hut and made it like a furnace. All the patients were complaining of the heat. Poor things! It would be bad enough in cool weather to bear wounds and pain, but it must be a great deal worse in the heat.

Another convoy came in last night. Someone said there were 300 men. We only had three beds to spare in our ward. Now we are full and every bed has a patient, some of whom are quite bad. One of the men from last night's convoy has been shot through the neck and his spinal chord is injured. The poor man is completely paralysed except for one arm. I don't know that he feels much except excessive discomfort and distress. It is sad to see him suffering. He cannot possibly get better. C's ward is very busy too, but more of her patients are able to get up. None of ours can except for one man who has been out of bed for a very short time. Some of the men are going back to England tomorrow I believe.

Had a very refreshing bath and that made me feel better. Matron is still away on leave. When she comes back, we shall hear whether or not we are to stay. I heard a rumour that C and I are all right. When shall we get home again if this rumour is true?! There is no prospect of the end of this war for many a long day to come. We heard gunfire the night before last. I didn't like it at all. Much too eerie. I had indigestion and couldn't get to sleep and kept imagining Germans approaching our camp and our line retiring and retiring in the night. However we haven't heard any more guns since, so perhaps the sound came from the ships out at sea or there was some practising going on. There are often aeroplanes sailing up and above the camp. One feels they are much more on business than those at home.

The news boy is calling papers round the camp, but I cannot summon up the energy to go out and buy one. I will wait to see the 'Weekly Times' that Mums is sending from home.

WEDNESDAY, 7TH JULY

What a wind blowing today! I am expecting momentarily to be enveloped in my collapsed abode. The rain is pattering on the roof and the wind is shaking and tugging the tent. If the ropes give way the worst will have happened. It has been stormy all day. Miss Rind and I have just been on a short walk along cliffs to get a blow – and accidentally a wetting – but clad in oilskins we were independent and defied the elements. Feel rather touzled now and certainly not presentable for tea when that time comes.

I was too busy yesterday to write my diary as Sister Cavan had half a day off. The afternoon was a great rush getting seven of the men ready to go off to England – getting their kits on and transferring them to stretchers. All the washing and beds had to be done too. We couldn't leave it to Sister Cowie who was busy with a 'special' case in the other ward. So I offered to stay on and remained on duty till 8. Mr Cowper came in late and dressed a man's arm and that took quite a long time. I was alone with him and we conversed pleasantly. Not quite so busy today with men gone and some beds empty.

Bridge, the man shot through the neck and almost completely paralysed, died this morning after being unconscious for two days. I am glad he 'went west' at last. There was no possible hope for him. His was such a sad case.

Sister Cavan is very nice to me now and I fondly expect this will improve more later on as she gets to know me better. C does not like her Sister Edwardes any better and Sister Cowie makes no secret of not caring for her either. She is such bad style; flirting with doctors and making patients gossip about her.

We have had lots of visitors lately. The Colonel keeps shepherding parties of English and French officers round the wards. The other day an English General came to inspect and a French General visited in the morning.

Our men are all so quiet and sober, yet they are nice and cheery most of the time. C's are very noisy and several are very young. Poor Bridge was quite young too. His few belongings have been sent home to his mother.

FRIDAY, 9TH JULY

Am having half day off and feel that I am not using it to best advantage, but it's really rather a joy to loaf for a little while. Have loafed absolutely since lunchtime. Went to Arnold and Tozer's tent and sat a long time gossiping. Before that Arnold and I made a tour of the camp with a message for the Sister-in-charge of each line. They have to report to Matron this very day on all of us VADs, and there is some trembling-in-shoes going on. I suppose that tomorrow we will hear the worst or best and also get some dibs which will be quite acceptable.

Matron and two of the Sisters came back from leave last night. They must have had a very rough crossing as the wind was awful yesterday. I really thought the tent would be heaved off several times. Great relief it is all gone and peace reigns again. Matron does not feel much better for her change, she says. She wasn't away long enough for a thorough rest. It's rather a relief to have her back. She seems to make staff more complete. Some of the Sisters wouldn't agree as they do not appear to like her much. She has a strange but interesting character, a very sad face but a pleasant, sweet manner when not on business.

Christie had a half-day yesterday and after tea I went into Hut 3 and worked – or rather did nothing – there until I was relieved at 8. I had the morning off and went alone to Tréport and shopped.

We have a new orderly in the ward called Anderson. He is more help than Diggle who was hopeless. He went off ill and Berry was alone for two days. I think we shall manage better now.

I can smell cooking! Look anxiously at the time but it is only 5 past 7. We have a new cookhouse that is palatial compared to the last (and a new Tipperary!* A vast improvement on the previously endured primitive arrangements – a little wooden erection quite inadequate for the numerous staff).

SATURDAY, 10TH JULY, 7.15 P.M.

Received my first pay today – great thrill – 190.90 francs.† It is not as much as I paid out but it is still a wonderful thing to really be earning money. I went to Matron's tent to receive the great sum. C came across for me after lunch and I left the ward for a short interval. We hear tonight whether we stay or not. Some have already been signed on. Two are said to be going. Poor things! It must be dreadful for them to be packed off. Though even this may only be rumour and have no truth in it.

The wards are being cleared of patients rapidly. The Colonel went round our hut today and marked nearly all the patients for England. I suppose they may be going tonight or early tomorrow morning. It is said that there is to be a big battle and there may be a great and sudden rush any time.

There was choir practice last night after supper in the chapel tent. One of the doctors taught and conducted seven VADs and a lot of orderlies. We kept at it till after 10, so I got to bed rather late. Matron heard us coming in and thought we had all been on lust. She was rather annoyed and said it must not happen again, so I suppose poor Mr Higgins will have to curtail his energies and give us a less thorough training.

* Origin of the name for the loo unidentified. Was it perhaps a 'long, long way to go'?
† The official military rate of exchange was fixed at five francs to three shillings and seven-pence, so Dorothea would have received about £7 (approximately eqivalent to £300 in 2013).

MONDAY, 12TH JULY

Have today signed papers committing myself to service abroad anywhere for six months and so the doughty deed is done and I am saved from dismissal. C also committed herself and this morning we were both summoned to Matron's office where the signing was soon accomplished and the die cast. Who knows how long we shall be out here? From the reports there seems a good chance of the campaigns being ended before winter, but all is uncertain.

Great changes have come to pass this day. All the night people have come back on day duty and Robertson (alias Little Tick or Tout Petit), Miss Wall Jacobs, Malet, Trotter and Miss Fletcher* are the chosen few to take their place. I must now get to know the haughty night people who were established here for some time before any of us came out.

THURSDAY, 15TH JULY

Am going on duty again in a few moments after having the morning off. C is having a half-day so I shall be on duty in her ward either this afternoon or evening. I don't like these mornings off but they must come about sometime, and C will have to suffer for me tomorrow. Windy again. Yesterday was an awful day of rain and wind. The weather is very bad just now, so much cold and storm.

There was a great clearing-out of the men in our wards early yesterday morning. We came on duty to find all the travellers ready to go. They were so pleased, the poor things, lying on their stretchers, waiting to be carried out and put on board ambulances. About ten went altogether. That left us only a few of the worst cases, but still there seems plenty to do in the hut wards even in slack times like this. We were quite busy all yesterday. In the evening I spent off-duty time sitting in Arnold and Tozer's tent with Jobson, gossiping and giggling in a very foolish manner, and then by way of sobering

---

* The use of the title 'Miss' is rapidly disappearing from the diary: from now on it was surnames or nicknames only.

influence I read Ian Hamilton's Dispatches from Gallipoli* aloud to the assembled company. Very little seems to have happened there these last days.

FRIDAY, 16TH JULY

More rain! St Swithin's Day has indeed lived up to its reputation and brought in bad weather this time. Just in from a long walk with Jobson. In spite of the unsettled weather we had a delightful expedition; we went off early after lunch, walked along the cliffs beyond Mesnilval and the next hamlet, Criel Plage, up to the top of the cliffs on the far side to see the view. It wasn't raining then so we sat and rested and looked from our viewpoint. The light on the sea was wonderful. Could just see Dieppe in the distance to the side of the wide, sweeping bay. Came back then over fields, skillfully negotiating barbed wire fences by rolling flat on ground underneath them and down to Criel-sur-Mer. We passed such a dear picturesque farm and old houses, some of which were very ramshackled but none the less pleasing to the artistic eye. Stopped for tea at a little café and were most hospitably entertained by the manageress and her daughter. Both spoke a little English and seemed to be well accustomed to visitors from the hospitals. We got as much coffee, bread and butter, raspberries and cream as we could eat for fr 1.50 and staggered away with bouquets of flowers and much goodwill and adjurements to return again.

Came back by rather long, straight road, trudging along in the wet but gossiping quite happily. We sat down to rest for a moment when an ambulance car hove in sight but got up at once when it shot past and we saw it was conveying Matron and a party back from Dieppe. It pulled up a bit further on and we pursued hotly and got a delightful lift all the way back to camp. Were very grateful for

* General Sir Ian Hamilton was the Commander-in-Chief of the disastrous Allied attempt to occupy Gallipoli peninsula in Turkey. See Chronology, p. 349.

otherwise the road would have been very long and we might have been trudging now. Passed a scene of great excitement. Three drunk soldiers had done something to a countryman and his little party in their country cart. The wife was clutching him wildly and, frantic with anger, he was struggling to pursue the soldiers and do battle. The whole party was in terrible distress. After waiting a minute or two we drove on but left word with the police at the outskirts of camp and one of them set off directly to the scene of disorder. Great shame of soldiers as that sort of thing brings such discredit on Tommies and makes them looked upon with disfavour.

SUNDAY, 18TH JULY

My birthday! Such a different one from last year. How little I thought then that another year would bring this birthday surprise.

Today was hard work. Another convoy of poor, tired, wounded warriors came in and our ward was full again except for the beds left empty by four of the patients who went away to Blity* this morning. Some of them are very bad at present. One or two of the wounds are pretty severe. Had so much blanket-bathing to do. Worked all morning and afternoon up to teatime. Sister Cavan had her afternoon off and came back at 5. Sister Cowie and I laboured away in the ward, the orderlies being of course mostly absent and not much use when they did appear. Very tired when I came off duty so was glad of a peaceful walk after tea, up to the cliffs with Rind – such a delightful companion – and a gossip lying on the grass together. Feeling much better now for the rest and change. Have just been reading all my correspondence. Had so many birthday and other letters; perusal has taken quite a long time and takes me right back to England, to Goily and Windermere† and to home and other delightful places. With such nice companions to fraternize with, though, I cannot but be happy here and with conditions as they are now it is a very pleasant existence.

---

* 'Blighty' was a new word to D – hence the misspelling.
† 'Goily' was Lochgoilhead, Dorothea's grandfather's holiday retreat in Argyll; Windermere was the home of Crewdson and Broadrick cousins.

The wind has gone which is a mercy. Yesterday was awful. Raging storm and rain. One or two of the tents were all but blown down. The Big Mess tent was nearly razed to the ground and was only saved by the frantic efforts of Miss Rogers and some of the orderlies coming to the rescue. One of the MO's tents was quite bowled over and flattened out. I saw an interested crowd gathered round looking at remnants. It is up now, a little flag proudly waving again over the front door.

TUESDAY, 20TH JULY

Am backaching after days of strenuous work. Our wards are still full, none of the men having yet gone to Blity. We have a lively crew in our hut, two of them keeping the others going. Have been working hard all afternoon, washing and tidying, while Sister Cowie made the beds very energetically. The wind is rising again and the very stormy sky does not look very promising for tomorrow. Since tea I have been with Miss Rind and we two and Sister O'Hearne went walking along the cliffs. We nearly got blown away and came back very much touzled.

Come in to try to get letters written but have made no speed so far. There was great excitement in Hut 3 yesterday. Miss Huntley was seriously overcome at the sight of a dressing being done, moved away a few paces and then fell headlong into a dead faint. Then she fainted again. Was so bad that Matron and doctor had to be summoned. She was conveyed back to tent on a stretcher. A great invalid but today she has come on duty again, though she is not looking too brisk. She bumped herself severely with her fall on the hard floor and must be feeling very sore and stiff. It is plucky of her to begin work again so soon.

Everyone seems tired just now, complaining of aches and ills. Feeling the strain of work more, I expect. Our orderlies seem to feel it very much. This morning, when he went for his breakfast,

Anderson said he was not coming back and he didn't come. He had simply absented himself and was not to be found in the camp. When he did come back he was immediately put under arrest. He will be sent to Dieppe to be court-martialled and is liable to be shot, but I hope it won't be seen as such a bad offence as that. Calder worked splendidly all day and another orderly came on late in the morning. Wonder how long he will stay. We seem to keep having changes, which is unsettling.

THURSDAY, 22ND JULY

Huntley is singing in the recreation tent. So many songs. She has had the day off, not being quite recovered from her sudden collapse on Monday. She looked very tired yesterday. I suppose she will go back to join C tomorrow. I have had a bath and feel so pleasant and washen. Am glad to be sitting quietly here writing as I had a very hard day up to teatime.

Only yesterday morning eleven of the last convoy went out of our hut on their way to Blity. They were so glad, smiling as they lay on a row of stretchers by the side of the road waiting to be put onto ambulances.

Very quiet after their departure but not for long, for another convoy came in last night and this morning we found nine new patients to be attended to. None are able to get up so we are very busy again. Means so much running about and extra washing. No one is very bad, but one boy with various wounds, including a punctured leg, seemed out of his senses with pain. He screamed at the pitch of his voice while Mr Cowper was dressing him. Awful to hear but think he must have lost his nerve as the wound is not serious, though no doubt very painful. C must have been very busy too as I have not seen her all day. No time for our usual lunch in the morning. Sister Cavan came back after dinner in her off-duty time to help finish dressings, but Sister Cowie chased her off after a while and bustled around getting through an amazing amount of work.

Had such a frivolous evening last night! There was a musical soirée in the recreation tent. All the officers were invited and a good number turned up. We all came in best bib and tucker to receive them. Our music and refreshments were much appreciated. The coffee and cakes were provided by ourselves, the music by C, Miss Huntley, Miss Urquart, Miss Laird and three MOs. We all sat round and talked and listened and amused ourselves very much if only by considering what a joke the whole affair was. Our guests all went or were cleared out by Matron at about 10, and then we went off to bed.

MONDAY, 26TH JULY, 10.45 P.M.

Such a lovely full moon shining down and a lovely sky – C has been to Abbeville with Matron and two of the Sisters. She seems to have much enjoyed the trip, especially the motor drive there and back. Says Matron was so nice and un-stiff and quite on the spree. I had the evening off duty and went down to Tréport with Arnold who I am getting to like better and better. She is so nice and liking seems mutual.

All the VADs received extra pay from Matron after supper tonight. C and I got fr 9 and the others 12, what for we can't imagine. It seems some mysterious arrears are being made up to us. Anyway, quite acceptable; never refuse a good offer.

Stacks of parcels arrived for us today. Have had such openings and arrangings and stowing away of contents. Some were eatable. Have not stowed them all away yet and I expect they will soon go in this greedy and ravenous place.

WEDNESDAY, 28TH JULY, 11 A.M.

Today I am having the morning off as Sister Cavan is indulging in a half-day. I have to be on afternoon and evening. Rather a bore! But must say am rather glad to have this morning's peace and quiet. Yesterday Rind and Sister Garnett were half-daying too so we planned to go out together. We thought of hiring a motor and driving to the forests of Eu. But it came on so wet at lunchtime that we were discouraged and lingered about till it cleared up again. Then we walked to Mesnilval, taking bathing dresses in case we felt like swimming. The tide was so far out, however, that we thought it wasn't worth the while, so we just wandered down onto the sand and took off shoes and stockings and had a delightful time splashing about and getting a bit of fun. Sister G is a most lively person. Kept Miss R and self in fits of laughter. We were all feeling rather mad and holiday-ish. The weather improved very much and it was a lovely evening and most beautiful sunset.

Got back to camp in time to tidy up and change for great do in the evening. The officers entertained the whole staff of nurses at 8.30 in their Mess with a grand soirée, the entertainment being a reciter who was making a tour of hospitals and giving recitals for patients and staff. He said he was an amateur but he was very good indeed and had a large repertoire of both serious and comic. We had refreshments at half-time after C, Huntley and Urquart contributed to the programme. Matron kept an eye on us all as our chaperone and we all behaved circumspectly but had very good fun all the same.

FRIDAY, 30TH JULY, 10.15 P.M.

Am tucked up in bed ready to settle in for the precious hours of sleep. Need it tonight, as may be busy tomorrow. A convoy comes in tonight and the ward may be full up with stretcher cases. A small convoy came in the day before yesterday. We expected it to arrive between 4 and 5 p.m. but it didn't come till nearly 7.30. Sister was having half-day off so I was alone in the ward all afternoon. I made all the empty beds ready and was kept expectant after tea till the arrival of the wounded. We only got four cases out of 150 altogether in my ward. Sister Cavan returned to receive the patients and Sister Cowie helped. As soon as they arrived we got them into bed. Clothes came off and we began blanket-bathing at once. Mr Cowper came in to look at them. None of the men are bad, two of them up and about today and leaving soon for Blity. One has a broken clavicle from a wrestling match and another with a kick from football playing. The other two had slight wounds. Three men went away yesterday morning. One of them was as Irish as one could be, but rather entertaining.

SUNDAY, 1ST AUGUST

Here we are in real summer at last. In the tents and huts it is almost too hot, but out here on the cliffs it is just gorgeous. Blue sea, fresh breeze, little sailing boat and a small steamer at anchor and everything so fresh and bright. All the same, felt very homesick this morning. Better now having had long chat with Arnold and also having received a parcel from home.

We have two men in the hut so terribly ill and one (Huntley) is a boy of only sixteen. Such a nice-looking lad but paralysed from the waist. He is in the little ward. Came in the convoy Friday night. Just dying by inches. So sad. Woe is me! The other one was hit in head and has fits continually. Also very ill. I am kept busy by these two invalids. Have not been able to get to work or do anything in the ward. We have an extra Sister, Sister Johnson, to help Huntley in the little ward before he goes to isolation in the afternoon.

Today I am off in the morning and Sister will want someone else to be with Huntley in the evening. Not looking forward much to this job; depresses me greatly. Had six new cases in, these two bad ones and two others fairly bad. Another has gone this morning and two or three have gone altogether. Last night the war news was so deeply depressing. Feel we are going to be out here ages and ages and even then perhaps the Germans will get the better of us. All the men in the wards were un-encouraging. I must try not to be so gloomy but cheer up a bit and look forward with hope to future.

WEDNESDAY, 4TH AUGUST

Pay night and we have all received a monstrously and wonderfully large sum of money amounting to fr 28.85. The Sisters of course have different pay and more of it. We all feel robbers of the Matron as our salary for the month comes to more than £10 and we only expected £20 a year. Just going to sleep now. Have had a very busy day. Thirteen patients went Blitywards at lunchtime. One or two of them were our older friends and the rest were from the large convoy that came in on Monday afternoon. The ward is full but for two beds. Lots of dressings to be done and not much time allowed for ward work.

When the convoy came in I was off duty but went back to the ward at 'fall in' bugle call.* The men brought in were so dirty as they had come straight from the trenches, no hospital in between. We got to work at once. Clothes off and blanket-bathing and nearly all our work was done by 8, much better than dawdling through the night and b-bathing left for the morning. One or two of the cases are quite bad. One boy with shrapnel through shoulder and chest was very serious. He was operated on today.

Poor little Huntley died last night. I was off duty. Sister said he couldn't live long. Poor boy! The head wound man, Peddar, has been having fits again today and seems worse. Otherwise he was getting on so much better and seemed more understanding. Three out of the new arrivals last Monday are Nottingham men. Rather strange.

---

* The sound of the bugle call punctuated days in the hospital camp. They sounded for breakfast, lunch, supper and 'lights out', but the call to 'fall in', signifying the arrival of a convoy, could come at any time.

Such awful wind yesterday, tearing and raging. Did hate it so. There was a thunderstorm on Monday afternoon so the weather is still unsettled. I have been down to Tréport this afternoon; I got my hair washed but not very successfully dried. Still very damp. C and I by lucky chance were off together yesterday. We took a walk in the gale along the cliffs and back by the fields and quite enjoyed it, alone together for the first time since being in the huts.

FRIDAY, 6TH AUGUST

How time goes on. Can hardly believe we have got into August already, and have been out here nearly eight weeks. I am waiting now for Rind and Tozer. We are going out for a walk to Mesnilval to have tea and be back in time to go on duty. All half-days have been stopped now except for very particular reasons. Consequently there has been much sorrow and sighing in camp. But we must expect busy times and have to be prepared for any emergency.

In our ward we have had two deaths lately – Huntley on Tuesday night and last night Moore died. They were both so young, poor boys and Moore suffered so much with the wound – two big lumps of shrapnel right at the top of his shoulder had carried the head of his humerus and part of his scapula into his side, broken the ribs and injured one of his lungs. The MOs operated and got the shrapnel out but could not save his life. He was very bad all day yesterday and so worn and fragile.

Rain and wind again today. Such a lovely morning yesterday, a wonderful glowing effect over the sea last night. I spent off-duty time with Rind, Tozer and Huntley, lying on the cliffs writing letters and looking at view. We watched little torpedo boats come right in front of the port and cruise past, evidently patrolling, and then turning Dieppe-wards again. Had three delightful and cheering letters yesterday morning from Mums, Alastair and Maggie, calculated to assist greatly in the curse of homesickness.

SUNDAY, 8TH AUGUST

What a nice place bed seems tonight. Have had such a day of work. A convoy came in at 9, or soon after, and it has been a great rush since. Every bed is filled except in the little ward. Had to get all b-bathing done as quickly as possible and was all finished soon after tea. We have seventeen new patients altogether. One poor boy is very bad indeed. Looks like he will follow Huntley and Moore. Left Malet looking after him. Other wounds are less serious at present. C had nine new people in. Three of the old patients should have gone today but railway officials would not allow it with one convoy coming in and another going out, so departure was postponed till tomorrow. Poor old Morgan still kept waiting. Does not seem able to get off.

Lovely weather all day. Went to the early service and glad I did, as there was no possible chance of thought for the Sabbath day after the convoy came in. Everyone is very busy and all the lines nearly full with some bad cases. Such a change after peace of yesterday when there was really only Peddar, who requires a lot of attention, to keep us busy. Arnold and I went into town in the evening and shopped. But I didn't get much time off today. Seem to have washed so many dirty feet cannot quite get rid of atmosphere, but a bath tonight has helped a good deal. Also quieted my fears of having contracted any livestock. Have seen plenty of creepy-crawlies today. C is busy doing her washing. Aha! I have done mine so feel relieved and happy.

TUESDAY, 10TH AUGUST

Very hot day – but not quite so much as yesterday. It was so sultry and trying and the poor men felt it terribly. Had another death last night. Poor little Watson, the Durham Light Infantry man and a miner who had had his arm amputated. He got much worse yesterday, was operated on but died in the night. Very sad. He was such a nice man. We also had a death the night before – Private Guy who came in with the last convoy – so we have had rather tragic times in our hut, one man dying after another. No more on DI list at present, but another convoy is expected in tomorrow and there may well be bad cases in that.

The great advance on our part has started. Bombardment has begun and rumours that we have won eight miles of trenches have spread abroad.*

Have been very busy all today up to now and yesterday we kept hard at it till 6.15 p.m. I went back voluntarily after tea to help Sister Cavan with the beds, as work was so much behindhand owing to Watson having his operation and coming back so collapsed. I helped Sister Cowie with him. We put him into a side ward, a sort of chamber of doom now for these poor men to breathe their last.

Great excitement yesterday about teatime. An aeroplane came down on the golf course just at back of our tents. The skipper was a young Belgian calling at Tréport to see his parents before going to the front. Everyone rushed to see the machine and when it went up again crowds were watching. Tozer and I went out to see the fun and it really was very thrilling to see the great bird go up and away into the sky. The Belgian's parents came up in their car to see him go and it must have been a rather sad parting for them.

Arnold and I have been to the new canteen. The most wonderful array of stores and necessities greeted us, all kinds of goods piled up, from boot blacking to tinned fruit and other delectable eatables. It will be a great godsend to get things there instead of having to trudge after them down into the town. The storekeeper is a Mansfield man. Must talk to him.

FRIDAY, 13TH AUGUST

Almost too dark to see now to write but must try to get something put down as I am getting rather behindhand. Seems dark and cold this evening – the days shortening I suppose, which is a bit dismal. After a busy morning I am having a peaceful evening off duty. A convoy came in about 8 p.m. We got nine cases. Two or three of them are what is called 'heavy'. One looks very bad. Two are partly paralysed. Poor things, très souffrant. Next door took in eleven cases. Talk of another convoy today but it has not come in yet. Perhaps it stopped en route.

---

* Unfortunately the rumours were without foundation. See Chronology, page 349.

Time of anxiety about who is going on night duty is over today. The change has been made, Arnold and Tozer have deserted our company for a month. I am very sorry, as Tozer was a great companion in off-duty times. Awdrey, Alabaster, Johnson and Gibson have also been selected. First two feel no great loss, especially Alabaster who is a queer creature indeed and would drive me to distraction to work with.

There goes the 8 p.m. bugle. So badly sounded. The bugler must be a novice. Matron spoke to C in ward yesterday and said such nice things about our capabilities as nurses. She tried first of all to make C think she was going on nights and then said no, neither of us were, and something about our being above average and worth taking trouble about, and we were to learn all we could. I feel now that we must do all we can to live up to this high estimation. Cannot think, truly, what I have done to deserve it. But I am certainly glad to be staying in our huts a bit longer. Do love them very much and Sister Cowie also.

SUNDAY, 15TH AUGUST

Have outstripped C altogether tonight. Had supper early before she appeared and now am sitting in our tent. It must be quite early still but I am ready for bed anyway. Blowy night. Not pleased to hear the wind getting up again after the last few days and nights of delightful peace. Tents in a wind are simply horrid; so noisy and unstable.

Have had such a day. Trotter has come from a spell of night duty to help in Hut 2. We share the work that Sister Cowie has mapped out for us in her businesslike manner. It is much nicer, though, to have all our respective duties made clear. Trotter takes one side of ward and I the other for dusting lockers, scrubbing and doing out the back rooms. We were both scrubbing and rubbing full tilt after the beds were made.

The latest idea is that the huts shall be kept for the very worst cases in transfer from the other lines. We had four in yesterday and another came this morning. Three trephines and two chest cases. The former were all brought in straight from theatre after operation. It was such a mad rush all day to get things done. Two bad patients

28

with paralysed legs kept wanting drinks and then to be shifted this way or that. Millard was worst and wanted something every time we passed. Poor man. His fate is sealed but he may hang on a while yet. He is going to be shifted away to Blity tomorrow if possible, along with Bennett, Peddar and several others so the ward will be much quieter and trephines will have more chance of rest.

I spent my off-duty time in town. It is so pretty down there. I went out to the end of the breakwater and watched a sailing boat come in before the breeze became too fresh. Most lovely scene – lots of busy fishers on the pier catching tiny little cuddies with a trout rod. They looked like sardines. Went round after to see what the fishing boats had brought. They had big drag nets aboard but their catch seemed to be a few flounders and starfish and crabs galore. The latter were thrown back into the water – only the fish and hermit crabs were kept – so the catch couldn't

have been very remunerative. Must go to sleep now. Christie has blown out her candle and is tucking into bed. I must do ditto.

TUESDAY, 17TH AUGUST

There is a 4.30 bugle going just as I have begun this diary and it is time now to go to tea. Have been reading one or two of my past day records. Find them rather entertaining. We were off earlier today as a special concession from Matron. We are all having an extra hour in our huts, so instead of 5 o'clock off duty I came away at 4. Quite nice and restful. The ward is very empty just now. So many went out yesterday morning including two very bad cases, Burnett and Millard, both with paralysis of the legs, and also poor Peddar who is still so wanting and inarticulate. But he had the Blity smile nevertheless. They are all so glad to go home. Millard is so bad that he had to have a special ambulance and special MO to look after him.

Watching futile amble of this 'insec' on floor!

FRIDAY, 20TH AUGUST

Yesterday evening Trott, C and I went to one of Lena Ashwell's concert parties in the YMCA tent.* Such a treat of music – Westminster Singers, the Letts and Carrie Tubb. The former were simply wonderful and were much appreciated. Phyllis Lett sang very well, as did Carrie Tubb. They must have been tired as they had given a concert in the afternoon and then in the evening they had to attend dinner at the Officers' Mess. Fifteen of our staff went over, including four VADs – Rogers, Rind, Hyne and Smedley. Sister Cowie went too. They seemed to have enjoyed the function very much. We had drawn lots for being the favoured guests as usual, but not with so much excitement as formerly.

Today we have had Royalty inspecting – Princess Victoria of Schleswig Holstein† – and a whole troop of grand officers and members of our staff. Our ward very much tidied up for the occasion and the procession passed through on its way to departure. The Princess looked very unassuming and kindly and she spoke to one or two of our patients on her way.

SUNDAY, 22ND AUGUST

Slack time in hospital still continues. Heard today from Anderson that there are only 191 patients in whole hospital of over 1,000 beds. Must be as empty now as it has ever been. The convoy that was expected the night before last never turned up and there is no definite word yet of another. Where is this awful war going to land us? News seems so bad, at least about Russia and Gallipoli, otherwise nothing is said.‡

---

* Lena Ashwell was one of the principal organizers of musical entertainment for the BEF. By the end of the war she had twenty-five different concert parties touring round the camps and hospitals. Phyllis Lett and Carrie Tubb were two of the most celebrated female singers of their day.

† There was probably a connection between the concert and the royal visit, as the Princess, Queen Victoria's granddaughter, in her capacity as President of the YWCA Auxiliary Force devoted much of her time during the war to organizing entertainment for the troops.

‡ News was indeed bad. See Chronology, p. 349.

Had such a lovely outing yesterday afternoon. Rind, Huntley, Sister Cooper, C and I went off in a specially ordered motor to the forest of Eu. The driver seemed to know what he was about but took us the weirdest way over grass-grown tracks and across fields. We landed finally at a single house called St Cathérine in the Haute Forêt and on the recommendation and guidance of our driver we went in and were greeted by a nice clean little French woman with a most powerful and strident voice but kind, hospitable manner. We wandered out through the gardens and at the end of a little plot were shown the most wonderful view right out over a deep valley,

all fertile, cultivated and wooded here and there. Were just at the border of the great forest. Spent some time wandering about and picking flowers and enjoying scene and change. Then went back to house to have coffee in bowls and lovely bread and butter and jam. Such an old-looking house, probably been there for ages and seen much coming and going. The coffee was delicious and we all did justice to it and felt very satisfied when we rose up to depart. The motor was all ready for us and off we sped again. Got back to camp in nice time to change and go back on duty. Rind stood us the trip at large cost fr 40 – dear, but still really worth the money.

WEDNESDAY, 25TH AUGUST

C and I have both collapsed feebly and are spending this lovely hot summer afternoon in the tent lying on our little beds. All our energies have vanished. Cannot help smiling at our feebleness but neither of us feels good for anything else.

I had to miss supper last night being overcome with an attack of innards and being only wishful to lie down quite quiet, C went to Sister Withers and got me excused and I went to bed very early and got a good long rest. Think collapse must have been partly due to very early rise on Monday morning. Convoy came in during the night at 4.45. Sister Blandy came to get me up for duty, to help get the men washed and settled in. I was much astonished at being roused up. C remained in bed, generously demanding why she had not been told to go too.

We had nine new patients in and there were thirteen next door in No. 1 and seven in No. 3. Pritchard is in our side ward – another case like Huntley and Bridge. Such a nice man, absolutely helpless and completely paralysed. Seems terribly sad that so small a hole in the shoulder can cause such a condition. The other new patients are doing fairly well. None seem very bad. This convoy is supposed to be going out tomorrow and thirteen of ours are marked to go. Will have a very quiet time ...

Stopped here to be roused by C to a campaign of tidying up and rearrangement in our tent. Am now in bed and trying a new way of sleeping with my head towards the opening and think it will be more airy this way. Have had a bath and am very glad now to be resting again. Had a very busy evening on with Sister Cavan and she was busy attending to two bad patients. Pritchard's temperature is up to 106 tonight, so must be very ill. He seems terribly restless and uncomfortable. The other bad one is Parkes, one of the trephine cases. He has been slowly getting worse and seems very poorly tonight. Both he and Pritchard are marked for Blity. Seems so sad that this should be another sort of going home.

SATURDAY, 28TH AUGUST

So slack in the wards now that last convoy has been weeded out. We have only five patients altogether in Hut 2 and two of them are up, though rather painfully limping. Poor Pritchard died on Thursday night and now Parkes is very poorly. Don't know whether he can get better. It is so sad to see him growing worse and more and more helpless. He is such a very nice boy, so anxious to be no trouble and always grateful for attention. Must come of nice people judging by the letter I read to him from his mother.

This morning an aeroplane passed over us very high up, shining like a gem in the sky and was said to be a genuine German Taube* and perhaps the same one that passed over Abbeville yesterday and dropped a bomb. Strange to think there really was an enemy passing overhead and might have dropped a bomb on us. We see lots of aeroplanes – two came over this evening but good English ones and real friends with no malice or uncharitableness.

Had such a lovely half-day on Thursday. Sister Cowie got me permission from Matron to go to Dieppe with a party to meet Sister Thompson coming back from leave. Five of us went: Sister Cowie and Sister Garnett, Wall Jacobs, Robertson and I. A motor ambulance took us all in fine fettle, rattling along at an astounding pace kicking clouds of dust and covering the distance in a little over half an hour. It meant we had time before going to the quay to potter about, shopping, having tea and seeing the lovely old cathedral. We were in a shop when the boat came in so had to bustle down to find Sister.

Dieppe is such a picturesque place. So very glad to have seen it and its glorious old church. The shops are nice too. Being overcrowded coming back, we were lucky to have no punctures. Besides Sister Thompson, we had two extra orderlies in front, an officer for the Canadian Hospital and piles of their luggage and belongings all crammed in somehow. But we got back quite safely with no mishaps, so our joyride was entirely unspoilt. Sister Cowie is a very nice person to go out with, she enjoys all jaunts so thoroughly. C and I spent long time in her tent last night gossiping and we didn't leave till after 10, breaking through all laws and orders.

There goes the bell for supper so must decamp into the Mess tent!

* The most common type of German aircraft in the early part of the war.

SUNDAY, 29TH AUGUST

Have had such a slack day and no prospect of more work as no convoys are coming in just now. Don't know what we shall do after next convoy goes out to Blity. Will all be absolutely unemployed.

In spite of slack times another invalid was added to the list today. Barton, who has been suffering from toothache for some time past, had to have quite an operation a day or two ago and is still very poorly, so has been shipped off today to No. 3 to join Gibson and be nursed back to health.* Hope VAD staff are not going to fall away one by one and go home crocked up.

Left Parkes much about the same – very poorly and so changed in appearance. His father came last night to see him and is staying on till tomorrow night or after. Poor man, so pathetic for him to see his precious son so ill. He seems a nice man too and very respectable, a soldier in the Sussex Regiment, stationed as a guard on a railway bridge near Aldershot. I wish he could see his son recovering but fear it will not be so.

Did not mention the excitement the other day. At lunchtime there was a fire in the Canadian camp. Three tents quite burnt up and another one damaged. There was great excitement and a crowd of orderlies turned out to the rescue. The fire was soon put out but not before good deal of damage had been done. No one was hurt and the patients in nearby tents got out with all speed. All round, a scene of great bustle and confusion. I went with four other VADs to see what was going on and we all got a scolding from Matron and were sent hurrying back to our camp. The conflagration made me

---

* No. 3 General Hospital, in the requisitioned hotel just along the cliff, had facilities for nursing 'Sick Sisters', so any No. 16 nurses who needed to be hospitalized were sent there.

realize awfulness of bad fire and having to get really serious cases away with speed. Tents go up like tinder in dry weather.

TUESDAY, 31ST AUGUST

Poor little Parkes died today about 12.40 p.m. His sorrowing father was by him at the last. So pathetic, but better the sufferer should go and he was quite unconscious at the end. Now we are left with less than ever to do in our ward. Letter came from Mother today. Says Jack Tennant* has been killed. Another tragic loss in the family. So sad. He was such a cheery lad.

WEDNESDAY, 1ST SEPTEMBER

Another letter with tragedy in it. From Al saying George† had been killed. Poor, poor Aunt Mary! Really seems as though G might have been spared for a little longer. He was getting on so well and had been made Commander of one of the Border Battalions. The news made me feel very depressed all morning. Wish this horrid, horrid war would end. The weather has turned cold and stormy. There is a concert this afternoon but I am not going to it. Must write letters instead.

Our tent feels very damp. It was re-pitched this morning and the floor scrubbed. Sister Williams warned us to take all possessions and furnishings out before going on duty. C had to superintend return of goods speedily after re-pitching operation finished as rain was threatening. Sure C and I shall both have rheumatics badly tomorrow. Mr Parkes went off this morning looking thin and worn, poor man, but more ready to smile and talk than before.

FRIDAY, 3RD SEPTEMBER

Heavy showers just sent us to our tent, but up till now we have been out this afternoon watching preliminaries of the Orderlies' Sports.

---

* Dorothea's second cousin.
† George Broadrick, a first cousin on the Crewdson side of the family. He was in command of the 6th Battalion the Border Regiment which was in action at Cape Helles in the Gallipoli campaign.

Real Sports day is tomorrow but some of the heats are being run this afternoon so as to leave more time. It was most amusing looking on.

It began with several heats of flat races. We were watching these from Rind's tent but when the fun grew fast and furious, we moved out to see things better. A few of the Sisters joined us and when we got to steeplechases, Matron appeared and added to the audience. The mop fighting and the three-legged race were very amusing, but we laughed most over the sack race. The competition looked so quaint and the participants rather like seals and all so much in earnest and anxious to win. There was a large audience of orderlies, MOs and patients.

Everyone ran for shelter when the rain came on, but this afternoon a fine interval was a great help. C and I both off together again. Sister Northwood is having a whole day off and we are all to get one in turn. Very exciting.

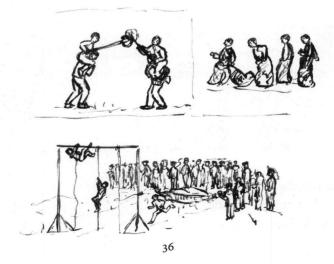

SATURDAY, 4TH SEPTEMBER

Am actually writing this while on duty. Reduced to this! I am in sole charge of the hut with two patients and no orderlies. Have to do everything myself, though getting tea ready will not be very difficult for so few. All this is not really worth mentioning save for the excitements of last night. After the Sports, the weather got worse and worse. There was more and more violent rain and wind and by the evening it was blowing a regular hurricane.

In pitchy blackness, under great diffi-culties, C and I wrestled with the tent ropes. We renewed three broken ones and then, with some doubt, crawled into our domain. We debated whether to go to bed and what preparation to make for the  collapse of our frail shelter. We finally got into our beds anxiously observing the acute angle of the tent pole and the straining ropes on C's side. The wind got so strong and sounds of straining and flapping all round so loud, that we got up and looked out and presently saw the complete collapse of our anteroom tent. It subsided quite calmly

in the middle of a violent gust despite the frantic efforts of order-lies and members of staff to save it from destruction. Short time later a wind arose from another direction. We looked out that way

and saw Parker sitting up unsheltered, Trotter being under ruins and rapidly suffocating.

After being extricated from difficulties, both were taken to Matron's tent and their possessions were covered with the remains of their home. Matron, the House Sister and a party of orderlies wandered about inspecting the tents and rescuing people in difficulty. The electric light having failed, the whole camp was plunged into inky blackness so all the rescue operations were carried out by lantern light, in howling wind and rain. It made the whole scene unique, one that we had never experienced before. Altogether four tents were blown down and the big one and one or two others were only just rescued in time. This morning we found the destruction even more widespread. The canteen tents were both down as was the big tent between the officers' quarters and ours. Sports should have been held today but have been postponed because of the weather.

TUESDAY, 7TH SEPTEMBER

Here we are, C and I, actually off duty till Thursday morning. What ho! and feeling as pleased as if we were going to have three months holiday. Sister Cowie worked the oracle today with Matron and in her teasing way, told us afterwards each in turn, trying to make us think the other one was not off. So we are at liberty now for a lovely long time and will have breakfast in bed tomorrow and then, if the weather keeps fine, go off for a whole day away. The past two days have been lovely but the nights are very cold and I couldn't get my feet warm the night before last.

Yesterday was a great day of Sports, a brilliant function held in brilliant weather. And so picturesque – all the watching men clad in khaki or light blue except for some 'kilties' here and there among crowd. The entertainment began at 2 p.m. I missed the first three items and came in at a tug of war in which several teams were competing. There were some thrilling moments and hard, strenuous tugging to great cheering from mutual supporters. The Officers' tug of war was very exciting and both sides, No. 3 Officers v No. 16, were well matched and determined to win. No. 3 won after a vigorous effort. Then there were all sorts of other competitions, with racing and mop-fighting and knock-out sack competitions. It was all most entertaining.

During the interval tea was served in the tent between the officers' and our quarters. Gullaravished fruit salad and ices and cakes and sandwiches. There were a lot of guests present, both French and English, and the MOs waited on them, doing the honours of feast. Smedley was closely pursued by Mr Rook all afternoon and Hogan had all her admirers round her, so much so that Matron pounced on C and me to go and do 'groseille'.* Which we felt was rather trying. Had to leave the brilliant scene at 5, to return to our efforts in the wards, but had seen most of the show, only three items left when we came away.

Drawing represents Mr Vilandré and Mr Pearce as they appeared on the course driving a ridiculous little donkey cart and dressed in bright red coats, large checked wide trousers and painted up like clowns and generally playing giddy goats. Quite the mountebanks of entertainment, they caused a great deal of laughter and amusement. How happy at breakfast tomorrow morning!!

* An early-nineteenth-century expression meaning 'to be an uncomfortably superfluous third person between two lovers'.

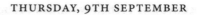

THURSDAY, 9TH SEPTEMBER

Our whole delightful day has been and gone and today C and I are at work again but feeling much refreshed, in mind at least, for our little holiday. It has really made a wonderful difference and I wish whole days off might come oftener.

We started away for our journeying fairly early, feeling we must get away as soon as possible and enjoy our complete freedom. So we set forth as happy as grigs down to Tréport, then took a motor – our first extravagance of the holiday. Got to Eu safely and wandered round the market, delightfully foreign in atmosphere, full of life and colours. Then we went into the fine, old cathedral and sat listening to a young priest play the organ. Afterwards, at the Hôtel du Commerce, we ordered our déjeuner for 12 and spent a pleasant time before lunch pottering to our hearts' content, shopping and buying presents of ink bottles for Sister Cowie & co.

Lunch was a rather entertaining affair. We sat at a big table with a crowd of French people. Most looked like decent country people probably in for the market, thoroughly French and foreign in every way. The meal was foreign too – no catering here to the English. One of the courses was boiled mussels, which C and I did not partake of but we ate the other courses with relish, much enjoying the change of diet. Departed rather replete to do some more exploring and find a nice place to lie back and bask and doze and rest. After walking some way we got out of town and, squeezing through a hole in the fence, went through a cornfield up into wood. We found a very cosy spot under a tree and had just a lovely time there, lazifying and sleeping and reading.

Came back to Eu for tea. Food formed a great part of our holiday-making. It was rather hot in Eu, so we were glad to get back to fresh air in Tréport. We stayed down on the front until the last possible moment before going back to camp. Interested to see a convoy of French wounded brought into hospital in Casino. They were so uncomfortably conveyed from the station in big motor transport wagons without springs. We sat on the shore for a while admiring the view and lovely sunset colours then we went up home again by funicular to our little canvas home, to end a most lovely day with sleep and rest.

Have had a bath tonight – a special allowance bath after the new rule. Too much water was being used for bathing so an edict was issued that no hot water was to be used from the boilers. We now have to wash morning and evening in cold water, except on our assigned bath night when the bath is to be left out during supper-time when it will be filled by an orderly and put into your tent ready for the weekly wash. New notice about this is giving rise to endless outcries and also laughter. Not at all popular but some thoughtless people have brought it down upon us.

Had such a pleasant time this evening with Rind and C, lying out on the cliffs, gossiping together. Getting to like Rind more and more. Enjoyed my afternoon in the wards so much too. Felt well and happy and was on with Sister Cowie and left pretty much alone except for her welcome appearances. We have six patients left now, several having gone off to Blity this morning. It will be rather slack again tomorrow with the ward so much emptier and the staff still augmented.

Yesterday was glorious and sunny and just completed our joys. We got up for a second breakfast and joined the night people. We tried porridge and were initiated into the mysteries of night-duty meals. Afterwards we had a grand turning out of beds and bedding, shaking out clouds of dust as far as our blankets were concerned.

SATURDAY, 11TH SEPTEMBER

Above picture represents an exciting interlude during this afternoon's duty time in Hut 2. Rippard, the concussion man who has been in some time, suddenly got out of bed and without any warning set off down the passage clad only in nightshirt. Had to hotly pursue him and with the help of Miles, an 'up' patient, I got him back to bed. He is quite dotty poor dear and really seems to be getting worse.

A big convoy came in early morning and now we have fifteen admissions in our hut. Next door there are twenty and we are all as busy as can be again. Had been expecting a quiet day ahead having heard nothing about the arrival of a convoy, so I was really quite taken aback to hear that the ward was nearly full again. C has had to go back to work again this evening in her ward. Their cases are worse than ours and there are more of them. Their side ward is full too. Captain Cowper was doing dressings all morning and afternoon and hadn't quite finished at teatime, so he was having a very full day and had no time to carry on his antics and treat us to his monkey tricks.

MONDAY, 13TH SEPTEMBER

Well-a-day! This is a jibe! The blow has fallen and C and I are both going on night duty. We learnt the news yesterday by degrees. Sister told us for a fact but only when the lists were put up at suppertime did we know where we are going to spend our time on nocturnal duties. We are still in our old Huts 2 and 3 and Sister Garnett is our commander-in-chief. We are really very glad for we know her and she is very nice. Rind is also on nights so we shall probably have a very good time. Have come to bed now for the afternoon and will rise up at 6.15. And then for the first spell of duty! Looking forward to the change with some anxiety. All will be so new. We are staying on in our own little tent today but will move into Parrot House* tomorrow. Besides us, Jobson, Bownes, Hynes and Parker are the other night-duty VADs. Great changes are taking place. The weather is still lovely. Long may it remain so.

WEDNESDAY, 15TH – OR THURSDAY, 16TH – SEPTEMBER

Well here we are established in Parrot House and having done two nights of n.d. am now in bed and will soon be trying to snatch precious hours of sleep to fortify myself for twelve hours of duty tonight. Don't know where to begin an account of all our doings. There seems so much to say. I cannot truthfully say n.d. pleases me. Life so very un-normal: it has some attractions certainly, though when novelty has worn off I may find it much more trying.

Have been doing special in Hut 1 with a man suffering from tetanus and glad to say he seems now to be getting better. C remains in Hut 3 and has been having dog's life there, as four men are terribly ill. One died last night and all the others seem dotty or violent. Poor dear, she feels rather worn.

Sister Garnett is no longer in command of Hut 3 and now looks after 1 and 2. I see a nice lot of her and the visiting tetanus man. C works with Sister Hewitt who relieved Sister Cross in 3 Medical, the latter not being considered competent to deal with the very bad cases there just happen to be there now. So I hardly see anything of C all night. She has supper in No. 4. Here, Sister Garnett and I – and Sister Banham who comes in from A lines – have our meal together in our sphere of action. Last night I was cook and prepared mushrooms in butter and fried eggs. Really very good.

---

* The marquee-type tent in which all the nurses who were on night duty slept was nicknamed the 'Parrot House', probably because of all the chattering which went on there.

Our workload is very light, nobody is really bad. I am rather enjoying this Parrot House. It is really very cheery being altogether. Rind is now snoring loudly on the other side of the blanket partition and there are sounds of deep breathing from other directions. Seems a sign for me to try to get to sleep now, and go on writing later tonight when keeping watch in the side ward. I got a letter written last night and night before.

8.45 p.m., on night duty

Slept like a top this afternoon, after I had settled down to slumber, and woke up feeling rather sodden. Until we get accustomed to the change, I don't know how we shall all manage after so many nights of duty. We have to make do with so much less sleep and longer duty. Am hoping none of our lot will break down, as one or two of every relay have collapsed so far. We seem all to be keeping well at present, except for Bownes who is suffering from headaches but not badly enough to keep her from duty. Will soon have to think of preparing our midnight meal – fried bacon again. Should be glad of any job to keep me awake as I am beginning to feel very sleepy and jaded. I find between 1 and 3.30 a.m. the worst hours, especially the earlier part, but have not felt any of the awful sensations about 2 a.m. that people describe. Can hardly realize that I really do sit up all night, as it seems a dreadful thing to get no sleep.

1.20 a.m.

Feel I am getting very sleepy and leaden eyed. Would be a serious matter if I dropped off while sitting here on guard, so I must pull myself together. I have had a very good meal – three rashers of bacon and buttered rolls, served hot, and also tea to drink and tinned peaches – so have done not badly. A Sister comes in to share our meal and she appeared this evening full of anticipation and seemed to quite enjoy the food. She is one of new Sisters and comes from Bagthorpe,* so knows Nottingham pretty well. The tetanus patient here is fairly quiet and really seems better.

FRIDAY, 17TH SEPTEMBER, 10.20 P.M.

Back in the little ward with Prior. He seems much about the same, though the Sister who is specialling him during the day says he was not so well and rather restless, but just now he is sleeping a lot so I hope he may be better. It is a nice night tonight, fine and warmer, rather a joy. I don't like wet cold nights at all, even when in shelter of the huts.

The Parrot House and birds at home

MONDAY, 20TH SEPTEMBER, 1 A.M.

A large convoy arrived early yesterday morning, so our peaceful time is over for the present. The convoy came just as dawn was breaking. I went into Hut 2 to receive them and Sister and I took temperatures and helped to get the men settled. Matron was on scene assisting and dividing her attention between our three huts. Sister Cowie came on duty early. We hadn't done any blanket-bathing, the time had gone so fast.

* One of the two principal hospitals in Dorothea's home town of Nottingham.

The ward is quite full and next door, all but one bed and the side ward is full up, as in Hut 3 too. At present no one is very bad except one man who is suspected of having pneumonia. Sister has been specialling him. Prior has been left to look after himself pretty much, though I have just been in to settle him up again. Now I am sitting in the bunk while Sister stays in the ward with Tidswell, the pneumonia man. Have had a very nice evening meal and feel fortified by it, not so sleepy as usual.

In the morning after breakfast, Rind, Jobson, Bownes and I went for such a lovely motor drive into the country to La Madeleine, a farm in the forest of Eu. The car had been ordered beforehand and came up to the camp for us. We had all donned new regulation, wet weather and windy hats and found them a great joy for motoring. We all packed into the little grey car – a very good goer – and set off. The countryside is looking lovely and the weather is so good. We went a new, very pretty way, past Criel.

At La Madeleine we had a most delicious spread of omelettes, home-baked bread, fresh butter, apple jelly, cider and coffee. Such a meal, and though we had only just finished a large breakfast, we were quite able to do justice to this second feast. Our table was out in the pretty little cider apple orchard, under the shade of trees, and we were all in excellent health and spirits. Afterwards, when we were settling up with the landlady, we secured a large loaf of bread and two bottles of cider, that Jobson and Bownes so wanted. They looked most dissipated and rather disgraceful. We drove straight to camp afterwards and went to bed as soon as we got in. It seems so funny to think this was all happening on Sunday. There was so little Sunday about it and now it is Monday and another week to come.

I have moved here, into the side ward, as Prior seemed restless. Mounting guard now and I suppose that Sister is doing same with Tidswell. Getting very sleepy and think I must take a walk up the ward to wake me up, or else I shall be nodding hopelessly.

TUESDAY, 21ST SEPTEMBER, 10.55 P.M.

Am sitting again in the little side ward, this time to watch poor Prior dying. A sad task for the night. He seems to have taken a bad turn during the day, as he appeared to be better this morning. He looks very, very ill, his breathing so strained and difficult.

A change in staff has come about tonight. Sister Garnett has gone – all of a sudden, she moved to No. 19 Clearing Station* on Miss McCarthy's orders. Matron came in last night and landed this bombshell on us. Sister G was absolutely taken by surprise and much perturbed. She went off at 10.30 today, by ambulance to Abbeville and then on to a destination up near the front. I was much distressed about her going. I seemed to have settled down so well and so quietly under Sister G's regime and was very happy indeed working with her. Such a toss up as to who her successor would be, though I am quite happy again now as Sister Northwood has been transferred tonight pro tem and I have every confidence in her and like her so much to work with. C is, of course, equally, if not more delighted. She has always had great admiration for Sister N as a nurse, anyway. Sister N is not very pleased with the change, coming back to night duty having only just been on, but she comes off when we do at end of month, so does not have so very long to go. It is now 3.45 a.m. and the day will soon be here again. The invalid here is still alive and seems just a little better. Sister Northwood and I have had café au lait to warm us up and we feel wakened and fortified.

All night staff were paid yesterday morning after breakfast. Matron dispensed coins, done up and packed as usual. VADs got fr 302 c 75, which is more than £10. Pay is a wonderful mystery and

---

* Casualty Clearing Stations were established as close to the battlefields as possible. See Glossary, p. xxiv.

seems always more than one ever expected. Have been kept waiting some time for this payday and some VADs have found their funds were getting very low.

THURSDAY, 23RD SEPTEMBER

The ward seems very quiet tonight and a great change from last night, for poor Prior died this morning about 6.30, just when Sister Northwood and I were making his bed. He had put up such a fight all night for life. It was terrible to sit there hour after hour and see him struggling for breath. He really had seemed a shade better in the early morning, his breathing was quieter, but the effort of having his bed made and being turned was enough to blow out the little spark of life remaining and he went quite suddenly, in a few minutes. Sister O'Hearne was summoned to see him and when she came in I went away to bed-make in the ward, while Sister N did the last duties for the departed. It seems strange tonight not to have anyone in the little side ward, and to see it shut up – dark, quite lonely and sad.

Mr Sinclair just been in and have had nice little tête-à-tête flirtation with him in the absence of our chaperone. Quite sad, as he is going home soon to be married to his lady love. We used to have great times when Sister G was here and he came in and stayed gossiping for some time. Now I must make a round of the wards and then investigate the matter of supper in No. 3 which we are all to have together, a very nice idea.

Between 3 and 4 this morning I was just dropping and my eyes were closing all the time. A most miserable feeling. All the same, time is slipping by and I shall soon have done a fortnight's night duty, practically half our term of service.

SATURDAY, 25TH SEPTEMBER, 9.30 P.M.

Think night duty must be affecting my nerves a bit, as I am feeling very jumpy tonight and not at all encouraged by the prospects of a sudden terrible rush of the wounded. There is an awful battle in progress and before long the harvest of sufferers reaped there will begin to come in.* I can just imagine the awful din and ghastly nightmare of it all. The whole place is to make ready for the arrival of hundreds tomorrow, in fact any time now. We are to have biscuit mattresses put down between each bed in all the huts. Hut 4 is to be made surgical and all the patients there transferred to other quarters. Every side ward is to accommodate three patients. Mon Dieu! What shall we do with such a state of things? I don't know how such numbers can be coped with. Even the convalescent camp is clearing out, to be used as extra wards. C and I hope we shall be able to rise to this emergency and not be absolute noodles, though I feel I really know dreadfully little if left to myself.

TUESDAY, 28TH SEPTEMBER, 2 A.M.

Well, here we are in the thick of it. I have always been told that one day we shall be busy and the time seems to have come at last but oh! the suffering and misery it means is heart-rending. There seems to be a tremendous battle raging. The general attack is from our side and the news from the men who came in with each convoy is encouraging. In fact if all the stories are true, the state of affairs is most hopeful. But it means a tremendous rush of work in all the hospitals tonight. We have had twenty extra beds put into the ward, brought in before midnight by crowds of orderlies and already we have 21 patients. There is hardly room to turn in the ward for all the beds.

The great rush began on Sunday morning. Now we are to have convoy after convoy and evacuations every day. What a life! I am still in No. 2 prowling around and rarely go into No. 1. Marsh reigns there supreme. We have two or three really bad cases here and another might haemorrhage which is rather agitating. I am not looking forward to the arrival of the next contingent of wounded soldiers. Have just been to No. 3 for light refreshment with Sister and C and am back to resume watching with Catterill. He is very pleasant to be with, most kind to patients, attentive and a good worker but rather a quaint creature, a little like an overgrown schoolboy, always ready to

---

* This was the beginning of the Battle of Loos. See Chronology, p. 350.

giggle and snigger at any joke or amusing situation. We had quite a burst of day orderlies when the beds were brought in, but after they had been established all the extra helpers went back to bed again till they have to turn out to receive another convoy, probably some time early in morning.

Have taken things quietly in the mornings over the last day or two and yesterday was not very fine, though it promised well. I went to bed as soon as possible to prepare for tonight. I find it very difficult to get to bed in spite of all my good intentions. Going to bed in the daytime is not the same as night, but I am very thankful to be able to sleep so well. It really is a great blessing … *Dorothea added a marginal note against next five lines:* 'sleep has made this nearly illegible'.

WEDNESDAY, 29TH SEPTEMBER, 11.45 A.M.

Here is C just back from town. She will find Parrot House still standing and inmates all in bed, mostly asleep preparing for a strenuous night. There is a most awful gale raging after a wet and wild night. The Mess anteroom tent collapsed again at breakfast time. We helped to do a hurried moving of furniture out into the Mess tent – made it only just in time. Orderlies and a troupe of volunteers did rest of the tidying up. There was no attempt this time to save the tent as there was no use struggling with it. No other occupied tents have gone yet but if the wind gets worse tonight it will probably cause wholesale havoc. Am in bed. C is anxious to get off to sleep to prepare for tonight.

Such a time last night. Came on to find a convoy occupying half the beds in the ward and the other half left empty by a departure in afternoon. Then at 4 a.m. we took in another convoy that filled every bed in all the huts and we were on the go all night long. Six operations, five of them head cases, were done last night. Rind came over from the enterics ward to help till 4. I was so pleased to see her.

The men all in very poor spirits about the fighting. There are a lot of very bad cases among the new arrivals, several on DI and SI lists. The day people will have a job. They already look very worn, hardly having had any off-duty time. I have no time at present for writing at night. Not much in the day either.

THURSDAY, 30TH SEPTEMBER

Parading tonight in a much emptied ward, 23 having gone out this morning at 6.30, and others this afternoon. So only the worst cases are left and two more are going tomorrow. Such a coming and going as never was. Do not think there is another ...

FRIDAY, 1ST OCTOBER, 11.30 A.M.

Never got further than this last night, as I was interrupted and never got back to writing again. Now I am in bed and have just read letters from Mums and Nurse Lee – such lovely long, long ones – Mummsie dear! I feel I want very much to see you and speak to you!!

Am not feeling very sleepy or really tired in spite of each night's happenings. Was indeed a night! After I began to write and was going to say that no convoy was expected, news came of one arriving at 4 and it turned up in very sooth. O Oh! the heart-rendingness of it. This time I felt sadder when looking at the men than ever before. They seemed so utterly worn and suffering and caked with dirt. All weary for want of sleep and dazed with horror of the ghastly sights and carnage up in the fighting line. Nearly all of them were wounded in more than one place. They came pouring in and every bed was filled, except for two that were left empty: one by a man who had just gone Blitywards minutes before and the other bed was poor little McGugan's, in which he died last night, very peacefully and rapidly, considering he was a bad head case. I watched by him all evening. He was ever so good and tried to take milk and feeds almost up to the end but he was unable to speak and not really conscious, though he could hold my hand and squeeze it which was so sweet of him. Sister O'Hearne came in and with her assistance I made him ready to be taken away, and not long after this, we were in throes of receiving another convoy.

After yesterday's mass exodus some more men went later from Hut 2. They are turned out now as soon as possible. What must the fighting be like? The men say it is sheer murder and simply horrible. They were too tired to speak of it this morning. One I asked told me the horror of it and turned away with a shudder from the thought of thousands of wounded lying unattended and trampled underfoot, not to speak of the dead.

I do not know how the day people will get on. Dressings will be fearful in all the huts today. One of new huts was opened and fifty stretcher cases put in. It must have been a very big convoy.

Besides all these excitements I had to keep a sharp eye on Williams and Knight. Both had a leg off yesterday and were in danger of haemorrhage and collapse, so we had to keep cooking to give them feeds and stimulants. They now seem to be getting on as well as can be expected.

Have nearly come to end of this book. Must begin a new one. Such an icy blast blowing in through our opening and chilling me to marrow. Must tuck down bed and get a sleep. C has had a bath and now is sleeping peacefully and Rind and Hynes both in bed too. Hut 3 very busy and added to patients they have Captain Williams in side ward very poorly. Was really bad yesterday and day before but better today. I don't know what the malady is.

MONDAY, 4TH OCTOBER

Just beginning new vol. of diary. How and where will it end? Am wondering very much just now what to do at the end of six months, as I have been suffering from an acute attack of homesickness these last few days. Must be partly a result of night duty, which is definitely wearing to the system, although except for a slight cold I have kept very well so far. Also, no doubt, a result of the very strenuous time we have had since the big battle began. Now the excitement seems to have died away again and we have not had another convoy in since the night before last. This is said to be a bad sign of fighting and everyone is really very depressed about the accursed war. Casualties during the past week must have been appalling, simply too much to contemplate. The day duty people have worked frightfully hard with no off-duty time for several days. In that way I feel rather glad not to be on day, but still don't think I shall be sorry to make the change when the time comes.

The last convoy, which came in on Friday, were really very depressed and seemed as though they had been through some awful times. They were quite dazed with sights and sounds and very exhausted and weary too. We took in 34 new patients and hut quite filled up except for two beds. Had such a job getting patients all in. Matron helped by taking nearly all patients' temperatures while I got on with other jobs.

Peace just descended on Parrot House except for murmurs of conversation, the time being after midday. Rind, at my back through the blanket curtain, is just getting into bed and I think she must be last to seek her downy. Will have to stop. Hope that I shall have time to add more tonight if no convoy comes in.

10.30 p.m.

Back on duty again and am sitting at the middle table keeping watch while Catterill is away having supper. We still only have ten patients and no word of a convoy coming in tonight, so I am expecting a quiet time. Except for Williams* and Knight, two amputation cases, we have no one bad at all. Sister has just been in for her occasional visits with Sister O'Hearne who is making her rounds. Now they have departed so I am left sitting in absolute quiet except for the sound of snoring coming from one of patients. Some of the men seemed very nice and I am sorry there's not more time to get to know them. They came and went so quickly amid such a rush of work that there was simply no opportunity for conversation. Large number of Scotches. Have four out of ten in the ward now.

WEDNESDAY, 6TH OCTOBER, 1 A.M.

Very quiet ward tonight. Catterill is keeping guard in there while I am here sitting in the bunk very cold about the feet and stuffed up with a cold in the head, but otherwise fairly flourishing. Have

---

* Unusually, the patient Williams was a commissioned officer who in normal circumstances would have been sent to an officers' ward. Too many officers must have been wounded in the great battle for this practice to be adhered to.

one patient less, Rippard having gone this afternoon to No. 3. He is a prisoner for some misdeed, so I suppose he is awaiting trial. Three more men are to go tomorrow, so if no convoy comes in it will mean a very slack time indeed in the night. C and I were energetic yesterday morning and went into Tréport and shopped and also had drink and bun at the little pâtissiers. We didn't get in till latish after we had performed all the commissions – our own and other people's.

Catterill in a blanket coat for the night

Have come back from supper next door feeling slightly restored but am still very cold. Very much looking forward to a delightful bed and a good sleep all afternoon.

10.25 p.m.

Just went for a little stroll up to the cliffs with C and Rind and looked out over a sea dotted with little sailing boats and wearing one of its more gentle aspects. Matron has been speaking to the original five VADs about us staying on another six months. The question has to be decided sooner or later, a very knotty point. Apparently there is not much prospect of leave at the end of six months, so it would probably be a long time before we could get home even for short visit and this seems appalling idea to contemplate, especially while I am still suffering from homesickness. Our time is not up anyway till 13th January 1916 which seems a long way ahead but the days will pass along fairly fast, just as they have done up to now. I can hardly realize that we have been out here four months already.

SUNDAY, 10TH OCTOBER, 1.30 A.M.

It's rumoured now that we don't come off night duty till end of this week so must make up my mind to peg along for a bit yet. Capt. Williams still very poorly and on DI list now. I'm afraid he will not get through which is sad after length of time spent here trying to get patched up to go to England. Others all seem to be doing pretty well. Not quite so cold tonight which is a mercy.

MONDAY, 11TH OCTOBER, 11.30 P.M.

Only one or two more nights left of night duty if the rumours are correct and then back to daylight and a more natural life. Seems much longer than a month since we came on night duty. I wonder where we shall be put when we begin day work. The hospital is ridiculously empty and I heard that there were only about 57 patients altogether on the surgical side and a convoy is going out tomorrow taking five of our six, leaving only Williams. Other wards are apparently clearing out in the same way. Was a rumour last...*

Sister just been in on one of her rounds, wondering too what we shall do tomorrow night with only one patient each in Huts 2 and 3 and two in Hut 1 and three orderlies and four nurses to look after them. Seems rather hopeless doesn't it? There was rumour of a convoy coming in last night so Catterill and I turned down all the beds in the ward, put out towels and made it all ready but no convoy came so we had to turn the beds back again and we looked rather foolish this morning when day people scoffed at us for ever taking notice of rumours. Catterill has just arrived back having had his supper. He brought a deck chair with him and will make himself comfortable with a blanket and pillow and probably go to sleep.

---

* As Dorothea was writing her diary while on duty, we can only guess at the interruption that caused her to break off writing this sentence.

WEDNESDAY, 13TH OCTOBER, 9.45 P.M.

A very different ward tonight with every bed filled. Catterill is at one table and I am up here at the other on watch. A convoy came in at about 4 this morning and all the huts have been filled up.* There are about 450 cases altogether – 170 or so cot cases. But none in our ward are really bad and seem such nice men. A good many of them have been in hospital before coming here, but not many seem to have been up in the part of the line that saw the last big actions. Such a chorus of snores going on. Hope it will continue through night. Such a change from last convoy of wretched, restless beings.

Had such a time yesterday morning after breakfast. All Parrot House sallied out together into town and gathered at the Regina Hôtel where a great meal was prepared for us. After waiting a short time and doing some shop gazing, we all sat down to a spread and feasted on delicious fried sole and omelette aux champignons. Most excellent coffee, rolls, butter, jam and pears completed the menu. We all did justice to our Parrot House party, celebrating with this 'blow out'. After the meal we adjourned to the photograph shop along the port.

FRIDAY, 15TH OCTOBER, 9.50 P.M.

Queer existence this with such ups and downs of work. Now, after the last rush, our ward is nearly empty again with just five patients all down at one end. Of the old stagers, Williams is still left but he is well on the road to recovery and will go soon. Am so glad as he has been through such a lot and deserves to get home safely. Three other patients are 'chests' and doing quite well and another one is GSC† man from Dieppe with a broken kneecap from a horse kick. He and

---

* This was the final stage of the Battle of Loos. See Chronology, p. 350.
† General Service Corps: the Army's transport service.

two of the chest cases are going to Blighty* tomorrow so if no convoy comes in before tomorrow night, we will have absolutely nothing to do. Catterill is going home on leave tomorrow. It has been quite suddenly arranged because his baby is ill with pneumonia. Am very sorry he is going, as he is such a cheery grig and so willing and kind to patients. I suppose someone will come in his place, but it will be difficult to get anyone as nice to work with.

No word of coming off night duty. We are all being kept in suspense. I thought this was to be our last night but one of the Sisters has to go home because a relation is very ill, so fresh arrangements have to be made and I don't know when new list will be ready. I shan't be sorry when the time comes to change, but I certainly cannot complain of overwork these nights.

Left off suddenly in diary on Wednesday night and didn't get back again with an account of our photography. All us Parrot House inmates grouped rapidly just outside photograph shop against the backdrop of a home and tried to look as photographic as possible. We had two groups taken with a slight change of position and

'A very happy Parrot House party.' Seated, from left to right: Jobson, Rind, Bownes, Hynes, Parker; standing: Christie ('C') and Dorothea.

* First correct spelling!

afterwards we came up home to rest. Yesterday we were in fits of laughter over our portraits. Bownes went into town and brought up sample copies – one better than the other – but there are some queer freaks among us and figures for fun. All the same I am glad to have had the group photographs, they will remind us of a very happy Parrot House party.

I went on a great expedition this morning. Was offered the chance to go to Abbeville and Bownes and I accepted with alacrity. Sister Cross and Sister Sims went too and we started off from in front of Matron's office about 10 to 10. Sister Mackay, leaving for an unknown destination, travelled in the ambulance, along with her luggage and a Major. Sister Mackay has not been here very long and commonly goes by name of 'Old Dugout'.

We all drove off in great form. The Major was going on leave. The ambulance flew along the road like whirlwind. Abbeville is a very different place from the last time I was there and I could only remember it in parts. It is more military now, the streets crowded with army traffic, mules, wagons and French and English soldiers galore. We soon left the Major at an office and Sister Mc at a hospital. We had half an hour to see the cathedral and then shop and have coffee and cake, so did it all in a bit of a bustle, but enjoyed it immensely. Most interesting trip to see a big military headquarters in full swing. Came back even faster than we went and arrived in camp just about 1.45.

On our return, everyone in Parrot House was asleep in bed, preparing to get up and go to a concert at 6.15. Bownes and I didn't go, having come in late and we had a longer snooze than usual, being rather disturbed with one thing and another. Motoring is rather tiring, the breathless speed of journey.

In the morning, after breakfast, the night staff went up to Matron's office to collect our pay. Rind and I only received empty envelopes having arranged to have our money paid directly to home. Rather sad to receive a hollow mockery in the shape of empty envelope with sum of £12 inscribed on it. Amount we receive grows bigger and bigger each month. What will they say at home when money arrives?

MONDAY, 18TH OCTOBER, 12.50 A.M.

Only just sitting down for a few moments to write this. The ward is full up again and there are several bad cases. Came in yesterday evening at about 9.30 and we were very busy for the rest of the time. Not much notice was given of the convoy's arrival so we had to turn down the beds in a great hurry. They were soon filled once the patients came in – poor men just down from trenches, all dirty and dressed in khaki. They seemed nearly all to belong to one or two divisions sent up to recapture Hohenzollern Redoubt, and from their accounts they must have had terrible time, though they succeeded in gaining position. Men from Notts and Derbys – the Robin Hoods and the Sherwood Foresters – were in it too. One man said both battalions were very much cut up. There are a lot of fractures and bad wounds in legs, and some men have lots of wounds to their heads, body, arms and legs. So many of them were out in the open without help for hours before they could crawl or be brought in, Germans shooting at them all the time.

I am waiting now for supper and quite ready for it; we have it rather late these nights. Poor little Sister flies from one hut to the other, doesn't know which to give attention to. They all have bad cases.

WEDNESDAY, 20TH OCTOBER, 8 P.M.

Well a day. Here I am back on day duty again. Such startling changes have occurred since I was last writing my diary. Heard only yesterday morning after breakfast that we were to come off immediately and do no more night duty till perhaps February. It took us all very much by surprise. Parrot House was in great flutter. Bownes, Hynes and Parker were hardly able to control ebullition of spirits at the news. I didn't like the suddenness of changing. I would almost rather have had another night before coming off but I was still prepared to enjoy a day off duty with the rest of the Parrot House party. The Sisters only come off today having stayed on an extra night. C and I are really upset having to part with Sister Northwood. Had enjoyed working with her so much.

There were no lists to tell us where we were going until we parrots were all tucked up in bed, so we had no idea till the morning. I am now working under Sister Sampson in Hut 1 and C has gone to A II lines and is not very pleased at going back to the tents. She finds the work rather dull as they are all very slight cases over there.

THURSDAY, 21ST OCTOBER, 4 P.M.

Seem to have very little time now for the diary and cannot keep it up to the standard of slack night duty-times, lengthy and illustrated, but here is me taking a solitary stroll along cliffs to get an airing and have just come in again to our little tent to sit down a few minutes before tea and get something more added to diary.

C has gone down into town to get her hair washed. Will be lengthy job, as it always seems to take more time according to French custom. I am feeling rather tired, not yet fully recovered from night duty in spite of an excellent sleep last night. I am finding work in

Hut 1 pretty hard and so chaotic. I feel inclined to laugh sometimes, in fact it's the only thing to do really and I would do it heartily if it weren't for the poor wounded men, so sore and ill. We have some desperate cases and I really don't think they are getting proper attention. It is all so muddled in the ward, Sister Sampson seems so hopelessly unmethodical and this morning I was kept on the trot the whole time doing first one job then another and not able to go straight on with anything and get it finished. It was Sister Banham's first morning on the ward and she was in despair at times but on the whole inclined to take a cheerful view and laugh at the situation.

One of our patients had his leg amputated this morning and is really desperately ill. When I came off duty Sister Sampson was sitting away at the other end of the ward looking after the gramophone turning on some figging tune that sounded most incongruous. Made me feel very sorry. I was quite glad to come away. Perhaps things will look better presently when I have settled down a bit. I am longing for the orderly businesslike Sister Cowie regime.

Last Tuesday, when we had our whole day off after hearing the exciting news that we were not to go back to night duty, we had to decide what to do with ourselves. We were keen on a motor ride but having adjourned to Tréport, couldn't get a motor. So we went on to Eu – all except Parker and Bownes who stayed behind and a while later turned up in a little conveyance they had got hold of somehow, like this:

They were very mysterious about it and as pleased as possible. They took Hynes with them and went off into Forêt for the afternoon.

SUNDAY, 24TH OCTOBER, 9.30 P.M.

Have been very busy in Hut 1. There are few patients left now but I keep on running about as they are all bad ones. We have six left, all the rest went off the day before yesterday. Sister Banham in great fettle, so very rumbustious, shouting at patients too much. She annoys me by scolding them in a loud and strident voice, but on the whole she is quite pleasant to work with and full of energy though it doesn't seem to me very finished in her nursing and dressing of wounds. Rather slapdash. Sister Sampson is being shown up more and more every day. She does dressings shockingly and the beds are awful with discharge from wounds not properly packed. Sister Northwood appeared this morning from op theatre and helped with every one of the bad dressings as Sister Sampson, having a septic arm, was forbidden to do them herself. Such a treat. Sister Northwood seemed to put everything straight and we got all the patients nicely settled up in clean dressings and sheets after a good morning's work.

Such a wet night tonight. C and I went to the Harvest Festival service. The church was nicely decorated with leaves and fruits and one enormous pumpkin at the foot of the lectern and a huge cabbage perched on top. There was quite a large congregation, including Matron and Colonel. C and I sat with the choir, four men and the VADs to keep our end up with about fifteen or so orderlies, but the congregation joined in heartily so we had plenty of support. Mr Clayton is leaving this week and a new Chaplain, a minion of Archbishop of Canterbury, is coming instead. Mr C has been splendid in getting the church started and people to come to services. The new chaplain will find it so difficult to carry on his work.

SUNDAY, 31ST OCTOBER, 4.30 P.M.

Just a week since I touched this poor neglected diary but what a week of change. Here we are very much established in our huts, the long-talked-of and much-discussed winter quarters. C and I are at home this p.m. in our quite palatial abode and next door on one side are Tozer and Arnold, and on the other, Gibbie and Johnnie; Rind and Jobson are further down. It really is very nice to be in solid dwellings again but still I miss our little bell tents, airy and flapping though they were.

We moved in here last Thursday – and what a scene of indescribable chaos. There was no word about any move until the order to pack up and go was given by Matron at second lunch. A motor ambulance was coming at 4 to convey belongings across. Meanwhile, I – and of course lots of others – were on duty, and I never heard a word of moving until Sister Chesters came over a little before 5 to say Sister Banham and I were to be quick and go over to see our goods were safely packed. Naturally we were rather taken aback! But we hurried over to camp and found the ambulance very busy loading up with beds and boxes and packages of all sorts. All our luggage was gone and C too, so I walked over to the huts and after some enquiring and hunting found our room with C in the semi-darkness amid a chaos of furniture. The beds were all tumbled about and everything else pitched in any way. C seemed rather distraught and distressed by the confusion and the way the orderlies had handled our belongings, however we both set to work and got some order out of the muddle. After tea we went on with arranging until the room got quite fairly decent. We kept running in and out of each other's domain to see how they were arranged and criticize the furniture and effects. Yesterday after tea, in my off duty, I had another arranging and altered the position of my bed and just now C is lugging her furniture about trying to improve her end of room. Really very pretty little interiors and could be made to look very nice if we had chintzes. The walls are stained brown and the ceiling is painted white. The curtains for the windows are not ready yet but will soon be put up, as well as a big curtain across the room. On Friday everyone rushed into town and besieged the menagerie for furnishings. We each bought, among other things, a small table and I expect we will add other things gradually.

THURSDAY, 4TH NOVEMBER, 2.30 P.M. (BUT NOW BED TIME)

Lying in bed and trying to scribble a few words. Arnold wanted to read my diary this afternoon and I wouldn't let her, but then there are no great secrets. I am getting more accustomed to our hut life and am really very fond of our little room. Very homely and comfortable, but I still have a lurking fondness for the tents we spent so many pleasant weeks in. One great event since last writing is the arrival of eight new VADs. They came yesterday at about 7.30 and were on duty today helping with a convoy that arrived during the night. Some of them are really very nice-looking. Three or four are Red Cross and the others St John. Matron was rather upset at news of their arrival. It meant great re-plannings. The night people all had to shift into the next hut further on to give rooms up to the new VADs. I helped to settle them in and was quite entertained at participating in their reception. Another event is moving of Mess into a new Mess room ...

Lights out alas! No more diary!

FRIDAY, 5TH NOVEMBER, 7 P.M.

Have just finished long letter to Mums. Seated alone in little wooden room. Candle lit beside me. Stove burning nearby. Really very comfortable and happy but would just *love* to see all the dear ones at home. There are ridiculous and wild rumours circulating that the hospital is to be shut for the winter and we are all going back to England, and another I heard today from Tozer who had heard positively from Sister Black that sixteen VADs were going to Serbia 'tout de suite'. I don't think!

We had a lovely little fireside gossip after supper last night in the anteroom. Two Sisters came in and Rind, Jobbie, Hopper, Malet, Tozer and I all gathered round a very cheerful and warming stove. It is such a cosy place at night and really quite an acquisition. Sister Maskell is now in charge of Hut 1 instead of Sister Chesters. She doesn't seem like a 'stripes'* and Sister Banham and I do pretty much as we like. Sister B is a very queer, excitable creature, but I really like her. She is so good-natured and kindly.

MONDAY, 8TH NOVEMBER, 5.20 P.M.

C and I are rejoicing in a whole day off. It seems such a treat not to have to bustle on duty or through our meals but to have time absolutely at our disposal. Have just returned from an expedition to Ault along the coast, now trying to settle down to get letters written.

---

* A Senior Nurse with stripes on her uniform, indicating the number of years she had served.

Fraser* had a day off too and persuaded us this morning to come down to Tréport and try our luck with a motor for an expedition. She went down first to order it if poss., and we met her later in front of Le Plage. She had failed to get a motor but hired a pony and governess cart at Mers and was going out driving with or without us, determined on some adventurous proceeding. She induced us finally to go too, so we all went by train to Mers and to the stable where we got on a conveyance drawn by a quiet, sober little steed – 'cheval de dames' – such a styled and neat little vehicle. A woman of hostelry and two very amateurish and unhorsey soldiers put the animal in, induced it with a bit of sugar and, after some urging, we moved off. It was very slow-going at first but warmed up a bit later. Fraser was the charioteer and didn't spare the whip, hoping to get some go out of our animal.

The country is looking so pretty, the trees very autumnal and rather bare of leaves but enough to give a lovely glow of colours with lighter shades over the sea and land, reminding us of a work of some great painter. We reached Ault after a not too rapid journey. A nice little quiet, unpretentious, seaside place. We put up at the Hôtel de Paris, ordered a meal and went out for a tour of inspection. There was not very much to see. We made a few purchases and came back to feed. The landlady apologized for disorganization of her establishment. She explained that fifty soldiers had been entertained during morning and this accounted for a shortage of food. However, we had two omelettes, a dish of shrimps, hot and fresh, and coffee, bread and butter and this thoroughly appeased our hunger. Three cats surveyed our efforts and received with gratitude gifts of shrimps' heads tossed to them. We went to look at the church after lunch, then walked down to the sea, admired a view of the cliffs and afterwards got our gee again and tooled off back to Mers. We took another, shorter way home and arrived without any adventure or mishap whatever.

Have had tea at Regina so am now free to spend the rest of evening, till supper, writing… Except for frequent invasions of

* Probably one of the new VADs who had arrived on 3 November.

visitors – Rind, Jobbie and Sister Northwood, Parker and Johnnie – so my correspondence is getting on slowly. C is now scribbling away at her little table in the corner and I must scribble too.

THURSDAY, 11TH NOVEMBER, 2.15 P.M.

Had to leave our rooms especially neat this morning on account of a visit from Surgeon-General Sir Arthur Sloggart* to our quarters. He came to inspect the hospital, saw the abodes of staff first and then came back to the wards. We had just finished dressings when he came through No. 1 Hut so there was a great bustle to get everything done in time. The orderlies were all scrubbing and scrubbing away in the passages. We got the ward very spick and span by the time S-Gen came through. I had to go into side ward to quiet Ford who was kicking up a fearful shindy as result of the anaesthetic he had had for dressing his legs.

Matron was very affable to Rind, Gibbie and me the other day. She asked us into her private sanctum to partake of chocolates and then stood talking for ages, telling us about her time over here in France. Was really very interesting. I think Matron has a soft spot in her heart for us little VADs. She would certainly never talk to the Sisters as she does to us.

Great indignation among our superiors because of the new cap we are all going to wear. It is something in the style of the Sisters' caps but not as big and to be worn differently, but some of the Sisters are very angry at our daring to wear anything like their particular apparel.

Sister Banham had whole day off yesterday, consequently the ward was very peaceful not resounding with shouts and giggles and 'old thing', 'muck and filth' and other Banhamish expressions. Sister Chesters comes back on Sat to resume her duties in charge of the ward. No sign of getting patients away yet. High time they went to get a change of air and treatment and surroundings.

It has been very rough and stormy over the last few days. Hail

---

* D had the General's name wrong: he was Sir Arthur Sloggett, Director-General of Medical Services from the beginning of the war until June 1918.

showers last night were deafening, pattering down on roof. Rain came in through the stovepipe and lay in pools. An eyesore in the morning – so, after all, huts are not much more rainproof than tents!

SUNDAY, 14TH NOVEMBER, 4.15 P.M.

Tozer has come to join me in Hut 1. Matron has been hard put to know where to put us all, and with the new VADs we are far too thick on the ground. After the wild storm on Friday, all staff were put into the buildings and no more tents were in use. Several had come down, including the church and recreation tent next door. A fine crucifix was smashed to atoms, which seemed strange after a sermon Mr MacMillan gave us last Sunday about the wonderful preservation of these things and the havoc wrought by bombardment on churches in Belgium and France. Now one of new huts is turned into a church. Sister Northwood and I helped to drape the altar yesterday and arrange hangings at the back and it really looked very nice when we had finished. It was a wild storm indeed and yesterday morning the wind was simply terrific. People about here very cheering – saying it is not nearly so bad as it will be. They never think of coming up here in the winter as a rule and they are sure that even the huts won't stand against the wind.

MONDAY, 15TH NOVEMBER, 7.45 P.M.

Had such a nice walk with 'Johnnie' up the high road towards Tréport. Gloriously fine, clear moonlit evening and the little town below was lit up brilliantly, the big silent sea stretching out beyond. Enjoyed J's society very much. She is such a nice girl. As we agreed, one of the nicest things about this life is the chance of making friends and really very dear ones too. Hope J will be source of comfort in these off-duty times when Rind and C are both of no avail.

I went into town yesterday afternoon, had a bath at Le Plage. On way down in funic I had three Belgian soldiers in my compartment. One of them leant forward and presented me with a nice button, then when I began to talk to them, he took one of the buttons off another man's coat and presented that to me and later, he gave me a third, so journey was quite fruitful in souvenirs and interest, short as it was. Two of them had been up to the front and were wounded. They seemed such nice men. The sea was just lovely yesterday, the colours so wonderful, and I saw little sailing boats plying to and fro and a ship just leaving the harbour Blighty-wards – big rolling clouds and a blue sky between and in the distance white cliffs and far away on the coast, St Valery lit up by sunshine.

FRIDAY, 19TH NOVEMBER, 6.25 P.M.

Simply shocking the way this diary gets neglected but really *cannot* find time to get it written these days and certainly not illustrated. Since my last entry various things have happened. Convoy in for one thing and that after wild rumours of packing and going to Serbia, Egypt, Italy, Étaples or Aldershot. Nothing of the sort has happened. The convoy coming had somewhat remedied the over-crowding of VADs, and Tozer, who had come to keep us company in Hut 1, was immediately removed to a new Hut and in 2 and 3 the ranks have been thinned also. This happened on Wednesday morning, the convoy having come in the night before. Our ward is quite full but all our patients except two or three slight cases are up and about. It seems a very different place to what it was when we had everyone in bed and in some ways rather upsetting – cannot get the ward to look tidy with so many men clumping about in big muddy boots except when they shuffle around in their ward slippers. Also, they seem to take up so much room and sit round the stoves blocking up the highway. However, they seem a nice set of men, and when they settle down a bit more will probably afford quite a lot of amusement.

Am finishing this in bed before preparing for sleep. Getting on for 10.30 and lights out time and C is talking and distracting me. We have got green curtains up in our room now to divide it into cubicles. We use one for modesty when we wash, but only because it happens to be there. Otherwise it is rather in the way taking up valuable space.

MONDAY, 22ND NOVEMBER, 9.30 P.M.

Tonight there is great excitement over the change of staff to night duty. The list was put up this evening at suppertime. Tozer and Arnold are leaving again, which is sad, also Hopper, Trotter, Malet, Hogan, Fletcher and Robertson. They go on tomorrow and begin duties of night work.

TUESDAY, 23RD NOVEMBER, 3 P.M.

Resume discourse, interrupted last night. C appeared on the scene when I got so far and after that I had to prepare for bed. Just been calling in on Arnold and Tozer next door who are getting to bed preparatory for their nocturnal rounds tonight. Matron made a new departure and arranged that VADs are to be in charge of their huts and to write their own reports; she thinks we should have more responsibility now, but I don't think the Sisters are very pleased. We still have most of our 'up-patients' cowering round stoves and gossiping together but most of them are very willing to help in any way they can and do a lot of work in the ward. Before we came on duty, three went away this morning to the base. Some more will be going soon.

C is singing at a concert tonight, very much alarmed in case she should have to wear the new cap. We are all sporting them now, not the St John people who have had no orders, but Red Crosses all have them. They are oblong instead of square like the Sisters' and worn pinned over at the back instead of under. Rind got the caps from England. Matron saw them in the evening and gave orders we were all to wear them next day, so at breakfast we all hurried in rather self-conscious and latecomers, who had more of an audience, were greeted with shrieks of laughter and remarks of numerous critics. Altogether the new caps caused great commotion and flutter but as all these excitements do soon die down, no one will think any more about it.

SATURDAY, 27TH NOVEMBER, 7.30 P.M.

A bitter, bitter blow has fallen since last writing. Both Sister Cowie and Sister Northwood have gone – to staff a barge* plying between St Omer and Béthune and perhaps journeying to Paris as well. C and I felt dismal and feel so still. Seems so odd without our two favourite Sisters and only one remaining to connect us with good old times. News came suddenly as these moves always do. They heard on Thursday morning and then, yesterday morning two Sisters were lost from us. C and I have both decided there is no use getting attached to any Sisters on active service. Perhaps later we will find the case is the same with VADs, but I sincerely hope not. At present we all seem very settled and while Sisters come and go, 'we go on for ever'. All the officer staff desponding about Sister Cowie's departure and she was sorry to go too, a sad parting altogether.

To counteract these sorrows, I have been much entertained for the two last nights by Mr Kinsella's concerts. Had half day on Thursday, so I was able to go to the ballad concert on Thursday and enjoyed it very much. C was singing and got a great reception and was encored enthusiastically besides various orderlies. Then at the end, there was a play got up by orderlies called 'Slasher and Crasher' that was simply screaming. It was a real farce and thoroughly noisy and full of incident and we were kept in fits and the acting was really very good. Two of the orderlies, dressed up as girls, were splendid – a little bit muscular and bony and rather obviously padded, but that made it all the funnier. Sergeant Preston, a great light in our choir, took a principal part and was very good. The whole thing went with a great swing. The large audience of patients, orderlies and staff were much enlivened. Then, last night I was able to go again to a second entertainment – Pierrots and Box and Cox – acted by Mr Pearse, Mr Chute and Mr Bowman, and Harkin our chief Mess orderly who played Box. It was simply splendid and it was really surprising how

---

* Barges were used extensively on French canals and rivers throughout the war as an alternative form of transport for the wounded.

spirited Harkin made his part. He always looks so quiet and sober in the Mess, but appeared very different on the stage. Mr Pearse was excellent too and Mr Chute made quite a dear old landlady in a white wig and bonnet and acted his part excellently. The whole audience were kept in fits of laughter, especially when actors threw in all sorts of local allusions in the course of conversation. The Pierrots were good too, but I didn't think they were quite as good as last time.

Sister Northwood and I went into town on Wednesday evening and had such a nice time. Then in the evening C and I entertained a select company of friends to a supper party and we ate up the Christmas parcel that Ruth sent me, plum pudding included, that stewed in a saucepan standing in my wash basin. Quite successful and seemed much appreciated. Sister Northwood was our principal guest and a great addition to party. No idea then of the blow that was about to fall and we never considered it was the farewell feast that it turned out to be.

Have been to choir practice this evening. Only Wall Jacobs and I were there of the ladies and there were not many male supporters, but Mr Higgins Junior was present – quite an addition personally, if not in the matter of voice.

TUESDAY, 29TH NOVEMBER, 8.45 P.M.

Rogers is in Hut 1 now, an extra VAD. She came this morning and was anxious to assist, very humble and ready to do any scrubbing required. She effaced herself for a long time cleaning up in the sink room. Perhaps she will feel more at home tomorrow. Sister Banham likes her very much and was quite pleased at her arrival. Can't say I was equally so, but I daresay we shall settle down to work together all right.

The other day the stove in the ward needed sweeping. The pipe was blocked up with soot and when we came on duty, Newton was rigged up in a patient's blue suit and overcoat and all with a red tie bound tightly round his head. Looked the quaintest sight I have seen for a long time. Stoves have been giving a lot of trouble getting choked up. Tiresome things and seem to be an unsatisfactory make.

Latest excitement is the question of leave. VADs are to have leave now if they can trump up any excuse of home affairs and probably will get it anyway. Sealy is going in quite a few days and Roscoe soon after. We get eight days altogether. Doesn't seem very long, but the idea is blissful. Will be just lovely to really be able to see all our dear ones again and enjoy a most delightful little visit home. Don't know when our turn will come. Not for some time yet probably. Very much hope will be able to go with C as much more fun to go together. Still miss Sister Northwood and Sister Cowie very much and long to see them. It seems so strange without them at mealtimes sitting at their respective tables.

FRIDAY, 3RD DECEMBER, 6.30 P.M.

Choir practice tonight and I must go in a minute or two and attend a function and help Wall Jacobs to support the female voices. We seem fated to be always left to do our best with the singing.

Wild night of wind after a wet day. Sealy goes for leave tomorrow and will have a tossing going over to England. Wish I were her though, tossing and all, but really I think we shall all go sooner or later and I don't know what I shall do for excitement when this comes. Will soon have to sign on again and pledge myself to another six months' service. This one has gone very fast. Hope next will go equally speedily and then perhaps the war will be over.

MONDAY, 6TH DECEMBER, 9.15 P.M.

Went into town this afternoon and had my photograph taken at little shop on the front. Rind was to have come with me but she had an unexpected day off and went to Dieppe instead with Sister Robertson and Sister Johnson. So I went alone and seance soon ended. Hope I won't look an awful guy – but am not expecting much as a flashlight was used and I had only one pose. Wore apron and one of new caps to show friends at home how they become me. C is still off at different times. We cannot get together, which is sad. Have not seen her all day.

Here she is full of vim and vigour having been in the anteroom while I was at supper. I got some Christmas presents in town to send home. Seems to be getting near Christmas now. Nothing more has transpired about leave. Great sounds of mirth coming from next door – Sister Whincup in great form, entertaining friends.

Went to church early yesterday. Not been for so long and felt I must really make the effort. C and Rind went too, very nice little service. Rind changed her time and is off with me, which is very joyful. Getting to love her more and more every day and every single person in camp who knows her likes her, which is saying great deal.

Getting late now and must get ready for bed. Time goes appallingly fast.

THURSDAY, 10TH DECEMBER, 7.15 P.M.

Another awful night of wind and rain after very wet day. I could hardly get along through the wind and rain, and the awful lakes and puddles and mud. Ground above the camp is now in a fearful condition. A convoy came in this morning and after a considerable time of slackness, we are all busy again. C and I docked our whole day off tomorrow which we were looking forward to, but we will get it later, no doubt. Three new medical huts have been opened as the convoy are mostly medical cases – trench feet as an effect of the cold. Not many wounded. Seem to have some nice men in our ward. The one with his eye out is in the Public Schools Battalion and comes from Chesterfield. Must find out more about him. Sad for him to have lost an eye. He does not seem very conversational but perhaps will improve later. He was stationed with his battalion at Clipstone Camp, so is quite pleasantly reminiscent of home. I had a fairly busy day in the ward. Rogers is still with us, working away in her apologetic fashion and annoying Sister Chesters at every turn and corner. Rather hope she will get a move on to one of the new huts now that we have got busy again.

Have got electric light now in all the rooms here and it is very convenient to switch them on and off as one requires, but I don't like light in the rooms as it is too strong and seems to show up all the defects and untidy corners. Gibbie went into town and brought back proofs of my photograph and gave it to me at teatime. I think it not bad but it does not seem to be generally approved of and has been treated with scorn by some. Do not think however that I shall bother to get another taken.

SUNDAY, 12TH DECEMBER, 10 P.M.

On Friday evening after supper, I took a decisive step and signed on for another long six months. Last six months have gone very fast but it seems a long, long time to look forward to and the news is so bad just now. Do not know what is going to happen. Out in the East things are going from bad to worse. Never had such bad position before.* So what is to become of us all? I can't think. Poor Rind received a rude shock at supper on Friday evening. She had a letter to say that her uncle had died very suddenly and now her aunt was left all alone and wanted her back badly. Most perturbing and sorrowful news. Rind didn't know what to do about signing on, but Matron advised her to take the step and then if the worst came to the worst it could be arranged for her to resign or go home. If that happened, it would be dismal. I can't bear to think of such an eventuality. We were out together this afternoon and then sitting in this room and having a heart-to-heart talk.

Six of the VADs are leaving. All the rest have signed on. Rogers is going as she cannot stand the cold or Sister Banham. Smith, Huntley, Trotter, Parker and Awdrey will make a big gap when they go which will be about 3rd January. Sealy is back from leave – she came last night – and has had a fearful time crossing. It is much colder again, wind is biting and feels like snow.

---

* D may have been referring to the Gallipoli campaign, which was being abandoned as a complete failure. See Chronology, p. 350.

TUESDAY, 14TH DECEMBER, 6 P.M.

A wholer! And such a lazy one. C and I both had it together. Have been slacking and enjoying ourselves. I stayed in bed until Gibbie came trotting in at about 8 with porridge, fish and other comestibles. Lazified in bed, gossiping and receiving calls from Rind and Johnnie before going on duty. Then Hopper came and stayed a long time, talking. Was after 9 when at last decided I must get up and, making a bold effort, scrambled out into cold. Later, after some delay of tidying up etc. went out with Hopper for a walk. Nice day, cold but fine, and the sea was so lovely again, dotted with little many-coloured-sailed fishing boats tacking in all directions. Walked along to Mesnilval. Hopper took us to see an old farm, a most picturesque place with a little chapel intersecting a row of ancient farm buildings. A suspicious dog prowled round, not liking our intrusions into his yard but made no further demur.

Went up a little lane on far side and then worked round to Dieppe road and so into town. Hopper went back by a shorter way having to seek her downy and prepare for night duty again. We lunched at Hôtel des Bains. The room was rather hot but otherwise it was quite a successful venture. Afterwards we did some shopping, then up homewards, toiling by the steps as the funic does not run till 2 now. Spent the afternoon very quietly, so the day has not been wildly adventurous or strenuous, but all the better for that.

SATURDAY, 18TH DECEMBER, 3 P.M.

This little anteroom is very warm and cosy. Have just come in to write letters, at Rind's urgent request. She is already ensconced and writing, as is Gibbie. One of the Sisters – I think it is Sister Chesters – is reclining by the stove, evidently in the arms of Morphy, and another Sister is reading the papers. Room is very peaceful. Am glad, as I have a lot of letters to write.

Shortest day of the year! How quickly will the weeks go past till the longest day comes again and where shall we all be at that time? Many changes may come to our little community, though it is better not to anticipate, and to make the best of bad jobs when they come.

Very sad at being without Rind even in my off-duty time now. Rind changed yesterday after a convoy came in, so I have no one to go out with. Sister Banham asked specially for me to get off in the evening, with her. We went into town at the double and bought some presents for Sister Chesters. Then I went with C to choir practice and enjoyed being with her again. We have not been off duty together for ages, except for the whole day.

There are rumours of a big convoy coming in sometime soon, possibly on Christmas Day. The Germans have made an unsuccessful attack and they will probably follow with another attack. This may make a busy time and so interfere with the Christmas festivities. Rather hope not, as it would be nice to have a fairly quiet day. A smallish convoy came in yesterday but there were one or two fairly bad cases. Two went to theatre in the afternoon and one, in a big dressing, took a long time this morning.

Gibbie has just been along to tell me I can have a bath in new bathroom. It is my night tonight, so I am going to step along and get a good clean on the premises.

SUNDAY, 26TH DECEMBER, 3.30 P.M.

Christmas past and Christmas gone! All the excitements of the day are over and this morning after it all, a convoy came in and we have eight cases in the ward. I enjoyed yesterday very much but am rather glad it is all over. Too strenuous altogether – and Christmas Eve, nearly as much so. Got on everyone's nerves rather when we were making preparations and decorating, but after dinner yesterday the feeling was quite different and peace and goodwill reigned throughout the camp. Rules were relapsed and conventualities dispensed with. Sisters and MOs ran in and out of wards visiting and eating, drinking and making merry. Must have had biggest crowd of visitors in our No. 1 of any in the hospital. VADs and Sisters and MOs, many and various, kept appearing in twos and threes. Our little bunk was nearly crowded out. The Major turned up bringing some Belgian officers with him. He had brought a Belgian band over from Criel and they played round and round the camp, then went and had tea and great festivities in the Mess.

Can't tell about all the happenings of the evening but the whole thing was an uproarious excitement. The men seemed quite to enjoy it, though when their tea was over they didn't get much more attention till we began to clear up for the night, except when Capt.  Cowper and Mr O'Neil brought their jolly boys in to give entertainment to the tune of the gramophone and performed a clog dance with great skill, after which Mr O'Neil obliged with a step dance, which was really very well done though he seemed to feel it. I called on Rind and C and I visited various other people in their huts and inspected decorations. I think that ours is really as pretty as anybody's. No. 2 runs us very close, but they are all nice.

Had a sumptuous tea with endless cakes, sweets and confections to tempt our visitors. Some came in at Sister Banham's special invitation from Lady Murray's.* In the evening we had a delightful supper awaiting us when work over and done. Trifles and cold chicken and salad and desserts. We had to clean up afterwards, as the orderlies were all over at a big dinner in the men's Mess. Then we cleared the floor in the anteroom and danced to the gramophone, Matron being one of the keenest. Some of the Sisters looked rather scandalized but Matron went on gaily to the very end and finished up with suggesting a set of Lancers, joining in with great gusto, even discarding her slippers and dancing in stockings. She was altogether most frisky.

* The officers' hospital nearby.

I can well sympathize with her. Delightful to frolic after rigid army restrictions enduring for so long.

On Christmas Eve, we caroled gaily all about camp, a very pleasant episode. The weather was not too good, windy and inclined to rain in short sharp showers, but anyway it kept off fairly well till tour was almost finished. A goodly number turned up. We assembled at church at 5.45 and were provided with hurricane lamps arrayed in red paper. We began our round with great verve. Chance conducted our party very well. All did our very best and Keenan made the thing go with real swing. I never heard singing so good. We got numerous invitations to sing in the huts and went to a good many where we rendered one or two of our repertoire in best style before moving on. Had a harmonium with us for part of time. We ended up at the YMCA and gave two carols outside there and then went in to sing 'O Come all ye Faithful'. All rather tired and hoarse when it was over and I was glad to come back to shelter and rest.

TUESDAY, 28TH DECEMBER, 3.15 P.M.

Another Christmas over and gone. Last night's fancy dress party was a first-class affair, a quite brilliant display of costumes. C and I were off in the afternoon so we had time to spend a good while over our preparations. We both dressed alike as Indian princes. We made trousers of glass cloths and wore overalls, turbans of bath towels and a broad sash of chintz that I bought some time ago. Crackers for cockades in front and we made our faces up with some grease paint that Urquart had borrowed from Mr Kinsella as well as some burnt cork for moustaches. Whole effect really quite successful. Marched in arm in arm. Were able to see entrance of most of the other frolickers. They were all wearing masks at first and it was really most difficult to tell who people were without very close investigation. Some of costumes really screaming. One of the very best was Assistant Matron as a Boy Scout. Most ingenious make up, a hat of her construction and knickers made from trousers split up the seam and turned in. She really looked killing, so thin and tall, and her face so solemn and spectacled. Sister Angel's Golliwog costume was

very good too and very cleverly done. Both of them got prizes in the judging at the end and quite deserved them. Other prizewinners were Johnnie as Joan of Arc in a sackcloth tunic, a tin box cut up for the breastplate and armour, the Colonel's sword and Hopper's rubber boots – and Conran as a brigand, really splendid. She was so well made up that for a long time I didn't recognize her at all. She acted the part well too. Awdrey took prize for the prettiest costume, her make-up of Watteau period and very becoming.

Haven't time to describe all the other costumes. So many and so good, but whole effect, variety and shade was really splendid. Event of evening was entrance of Matron, after everyone was in the room. She came in with two ladies from the YMCA to a general chorus of shrieks of surprise from whole assembly as she appeared dressed in Colonel's uniform. Everything complete. She saluted to the company and then walked about for a bit looking at the costumes, causing much mirth. In a way she looked rather well but it wasn't a becoming get-up. Too stagey. Looked better in costume she changed into after, sort of Grecian effect. Really suited her very well. Was as nice as she could be, quite entered into the spirit of thing and enjoyed it as much as anybody. She stayed on till the very end and it was after 11 before the show was over. A large proportion of the company were in male dress of some sort, but being a 'hers' party, it didn't matter the least. All the windows were well covered over and the curtains pinned down to prevent any peeping Toms from spying on our goings on. If it got about widely that Matron had dressed up, especially in Colonel's clothes, there might be a great commotion at headquarters. Sister Robertson and Sister Blandy dressed up as 'Scotties'. Kilts both very good too. We danced in the big Mess room, cleared of tables and chairs, to the tune of the gramophone and had refreshments in the anteroom. Really enjoyed ourselves immensely and had a ripping time. Feeling now rather as though we had several nights out. Weary about the feet and eyes. Anteroom this p.m. a very soporific place.

THURSDAY, 30TH DECEMBER, 9.15 P.M.

Johnnie is paying a call and sitting garbed in a pink dressing gown discussing C's performance at the next patients' concert tomorrow, which she is to accompany. C and I have had lovely half-day together. By lucky chance our Sisters asked for us on the same day so we have enjoyed each other's company for a whole delightful afternoon. Nice weather too, so we have been out on a walk by the high road to Eu and through the park. We had tea in Tréport and came back again to our little room directly after. Early supper and now to bed to have a good sleep and prepare for hard work tomorrow as convoy is said to be coming in at 3 a.m.

Had a late night yesterday. Went to the Canadian concert at the YMCA. Was a sort of revue, based on a show of waxworks, and a man dressed up as Mrs Malaprop* showing off the figures – wonderfully well made up and dressed most beautifully in fashionable attire. Quite made the performance. A lot of people took part. They all did a little turn either singing or dancing. One of the best was a man who recited, garbed as Shakespeare, and a girl who danced as a glowworm was quite good. The effect was chiefly attained by limelight. We weren't out till after 10.30 so got very tired and longed for bed. Tumbled in as soon as possible after we got back.

Big evacuation for the hospital yesterday morning and at last Ford and Davis departed. We really felt quite sorry to see them go. Poor little Ford at very end just couldn't say goodbye. Had to cover

* A character from Sheridan's *The Rivals*.

his face to hide the big tears. Was really regretful to be departing. It is rather slack in the ward now but if a convoy comes in we will be busy again. Must settle down for sleep now, can't write any more. Am expecting to be on night duty next Sunday and not looking forward at all to the prospect.

SATURDAY, 1ST JANUARY 1916, 5.40 P.M.

New Year's Day! What a wild, stormy one, wind now tearing and whistling around our 'little wooden huts' like a mad thing. Wonder if it presages anything in the coming year. There is a feeling of unrest just now and rumours of big fighting in the near future, but where, when and how, no one can tell. A convoy came in the night before last. Not a big one and not many bad stretcher cases. We had six new ones. One was operated on today and seems to be a trephine. Have not had a trephine in the ward for quite a long time.

I wasn't awake last night to see the Old Year out and the New Year in. Was fast asleep and dreaming of home. Had a huge longing when I woke to be really there. Leave seems so far away. Nothing more has been said about it and Matron adheres to the fact that we cannot be spared. The fear of night duty is gone. To my great surprise, I found that all the new VADs are going on and we old ones are allowed a longer lease of life. Feel really overjoyed at thought of enjoying daylight a while yet, though work with reduced staff will probably be hard if there is any rush. The change around is made tomorrow and Hopper and Malet will come to life again.

Had a grand Christmas dinner last night. Got in a little late waiting for Sister Chesters and had to sit at a table nearest the door, but C came to join me – couldn't be parted at such an occasion – and we quite enjoyed ourselves. Had a very good soup and fish and then the turkey and its accompaniments and inevitable plum pudding, after which there was dessert and coffee and much laughing and daffing. Cap masks and moustaches caused much amusement. It really was quite a gay time. The decorations were very pretty for Mess. The only thing lacking was toasting at the end. No one proposed any health and when Matron got up we all got up too, so the grand dinner ended like any other evening meal. We should have celebrated the occasion with one good 'caller' but no one felt inclined to take the lead in the matter. However, afterwards Jobbie gave three cheers for Matron and House Sister and House Sister's Assistant. Then we had some dancing and frolicking in the ante-room. And then, to bed.

MONDAY, 3RD JANUARY, 5.30 P.M.

Night duty change has taken place. All the new VADs have gone from the community and others have come back to us. So pleasant to see such friendly faces as Hopper, Arnold and Tozer again. The latest excitement is that little Robertson is a scarlet fever suspect. She developed a brilliant rash, has a sore throat and suspicious symptoms and had been working in a ward where there was a scarlet fever case. So it sounds rather like it. Now isolated in room by herself and no one is to go near except those in attendance.

This morning was marked by the departure of six VADs – Awdrey, Trotter, Parker, Smith, Rogers and Huntley. Great leave-takings and farewells last night and again this morning. It makes a difference that they are not here. Our party seems so much smaller and it will be odd at first without them, especially such a personality as Huntley with her loud voice and virginal deportment.

Am now working as the only VAD in Hut 1 and tomorrow I believe Sister Chesters is taking both Huts 1 and 2, while Sister Street has 3 and 4, the latter to be surgical now. This will make work rather harder, but I like it. I never mind hard work so long as I am feeling well and brisk. Rind and Roscoe are expected back this evening from leave. So looking forward to seeing Rind again, dear person! They must have had a rough crossing. The wind has been so strong all day but it is lovely and bright and sunshiny. Private Chant came into ward this afternoon. He is going home for seven days' leave tomorrow to his father who is very ill. Such a nice man. My one little flutter of romance in this unromantic camp. Sister Chesters is having half day, so Sister Banham is in all afternoon. Consequently I have been going spasmodically at the double.

THURSDAY, 6TH JANUARY, 3.30 P.M.

Rind and Roscoe returned to us safely on Monday morning and got in at about 6, earlier than anyone expected. But they had had the most ghastly journey, both being bad sailors. Captain Wortham, who was supposed to be looking after them, turned out to be a worse sailor, so all three were as ill as could be and really suffered the worst woes of sea sickness. They are slowly recovering now, but vow not to face such a journey again, even if they are offered six months' leave or more. Gibbie went yesterday and must have had nearly as bad a time, poor dear. No word of any more of us going on leave. I suppose we must just abide in patience and hope for the best.

Have a very happy time now when off duty – just our nicest party of select friends, Rind, Arnold, Tozer, Hopper and Johnnie.

TUESDAY, 11TH JANUARY, 5.30 P.M.

C and I are having half-day together again. Another lucky chance and we are much enjoying an indolent afternoon. Just got in from taking the air. Not very energetic. We went down to Tréport, to the quay on other side of harbour to watch the waves. Really splendid as they are dashing up, then hurled back from the wall to rise in great columns of spray high into the air or shooting right over the esplanade in a most thrilling manner. Went up to end of the pier and watched a little Norwegian boat come in bobbing up and down in waves and looking very weather worn. A little piebald Aberdeen dog was standing on deck anxiously surveying terra firma, no doubt looking forward to wider spheres of exploration when safely arrived in port. We went along the sea front, and then C took me to a nice little patisserie to have tea. We burst in on Johnnie, Hynes, Sealy and Arnold just finishing a meal, and when they departed we had ours.

SATURDAY, 15TH JANUARY, 12.45 P.M.

Nearly time to go back on duty but must just begin my entry for today. Busy again in the ward as a convoy came in during the night before last. Not a very big one and a good many medical cases, but we got seven of them and two rather bad ones. One turned out to be blue-pus and has now been put into the side ward and isolated from others, which makes a more complicated arrangement for the staff. Sister dressed him in the morning and I helped. First time I had seen the real thing. The dressings are most extraordinary when taken off. Stained the brightest metallic green shading into blue at the edge. Discharge only from one leg so far. One poor man had a wound through both thighs, the result of one of our own maxim guns that another man was 'messing about with' near to him. The patient was unsuspectingly looking after dixies* for dinner when the gun went off and caught him in the legs. He seems very sorry for himself and rather nervy, but then the wounds must be very pain-ful. We had another man brought in at midday yesterday from the Indian cavalry camp who is suffering from a kick in the eye. Really bad, poor man, and he went to theatre in the afternoon. Had his eye taken out and in theatre it was discovered that he had compound fracture of orbit. He was dressed under anaesthetic this morning and is bad enough to be on SI list.

TUESDAY, 18TH JANUARY, 3.30 P.M.

Fire in our little stove crackling away so cheerily this wet damp day. C has a bad cold so given a half-day and now sitting up in her bed, drawing in Rind's album. R and I have been down into town rather languishingly; weather not conducive at all to brisk exercise and, having done our shopping, we came straight up here again to rest till teatime. Have been the only pro in my ward again this morning. Tozer is off duty for the day also suffering from a cold and general collapse. She was very poorly yesterday and the day before and came away early from duty in the evening. I quite enjoyed the morning and got through a good deal of work.

Arnold just come to call and is now sat down on my bed, darning stockings. Rather a boring job, but necessary at times. Great excite-ment amongst the nursing staff, rumours having spread that all

* Metal cooking pots.

allowances are to be cut off and we, and the officers, are to get nothing but bare pay. This has been the subject of much discussion and tribulation, but it really is fair enough when considering the rather extravagant allowances.

MONDAY, 24TH JANUARY, 2.30 P.M.

Today, a new blue-pus case arrived to join Brown in the side ward. Came from No. 9, one of Rind's huts. Arm case and looks rather souffrant. He will be company for Brown who is a melancholy creature and not an interesting patient. Sister does his dressing always and nothing else in the ward, so I am not to have any danger of infection.

No more convoys in and no word of any just yet. Will soon be time to go on night duty. Not looking forward to the prospect at all. The leave question is still in abeyance. Gibbie is away ill and till she comes back, apparently Johnnie and Malet can't go for their turn. Matron is at Hardelot, rest curing for a week. Seems different without her. Sister Johnson, who is taking her place, doesn't suffuse her personality throughout the camp as Matron does.

TUESDAY, 25TH JANUARY, 7.15 P.M.

Convoy supposed to be going out tomorrow afternoon or the next morning. Men have all got their kit and are much excited. No one will be left in the big ward apart from O'Meara and Paddy, our nice old Irishman, so there will be very little to keep me employed.

THURSDAY, 27TH JANUARY, 7.15 P.M.

Staff very busy again yesterday, a convoy having come in Monday evening at 9 p.m. Not very large, but some fairly bad cases. None in our hut are very bad. Sister B rather annoyed at light dealing we received. However we did have eleven cases, all the men are in bed and nearly all the GSW need dressings and foments, so it is not very slack on the ward. It was a great rush yesterday morning settling the newcomers in and then at 1.30 seeing the Blighty ones out. The sergeant was so excited that he was shaking all over when he was dressing into his pyjama clothes. I had to go to lunch before the stretchers were borne off, so didn't see the last of our friends leaving. They were all very happy and more excited than many of the departing patients have been.

Gibbie is expected back tomorrow, restored to health again. Will be pleased to see her and Matron should be back from Hardelot now. The invalids at No. 3 are doing well, but Tozer has had a bad time and was put on the SI list with her bad heart. Her sister has been transferred from another hospital to No. 3 to work as a VAD so she can be with Tozer in case anything happens. Don't know how long it will be before she can come back to work. May be some time. Conran is better too so her disease cannot be enteric as at first suspected.

In the evenings, I am very happy in the company of Hopper, Johnnie, Rind and Arnold. We have inaugurated the Reading Society for Improvement of the Mind. We were to have our first meeting last night after supper, but three of the mind improvers wanted to get baths for cleansing of the body, so the meeting is deferred till tonight. Stock of improving literature is wanted, but C has a book of Hilaire Belloc's essays and we are going to make a start with that, to let us down gently.

SATURDAY, 29TH JANUARY, 6.45 P.M.

Arnold has come to No. 1 to relieve the pressure of work. She will be helping Sister with dressings in the side wards of both huts, so I shall not be required there any more. Am delighted to have her to work with although I probably won't see much of her as she will be busy with Sister all morning and then off in the afternoon, when I am on. Brown and Arnold both had anaesthetics this afternoon and operations performed so I was left on lonesome from nearly 2 till teatime, while Mr Chase, Sister and Arnold managed affairs in the side ward. Have been a lot of operations over the last two days: three yesterday and today. One or two of the patients are bad, especially a Scotch boy with a wound in the neck, a very nasty place and rather serious. O'Meara had something more done to his leg and was kicking up great fuss all afternoon in consequence.

Hopper, Rind and I have been out for a walk this evening; our usual one up to the view point to look down on the town lights and then back again, just a nice little constitutional. It has been such a lovely glorious mild day, a sort of foretaste of spring, which is so cheering and refreshing. Lovely for Johnnie and Malet, who have gone on leave. They only heard they were going yesterday at teatime so they packed up last night and were off this morning. Lucky creatures. Will have had a glorious crossing. Gibbie came back with Sister Cooper last night. She arrived at dinnertime and was ushered into the room while we were all seated there. Looking certainly a lot better, not so haggard, but she is not very strong. Hope she will keep well and not break down again. Tozer is said to be going home quite soon, probably never to come back again. Her heart is in serious trouble, from over-strain and continuous coughing.

Yesterday Rind, Arnold, Hopper, C and I had a lovely walk to Mesnilval in the afternoon where we had a tasty meal at the very enormous Madame's of coffee, bread, jam and butter, an omelette and then, as a surprise, a dish of toast. When we had all put away practically as much as was humanly possible, Madame and her daughter came in radiant, bearing a plateful of pancakes, delighted to have thought of such a pleasant surprise for us. Was indeed very nice of her and we all ate up the pancakes somehow, but we could hardly stagger home afterwards. I felt rather ill for rest of evening. Dreadful to make pigs of ourselves!

*Fat woman
of Mesnilval*

MONDAY, 31ST JANUARY, 7.30 P.M.

The light has just failed again but fortunately not for long and is now back once more in all its resplendence. Have been into town with Rind shopping and we picked up Gibbie along the front. She looked tired and worn tonight. Do hope she will be able to keep well this time as another breakdown would just about finish her VAD-ing. Went yesterday afternoon with Rind and Hopper to call on the invalids at No. 3. Hopper went up to Tozer's room so Rind and I went along to Conran's and sat there a little while conversing. C is much better so it is not enteric after all. Only 'flux' of a rather aggravated kind but she must have been pretty poorly as she is still in bed. Tozer is still far from well. She looked so flushed and purply and still coughing a great deal. She is on the SI list and her father wanted to come and see her, but was not allowed to by the War Office. Seems very hard lines when Tozer is so ill. She will be going home as soon as possible, probably never to come out here any more. It is said that VADs are crocking up everywhere in hospitals throughout France, but here, the Sisters have crocked up as much as we have. Three are off duty now, the strain of winter probably and this rather rigorous life, day after day.

Getting great pangs of homesickness and longing to see all the dear ones again and would love to get leave, but oh! it would be sad to have it over and have nothing more to look forward to for ages. Still very busy in the ward, but this afternoon the blue-pussers were spirited away from all the white huts to Hut 18, to be isolated there and nursed separately. There are six altogether, so it will mean quite a business for someone. Arnold has gone with them and I am very sorry as she is so nice. Loved having her nearby though I saw very little of her really. Got a new patient shoved in on us after his operation this morning and another one yesterday. Blair, the boy with the wound in his neck, has been as bad as possible the last few days. Haemorrhaged twice, had three operations and is on saline constantly. Will be a wonder if his life is saved, the poor Jock. Nice boy too and always very quiet. Will be a convoy out soon and quite a lot going so ward will be much lighter unless another convoy arrives, which seems quite possible. Two of the Sisters, Davies and Maclennan, got orders to go today, packed and were off by 2.45 to a clearing station. So suddenly are things worked in this army system.

THURSDAY, 3RD FEBRUARY, 8 P.M.

Poor Blair died the night before last. Had a busy day with him and Sister was practically specialling him, with salines, hypodermic injections and frequent feeds, but all to no purpose. He was operated on in the morning, the artery that had been cause of haemorrhage was tied. He never properly recovered. He was dying when we came away at night and died at 11.30 p.m. We came on in the morning to see another bed empty. Another poor brave Tommy had given his life for his country. His mother had just arrived at the hut when I came in. She was too late to see her son but had come to get details from Sister and to speak to the men. Was a very decent woman from Glasgow and she looked so wayworn and sad. So dreadfully sad for her to be among strangers and too late!

Sister Chesters went to Abbeville with Matron yesterday afternoon, so Sister Banham was on all day and she and I had great time together after dinner. Had our tea in the bunk with great feasting, Sister B in great form, shrieking with laughter. We got the gramophone going in the ward and the men shouted choruses with very lusty voices, 'Down where the breezes blow – Oh-oh-oh-o-o-oh' was our favourite refrain and we all got quite giggly and foolish.

SATURDAY, 5TH FEBRUARY, 4.55 P.M.

Just in from such a lovely walk with Arnold, Hopper and Rind. Went daffodil gathering in the park. Found just a few far enough on to pick but still rather too early. Everything looks just so good in the sunshine. The sky is cloudless and it is so warm and spring-like. Promise of gentler days coming, regardless of the destruction. We boldly tackled Madame of the Lodge at the top gate on the subject of coffee and omelette and she promised to do her best. So after daffodil picking, we came back to the Lodge and before very long, we witnessed the preparation of the delicious omelettes, coffee and cider that the old granny pressed on us very insistently. Rather an unsophisticated meal, but very excellent. La petite of nineteen months old watched us most solemnly all the time from her high chair. Thought it must be an invasion of gibbering lunatics into her house and home. Have had rather a bustle back to be in time for duty, but with Hopper and Arnold I always expect bustle to end our promenades.

WEDNESDAY, 9TH FEBRUARY, 10 P.M.

Busy day again today. Convoy in last night of 350 or so cases, but not many very bad surgical ones. We have sixteen in Hut 1 and there are about the same number in 2 and 3. There is one very bad case in Hut 2, so I have seen very little of Sister Chesters today as she has been practically specialling this case. Sister B and I got on with dressings. Mr Chase's non-appearance made us rather late so I didn't get the afternoon off till 3.15. Seem a nice lot of men, though they are subdued and tired, but I think they will soon be quite merry and bright. Sergeant, Godfrey, Paddy and Weekes worked splendidly in the afternoon getting washings and tidyings done. They really are the most useful up-patients.

THURSDAY, 10TH FEBRUARY, 8.25 P.M.

Just got into bed, under the amused inspection of Rind and Urquart. It is a great business spreading out the first blanket and the sleeping bag, lying on the top, getting into the latter, pulling the rugs over the top of me and then tucking down comfortably. C and I laugh at our night costumes as they are distinctly funny and original. This was mine the other night when it turned very cold and frosty. I wear a nightgown and pyjamas with assorted bedsocks and I don't know what else besides.

Feeling tired tonight so got to bed very early. Went at double this afternoon. Sister Banham wanted me to do all I could so I got temps taken and beds done. Sergeant and some assistants did the washing. So saved me all that. Have two more patients up today so there are plenty of helpers rendering valuable assistance. Nobody bad among the patients – one man has a bullet embedded in his knee, which is unpleasant and will have to have op. of some kind. May turn out to be serious.

Matron is still threatening to move me from Hut 1 to let someone else have the chance of better experience. I have certainly had my share of best work. Been in Huts 2 and 1 for nearly eight months, but will be dreadfully sorry to go. I hope plenty of convoys come in to keep me there as I cannot be moved till we are slack again.

Great undercurrent of feeling just now between Sisters and VADs. Think it partly, if not largely, arises from the everlasting money question and also from real resentfulness and good deal of jealousy on the part of Sisters. Not an individual feeling but just an atmosphere of disunion.* It is a real pity as we should be able to combine quite peacefully to work for King and Country. I see no way out of this difficulty at present.

SATURDAY, 12TH FEBRUARY, 6.15 P.M.

Nice to be off duty, no more work till tomorrow morning. Have been fairly hard at it all afternoon but Matron has decreed that no beds are to be made before tea. They are all to be left till evening. Have got such a lot of up patients and some very useful ones. The Nottingham Sergeant is most helpful and can get others to work, having the authority of his promotion. Paddy does a good deal and talks a good deal and guffaws occasionally in the most inspiriting manner. He is a real old soldier, but quite entertaining. There is supposed to be an evacuation on Monday or Tuesday and possibly a convoy in tonight. Must be some more fighting as the convoys are coming in so thick and fast.

Concert party came to give two entertainments and then a dinner party over at the Officers' Mess, to which several of staff went. Sealy and Jobbie and Urquart represented us VADs.

The latest departure in camp is the inauguration of a Choral Society for the three camps, to perform oratorios and such like for the edification of personnel and the hospitals' wounded. I think if it ever gets started it would be a quite interesting and entertaining

---

* If this tension was money-related, it must have been because the professional Sisters felt that the VADs were being overpaid.

effort. Mr Kinsella is likely to be the conductor, though this has not been received with much approbation. For now the whole thing is very much en l'air, only at the preliminaries of arrangement.

MONDAY, 14TH FEBRUARY, 7.45 P.M.

Valentine's Day! But not much Valentine to be got here. A military hospital of BEF is a very unromantic place and when a small affair does blaze out, it instantly becomes common property and discussed in and out till quite threadbare. Nothing can be done in camp that isn't immediately discovered, but all hospitals are alike I suppose, as there is so little outside to talk and think about except the everlasting topics of the war, leave and home. Anything out of the ordinary is welcomed with delight, as food for gossip. The latest is that today Sister Blandy received her marching orders. She was given half an hour's notice this afternoon. She had to come off duty, throw her things into boxes, and now she is gone from our ken. Perhaps I will never see her again, but cannot say I am heartbroken. Such an odd world of rapid change this hospital is! Mr Chase is leaving to go on a barge. The Major came looking to break the news to him. I wonder who we shall have instead.

Great movements are going on up the line in preparation for the convoy that came in to the Canadians last night. And another comes in tonight. I cannot imagine where it is going to be accommodated.* There are no beds at all in No. 3. The church and Mess tent will have to be filled up, and what will happen then? Must be preparing for some awful fighting soon, poor, poor things. Do hope it won't be another time like Loos. I never shall forget the dazed horror on the faces of the men who came in then, worn out and nerves shattered – and some of them with such dreadful wounds.

The big huts are now full up – every bed. Nobody is very bad in Hut 1 except one boy with wounds in both thighs and gas gangrene in one. He was operated on yesterday and 'cleaned up', but his leg is

---

* These would almost certainly be soldiers wounded in a German attack on 'The Bluff'. See Chronology, p. 350.

a dreadful sight. Expecting big evacuation tomorrow, cots, crawlers and sitters, including the invaluable Sergeant Godfrey and Paddy. Don't know what we shall do when they are gone.

WEDNESDAY, 16TH FEBRUARY, 6.10 P.M.

This has been an awful day of wind and this morning there was a violent hurricane and a tornado of rain. It just poured in through the roof of the hut and the cracks in the windows. The floor was like a veritable lake and everyone was paddling about wondering when the flood would end. I have never seen anything like it – the rain came down in almost solid sheets and the wind was terrific.

The convoy yesterday got away safely at 2.30. I went back on duty after lunch to help with clearing up and got away again at 3.15. The cots and crawlers went but the sitters were stopped because by the time it was their turn, the wind had made it impossible for the hospital ship to cross. They have been spending the day, poor things, in a state of uncertainty and expectation, but are to go tomorrow morning unless there is another delay. I don't know what any other cases are doing and where they are being housed. I suppose they will be on board the ship and being nursed there. Rumour was that they would be brought back here till they could really go, but they didn't turn up which was a good thing for them, poor things. Would have been a bitter disappointment to be popped back into their old beds, no nearer Blighty than before.

Have to go to the YMCA this evening for a meeting of the new choral society, to get this new venture started. Several of the staff have joined and Matron and Sister Johnson will chaperone us. C is getting ready for a bath. She seems in fairly good fettle just now, but most of us are a bit tired with busy times this last week.

FRIDAY, 18TH FEBRUARY, 6.20 P.M.

How joyful not to be out or on duty. Awful weather again but our fire is burning up very cheerfully, I having lit it after tea. C is drying her bedclothes in front of the stove. A result of the windows being left open all afternoon and the rain pouring in onto C's bed and belongings. She was much disgusted at the discovery when she came in from duty. In some ways I certainly score by having the end of the room.

Blighty ones all got away safely this morning. Godfrey, Weekes and Wadsworth had all gone when we came on duty and later, as smart and brass buttoned as possible, Paddy and another patient departed in a second convoy. So the ward is a good deal depleted though I have all the long dressings still to do. Brookes has been finally moved this afternoon, so beginning his career as a theatre orderly and Newton comes to take his place in Hut 1. Wonder how this change will turn out. Very sorry Brookes has gone; he is such a nice boy and always so friendly and considerate.

Meeting the other night about choral society matters was an amusing affair and quite lively, almost crackling at times. Preliminaries are all arranged and a small committee was elected. We had to vote on paper for a conductor, between three names: Mr Kinsella, Chant and Captain Rainey, a Canadian candidate. Captain Rainey won the vote and was duly elected. I thought Mr K looked rather grumpy about the whole affair and he subsequently absolutely refused to have any official position whatever. Wonder how the Canadian will manage. He seems a nice man and is full of views on the subject. Quite a lot of us VADs went, as did Matron and Sister Johnson. Other camps were fairly well represented but ours was in the majority. Sergeant Preston had a lot to say and was rather tiresome and argumentative but he certainly kept things lively. Chant didn't appear at meeting as he was suffering from influenza with a temp of 104. Hear he is better today but not looking well. Wall Jacobs looks after him and brings us the latest news of his condition.

SUNDAY, 20TH FEBRUARY

Have got two letters to patients written and feel a great load off my mind. C must be in the anteroom making music or gossiping. Went to church this evening and had an early supper, so have had nice long time to get writing done before bed.

Sister Banham showed me how to give a hypodermic injection

and yesterday let me give it myself. Quite exciting considering what a special job it is. But really it is very easy to give an injection. I do a lot of dressings now – just minor ones – while Sister gets on with more difficult cases. We do the worst ones together.

Pay night yesterday and we got fr 334.90, the last big pay we shall have before allowances are cut down. But am glad as I think it is a waste of English money to pay us all so much.

TUESDAY, 22ND FEBRUARY, 8.30 P.M.

It has turned so cold. Snow fell in the night and it is bitterly chilly this morning. There will be more snow this evening, so this cold spell is by no means over yet. Wish it would go soon as it is so miserable getting up in the morning and going on duty with aching fingers. Everything you touch is colder than the other. I suppose we were lucky to have had as mild a winter as this for a rigorous one would just about have killed us all.

It is rumoured that the 'nights' come off next Monday or so and I am wondering very much who will go on. It is quite possible that C and I will still escape, but in a way I rather hope not. Would like to get it over and done with.

SATURDAY, 26TH FEBRUARY, 1.30 A.M.

Well-a-day! back again on night duty and not looking forward to a month – or very possibly two, if Matron so decrees – of this unnatural existence. I am still in Hut 1, with Sister Banham in charge of 1, 2, 3 and 4. She seems in a regular kerfuffle tonight, worried and tired and very busy, which is not very helpful when one is rather struggling with the first night of a new regime. Sister Chesters is the Night Super, so the whole staff of Hut 1 is changed in one fell swoop. I am rather – in fact, very – woeful because Rind is not on. She was kept out because of being so good in the nephritis ward where Sister Williamson begged to be allowed to keep her. Sad for the rest of us. Jobbie is desolée. She, Hynes, C and I are the ones to go on. It is such awful weather – blizzards all day and deep snow tonight, a searching, bitter cold.

SUNDAY, 27TH FEBRUARY, 12.50 A.M.

Just come to sit down in the bunk for a short time. Not very busy tonight. There are three operation cases to look after, but fortunately none are bad. Another night of this queer existence is speeding away. Time passes wonderfully quickly, considering the long hours of darkness, broken up into periods by meals and then work at 4. This morning was very busy and I had to write a report for first time. It was not a difficult job really, but it was tiresome to begin with as I didn't know quite what to put in and what to leave out. However, it was received graciously by Sister Robertson when she came on duty, so all was well.

Took on house moving this morning, after breakfast. Did a great job carting all the furniture along, even though everybody was colliding in the passage, staggering under bundles and boxes and household goods. Got settled without very much delay and tidied things up at the double. We were able to go over to the canteen before going to bed. Slept soundly till after 5.30, so woke up fairly refreshed, as much as one ever is on night duty.

I believe there is convoy going to the Canadians tonight. Thankfully we have escaped it, so it remains peaceful for yet a little while. C having a better time in Hut 3 and Johnnie in Hut 4 as their bad cases both died last night, poor things, and there was

great turmoil and commotion. Sister Banham was thoroughly worried and upset until it was all over. Tonight things were different. Sister B has been in here for supper and we had it very comfortably together, in peace and amity.

TUESDAY, 29TH FEBRUARY, 2 A.M.

Have not long finished supper, Sister and I. She comes in at the double for supper here, and does the cooking, which saves me a lot of bother. She made a sweet omelette tonight with cherry jam and it was really very good indeed. We sat a long time over our meal, gossiping. She has bustled off now but will return before long to have a cup of tea. Then, we shall do the dressings of men going to Blighty.

Berry is quite amenable but he comes off duty tomorrow and then alas, I believe we are to have Jones of ill repute. Hope he will be decently civil and not make things unpleasant, as night duty with an absolutely uncongenial orderly might become a dreadful burden.

These bright fires make good deal of difference to night duty this time. We can always keep good fire burning in the bunk to cook supper on and sit by when we are not wanted in the ward, so that's very nice and comfortable.

THURSDAY, 2ND MARCH, 12.40 A.M.

Ward quieter than ever tonight. Patients are dwindling away by degrees. The ward will soon be left practically empty. Hut 4 is closed now and Johnnie gone to the medicals. C and I had our supper together here tonight as Sister B wanted to make herself some bread and milk and said she would rather stay in her own hut. I cooked two chops for our supper quite successfully. The new regime has begun with the arrival of Jones instead of Berry. So far Jones has been all that is pleasant and obliging, but he is like that when not in an ungovernable fit of temper. Wonder what will happen though if a convoy comes in and makes him very busy again.

Still feel very cut off from Rind, Hopper and Arnold. They have paid us visits in the evening when we are getting up and declare they are very dull now without our company. So it is a sad case for everyone.

TUESDAY, 7TH MARCH, 11 A.M.

Alas! Have broken my record and been invalided, off duty for two nights! Succumbed to bilious attack, a result of a cold and chill. Was sick, sick all through the night before last and into the morning so was quite glad of a rest in bed till today. I am up now, restored though still rather weak in the legs. By tonight I think I will be pretty well able to cope with night duty again. I was very sad to collapse like this when I was hoping to get through my time here without a single off duty for illness. But such things happen and I really couldn't have gone on duty in the state I was in. Everyone has been so kind and attentive. I couldn't have been better looked after. Malet has been running in and out, bringing me meals and water for washing, making my bed and looking after me like the best of nurses that she is. Poor C was turned out of our room yesterday afternoon and had to take a bed next door and sleep with two others there so that she shouldn't be disturbed by me. She was very willing to go but quite glad to be re-established here today!

Captain Paulley has paid me two visits today and yesterday, but I knew as well as he did what I was suffering from as it is by no means the first time this enemy has attacked me. I felt very mean being off duty just now as a large convoy came in the night before last and filled every bed in all four huts. Some of the cases are quite bad too and made the depleted staff very busy. Last night, rather under protest, Jobbie took my place in Hut 1. She has no pleasant recollections of her last night duty spent in Hut 1. I expect she will go back to enterics tonight and I shall be in old haunts once more. Waiting now for Sister Banham who wants to take me out for a walk. It is a lovely morning so I must go and get some air before coming to bed again to prepare for the exertions of tonight.

Just come back to bed for the afternoon having had a second lunch after a nice walk along the cliffs. Now I must try to get well reposed before wrestling with work tonight. A large convoy is coming down, to be divided between the three hospitals. There must be some tremendous fighting going on up at the front.* It is supposed that the Germans are attacking and making furious assaults on our lines. C is safe in her bed and I think she is sleeping. Anyway, she seems very peaceful.

---

* This was the final stage of the Battle of The Bluff. See Chronology, p. 350.

THURSDAY, 9TH MARCH, 3.30 A.M.

Very chilly just now. Sitting on my rug in front of the fires, drinking some hot milk before beginning work. Very different tonight to last night when I hardly sat down at all, tending to the wounded. There was a tremendous clear-out this morning. We are left with fourteen but several of them are up-patients and two are going this morning to convalescent camp, so unless a convoy arrives today we will have a much more unexertive time.

Had another of many – and constant – wiggings from Sister B tonight about supper. The fire was not kept up – altogether a great grievance – so I think it better for her to have her meal in Hut 2 and not to bother about coming in here. Have had so many scoldings and tirades on the subject I think it is better not to try to experiment any more. I was too tired and becolded tonight to argue, or even answer Sister B when she scolded me. Have only seen her once since. She is an odd, hot-tempered creature. But really tonight wasn't my fault. A concatenation of circumstances and things weren't really as bad as Sister made out. Very different from my happy meetings with Sister Northwood. Anyway, I was in high dudgeon so social intercourse tonight was rather brief and chequered! Have not seen anything of other two. Never get a chance nowadays.

SATURDAY, 11TH MARCH, 2 A.M.

Have a bad case in here tonight, a boy who had a leg amputated today. Has a bad wound in shoulder as well. Unlikely he will make it. Sister Banham is specialling tonight, while I sit in here, relieved of all responsibility in looking after him. Very quiet time last night. Went to Hut 2 for a supper prepared by Sister Wright. We had it together in spite of a tiff on the subject the other night. Sister B soon gets in temper and soon gets out again. I have been round visiting other wards, doing Sister's inspection for her. Made pleasant calls on Johnnie and Ellis. Arnold is ill now, with a temperature of 104 this evening. Do not know what is the matter but it must be pretty bad.

SUNDAY, 12TH MARCH, 10 P.M.

It is with heavy heart I am writing this diary tonight. A dire, dreadful catastrophe has befallen us. Our dear beloved Arnold died last night over at No. 3, quite suddenly, quite quietly after being ill for only two days. Seems inconceivable and we can't realize it a bit. I heard this morning when we came off duty. She had acute double pneumonia and her temperature was so high and the disease so virulent that her heart just couldn't stand it and failed quite suddenly. Oh! It's a dreadful thing and such an overshadowing of our little community here. Arnold was one of the very best, the nicest girl you could find anywhere. Straight, true and sterling and loveable. There isn't one person in the camp who won't be sorry that she has gone.

Poor Matron is dreadfully upset and worried, and looked this morning almost at her wits' end. She requested that we should go to the Park and get some daffodils to put on the coffin, so C and I went out soon after breakfast each armed with a basket to try to get some flowers. Such a lovely spring morning, the air so clear and pure and the countryside looking so fresh and sunny. If our hearts hadn't been so heavy we could have enjoyed our expedition very much. We found quantities of daffodils in the Park, nodding their yellow heads and looking so pretty among the trees. C and I filled our baskets, then after sitting on a trunk a little while resting and reflecting, took our homeward way. It was almost too hot in the sunshine, though it was lovely after the cold weather. No word yet of Arnold's mother and father arriving but I expect they will come for the funeral, poor things, and Arnold will probably be buried in the little quiet bare active service cemetery where all our brave soldiers who have died at the different hospitals are resting in peace.

Saw Hopper for a few minutes after supper. She looks dreadfully cast down, as indeed we all are. Too sad that Rind and Hopper are segregated from us by this wretched night duty; we could have given each other such mutual support if we had been together. Do not feel as if things could ever be quite the same again, after the happy times we have all had together.

MONDAY, 13TH MARCH, 9.25 P.M.

A peaceful night in here, but I expect to be running in and out of the other huts as I did last night. Sister Banham has a bad case in Hut 2 and two or three of Johnnie's men in 4 are bad. Poor dear was in a sad state herself last night. Feeling rotten and sick herself and all these bad cases to look after and to be responsible for. I was in for a little while and helped her with a bad spine case, which relieved her for a little while. C was also struggling last night with very bad patient who died at about 5.30 of some mysterious brain trouble that made him very ghastly to see. So she was busy and I helped her at suppertime and had my supper in her hut. Am glad they are all quite well in here, as I feel this is a haven of refuge where I can get rest and relaxation. Must have been a lovely day today and feels so much warmer tonight. Clear starlight sky and moonshine, but away in the distance there seems to be a bad thunderstorm. Sheet lightning keeps flashing brilliantly behind a big cloud.

Matron has been very worried lately about an injudicious proceeding on the part of Tozer's sister. She seems to have championed our cause rather unnecessarily, without consulting any of us. She wrote off to Mrs Furze about our not getting enough off-duty time and leave. Mrs F wrote to Miss Becher at the War Office* who wrote to Miss McCarthy who wrote to the Colonel here and the Colonel came to ask Matron about it, so the whole thing has created great commotion. Tozer's sister has stirred up an ants' nest with no very good results. We are all indignant and Matron is indignant and the whole thing is not going to do anybody any good. We are treated just the same as the Sisters here and, if sometimes rather hardly dealt with, it is the case with everybody. After all it is active service and we must expect to have some hardships to put up with. On the whole we have a very good time here, even if this hospital is known as the 'convent' all over France.

* Mrs Furze was now the Commandant-in-Chief VAD Women's Detachment. Miss Becher was Matron-in-Chief, War Office.

TUESDAY, 14TH MARCH, 9.25 P.M.

Can hear the rain pattering down on roof which is sad after such a glorious day. Matron wanted more 'daffies', so Johnnie, Gibbie, Jobbie C and I went off armed with baskets to the Park, which looked even more lovely than it did the last time we were there. The sky seemed bluer and clearer and the sunshine warmer. A perfect spring day. There were so many daffs growing among the trees, that it looked like a yellow carpet had been laid. We soon filled our baskets. Sister B and two other Sisters had come on the same errand, but after we passed them in the Park we saw no more of them, rather to our relief. The deer were so pretty, stopping to look at us with their anxious, frightened eyes, then scampering away as we came along.

Went to No. 3 to leave our flowers and saw Miss Stevenson, the Matron, who was very nice to us and accepted the flowers gratefully. Then coming home we met Mr Arnold, dear Arnold's father, as well as one of her sisters. They have come over for the funeral and were just coming out of the Colonel's house. I hesitated a few moments then went up and spoke to him. They seemed so nice and are bearing up wonderfully bravely. They were interested in the place and all they were seeing and were intending to have a good look round to see everything they had heard so much about from Peggy. Their composedness helped us to keep up, otherwise I think we might all have broken down which would have been rather harrowing in such a public place.

The funeral is to be tomorrow at 2 p.m. and we are to go to bed early and get up for it, then go to bed again and come to the second dinner instead of our usual first dinner and come on duty late for once. It is nice of Matron to arrange it so that we should have the opportunity of paying our last respects to our dearly loved friend.

WEDNESDAY, 15TH MARCH, 9.30 P.M.

This is another of our quiet, peaceful nights and I am rather glad as we have had a campaigning day – with somewhat broken rest.

The funeral was held at 2 p.m. and passed off very quietly and very reverently. I was afraid the weather was going to be bad but it cleared up quite nicely and the sun was shining when the cortège came winding down the hill. The night VADs all went to bed directly after breakfast and we got nearly two hours sleep, C and I did anyway, before Malet called us at 1 p.m. We had a cup of tea and a biscuit before setting out to join the whole party of VADs. Nearly everyone went except for Urquart who is away ill at No. 3 and De Burgh and Conran who are both ill with scarlet fever and relegated to isolation. We all wore our indoor uniforms and overcoats and looked fresh and clean in our white caps. A few of the Sisters came as well and a contingent of Canadian and No. 3 staff attended ceremony too, so there was a good muster.

All the MOs and a special escort of orderlies accompanied the cortège along with the chief mourners, Mr and Miss Arnold. They were remarkably composed, not to say cheery at times. They seem to be philosophic people and not likely to make an open show of grief, though no doubt they felt it all dreadfully. Matron escorted Miss McCarthy, who came over specially from Abbeville. She looked so white and tired and sad – almost the saddest and nearest to breaking down of anyone. We all kept up as well as we could and there were a few sniffs and sobs, but it was all very impressive and touching.

Mr MacMillan conducted the service and our batmen from the Mess were the bearers, lowering the coffin into its last resting place. The inside of the grave was so prettily lined with ivy and flowers and moss. I believe Dalrymple and another VAD had been at work in the morning. The flowers were lovely – big wreaths and crosses and bunches. There were gifts and tributes from the orderly officers, Sisters and VADs. The coffin was covered with the Union Jack with just a few flowers laid on top. It was all so simple and yet wonderfully impressive.

When the prayers had been said and the service was finished, the buglers blew the Last Post over the grave and the call that Arnold had heard every night for the last nine months, summoning the camp to rest, now came to summon her rest with no more toil and weariness to wake up to when morning came again. We all quietly took a last look into the grave and then came away and the ceremony was ended.

I lingered a little while afterwards with Rind and a few others to take leave of Mr Arnold and Ruth and then walked up to No. 16 and back to bed again. It seemed like a sad, strange dream had broken into our afternoon sleep, but I am very glad we were allowed to go.

SUNDAY, 19TH MARCH, 1.20 A.M.

Very sad. Have left my book behind and have nothing to read in spare moments. Feel rather stranded as we are not very busy. All our patients seem remarkably quiet and peaceful and there is no one needing constant attention. I can sit here in the bunk, at ease, while Jones sits in the ward, sewing by the light of a lamp. J is still quite amenable though gets rather grumpy at times if he is asked to do anything he doesn't approve of. But he is a good orderly and it is a great comfort to have him in the ward and know that the patients are being looked after. C and Johnnie are very woeful about their 'joint' orderly, Boyce. He must be a most trying little man. His one idea is to get out of doing work if he possibly can. He likes to sit down and sleep and doesn't at all approve of being at the beck and call of patients the whole time. I think he will go sick tomorrow which is quite a good plan for he can't be worse or more useless than he is now.

I am getting dreadfully sleepy and really must do something to keep awake. The other night I took some spasmodic walks while there were so few in the ward and I believe Jones did too. Seemed such a good opportunity when the ward was so slack.

Latest excitement is that Hogan has confessed to being engaged to Capt. Hendry. Matron and Miss Stronach saw them out walking together a few days ago and afterwards interviewed Hogan who admitted she was engaged. Matron is rather pleased with the romance but it means that one or the other must leave the camp and the Colonel says he will not part with Capt. Hendry and Matron does not want to part with Hogan.

MONDAY, 20TH MARCH, 9.45 P.M.

Seems a long time since I wrote this diary – on Sunday morning – in the stilly hours of the night. Longer ago than 'yesterday' but time becomes all upset on night duty. The days seem longer in some ways and yet shorter in others, but on the whole they slip by wonderfully quickly.

1 a.m.

Have just come back here from supper in Hut 2. Now the accustomed order is to go in to Sister B to have our night meal. Rather boring in some ways but it makes a change of surroundings. Sister Street joined our festive board tonight. She sent over her supper and a message to say she wanted her eggs scrambled. Sister B was indignant, being 'put upon' like this, but she still made Sister S welcome and we all had scrambled eggs and toast and a tin of baked beans mixed up as confection. It turned out successfully, though the beginning of cooking operations were not at all encouraging.

THURSDAY, 23RD MARCH, 1 P.M.

Last night around midnight, a convoy burst in on us in quite an unexpected way. It was only a small one, divided between three hospitals. This arrangement made it very slow in coming in so it was a long time before we could get patients settled up, the ward tidied and lights put out. We came off very lightly in here with only five new cases.

Sister Banham continues to provide Johnnie, C and me with much food for gossip. Her ways are quite incomprehensible at times and Johnnie cannot get over them. I have got accustomed to her rowings so take no notice, the only thing to be done as she forgets quite soon and never seems to bear any grudge. She comes stumping down the ward, waking up patients and calling out in loud whisper, sometimes even not at all disguised effectively, arousing all the patients from their slumbers. She will be in soon to do Jackson, our head case's, dressing, so I must be ready for her. Jackson is going to Blighty tomorrow. He is so pleased, poor boy. Seven are going altogether but only two of them are cots.

THURSDAY, 23RD MARCH, 9.10 P.M.

I was very sleepy last night when I was writing my diary and in the end could hardly keep my eyes open. In fact, I do believe I winkled for five minutes or so, absolutely overcome by the charm of Morpheus and my little bunk fire. It has been so cold again today and last night, it was trying to snow very unpleasantly. I went down and got my hair washed at the little Madame's whose *mari* is still very ill. She looks tired from the continued efforts of keeping on the shop and the household as well as nursing the invalid, who is probably rather exacting. I was glad to have got my hair washed. It is so difficult to bring one's mind to get these things done.

Have a fairly slack ward tonight with a convoy having gone out this morning and four of our up-patients transferred over to the black huts.* There seem to be a good many Nottingham men in the hospital just now, their familiar lingo very pleasantly reminiscent of home. One man in C's ward lives in Park St Lenton and has quite the familiar countenance and type of a regular Lentonian of rougher sort. Can quite well imagine him loitering about waiting to go into the Wheatsheaf Pub on Sunday mornings as soon as it opened. His name is the singularly uncommon one of Brown. He is a rough enough specimen but plucky about his wounded legs.

Tomorrow night, I shall have done just a month of night duty. Wish it were the two months. Don't think I shall be at all sorry to come back to daylight and normal life once more.

---

* At No. 16 the ward huts were divided into 'white' huts, which were for 'surgical' cases of wounded and injured soldiers, and 'black' huts, for 'medical' cases, those suffering from diseases.

SATURDAY, 25TH MARCH, 9.45 P.M.

Jones is in a very amenable mood tonight. Have been chatting with him about things in general, chiefly leave and questions of that kind. He was very pleasant too last night and gave me a pot of honey and a share of some broth he had been stewing for his 2 o'clock feed. Excellent soup, best I have tasted for a long time. When Jones is feeling pleasant he can be very nice indeed, but once his temper gets up, he is anything but pleasant to deal with.

Last night Sister B was in great form, decreeing that we were all to sup in Hut 3 with C. She bounced in about 11.30 and the place was in a hubbub at once as she stumped about clattering plates and cutlery and cooking apparatus, talking and laughing, loud and long. Poor C was on tenterhooks for her men, knowing that they would all be much disturbed and would keep her busy when she went back into ward. However Sister B didn't seem concerned. She thoroughly enjoyed herself making omelettes and keeping us all employed. Johnnie came from 4 to join in the feast, not altogether willingly. She and C usually have their meal together when we are slack and preferred their usual arrangement to this united gathering. I am hoping it will not occur again tonight, but I shall have to go to 2 again as usual I suspect.

Things are not harmonious like they were during the last round of night duty. We have much more responsibility and are far less sociable. We are such a small party of VADs too – only five of us to keep each other company. Rumours are afloat that Johnnie and Gibbie will come off night duty at the end of week and then perhaps Rind may go on. It would be lovely if she did. Dalrymple went off to No. 3 this morning suffering from 'glands', probably influenza. Matron doesn't mean to take any risks, packing off the invalids all double quick pace. And so our staff is sadly diminished.

Heard last night that a cross-Channel Dieppe to Folkestone boat had been sunk. Rumours said by a torpedo and that possibly 300 were lives lost.* A dreadful catastrophe and it was just chance that

* SS *Sussex*, a cross-Channel passenger ferry, was torpedoed by a German U-boat on 24 March, killing at least fifty of the civilian passengers on board and sparking international outrage.

none of our people were on board coming back from leave. No one seems safe in wartime at home or abroad, and crossing the Channel now certainly seems to be a risky business.

WEDNESDAY, 29TH MARCH, 12.15 P.M.

And time I was asleep! But have not had the opportunity or inclination all this night to write, so must put in a short entry here to bridge the gap. Just had such a lively episode – Jobbie, Johnnie and Bownes triumphantly bearing a small dish containing a family of very repulsive and miserable little mice, discovered in Jobbie's box. Jobbie of all people, who is particularly horrified by mice! Don't know what is going to become of the gruesome little things, but they won't be long for this world. Fancy babies being born in the Sisters' quarters of a military hospital on active service – what a scandal!

There have been a few changes and excitements since last writing, chiefly in the wards. But Rind, our dear Rind, has come on night duty. She changed yesterday to take the place of Gibbie who, after going sick with a bad cold and neuralgia, has now been put on day and is working in medical. There is such a nice little party of VADs on night now. I hope Johnnie will stay on. If only Hopper could join in, then it would be even more uniting and delightful. Hopper is expecting momentarily to go on leave. She had notice to go in the afternoon and she and Sister Johnson got ready – very excited and pleased – and got as far as Dieppe. Then, either because of a storm at sea, or for some other reason, they were turned back. They will perhaps be going tomorrow.

Am now temporarily out of Hut 1 and banished to Hut 2's side ward, where I am specialling a man with tetanus, so reminiscent of Prior on my last night duty. This man, Riley, has been very badly burned down all of his arm, side and leg. The tetanus was only discovered two days ago. He is pretty bad, not as much with tet as with his chest, which sounds very ominous. Have spent the last two nights with him doing nothing at all and am very sad to have lost sight of all the dear things in Hut 1. Am afraid they may have gone when I get back there. Meanwhile, Jones is proceeding in charge and getting on quite well. He is reasonably competent and he can manage without help as long as the ward is fairly light.

There was a great upturn last night – one of the patients discovered in ward, Hut 2, having died unperceived. He slipped away as the result of a haemorrhage. He was very ill before but it seems dreadful to think that no one should have noticed. Sister B is talking and bustling and thinks this was the result of a new orderly who is very careless and unobservant. There was a great flutter and commotion and Sister Street was summoned at the double, Sister B almost beside herself with distraction at the whole affair.

Another excitement of the last day or two was an interview with the Colonel. Each one of us VADs was called in separately to Matron's sitting room and interviewed alone by the Colonel on the subject of our treatment here and whether we were happy. This is all the outcome of Tozer's sister's letter, which has been causing great trouble to those in high authority.

THURSDAY, 30TH MARCH, 1.30 A.M.

Am free again, no longer exiled in the side ward of Hut 2. Poor Riley died yesterday at 1 p.m. He must have gone very quickly for somehow he didn't seem as bad as that when I left him in the morning. Anyway, here I am back in Hut 1 with nothing to do, Jones having taken charge of things in my absence and running the hut very successfully on his own. While I was away tonight having supper with Sister B in Hut 2, Jones gave a saline to a patient here and when Sister came in to give it, the deed was already done. J is certainly invaluable as an orderly. If only he could keep his temper. Sister Banham tells me in great confidence that the doctor was questioning now whether it wasn't cerebro-spinal that Riley died of and not tetanus. Either of them are dire complaints, whichever it was carried the poor patient off quickly.

THURSDAY, 30TH MARCH, 9.45 P.M.

Writing under some difficulties, having fomentation on my first finger for a septic spot up by the nail. Not bad yet but I am always rather nervous of septic fingers, you never know where the mischief will end quite. Jones put on the fomentation in best style. Must get him to do another later on.

Alas! There are more changes, another dismal break into our really very happy existence here. Poor little Hopper, who has gone on leave today, heard yesterday from Matron that she has had marching orders – to go directly after her leave to No. 20 General at Étaples. She was dreadfully upset and so are we all, for it means not only parting with her, which is dismal when we have grown so fond of her, but is probably a series of moves and changes for our whole party. The only question is who will be next and if C and I were parted and sent to different destinations this would be the comble of all malheurs.* Must all be the outcome of wretched disturbance about the letter and the enquiries made from headquarters about our treatment. I do wish the mistaken person or persons, who have been agitating on our behalf, had left matters alone and let us go our own way, for they haven't done any good and now we are to be torn asunder and sent in different directions to begin active service all over again. Our VAD community is dwindling sadly and only thirteen are left of the original twenty-six. Hogan went home today, summoned to her mother who is dying. She means to resign when she gets home, so we will not see her again. One by one they drop away, a miserable existence. Hopper, tear-stained and not at all in holiday mood, came in to say goodbye this p.m. after we got to bed. She is just heart-broken and seems sad to be going off on leave in that state of mind when she might be enjoying the prospect of home so much. I daresay she will cheer up though when she gets to Blighty.

We seem likely to be spared a convoy again tonight and the ward is very light, only the one little boy, McFadden, who is not bad at all. The little monkey is only seventeen and such a child. He looks younger. He has bad wounds in his legs. I hope he will get on all right. He is getting plenty of care and attention and is well fussed over.

Able to have supper with C tonight in Hut 2 while Sister B ate tinned lobster with a very unwilling Johnnie in Hut 4. This is Sister's

* 'The height of misfortune'.

new arrangement. As far as I am concerned it is quite a good one, though for other people it may not be so pleasant.

SATURDAY, 1ST APRIL

It is peaceful again tonight and I am very thankful as I am not feeling as well as I might be. A bit bilious, but expect I shall weather the night through again. Still have large bandage on my finger and this morning such a doing with it, causing quite a disturbance in fact through the absurdity of Mr Wells, the MO and then my own foolishness. When he came in last night to see the patients, he saw my bandage and made enquiries about my finger. I told him how I got it, probably from Riley in the side ward. He looked rather solemn and advised an injection of anti-tetanus serum. Seemed a simple enough process, mere precaution, so not really thinking he would take any such steps, I said if he really thought it advisable he better see Sister or tell someone in authority. But it seems he bustled off to Sister Street and she was very indignant and when she made her next round, she told Sister Banham that she wouldn't have us gossiping with MOs. So Mr Wells' advice didn't meet with very cordial reception.

It being a very slack night, I was able to nurse the offending finger very thoroughly. Spent a good part of time in Hut 2 soaking it and having it fomented. Sister B put a needle in it and let out lots of horrid pus. It really was in quite a bad way, especially for me as I am so unliable to ailments of this sort. The outcome was that I had to stay in this morning to let Captain Paulley see my finger. He advised that it should be opened more and I was sent over to Hut 3 for Mr Higgins to inspect. I was also warned by the medical advisers to take no notice of alarmists, meaning Mr Wells. In fact, Riley did not die of tetanus but from meningitis, the result of his burns. I suppose I had been thoroughly frightened by Mr Wells, not to say panic struck, and after Capt. Paulley's I received some more good advice from Matron as I made my way to Hut 3. She called me over and warned me to take no notice of these young doctors full of fads and fancies. She was very nice about it and didn't straf at all. The operation was performed successfully in Hut 3's bunk. Quite a paraphernalia. Mr O'Neil did the slicing with a very small fine scalpel while Sister O'Donoghue was ready with swabs, meths and iodine, and Robb was assisting with the fomentation. New-fashioned freezing stuff was squirted on first and then Mr O'Neil made quite a deep cut and in surgical parlance opened it up thoroughly so now my finger is cured or anyway ought to be, after all that doing. It is certainly much better tonight and I can hardly feel it.

WEDNESDAY, 5TH APRIL, 2.30 P.M.

Well, real change this time, as I am now in medicals and seated in bunk of 31, one of three huts I have to look after of less acute medical cases. This startling change occurred yesterday, or rather the day before. I had just got on duty and was getting ready for a new convoy that was coming in, when Sister Street appeared and said I was to come over here at once and Rind would take my place. So I was suddenly bustled away and it felt dreadfully strange being out of my familiar surroundings, planted down alone in these medical huts with only occasional visits from Sister Sims.

I don't know anything about medical work at all, but there is nothing much to do – aspirin and hot milk seems the resource for the wakeful and cough tablets to the barking people. It is not busy at all here, not even after the convoy. Only took in eleven patients altogether and they could all look after themselves, except for one man with acute rheumatics who I washed in the morning. This tiresome finger is responsible for all the change. I am not supposed to touch anything septic till it is cured, so with a convoy coming in it was considered unwise for me to be dealing with those patients and consequently I was spirited away here. Poor Rind is feeling rotten, as she had to receive the convoy and struggle with a nearly full ward of mostly new patients. She has now gone off sick and probably will end up going to No. 3. Another prop and stay that has gone for the time being is Gibbie, who has fallen victim to the odious disease of scabiosis. She must have been in a low state of health to catch it. She has got it on her hands and face. Very depressed, poor dear, and no wonder.

Staff in the white huts are now being rearranged tonight owing to the departure of Rind. A newly arrived Sister has been put in charge of 1 and 2 and Sister B remains in 3 and 4 with Johnnie. C has gone to Hut 1, so she has taken my place.

THURSDAY, 6TH APRIL, 9.30 A.M.

Something even more startling has happened since last writing. For here I am at No. 3 Hospital, packed off all of a sudden for no earthly reason that I can see, to have my bally old finger doctored up. Went over to Hut 3 in the morning to have it fomented and seen by Mr Higgins. He threw me some dark hints about No. 3 and having the nail off, but didn't say anything that I took to be meant seriously and I went off quite happily after having the fomentation done. Meanwhile Mr Higgins went off to Capt. Paulley and the result, to my consternation, was that I was to be doctored till the offending spot was better. I was undressed and just getting into bed when Rind came in to help me to pack up. Received a great shock when she told me and I had to get ready as quick as poss. and prepare to adjourn over to the company of invalids. Very sad too at leaving C and separating from her, for I do not know whether we shall be able to get together again.

Got my things packed as far as poss. and was then hustled away by the House Sister for being in C's room at 1 o'clock. Left my packages very uncompleted, departed to Mess, had a second dinner and afterwards walked about for a little while before being chaperoned over here by Sister Rawes. Matron called me back just as I was going and said goodbye very sweetly and gave me such an affectionate kiss which was somehow unexpected when we are all so much in disgrace for going sick like this. I didn't want to come here at all, though I must say we are splendidly treated and should certainly be happy. I am in a room with Sister Reid who is suffering from bad eyes, little Robertson who came here a while ago with bronchitis, and a Sister from this hospital who is convalescing after influenza and general breakdown. Robbie departs tomorrow at 6.30 with convoy for England if no fresh orders arrive – she is going on sick leave but can't quite make out why. It may mean that she can't come back here again, so she is rather depressed about it. Dalrymple is here too but goes back to No. 16 tomorrow to begin work again. There are two Sisters in the room Dalrymple sleeps in, and Sister Watson, suffering from eczema, has a room to herself. So there is quite a party of us. A rather young MO saw us all yesterday morning. He prescribed fomenting and bathing for my finger, no terrible measures in the way of taking the nail off as hinted at by Mr Higgins.

Have a nice Day Sister to look after us and another for night and a little, bright, brisk VAD who has been christened 'Twinkle' by Miss Robertson. We have rooms in the officers' medical corridor and see lots of officers wandering about to and fro from the men's rooms. A convoy came in last night so several men arrived and we watched them coming in. Went to bed very early and slept like a top in my most comfortable little spring bed covered with nice soft quilt, resting between the luxurious sheets. Feel such a fraud being here, for really I am very well. Don't feel finger at all.

FRIDAY, 7TH APRIL, 7 P.M.

Just had a most sumptuous meal – four courses, washed down with lemonade. Shocking state of overeating and laziness. Had breakfast in bed and early morning tea before that to wake us up. Little Robertson departed at 6.30 by convoy en route to England. She went away quite cheerfully but rather regretfully, really being so unwilling to go on sick leave. Her place has now been taken by Rind. Not at all surprised as Robertson has been poorly for a long time past. She is now in bed with a temp of 100 but all afternoon was up and looking rather poorly. Rest of invalids all going on very well. Dally returned to 16 this afternoon to go on duty tomorrow morning. My finger is getting on like a house on fire. More convalescing prescribed and now it is to be anointed with repulsive-looking yellow ointment instead of foment.

Matron has just gone in to see Rind. She has such a sweet face and charming manner and everyone seems very fond of her. She seems to regard 16 and our Matron as awesome in the degree and considers we have a very hard time. I am not sorry as it is nice to feel we really are on active service and enduring some hardships when so many people have to endure them in a much severer form.

This corridor is quite an entertainment. Officers wander in and out, sometimes apparitions appear in pyjamas and dressing gown and one wag, whose khaki is being stored, goes about in patient's blues and looks very anxious to come in and join us behind the screen here.

I wandered down to Tréport this evening after tea and did some shopping and bought a little pot of tulips to put on dear Arnold's grave. Often think I see her coming along or working in the wards.

SUNDAY, 9TH APRIL, 9 P.M.

Poor Rind will be an inmate for some time yet. Matron said airily that Rind was being sent in for a couple of days to be restored to perfect strength, but it looks more like being a couple of weeks. Yesterday she was quite bad and I really began to feel anxious. She was kept in bed all day and had an agonizing pain in her side that sounded like pleurisy. Rather better today I am glad to say, but she still has a bit of pain.

A lovely day today, so light and spring-like. Had a delightful trip this afternoon with Seely and Hines. We got hold of a quaint little conveyance, like a wagonette with a cover that was drawn by a very spirited young horse. Drove into the forest and had tea under the trees in the orchard at La Madeleine. Picked bluebells in the lovely woods and trod on carpets of wood anemones coming up among the dried leaves.

Time I was now settling down. The night sister has just been in with hot milk.

TUESDAY, 11TH APRIL, 4.45 P.M.

Still at No. 3 recreating but very convalescent now. I don't even have a bandage on my finger, which is dry as a bone and quite better. Suggested to MO Capt. Sundell this morning that I should go back to 16, but he said that there was no urgent necessity for that and so the matter was left, so I am still enjoying the rest and holiday. Sitting now beside poor Rind. She is quite invalidy yet and still suffering from pain in her side, a cough and general collapsedness. It is pleurisy, so she is an interesting case. Matron came up to call yesterday morning. She was very kind and sat and talked a few minutes and looked very sympathetic.

Have been into town this afternoon, shopping and pottering round. Several fine sailing ships have been in the harbour for some days now. One is English and I longed to have a talk with some of the crew who were pottering about on deck but I didn't quite see an opportunity of proceeding.

Here comes Twinkle to see to her patients, so I must move away to a more unobtrusive situation. Stormy and unsettled today, a south-westerly wind driving up the Channel and bringing some big white-topped rollers along with it. Yesterday was so lovely all day. Went out for a long walk with Sisters Watson, Reid and Burnett after lunch – we tramped off to Bois de Cise. Various 'easies' on the way

and light refreshments in way of oranges and biscuits. Bois de Cise is just lovely. Rested for some time down near the shore and to stave off pangs of hunger and thirst, we ate more oranges and biscuits and economized on the matter of tea. Funny little seaside resort – houses and hotels all shut up but evidently it is a very gay spot in summertime. We wandered through the woods picking primroses, violets, daffodils and anemones. All growing so prettily among the trees. Really felt as if spring was here at last.

Have just got into bed and now prepared for sleep. Such a lovely night, the sound of surf beating on the shore right down below cliffs, rising so clear and distinct. This former hotel has a wonderful situation, but is also an excellent place from which to signal to an enemy craft.

FRIDAY, 14TH APRIL, 9.30 P.M.

Back again at 16 and sitting up now in this camp bed – old, narrow couch – writing, while Alabaster, whom fate has thrown me with as my stable companion, sleeps on the other side of the curtain. Dally is away being sick in the room given up to new Sisters, and my things have been shifted in here. We have a big room at the end of the corridor, so it is really very nice as there is lots of room and have window here all to myself. Arranged things yesterday afternoon after reporting to Matron at her office. She was very pleasant and chatty yesterday so I ventured to ask if it would be possible for C and me to go on leave together and she seemed hopeful about it and said she would try to arrange it if she could.

My sphere of work lies now in medicals. The days of white huts are over after nearly ten months of them. Must say I am rather glad for some things – the rest and none of the everlasting cleaning paint, scrubbing and tidying of 1 and 2. I am working with Jobbie and found it very pleasant this morning, making beds, dusting and straightening my ward – number 33 – and cleaning till lunchtime. J has 34 to look after but this afternoon I was in and out of both the whole time. Have Sister Armstrong, one of new ones, and she seems very nice for a Staff Nurse and Sister Chesters for S/C,* which is quite nice, for I know her and like her, so at present all is absolutely A1.

Went to choral practice last night and did so enjoy it. Kept pretty hard at work but the performance is next week, so the cantata had to be taken right through, as if we were singing in public. We are doing Stainer's 'Crucifixion' as it is suitable for Easter. Parts of it seemed to go very well but some parts seemed to need a good deal of rubbing up. The soloists are quite good. Mr Higgins has one solo. The other soloists are Capt. Brown from No. 3 and an orderly from the Canadian camp who has a very good voice. Got back at 10.15, but the rehearsal didn't seem a bit too long.

Today and last night was so rough and windy. The sea was all white horses and big rolling waves. After tea I went with Fletcher to No. 3 to see the invalids. Thought Rind was much better. Better than she has been for long time.

TUESDAY, 18TH APRIL, 7.30 P.M.

Another move today, but not far this time. C is off night duty and has come in here to join Alabaster and self. Very pleased to have C back again but having three together certainly makes things a bit crowded. When I got over this morning for a little time off, I found the room in turmoil again and C trying to get her belongings straightened up into corner opposite in a sad conglomeration. Set to and did some tidying at once but hopeless to make the place look anything like presentable when household furniture and belongings are so pushed together. Alabaster seems quite happy on the other side of the curtain and still looking forward to leave, which is supposed to be beginning again on 25th. She had a sad blow when it was all cancelled a few days ago, just as she was on eve of departure. No reason given so it may have been something to do with storms and wind or submarines and the dangers of the Channel.

---

* Sister-in-charge (of ward).

THURSDAY, 20TH APRIL, 9.45 P.M.

The first great performance of Stainer's 'Crucifixion', as rendered by Tréport Garrison Choral Society, took place this evening to an audience of men from the convalescent camp. To be truthful, I don't think it was very brilliant performance. Still, it certainly went better than at dress rehearsal last Tuesday. We made a false start at the beginning and there followed various shaky and uncertain leads. Capt. Brown was not at his best, being mostly out of tune and rather reedy. The other soloists rendered their items very well. The anthem seemed to go quite well as far as one could tell, being in the choir. YMCA was packed with convalescents, among them no doubt many well-acquainted old patients.

Have had change of sphere of work, being moved down to 30, 31 and 32, while C has charge of 33. Don't like this move much as the patients in 31 and 32 are not nearly so nice and Sister Webb rather encourages them to be lazy. She spoils them too much and they get cheeky and unwilling. However some of them seem nice enough, and must struggle along as well as possible.

Hogan goes home tomorrow intending to be married as soon as possible if Capt. Hendry can get leave, so when she goes camp romance will fade into the annals of the past. Rind is off to Hardelot* tomorrow to recuperate. She needs the rest, for she is not looking very well yet. Saw her this afternoon for a few minutes before going to tea. Seems odd and lonely without her and Hopper, two of our dearest friends.

EASTER SUNDAY, 23RD APRIL, 10 P.M.

And St George's Day, as Mr MacMillan reminded us tonight in his sermon. Such a nice Easter evening service. The weather has been glorious today, so lovely after yesterday when it was ghastly, blowing and pouring from morn to eve. 'Day Off' people had a very

---

* A seaside resort between Étaples and Boulogne where there was a convalescent home for nurses.

thin time, could get nowhere and do nothing. I had very delightful half-day today and wandered off after dinner with Ruscoe, also half-daying, away into country through Flocques and Étalondes. We found ourselves eventually in lovely little wood full of wild flowers and so remote and peaceful, just a paradise of quiet and rest. Could forget all about No. 16 and nursing and just enjoy nature in one of her loveliest garbs, signs of spring everywhere. Saw first swallow today, so that looks like warmer weather coming.

Last night C, Jobbie and I were all on duty and it was so slack that I paid a visit along the lines and found J and C just going into 35 to hear one of patients, a boy called Perry, sing. So I added myself to the audience. He has a high falsetto voice that is well trained and rather nice to listen to – as nice as falsetto ever is. Sang really very well indeed and of course without accompaniment.

Third and last performance of 'Crucifixion' took place yesterday at 2.30 for patients. Not quite such a big audience what with the weather being so bad and rain dripping through the roof, flooding the floor in places. It was quite a creditable show on the whole. The conductor was quite pleased with it and congratulated us all afterwards, but our performance still left a good deal to be desired. Rather uncertain in places. Perhaps 'Revenge' will be more perfected. We start with the first practice on Thursday night.

WEDNESDAY, 26TH APRIL, 2 P.M.

Another gorgeous day. Hot sun and blue sky, such a lovely change from bad weather lately. Too lazy and too conscience-ridden about letters to go out – anyway just yet – and C doesn't seem very energetic lying on bed and lazifying while I sit at the window writing. I like this end of the room very much. See all that is going on up and down the road and over in medicals. Last night, I had a first-class view of a convoy coming in, directed by brilliant flares of acetylene. Sat up in bed being roused up by the arrival of the first cases and when I lay down again they were still coming – but not a large convoy, all the same. Only got a few new patients in our wards, four in 31 and three in 32 and one poor solitary man in 30. Few more in

C's domains but no one is very busy. Rather a joy to have a convoy in, for it will make a little more work.

Alabaster expects to go on leave tomorrow. Will be quite good when she gets away as she does nothing but talk and complain and discuss the matter. Another disappointment would make life unbearable.

Choir practice last night and quite a good muster of female voices to rejoice Mr MacMillan's heart. He is desperately anxious that the numbers should keep up.

FRIDAY, 28TH APRIL, 9 P.M.

Had the first meeting of our second session of the choral society last night. I haven't laughed so much for a long time as we all did over our efforts to tackle the 'Revenge'. Never heard such an infernal sound or such dismal wails. Capt. Blaney endeavoured desperately to get us along over the rough and smooth. Fairly large numbers turned up. Hope the choir will continue to exist as it really is a very pleasant distraction and I do get real enjoyment from it, even though I am tired after being on duty all day. L/Cpl. Chant did the accompaniment and was much amused by the hopeless efforts and wandering wails of the choir. He suggested we should have more practices and we really will need them to tackle this piece, as it is much harder than the 'Crucifixion'. We have gained much 'kudos' for that and seem to have acquitted ourselves quite well, considering it was our first effort.

Jobbie is getting excited at the prospect of leave. She goes with Matron, probably on Wednesday next and now we hear that we are all to have fourteen instead of ten days, as the Le Havre route – which we have to go to instead of Dieppe – takes so much longer. Dieppe seems permanently closed but I do not know why. While we are having a peaceful time here, disquieting news comes from Ireland and though we can only get the newspaper version of the disturbances, they seem pretty serious.*

* The Easter Rising in Dublin. See Chronology, p. 350.

SUNDAY, 30TH APRIL, 3.30 P.M.

Had a most successful day off yesterday, albeit a little lonely. There
was no one else of kindred spirit to go out with so – after breakfast
in bed, brought to me by kind Gibbie – I set off all by my lonesome for a day's outing. The weather was just halcyon, but with a
strong east wind and it was very dusty along the roads. Went on
a voyage of exploration partly over the same ground that Ruscoe
and I covered on our half-day walk. After good deal of tramping
and various pauses to look at Malet's map, borrowed for the occasion, I got down to a dear little village called Pierre en Val which
seemed an appropriate place to have lunch. I went into a not over-
clean little inn where they served me with quite a
good omelette and coffee, the two things one
can always be sure of getting. The church
is very pretty and quaint. I slipped into
it for a moment while waiting for the
meal to be got ready.

Then I tramped on again and found
myself on the main road to the forest, so without thought set off
towards the world of fresh green that looked so alluring in the
distance. Was well worth the extra tramping when I got there.
Found a little by-path and followed it up some way into a maze of
dried bracken and small trees and undergrowth and there lay down
full length. Had a delicious repose, barring the flies. Ate an orange
to appease pangs of thirst and after a bit I wandered on my way and,
having picked a huge bunch of most lovely wild hyacinths in the
forest nearby, arrived finally at Madeleine. Wished so many times
that I could have painted the scenes I saw as I came along. The colo-
nies of bluebells under the trees, the blue sky above, the colours of
the village and farm – indeed of the whole country in sunshine and
shadow – were so delighting to an artistic eye.

Had an excellent tea of fresh whipped cream, apple jelly and
bread and butter at La Madeleine and a most restful and reposeful
time under trees in the orchard. Then homewards, tramping fairly

steadily down the long road into Eu. It was very hot and
dusty but I quite enjoyed the tramp and was lucky in not
having to wait very long for a train into Tréport.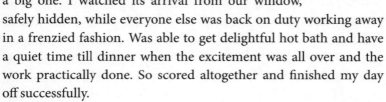

Arriving up at camp, I found that a convoy was quite
shortly expected. There were supposed to be 600 cases,
but I don't think so many came, though it was quite
a big one. I watched its arrival from our window,
safely hidden, while everyone else was back on duty working away
in a frenzied fashion. Was able to get delightful hot bath and have
a quiet time till dinner when the excitement was all over and the
work practically done. So scored altogether and finished my day
off successfully.

The big convoy is the result of a severe gas attack by the Germans,
two attacks at least and a second one that the men were apparently
not prepared for or couldn't protect themselves from, so they got it
in full strength.* All our medical huts are full and nearly all the men
have gas poisoning, mostly very slight so a good many of them are
up and about today. Kept us pretty busy, running round tidying and
looking after so many patients.

Evacuation at 4.30 today. Nearly that now, so it won't be long
before Blighty ones are on their way. I must get ready for stand-up
Sunday tea. It is quite a long time since I attended one of these func-
tions and I am not wildly thrilled at the prospect. I quite enjoy going
back to the wards these days. I really like the patients: though some
of them are a bit grumpy and complaining, others are very dear
things and I get really fond of them. Fonder in a way than I ever did
in the white huts where everything was more formal and strenuous.
C on duty this afternoon, so I shan't see much of her till evening.

THURSDAY, 4TH MAY, 6.45 P.M.

Just going to supper in a few minutes. First time today that I am
up after being laid low again with another wretched bilious attack
and general knock-out. Feel very chewed-stringy now but think I

---

* Fighting continued in the Loos area. See Chronology, p. 350.

will avoid going to No. 3 again which was threatened if I didn't feel well enough to go on duty tomorrow morning. I went to bed on Tuesday afternoon and have been here ever since till this evening when I crawled out of bed and went for a walk along the cliff with Sister Banham …

Am back in bed again, supper over. C has just departed to choral. Am sorry to be missing it, as last time was such entertainment, besides which it is interesting to hear something beginning to emerge out of chaos.

Matron and Jobbie have gone on leave, departing yesterday morning. Bownes, or Hynes, goes next, then two of the Sisters – and then C and I! If all goes well and leave keeps on steadily every week, which is the present arrangement, then we should be turning our faces homewards on the last day of this month or the beginning of next. Hardly dare think about it too much in case something should happen to alter this pleasing outlook. It will not be so long in coming anyway now, even if there is a slight delay. Will soon be having Allybuster back again, I suppose. She only gets ten days having gone before the fourteen-day regime was brought into force. She did not score very much by being in such a hurry to go.

SUNDAY, 7TH MAY

The first wet, unsettled day we have had for some time, but now the weather is improving and glints of sunshine are showing every now and again. A convoy came in last night, not a big one – not for medical anyway. Had one new patient in each of our wards and five in 30, all TB cases and staff are still stumbling over each other, so things are pretty deadly. Sister Withers hands our domain over to a new Charge Sister tomorrow who is just down from isolation and goes by the rather discouraging name of Rottenbaugh. She doesn't look very lively but perhaps will turn out better on further acquaintance.

8.30 p.m.

Just into bed with a delightful hot bottle to comfort my cold tootsies. It has turned very chilly with the rain and damp and we are glad of anything warm to feel or wear. Did not go to church this evening, after all. Had a headache all afternoon and so went and lay down and read. Took things very easily and now feel better.

Very lively and busy Sunday tea with lots of MOs as guests. Making pleasant conversation as we handed out cakes and tea. Capt. Paulley was there, critically eyeing up his flock of erstwhile invalids; he detected I looked pale in a most unkind manner, especially when I was trying to put on a pleasing aspect for our visitors.

Sister Chesters has had her moving orders and goes tomorrow and both Sister Williams and Sister Bownes go on leave on Wednesday; so things are humming. Changes always seem to come when Matron is away. Sister Johnson is carrying on in her absence and managing quite successfully, being quite stern in her ordering of the camp. She says she enjoys wrestling with the difficult problems that crop up every day. I wish she would wrestle with the surplus of staff on our line – orderlies and Sisters are far too thick on the ground and always getting in each other's way. Such a lot of our men have gone – some to convalescent camp and others to Blighty. The CC men often turn up again, generally looking much better and more workmanlike. We always exchange great greetings, especially if they have been my rather favoured patients.

TUESDAY, 9TH MAY, 2.30 P.M.

Horrid day again today, cold and windy and wet, so am just sitting indoors in our room taking things easy. Went into town yesterday, met C and had tea, or rather coffee, together at one of the popular bun shops. Alabaster turned up last night full of beans having enjoyed leave very much. Now we are back to our old three-in-a-room squash. Bownes goes tomorrow. I wonder who will go on night instead of her. She will have a tossy crossing if this wind keeps up.

THURSDAY, 11TH MAY, 5 P.M.

Rejoicing in a half-day and have wandered up into the woods and here I am sitting back up against a tree in what seems as remote a spot from the hospital surroundings as one could possibly imagine. The woods are all green now and so fresh and lovely with horse chestnuts, lilac and laburnum all in bloom. Seems so strange to have seen this place through all its seasons. It will soon be looking as it did in its early summer garb and then it will have shown us all its various aspects and changes.

Went out this p.m. with Malet, Fletcher and Gibbie but our party gradually dwindled away and I was left forlorn. We went to Eu by the canal bank through the docks, which was very interesting. Malet stayed there, to sketch a very pretty view looking along canal with its brightly wooded banks to Eu Château and the wood behind. Gibbie went off next, to walk back home by the park. I went with Fletcher to do some shopping, then she had to hurry off to get into camp by 5 and so I continued my sauntering alone, till it has brought me here to this haven of rest. Must be moving off again soon on my tramp home before it gets too late.

In the Park farm, I passed one of these lovely birds making such a display of tail down as I came by. They are wonderful when they show off all their colours.

SUNDAY, 14TH MAY, 8 P.M.

A new week begun and a day nearer leave. Am not thinking too much about it, but I cannot help giving such a tempting subject a thought now and again. Another convoy coming in tonight, thought only small one, so we hear. The Canadians are taking one in now, so things are still pretty active. I expect these are the tail end of the rush and may have a slack time again after this is all over. C is still over in Hut 4 helping there, but she expects to have to leave again at any time as Sister Johnson doesn't want Matron to find that the Hut 4 sisters are having extra help. Everything is considered in this light while Matron is away. Though absent, she still makes her authority felt and Sister Johnson seems fearfully afraid of making any alterations or rearrangements in case Matron should straf when she comes back. She is expected back on Wednesday along with Jobbie too, I suppose. Their holiday time is getting very short now. Just for the present, I have moved into 33 and 34 instead of C and am finding plenty to do, tidying and dusting and making beds. Really quite busy this afternoon and the time passed quicker than usual.

Quite a nice service tonight in our wooded church. Mr MacMillan is said to be leaving soon and I rather hope we shall get someone more inspiring and more likely to stir the souls of the patients. Little Mr Clayton, our former chaplain, came back to visit the camp a day or two ago. He was full of smiles and nods and cheeriness, greeting everyone with overflowing cordiality.

TUESDAY, 16TH MAY, 7.35 P.M.

Just come in from a prowl on the cliffs with C. It is such a lovely evening, after the shocking weather of yesterday. We just sat near the edge of the cliffs and looked and looked at the colours of the sea, sky and town.

This has been great day marked by a visit from Princess Victoria of Schleswig Holstein, on a round of inspection. She was expected to appear any time after 11 this a.m. but didn't turn up till 1 o'clock. There were great scrubbings and tidyings and cleanings in the wards and everywhere else. Everyone was on tenterhooks when the inspection was drawing near. One of the choicest things about the show was the sight of the orderlies along the medical lines. They were all got up in their spotless overalls like good little boys cleaned up for a party, excited as children. We were all clean and starched and trimmed up too. We couldn't go to lunch till 1 – any of us – so we were waiting and standing about a long time looking out of our front doors to see what was going on, gossiping with the MOs. The Royal Personage didn't however honour us with her presence, only passing through 36 and then straight across to 26 opposite and through there, to surgical. We watched the little procession on their way over, the Princess in sober black and not too fashionable. Lady Murray* was conspicuous in her white Red Cross attire while Sister Johnson was looking very tall and angular and anxious.

---

* The Hon. Helen Mary Murray, Lady Murray, was the Director of the nearby officers' hospital that bore her name.

Am feeling very virtuous, just having written three letters. Has taken me from 5.30 or thereabouts till now, so it just shows what a brain effort such an accomplishment means. It is now dinnertime and I must get ready in brace of shakes. Suffered a slight downfall this morning – C came back to Med lines again and I was pushed out of 33 and 34 and back into 30/31 etc. to a lot of strange patients, Sister Angel and nothing to do. I wasn't a bit pleased but C was more than unwilling to give up 33 and 34 too, so I made no great stand about the matter and as a matter of fact quite enjoyed my morning. Found a delightful set of patients in 30.

Matron and Jobbie came back on Thursday night, neither looking much refreshed from leave but having had quite a gay time. Jobbie acknowledged feeling more tired than when she went away which is not very encouraging to anyone looking forward to their leave as time of rest and recuperation. Rind is also back from Hardelot, stronger and restored to health but not yet quite her old self. She and Jobbie plunged straight into the white huts and have been very busy consequently assisting with all the bad cases. A good many of the patients have been evacuated, but we still have quite a number, enough to keep the staff very fully occupied.

Hynes and Sister Angel have not gone on leave yet. The Dieppe boat is suspended indefinitely for unknown reasons and it is a matter of extreme doubt as to whether – or when – we shall get away. C and I depend on them for our leave, for we go when they come back. Capt. Paulley and Mr Kinsella got away via Boulogne, making a pretence of special leave which enables them to get round that way and not have to stick here till the authorities choose to make it easy to cross the Briny.

It was lovely out on cliffs this evening. Sat out with Rind for a while gossiping and taking the air and I found the scene and the cool evening breeze and the diverse colours to be just delightful. C has come to bed now having been practising in the anteroom with Miss Little, one of the Canadian sisters. They are singing in a quartette together and practised last night with great vigour. They are to perform at the next concert, whenever that is. Must put this away now and compose myself to sleep.

WEDNESDAY, 24TH MAY, 7.45 P.M.

Days have slipped past by since I last wrote up the events of life here. Since last Saturday there have been great changes as far as I am concerned. Am now up in the redoubtable and strenuous 'enterics' and enjoying life very much. Went there yesterday morning to be second VAD and to assist Malet and share duties with her. Had half-day, so got off lightly for the first experience, but today I have been very strenuously occupied all afternoon, plunged into feeds and blanket-baths. I am much enjoying working with Sister Watson who is very nice and an excellent nurse withal. Matron has some funny ideas and the move seems partly brought about by the fact that C and I, being in same line, could never get half-day together or be off at the same time conveniently.

Am quite sorry to have left medicals and the nice cheery men but it was so slack at times that I think I should have got thoroughly fed up before long – and between Sister Angel with her affectations, Sister Webb with her sentimentality and Sister Maddison who is really almost mental, I couldn't get much pleasure out of working with the staff.

Had a day in the black huts on Sunday. I was sent over to take Ruscoe's place as she was laid low with inoculation. Found a very busy ward with some really bad cases and in addition, things were in a general upturn because of an impending visit by the DGMS – i.e. Sir Arthur Hoggart – who elected to come round at the busiest time of the morning. Sister Treloar and I bolted round tidying up and doing beds at the double and locking and hiding things away, making general clearance and orderliness in ward. Then the DGMS never came round to us after all. So after a fearful scrum, we finished morning in comparative peace of mind.

Ruscoe was restored to health on Monday morning and returned to duty, so I went back to my old haunts in Med. Line. A large convoy came in during the night, at about 10.30. C and I watched most of it from our window and saw car after car go past, but the patients are mostly surgical. Expecting another tonight. Must have been some severe fighting to keep us so busy. However, convoys won't affect me now in the same way as in enterics: we get our patients any time and every time.

9.45 p.m.

Still no prospect of our leave. Hynes and Sister Angel are waiting and getting no word. Bownes and Sister Withers are back from their leave having had a very nice time and Bownes is now to take Gibbie's place, as she is going into the white huts soon. Bownes is so much thinner that I hardly recognize her, but she seems full of beans so must be in good health, despite her decreasing girth.

FRIDAY, 26TH MAY, 9.45 P.M.

Just into bed and quite glad to be there after a strenuous day. I find bed *very* comforting, even though it is getting rather shaky on its legs and descending gradually nearer and nearer to terra firma. Don't know what is to be done when it finally rests flat on the floor and I extend myself on a veritable stretcher. I have been next door in Malet's room, eating strawberries. First 'straws' I have tasted this year and very delicious, so have been having little galavant on my own account. Before that I went to Compline service at church, which I always like because of the peace and quiet it brings after an active day.

Am enjoying enterics very much and the work there is certainly pretty hard, especially afternoons with blanket-bathing, but I really enjoy good, hard work if it is straightforward and one feels one's helping usefully and not doing any made-up kind of job. The spirit amongst the orderlies up there is congenial. Philp is nice and obliging and Walker is quite a respectable and pleasant Scot, with a broad unmistakable accent. I enjoy working with Sister Watson very much and of course Malet is a dear and quite extra special to pull together with, so I should be very happy in my new sphere of labour.

Latest development is an influx of seven new VADs, all St John's, to our harem. All of us are rather bored at any new additions to our contingent. No more news of leave alas! Hynes and Sister Angel are still waiting grimly, longing for the moment to arrive when they can begin their homeward journey.

SATURDAY, 27TH MAY, 3 P.M.

A glorious summer afternoon. Doing a little nursing chez nous instead of over in the wards. Poor Alabaster is the sufferer. Just after lunch I was here in the room with her and as she was diving after something in her box, I saw one side of the window slip off its hinges and come crashing down on her head. At first we didn't treat the matter seriously, although it was an awful dunt, but when I went over to her I could see that she had practically collapsed and was not conscious. She seemed in a sort of fit. I got the poor dear up into her bed and went to get help next door from Malet. She went for the Home Sister and we all did what we could to make the poor dunted one comfortable. Mr Higgins has been in to see her and now she is lying in bed half dozing, evidently with a very sore head and not looking up to much. She still has a most peculiar look about the eyes as though she had lost control of them. Don't know whether she will be a case for No. 3. I am mounting guard to see she stays quiet and to keep the room dark and peaceful at her end. Can't do much else except leave her quite alone. She went absolutely cold and almost pulseless at first so must have received a dreadful shock and certainly the bang of a heavy window is no trifle to receive on the top of one's head. A horrid accident and just like the poor unfortunate Alabaster to come to grief like that. Think she looks unlucky, as though she had been born under an evil star.

C is away to Dieppe with Matron and Sister Simpson. She left a note for me on the dressing table to say she was having a half-day and had gone at 12 so will have a nice trip on a day like this. What it is to be in favour! Malet is also having a half-day and has gone out somewhere after excitements of the mishap.

TUESDAY, 30TH MAY, 7.15 P.M.

Must be moving back home in a minute or two, but the sunset colours of this evening are so lovely and I have been enjoying a quiet, peaceful time, writing in a secluded spot, ensconced just at end of golf links behind the gorse bushes. Will soon be the longest day again and it is amazing how the year has gone by since we first stepped out of the ambulance on our arrival here.

No more word of leave but Sister Angel got her moving orders yesterday and left in the evening for an unknown destination. Poor thing was much upset – this was not at all the change she was expecting but I expect she will get leave more easily from there as we all seem to have come to a standstill here.

Alabaster is restored to health again and back on duty today but she had a narrow shave of being sent to No. 3 and still looks rather goggle-eyed and shaky. Must have had a very sore dunt on her poor head.

WEDNESDAY, 31ST MAY, 8.40 P.M.

C and I are in an inward glow of excitement, for at last leave has definitely come nearer. We signed for it today at lunchtime and now this evening we hear that Sister Treloar, who was going the day after tomorrow, won't now be able to go as the district she was going to is out of bounds, owing to an outbreak of infection of some sort. We don't quite know what this will mean. Our leave can't get through for a day or two but we might be packed off quite suddenly now that events are really progressing. It will be lovely when we are actually speeding homeward and I can hardly realize that the great and longed for occasion is so near.

One of new VADs seems to have disappeared. She didn't turn up for duty this evening and Sister Reid is quite agitated about her. Such a thing has never happened before. Perhaps she will reappear quite safely tonight and allay all fears, but it seems rather queer of her to vanish so completely.

10.10 p.m.

Excitement has been great over this disappearance, as it seems to be a real absconding, from all we hear. Had great gossip in Johnnie's room. Everyone has some version of the tale and we are all agog for more news. It is the most exciting event that has happened for long time in the camp. She walked off with a little suitcase in hand and has not been seen since. All the new VADs are much upset. There are great comings and goings between the Colonel and Matron and the staff in general. I just hope it won't affect our leave. It will probably result in some new rules which will be tiresome, but it is always the way. When anyone kicks over traces, other people suffer for it.

THURSDAY, 1ST JUNE, 7.45 P.M.

Matron told me today that we would probably be going on Monday for our leave, so there's a pleasant 'prospick' and really something definite. Sister Cross goes tomorrow. Haven't heard anything about Sister Treloar.

Very sudden departure of Sister Banham and Sister Sumpsion from our midst this afternoon. They got their moving orders in the astonishing way that these things come and were packed off at 6.30, almost before we had recovered from the first shock at sunrise. They were both rather regretful at going and in a great kerfuffle getting their things packed. I went into town so didn't see the last of the departing couple, but I don't feel any very, very great regrets at the thought of not seeing either of them again. Sister B and I had knocked about together a good deal but she was a queer creature and made herself cordially disliked by her rude manner, though she had a really kind heart under it all.

Latest developments of the runaway affair: she was found at Dieppe at dead of night by Sister Johnson and Mr Horsburgh who went in pursuit by ambulance and brought her back to camp in ignominy. Apparently nothing will be done beyond sending her away at the end of the month. She is said to be heartily ashamed of herself and is hardly daring to show her face in the Mess.

SUNDAY, 4TH JUNE, 3.50 P.M.

Have been feverishly tearing and tidying up letters and now must write a line before getting ready for tea. Am in a state of great anxiety about tomorrow, for there has been some muddle about my leave coming through and I have not heard yet whether it is alright and we really will depart on our adventurous career in the morning. My leave didn't come through when C's did and then when it was sent for specially, it came back marked 'Special Leave via Boulogne' for seven days only, which was not at all same thing, so Matron despatched it back again and it was to have been returned today but we have heard nothing yet. I am feeling rather anxious and uncertain what to do about packing. It won't take long once I set to and C does not seem to have begun hers. She is off this evening, so I shall not see her till tonight when the awful question of tomorrow will be decided. It would be maddening if, through a bungle, we were stopped or I was alone, and C were to go off leaving me behind. Hope profoundly all is well but must make up mind to fortunes of war if it isn't.

The weather has turned very stormy and wet today which is a drawback and promises a rough crossing for us, after all these weeks of the lovely weather we have had lately. I think we go by Dieppe, so it won't be a very long crossing and we don't lose a day over it, as we should by either of the other routes.

Had a great do last night. Fourteen of us VADs – that is, all the ones of the original party who still remain – took a trip to Mesnilval to celebrate the anniversary of our coming. Ruscoe and Sealy, C and I were included with the main body, as we all belong to the same family party who have worked together so cheerfully and smoothly for past year. The affair was a great success and Matron's presence was a crowning addition. Had a great supper feast at the Bosquet down in M-val of omelette, pear and compote and cream. Matron was in great form and quite one of us for the time being and very pleased at being asked as a guest. She gave us all a present, handed out of a basket like a bran tub. The presents – little toys – were a marked feature of the entertainment and provided us with a lot of amusement, which we thought extremely thoughtful of Matron. Mine was a very fine cock and C's a sailor in a boat and some got rattles and various noise producers, which were used with great effect to keep the party lively. However, we were lively enough anyway and the anniversary celebrations were a great success. Rind and Wall Jacobs got up early to come with us. They had to leave early to get back on duty, but not before we had nearly finished the feast. We all walked back to camp together, Matron setting a very smart pace, and got in at 8. Were excused supper so we all got to bed early.

MONDAY, 5TH JUNE, 12 P.M.

Well! Well! Here we are, C and I, fairly off on our travels. On the train to Le Havre from Dieppe and turning our faces homeward, after a whole long year away, strenuously at work practically all of the time. This train is not a rapide and we have stopped twice since leaving Dieppe, only a very short time ago. We had a good send-off and much counsel from Matron beforehand in her room. She seemed to have some qualms about our going off together without a Sister, or presumably a responsíble person in charge. Great favour is accorded to us: we are considered sufficiently sober and are to be trusted not to get into any pickle en route. Certainly feel the journey could be fraught with a good many complications in which RTOs and SHLOs* loom very large. However, I daresay we shall wrestle through somehow. It is rather a good joke that C and I are in charge of a party of ten men of various ranks, us being the only members of the party of officer rank and consequently in authority. One of the Tommies brought us the railway ticket and seemed rather anxious at the situation and no wonder, when two poor little VADs had to shoulder such a burden of responsibility.

We cross over tonight at some midnight hour and will reach Southampton about 6.30. Quite expecting to have a rough time on board as the sea looked very turbulent and the wind has been

---

* Rail Transport Officers and Senior Home Leave Officers.

raging all night. We were very busy packing after supper till lights out and this morning we were up early to finish off and make our final preparations for the journey. Matron had a great celebration dinner party for the stripe Sisters last night, having heard that she had been awarded the MRRC which is the coveted distinction of the Sister nursing staff of the BEF. I think Matron quite deserves to be recognized, for she has really worked very hard and managed the large convoys wonderfully, though perhaps a little brusquely and undiplomatically at times.

THURSDAY, 6TH JUNE, 10.20 A.M.

Now at Southampton and having a long wait before the train starts. Boat was very crowded and we just had the number of our berths shoved at us. There was no chance to get cabins or for any picking and choosing. Didn't start off till quite late and trouble soon began when we got outside the shelter of the harbour. It really was very rough and some of the passengers, well within our hearing, spent a most miserable and suffering night.

Dear old Blighty, very, very nice to see it again and looking so very bright and pretty, though it is cold now that the storm has blown over a bit. Am just going to enjoy these precious moments of leave to the full and make a real holiday of it, which in fact is what it is meant for.

TUESDAY, 20TH JUNE

During her leave D divided her time between Nottingham and London, seeing as many members of the family as possible, and visiting Harrow School to see 'little A', her brother Alastair, in his last term there. She made just one diary entry, which included the following:

The introduction of women into various professions and callings to replace men is a new development. Still cannot help feeling much amused when I see women window cleaners clad in their overalls and trousers looking as though they had stepped straight out of some musical comedy. Tramway conductresses are quite established in their job and looking as though they have done it for years and have nothing to learn.

WEDNESDAY, 21ST JUNE, 11.45 A.M.

No. 16 once more! and back again in all the old familiar surroundings. Same old room, same belongings resuscitated from boxes where they were stowed pro tem. Same friends to greet us, same old view from the window – everything in fact as before and yet somewhat changed. Don't feel back in the swing of things yet, but after this afternoon suppose I shall more. Fourteen days of leave goes like lightning. Yet in a way I seem to have been away from this place a long time and a far distance removed from it.

Now is just lunchtime. C and I have both to go to enterics this p.m. for some hard work. It seems very busy up there.

4.20 p.m.

Have just come from first spell of work – up at enterics. I am back again there apparently, and permanently, and C is there too – for this afternoon and evening anyway. Have some very very bad cases, two with dressings to be done. Poor things, with not much, if any, hope of life. C and I and Sister Watson were on this afternoon. We have been blanket-bathing and working away pretty hard, but by no means to distraction. Malet is off with splitting sick headache. Hope it is only that that is the matter, but one always wonders with the enteric ward. The new VAD who was there has been inoculated, so she is off too. Robb will be on this evening so it will be a goodly crowd to do the work. Nearly all the patients I knew have gone but there are just a few left who greeted me cheerily. Same for orderlies except for Mann who is taking Philp's place. Tea now calls us, so I must break off again.

FRIDAY, 23RD JUNE, 2.20 P.M.

Returning from leave we were met at Dieppe by Sister O'Donoghue and Sister Roethenbaugh who both came in for joyride and shopping. The ambulance was then lost along with Sister Mary Jane, who had come in too. We had to go in search of them and found them both coming along after much delay. We got back safely by rather a long way, so what with the extra joyride and lateness in starting, it was after 10 when we got in. Matron was displeased and rather agitated. However, she soon calmed down and was sweet to us. She greeted us so warmly and lovingly, our hearts were really warmed to her. We all had a refreshing meal together and then went off to bed, calling on Jobbie, Gibbie, Fletcher and Malet en route, where we were received with great jubilation.

Had to get to bed after long and weary travelling, and we were allowed the morning off and a second breakfast the next day. So we had a nice long time to get our room straight and tidied up. We are back in the same old room with Alabaster, who is not very well just now and is helping in the refuge for the broken down.

We were both sent up to enterics in the afternoon and worked hard there for rest of the day. C gone to 36 Med today, to serve a period there. We had a convoy in last night at about 9.15. It was not a very large one but there are a good many medicals. Hosts of new VADs have arrived. The place seems to swarm with them – unattractive-looking specimens too, mostly. Hope some of them will improve on acquaintance.

We have four VADs up in enterics. Robb, Malet, Bates, one of new ones and self. But there seems to be enough for us all to do and we have one or two very bad cases. One poor man died this morning about 11. We tried oxygen and an injection at the last minute but couldn't save him. Two others have both been wounded, which makes it rather complicated. One is an amputation case and the other, poor boy, has a wound right in the back – a bullet embedded in bone. Both as much in DI as they can possibly be.

SUNDAY, 25TH JUNE, 5.30 P.M.

A really lovely, sunny Sabbath day and so peaceful just now. Rumour has it that a convoy is coming in at 7.30, but this may only be a rumour as these things so often are. Have cut Sunday tea today as up at enterics Sister Watson prepared such a feed of scrambled eggs, bread and marmalade, for Sister Walsh and self, that I feel quite fortified till suppertime. Quite the slackest afternoon I have had since going to enterics.

Poor Greenaway died last night and everyone was so sorry. He has been so dreadfully ill these last few days. Such a dear boy and only nineteen and as nice as he could be. Now that he and Cross have gone, this leaves only Lee who looks like pulling round and was out all afternoon today enjoying the warm weather. He is not really conscious yet and looks pretty bad still, but he is decidedly improved from a day or two ago. It would have been so much better if he, not Greenaway, could have gone, as he has really nothing to live for. Has a leg off, no friends and a wife who has deserted him. Poor man, doesn't seem much of an existence to pull round for. Greenaway had very nice relations and was evidently thought all the world of.

Robb had half a day off today. Things are going much smoother under Sister Roethenbaugh's regime now that Sister Street has gone. Perhaps not so systematically but certainly more pleasantly, as the staff are not driven and harried into a frantic state of irritation.

Great day of sports yesterday. Began at 2. Had the afternoon off so went up soon after to watch. Held on the golf links behind enterics, being convenient for us. Very much the same sort of show as last year but not quite so enthusiastic, though it all went off very well. No. 16 won quite a lot of events. I saw the sack competition and greasy-pole fighting and some exciting tugs of war. Missed the obstacle race as I was by then on duty, but I was able to watch some of the events through the fence of the enterics division. Sister Watson and I surveyed the scene from that point of view. Had an excellent tea of fruit salad, cake and ice cream and gullaravished with excessive greed, thoroughly enjoying the feed.

Downey and Campbell this time dressed up as clowns – two very rakish swells – the former having a straw-coloured wig and big corporation stuffed out with pullovers, giving him the most extraordinary figure to raise a laugh.

TUESDAY, 27TH JUNE, 7.20 P.M.

Matron threatens to dispense with orderlies in the house and put in VADs instead. C and I are to be the first because we remarked once when she mentioned it that we shouldn't mind the work. Don't know whether anything will come of project though.*

FRIDAY, 30TH JUNE

Ought to have been out this bright afternoon but have been reading an absorbing American novel and not able to tear myself away from it. C is spending lazy off-duty time too, tidying and pottering about and now writing a letter in French. A small convoy came in last night, or rather a big one, divided between three hospitals. Rumours of another tonight. 'On dit' has it that the rush has begun. Our men were supposed to be 'going over the top' yesterday morning at dawn to begin the great offensive.† Am afraid this will mean thousands of poor wounded men and a good deal of suffering. All leave is supposed to have been stopped. Sister Watson was very downcast about it and also because yesterday she was moved at short notice from enterics to be in charge of acute medicals, taking Sister Withers' place. Sister Withers and Sister Treloar had their moving orders and were off to new work yesterday afternoon in very short time. These changes came with startling suddenness and heaven knows who will be moved or what will happen next. Sister Walsh, the Australian, is carrying on for the present instead of Sister Watson.

Another wild rumour going about yesterday was that two more VADs and five new Sisters were coming, but this resolved itself into the arrival of one new stripe and no sign of the numerous other

---

* Miss McCarthy recorded on 7 July that No. 16 had 'officially asked for more help in the way of Mess servants', and that she had replied that VADs should be employed.

† Dorothea was correct that the Allied offensive was originally planned for 29 June but was delayed until 1 July. The artillery barrage had already begun five days earlier. See Chronology, p. 351.

additions. Robb is having whole day off today. She will be having a nice time now, but this morning was very wet and windy and disagreeable.

A lovely afternoon and here I am having half-day when everyone else, except the enteric staff, are rushed nearly out of their senses. Can't realize – lying out here in the sunshine, in this beautiful place – that war is raging so near. The advance, if it is to be one, has begun.* Our men went 'over the top' yesterday and since then the camp has taken in three convoys. The news is none too cheering. After all the bombardment the men seem to have gone over expecting to find the trenches empty, instead of which they were full of Germans all ready and waiting and receiving our charge very murderously. They had such good dugouts that our bombardment didn't affect them and they were all hiding safely until the critical moment. Will see what today's news is but I feel afraid it is going to be awful too. Can hardly bear to think of the thousands of wounded streaming away from the firing line and thousands more to come.

This is a lovely spot that I have found in a little quiet corner of a wood at the edge of a ploughed field. Birds are singing beautifully and there is absolute peace except for their voices. Have come up through Mers, over the hill and through fields, picking flowers en route. Corn seems quite far on. I came through a lovely corn field full of poppies, corn cockles and cornflowers – just a feast of colours. I am lucky to be having a half day off and for it to be so fine too. If it were not for our numerous staff and few patients I shouldn't be sitting here now. Left C off duty for the day with her foot. Has same pain in it that she had last year, only rather more acute and she really was very lame indeed yesterday. Très souffrant as reported by Sister Paynter to Matron, and now Capt. Paulley has seen it and she is resting today to see what result that will have.

Alabaster, Gibbie and Hynes depart tomorrow at 7.30. Think they

* After months of preparation, the Battle of the Somme began on 1 July. See Chronology p. 351.

are really sorry to go just at this very busy time. They gave a great party on Friday night, all the old VADs being invited. Robb and de Burgh were invited in too, as well as one of new ones who was in Jobbie's room and couldn't be left out. Feasted on strawberries and cream and cakes, made an appalling noise. Dressing gowns were de rigueur, deshabilly being right apparel and some very smart toilettes were to be seen. Alab had just put on her very best nighty to show off to the assembled company and was going to slip off her rather old dressing gown, so as not to hide the beauties of the embroidery, but everyone began to laugh very unkindly and teased her so much when she took her d.g. off that she had to put it on again.

Matron came in to see C just before I came out and sat quite a little while talking. She is so charming when off duty and not wearing her official manner. Our nice Australian Sister has gone to a surgical hut and we only have Sister Reid now who came up yesterday morning having just got back from leave. There was a great to-do because of the Colonel's inspection yesterday morning. Wind up very much, in fact a great gale was blowing and everyone was hurrying hither and thither trying to get things straightened. The Colonel had nothing much to say so I suppose he found everything to his liking, much to Sister Roethenbaugh's relief. His visit worried her dreadfully.

MONDAY, 3RD JULY, 5.45 P.M.

Must go back on duty in a minute or two, but have time to scribble a few lines first.

Malet and I have been left alone in our glory up in enterics, as Robb and Bates have been snatched away to cope with the awful influx in the black and white huts. Huge convoy in during the night and nearly all the huts are full with really bad stretcher cases. No evacuation yet, so if as expected more come in, I don't know where the new arrivals will be put. I do hope the advances we've made compensate for this dreadful loss of life and casualty list. Seems really awful to think of it. All staff are up to their ears in work and we only have peace and quiet up in enterics. I was off this morning and have been on all afternoon.

The three old friends and the four departing Sisters took their leave early this morning. Alab, Hynes and Gibbie came in to say goodbye. I hope for Matron's sake that there will be no more startling changes just now when things are in such a turmoil. I should go back on duty now. C is still off with her foot and has been helping in Matron's office all afternoon, rolling up dressings etc. She seems to be quite enjoying it.

WEDNESDAY, 5TH JULY, 5 P.M.

Camp is still in a whirl with this big rush and the wards are terribly busy. Operations happening by the dozen. Matron has been helping in theatre for the last few days. There are three tables going all afternoon and practically all the MOs are in at one time to operate or assist. Everyone who has been in says it is appalling but the ops must be done and many of them tout de suite. There have been several deaths in both the white and black huts. Some of 'blacks' are filled up with even worse cases than 1, 2, 3 and 4. Yesterday was breathing space. No convoys came in during the day or evening but an evacuation and a convoy this afternoon has made things hum again.

Still get varied accounts of news. The papers seem cheerful on the whole but wild rumours float about the camp of repulses and huge losses, and the worst of it is that they generally have some foundation. Our four, poor convalescents are still waiting to go. Three of them were told to get ready. By this afternoon they were all dressed in khaki, waiting, but I don't think they will get away after all. Schermuly the sailor man – my especial friend – gets rather depressed at repeated disappointments but bears up wonderfully all the same. They are all such nice men. Do wish they could get safely away. The poor one who is being left behind looked very forlorn this afternoon. Malet and I gave them all a big tea of scrambled eggs and toast, syrup and cake and cream cheese and Mansion House tea.

THURSDAY, 6TH JULY, 7 P.M.

Well here's a go!! Such a change has descended upon me since last writing in the diary. Matron informed me yesterday evening that she wanted me to go into the Mess to do batman and my face must have fallen yards. Really was dreadfully, dreadfully sorry to leave enterics. Last few days there have been so nice just working with Malet. However, all for King and Country I suppose. Sealy is my co-worker put in here because she has a boil on her neck and Matron didn't like her being in surgical ward with septic cases. She really looks quite poorly though with the boil – it must be painful. We were allowed to have breakfast in peace this a.m. then afterwards the clutter began. Lunch went fairly smoothly, waiting got through quickly. I was on alone all afternoon. Got rather worried at times over Matron's tea and such like. Have to go back presently for 8 and make supper arrangements and then a scrimmage round clearing away. Work seems pretty hard but will go better when we get more into the way of things.

Sister Jones is a funny old thing. So far has been very considerate but has her little affectations and mannerisms. The French woman got in to be an extra help is not turning out a success so far. She is much too grand for the job and gives herself such airs. Has a little girl called Grazia, a real monkey, but she has been doing the shopping the last two mornings and seems to manage all right. C is still in the office helping. Wish she had been put in the house helping but hope she will by and by.

FRIDAY, 7TH JULY, 2.30 P.M.

Am still wishing myself back in enterics. My old patient Schermuly has written me a letter in his seadog style. The poor things are still waiting to go to Blighty and I don't think any moving orders have come yet. This morning Sealy has deserted me and now C and I are running the show. Sealy's boil on her face was worse so Capt. Paulley came to the rescue and had in Mr TT* to consult. Now she has to foment and attend to it and is off duty today anyway. This is the first occasion during the whole of her time here that she has been sick. A pretty good record.

C and I have had bit of a rush round this morning with a few

* TT's identity is never disclosed.

things forgotten and a good many scrimmages. Don't think the men in the kitchen are very helpful. They seem quite willing to help in little things but don't like getting on with their work and are very unobliging to Sister Jones. She irritates them I think. Jackson the cook is inclined to give himself airs and a dreadful growser withal. He has been second cook at some swagger club in Piccadilly and turns up his nose at our fare, so much tinned stuff that he doesn't approve of. Matron is going to get rid of the washers up, Diggle & Co., send them to their wards and get French women instead. I hope the latter will turn out better than the first attempt or it will indeed be a failure.

The great push up at the front seems to be progressing but there is a lull just now, no convoys are coming in and the wards are emptying quickly. Another seven VADs descended on us last night, making for a huge staff – 91 in all – which means some waiting for us poor little batwomen. Shall have them all at breakfast tomorrow and don't know how we will manage for crockery etc. and space.

TUESDAY, 11TH JULY, 3.15 P.M.

The days are flying by while I am working away at batwoman job. It really is a busy life and more physically hard than mentally. Feeling very tired and sleepy this afternoon as I lie out on the golf links. C is beside me sheltering behind a bunker and enjoying the lovely fresh air, sunshine and larks singing. Bownes and I are now running the Mess, which we like much better, but it means harder work and we aren't able to be quite so thorough. Walker, the assistant cook, went this a.m. and the French woman, who came yesterday, has taken his place. She seems very nice indeed but has to leave at end of month to go back to Paris, so there will have to be someone then to replace her. Once we begin with these people there will always be some troubles.

Kelly (VAD) is established in the kitchen now with Tennant to assist her and they really do splendidly, turning out some excellent and successful dishes. I expect they will find it a hardish job now that Walker has gone. Diggle is going soon. However, so far it has all worked well and Sister Jones is very delighted with the results of this experiment. Bownes and I get up quite early these mornings as we have to sweep, cut bread and finish setting the tables before 6.55 and that takes some doing. Breakfast and dinner at night are the hardest times of the day, but so far we are getting on all right. Am afraid it will make us both pretty tired.

SATURDAY, 15TH JULY, 3.45 P.M.

Spending a lazy afternoon off duty sitting in our room by the open window. Seems to be a pity to be inside during such lovely weather when it has been so unsettled of late, but I feel too slack and exhausted to be in the least energetic nowadays when I come off duty. Still am really enjoying my work and Bownes and I think we are getting more into the way of it now. We can manage pretty well really, with occasional lapses through want of observation at mealtimes and irritation caused by Sister Jones's slowness.

Our ménage is settling down by degrees but the French women are rather a problem still. One of them has left today, finding the work too much for her. Knocked her up and made her ill, which was quite likely considering she had come down for a rest cure to Tréport having been made very ill by inoculation for typhus. It is a pity she wasn't strong as she was a nice woman. The other little Madame works away like a Trojan and today is doubly busy owing to the absence of Mme Moreau. We have to do all the washing up, which is a tremendous business, especially when there is any rush between meals.

The staff seems enormous now to wait on. Five new Sisters have lately arrived as well as a new Assistant Matron who is a very imposing and capable-looking lady, really very good-looking indeed. She and Matron make a very imposing pair to head our establishment. Matron often drops in at odd times to bring us a message or just to have a crack and she is so nice when she comes off duty like that, always so friendly and considerate.

We hear very little nowadays of the outer world or the wards. The hospital is slacker now than it has been for some time, several evacuations having taken place; but I expect there will be another convoy in soon as, according to the papers, another advance has taken place.

Am feeling very sleepy and tired and not at all inclined to take up the evening's duties of laying tables for supper and running round trying to serve people in double quick time. Bownes and I were not back in our rooms last night till 10.15, having been busy setting tables and making preparations for breakfast overnight. I am finding it a very busy and strenuous existence. There is such a crowd for breakfast that cups and crockery have to be washed up again to supply latecomers and we get in a bit of a pickle sometimes. The two cooks are doing wonders and turning out excellent meals, which pleases the staff immensely, so much so that sometimes it means we have to run for second helpings, which all takes up valuable time.

MONDAY, 17TH JULY, 6.15 P.M.

Matron had Miss Stronach, Matron of No. 3, in to tea today. I waited on them discreetly setting out the tea in Matron's little sitting room. Both were busy darning stockings and gossiping and very affable when I went in.

The ménage seems to work quite well now. Mme Férange and her birdy-faced, thin little daughter are firmly installed, looking after the kitchen and washing up and little Mme Desfanu is aiding and abetting. Everyone is loudly commending the efforts of the two cooks who seem to be getting on better and are less worried than they were and not so tired-looking. Over the last evening or two Matron has taken hand with the clearing, seizing on a crumb brush and shovel and running round the tables very busily, all the time keeping an eye on us to see what impression she is making. Last night Assistant Matron and Sister Latham, who were with Matron, had to join in too. They must have been very bored but they still lent a hand quite willingly. Bownes and I quite enjoy our evenings after Sister Jones has gone to bed which she does quite early, as we then potter about finishing preparations for the next morning's breakfast and generally don't get to our room till after 10. We are up in the morning at

6 or soon after, so we have a pretty long day and it is hard work, but really enjoying it, so long as I can keep going.

News from the front is hopeful, if only we can keep up this push. Can't understand why convoys are so few and far between. The hospital is really quite slack and many evacuations have taken place since the last convoy came in. The one last night was conducted by lady ambulance drivers in the pouring rain – poor things! – and at night in pitch darkness. They must have had a dreadful time.

WEDNESDAY, 19TH JULY, 10 P.M.

Had a really delightful birthday yesterday though the weather was not too propitious. If it had been today, the sunshine and cloudless blue sky would have given a finishing touch to a very pleasant day.

I was on duty till lunchtime as per usual, looking forward to a half-day's rest. Matron called me up to speak to her at the table and asked me if I would like to go to Dieppe. I jumped at the idea and hurried up with my lunch, dressed and was ready by 2.30. Sister Rawes came too. We had Colonel's car, which was a great concession and only lent to us because it was a business expedition to change the pay cheque. There are no more joyrides now on account of a shortage of petrol. Matron and I sat at the back together and Sister Rawes and driver sat in front. A nice arrangement as far as I was concerned as the back seat was most comfortable. Matron chattered away en route on all sorts of subjects and we had a very nice tête-à-tête tucked in with the Colonel's fine fur rug.

The ride didn't take long at the breakneck speed we went. Drove straight to the bank and there Matron and I parted from Sister Rawes and the car, who went on different errands while we pursued our friendly course. We spent a good time at the bank getting the cheque changed. Matron was airing her best French on the little clerk behind the grille who was not at all particularly cordial and seemed very worried. Got away at last and wandered down to shops buying various things en route till we were joined by Sister Rawes in the car. After a little more shopping we set off on our homeward journey – another breathless run along the fine main road. Landed without mishap at our quarters, then Matron asked me to tea in her room. She also said I might ask C if I could find her. I waylaid her just going into Mess to tea and we two and Matron foregathered in her little sitting room. Bownes brought in tea and we boiled eggs on a spirit stove and had a grand spread and thoroughly enjoyed the feed. Matron was quite enjoying herself and looking at us with broad smiles of pleasure. We felt ourselves to be very honoured guests, no invitation having been accorded to Sister Rawes or anyone else. After this great tea fight I went to my room and had a very quiet evening.

We do have some times, behind the scenes, over the culinary arrangements for the staff. There were great scenes today when the chicken that had been ordered for dinner appeared to be about the size of crows and very thin and costing fr 100. It was quite absurd and the cause of great argument. Bownes and I have many a good laugh at night over the day's incidents.

SUNDAY, 23RD JULY, 3.45 P.M.

Still working away in capacity of waitress and Mess attendant – a strenuous life certainly. Have never worked so hard in my life before, such sheer physical hard work, but I must say I am enjoying it. I never find the work too hard if it is straightforward, and the rushes at mealtimes provide a good deal of excitement. It is irritating when people will ask for things just when one is in full career, or make complaints at not being served quickly and think they are being forgotten because you happen to be waiting more on another table just for the moment. Bownes and I have learnt a lot about the manners of the staff since we took up this job, who is considerate and who is not, and some of the staff – both Sisters and VADs – are sore trials to the temper. None so much, however, as Sister Mary Jane. She really is the limit and provokes me almost to the pitch of rudeness at times. Bownes's irritations break forth frequently but that doesn't do any good and the best way is to go on steadily taking things calmly and avoiding, as much as possible, all cause of provocation. Ruscoe has now joined our little throng and works as a VAD and general assistant. At first some confusion as to her share of the work, but Bownes and I have managed to arrange it this way which is quite to our liking and still keep to our own job which we guard jealously.

This is a disagreeable day, a dry, hot east wind sweeping over heights, making doors and windows bang. C has a half-day and has gone out somewhere. A new VAD has arrived, sent here specially as a cook but apparently she doesn't know a great deal about it. She is taking Tennant's place, which I am sorry for as she is such a nice girl and I shall miss her very much. The new one is tall and thin and not very strong-looking. A little bit like Huntley in style but more gathered. She seems to go by the name of Austen Leigh. Another funny little VAD turned up a day or two ago, very plain and bespectacled. Don't know why she was dumped here. Seems to feel it a personal insult.

No more convoys since night before last and the hospital is still rather slack, but it seems the same everywhere. Today, six of the MOs – some of the old original staff including Capt. Cowper, Hendry, Day and Millsom – are going up the line to more dangerous work. Hope none of them will get killed, poor things.

WEDNESDAY, 26TH JULY, 5.30 P.M.

A dull grey day and heavy, not very enlivening weather and all the time the battle is raging, raging, not so very far away. Yet the hospital is very peaceful. Someone must be getting scores of wounded. I expect Hopper, over at Camiers, is very busy. One explanation of our slackness is quite probably that we work for one special Army – the Third – which is not so fiercely engaged just now. If they come into it, we shall have our turn for a rush. I see ward work looming in the distance again. Matron keeps asking me how long I have been in the home and it is three weeks to the day since I began the job of batwoman, so when the month is up I expect I shall depart and someone else will be dashing round with plates and dishes while I sit watching, with the eye of the connoisseur.

Kelly has been having a day off, so Miss Austen Leigh has been coping with the situation, looking rather worried but managing quite well, considering her inexperience. She was at Malta before coming to France. She seems to have enjoyed herself there, having had a pretty easy time, which she certainly isn't getting here. She is related to Jane Austen and evidently rather of literary origin. She is probably a very interesting girl but looks rather sad and extraordinarily different to Kelly. Will be rather relieved when K's whole day is over and we get her back again, as the poor descendant of Jane Austen doesn't look very capable of coping with unforeseen situations and Sister Jones is too vague and un-businesslike to be a great stay and prop.

One of the French women – the one with the daughter – packed up and left on only a few moments' notice at teatime on Monday afternoon, because she found that her daughter wasn't going to be paid at the same rate as herself. She was fearfully angry and jabbered away fiercely at Sister Jones who didn't understand a word – on her side poured a flow in retaliation, equally incomprehensible to the indignant little Madame. Anyway, she left and the other little woman is working alone now with Diggle's help and really doing very well. There have been plenty of applications for place so I expect it will not be vacant long, but Sister Jones is such a bad manager and for as long as she is in the home, I am sure we shall have trouble with the hired staff.

SATURDAY, 29TH JULY, 3.15 P.M.

A really sweltering afternoon, with a white thin mist driving over from the sea to add dampness to the frizzling atmosphere. Still, it does shade the sun a bit and make everything look very mysterious and rather picturesque. Am feeling very sleepy after early risings and late bed-goings. Next Wednesday will see the end of the fourth week of my existence in home and perhaps Matron will then decide that I must go back to the wards. Things seem to be working smoothly though the ménage doesn't seem quite like it did when Kelly and Tennant worked together in the kitchen. Miss Austen Leigh looks so sad and seems so lacking in energy, not calculated to brisk up one's spirits very much.

Another woman has come to take Mme Férange's place, a Belgian girl who is married, I believe, to an English soldier. She seems quite nice and very quiet and an extremely good worker so far. This morning, instead of having the latecomers' scrum at breakfast time, trying to find places and having to have these reset where other people had been, the letter table was laid and all homeless people went to that and found provision for them there which greatly relieved the congestion and made things easier for us. But it is always a bit of a scrimmage and people are so impatient if not quickly attended to.

A large convoy came in last night, but not from the scene of fighting. It is being said now that the real push is coming off in first week of August; this is only preliminary. But what will the loss of life be in the fighting to come if this is only preparation? Awful to think of.

SUNDAY, 30TH JULY, 6.15 P.M.

Another gorgeous day and a peaceful Sunday afternoon. Am going to church in a few minutes. Not been now for quite a long time, but this life is not conducive to religious exercises in any form. Somehow seem to get shoved aside in the hurry and bustle which I feel sad indeed about and wish it was otherwise, only it is so difficult to concentrate one's tired mind and be fervent and composed. Today Bownes and I induced Sister to let us arrange tea out of doors, so we had tea fight just outside the Mess room and our little patch of lawn looked very nice and summery, especially when the party was gathered round the tables in clean white aprons and print dresses.

THURSDAY, 3RD AUGUST, 3.30 P.M.

Notice with pain how the days have flown since putting my first entry into this diary. Now it is the month of August and the year is flourishing in a marvellous rapid manner. For days now the weather has been perfect and today is glorious. A cool soft breeze is tempering the heat and Malet and I are reposing comfortably in the shade along by the night people's quarters and writing and reading very peacefully.

The Mess goes on through various ups and downs. Sister appears to be in a rather ruffled temper, tired I think and rather fed up with us all, especially at breakfast time when she tends to get very irascible. Little cook Kelly is back on duty again and staying up the kitchen arrangements very efficiently, and bustling up the rather idealistic and languid Miss Austen Leigh. She had half-day on Tuesday too and went to Abbeville with Matron and was able to see her brother there who has been severely wounded. She found him going on nicely, so came back comforted. Miss Tennant was in the kitchen for a day or two assisting during Kelly's absence. She is such a nice girl and I am sorry she is going back to the wards again. Bownes has whole day on Saturday and well deserves it. Will have a racketing time in her absence, I expect.

FRIDAY, 4TH AUGUST, 7 P.M.

Have had a fairly busy afternoon on duty. Must go along to supper now, then to work again. More changes in staff and the reappearance of Miss Tennant who bobs in and out of the kitchen like a jack in the box. This time Miss Austen Leigh is the disappearer. She had orders this morning to remove to No. 2 Stationary at Abbeville where her brother is and went off at short notice. Said she was sorry and perhaps in some ways she was, but she has made a very short sojourn here. I liked her very much and probably would have liked her more on further acquaintance but didn't think her very practical. Rather vague and not at all strong, looked wretchedly tired and I don't think she would have stood the work much longer.

TUESDAY, 8TH AUGUST, 9.15 P.M.

Have had very delightful half-day and been out with Malet, disporting ourselves in the little wood this side of the Bois de Cise. Found a cool and refreshing spot under a tree where we reposed ourselves very pleasantly and talked about all manner of things. Malet is a dear and, by the way, belongs to the sect of Plymouth Brethren and adheres thereto with firm conviction. Another lovely, hot, cloudless day and evening. The summer comes now anyway, if it lingered or delayed before.

C out at choir practice, but must be gossiping now in somebody's room. Seems too hot tonight to settle down in bed, but must do so to prepare for 6 o'clock rise tomorrow.

SATURDAY, 12TH AUGUST, 7 P.M.

A stifling day! Hot wind and now it is growing overcast and looks uncommonly like thunder that probably will end in a storm. Have just come back from a rapid trip into town to make a few purchases and was intending to write letters but alas! The opportunity has gone by and I must settle down to correspondence tomorrow.

MONDAY, 14TH AUGUST, 6.40 P.M.

Have a half-day today that I have acquired rather on false pretences as Bownes was having it really and mine was tomorrow. But cut my finger rather badly after first lunch, a good slice through the tip, which seemed to horrify Sister Jones considerably so she decided I must take a holiday to recover from serious shock. Injured member is now well done up in sticking plaster – to keep it together! – as Sister Jones seemed to think necessary but I don't fancy the case is as serious as that.

Just got back from supper, waited on by poor Ruscoe who had to move pretty fast owing to an unexpectedly large crowd turning up, but it will relieve pressure at the next meal, which is always an advantage. Tables look very smart now with our new cutlery spread out. Matron sent for eight doz. knives, forks and spoons, so as to be independent of army material and our rather nondescript private property, so we can lay the tables very nicely now. If we had new cups and saucers and crockery, we would be very well set up and equipped.

Seems to be blowing up for quite a fall tonight and the fine weather has temporarily departed, which is rather melancholy.

FRIDAY, 18TH AUGUST, 7 P.M.

Nearly finished vol. III of diary and completed fourteen months of service abroad. Not such a bad record when one comes to view the matter squarely. All VADs with twelve months' service under the military are now entitled to wear a white stripe on their arm, but the idea hasn't so far received much encouragement here. We think it would look rather like swank.

It is just suppertime and I must go back to Mess in a minute or two. It turned cold and cloudy this evening and the fine weather has disappeared for the present, the last few days being very unsettled. Matron got up a picnic to the forest the other day and we ate our tea under the trees to the sound of falling rain and received a good many drips on ourselves and the eatables, but nevertheless we contrived to enjoy ourselves very much. Poor Matron was rather discouraged about her little frivolity at first. Sisters wet-blanketed it considerably, but in the end it turned out quite successfully. I got an extension of off duty and was very lucky altogether, for Tennant and I were stowed into the Colonel's car, which conveyed our Matron, Matron of No. 2, the tea things and us to the place of meeting. We got there most comfortably and successfully.

About sixteen turned up, some VADs and sisters arriving in shays hired from the town, while some came on bicycles. Got tea made at the Madeleine and the eggs, milk and cream and conveyed everything up into the wood. Had our feast there under the trees very happily, a truly Matronish scheme and she enjoyed herself no end, which was very nice. On the way to the forest in the car, she suddenly discovered a nickname for me and now calls me 'Button' with great gusto. The waitresses are 'Button' and 'Podge'. Not quite what one would expect for a dignified Sisters' Mess, but I think the names are both quite suitable to our present calling. Sister was off the whole day yesterday and things were very happy and peaceful. Really enjoyed her absence. She seems depressed and tired still and Matron is very antagonistic, which is rather a pity as it creates a feeling of friction. Must go to supper. To work, Button!

TUESDAY, 22ND AUGUST

Begin this new little vol. feeling very much under the weight of sad impending changes. News came today of Matron's departure the day after tomorrow, to a hospital at Étaples. C and I are both wondering how we shall get on and what will become of this place. Matron has her faults certainly, and seems to get on wrong side of nearly all the Sisters, but to anyone who understands her she is very charming and lately, since being in home, I have got to like and appreciate her far more. She has been just sweet lately and now I feel sad indeed at the idea of her going away. Don't know who will take her place. No one could be such a personality anyway or so efficient in running the camp.

WEDNESDAY, 23RD AUGUST, 2.30 P.M.

Another sad departure just witnessed, that of Sister Roethenbaugh. She got her moving orders last night, and was seen off in the fore-court at 2 p.m. by a little group of sisters and VADs and Matron. I think the Army is a horrid institution, most unfeeling, never leaving anyone alone and making such an unhappy feeling of unrest. Another Sister who has been on night duty and only just come lately went too, and Malet and Sister Rindon went in the car with the travellers to see them off at Abbeville.

Matron's departure tomorrow is a time to be dreaded. I hate these leave-takings and goodbyes and wish I could keep out of it all, yet I will be wanting to see the last of her when she goes. Bownes, C and I were all in bed last night and just preparing for sleep when Matron came mysteriously to the door and was immediately welcomed rapturously by her adoring satellites. Much grieved and lamented over, her departure was discussed in all its aspects. She sat down on Bownes' bed and the party was augmented by Malet and Fletcher, who heard our voices and came in from next door. We all sat round in our night attire like a family party, Matron mothering us all. She couldn't have been sweeter and so affectionate and full of regrets at leaving us all. Altogether had a most uniting time and I really believe that if Matron came to us for a little comforting, she must have got what she wanted, for a more unanimously adoring party of VADs there never could be. Seems odd, after all the many hard things we have all said one time or another about Matron and the bitter enmity she has roused up in some of her dependants. The Sisters seem to be hugging themselves with joy over her departure but that is perhaps not to be wondered at as she has, latterly anyway, been much more a VAD Matron than a Sister's and never showed her best side to them.

Kelly and I went together to the pictures last night. Matron, who was to have taken us, was under the Major's wing, so we were deprived of her company. I really very much enjoyed the show. It seemed to take us away from the hospital and gave us something new to think about. One film showed Charlie Chaplin in a characteristic performance, but I didn't care for it. He was rather vulgar and the piece was so utterly footling. Must go again some other time to the entertainment. Really seemed quite a frivol here in this camp where, up to now, there has been no chance of seeing any show like this.

Hospital is still very slack indeed and I wonder very much what will become of it at this rate. Seems such a waste of valuable staff and material when other places are beside themselves with work. The Mess staff continues to be hard at work though. I have just a week more of the home, if Matron's arrangements hold good; but I don't know what Sister Barton, who is carrying on for the present, will do. A Matron called Miss Ram is coming in due course, but I feel no enthusiasm for Miss Ram or Miss Goat or any other ruminating animal.

THURSDAY, 24TH AUGUST, 6.30 P.M.

Matron has gone, and the place seems very strange and deserted and headless. Cannot really believe that she has departed altogether and keep expecting to see her coming over from the office or into the Mess at the accustomed times. Rind, Bownes, C, Sister Burnell and Sister Hannah went in the car to Abbeville with her this morning. Didn't have a very interesting trip though, as Matron was depressed and apparently had a very trying interview with Miss McCarthy for she came out almost on the verge of tears, much upset. Seems too bad to treat her like that and give her this thankless job with smaller pay after all that Matron has done here.* Really, the Army is a hard, unfeeling machine.

* See Appendix, p. 357. The reference to 'smaller pay' is unexplained.

The escorting party didn't get back till about 5 and Bownes carried on when I came off duty. Great difficulty now in the absence of both light and water. The electricity supply has failed from the main station at Eu and consequently our electrically operated pump for the camp water has broken down too, so that the precious liquid has all to be conveyed up in water carts and doled out in meagre quantities, baths being discontinued and the staff going about unclean, having to wash in the merest drop as best they can. Rumour has it that if this plan doesn't work, the hospital will have to close down for the time being till repairs are completed. As it is it is slacker now than it has ever been and the staff is simply kicking its heels with idleness and getting very much fed up altogether.

SUNDAY, 27TH AUGUST, 3.48 P.M.

Feeling rather 'fed up' today, tired and extremely irritated by our most unreasonable overseer [Sister Jones]. She didn't go into town this morning, so instead spent the time running after us all, grumbling and scolding about everything and reducing us all to the last stages of irascibility. It has been getting worse and worse for the last day or two. I don't think she can be feeling well but I feel she also thinks we are trying to get the better of her, to usurp her authority and she is doing her best to keep us in proper subjection but she does it so grumpily, enough to rub up the crest of the best-tempered person.

We haven't seen much yet of the new Matron. Yesterday thought of a good name for her – 'Black Mumbo' – because she is so small and tubby and dark. Am sure she must have a dark strain in her. She is very musical indeed and yesterday when C was singing in the anteroom, she went in and was most affable and admiring and played some of C's accompaniments for her. She and Sister Barton are a funny contrast. One is so tall and thin and the other so fat and short.

I have just been writing to Sister Cowie – delightfully reminiscent of the old days, so long gone by. Am always sighing for those times again, even though they had their ups and downs. Am thankful that we once more have light and water and are able to resume the normal course, supplying these necessaries.

WEDNESDAY, 30TH AUGUST, 3.45 P.M.

More changes and yet more changes! This afternoon has witnessed the departure of nine VADs who received moving orders yesterday and are now all packed off to No. 23 General at Étaples to be under Matron's care and command! Matron must have said something to Miss McCarthy about wanting some of the VAD staff to accompany her when she went to the Matron-in-Chief at Abbeville and this is the result – not at all the ones she wanted, none of the older ones, with exception of Elridge. So a great clear-out has taken place and a great sending off this afternoon, though very much under difficulties because of awful gales of wind and rain that had been raging all day, the poor departing ones not going under very favourable weather conditions. They looked rather miserable altogether and found it a great job to get packed and prepared. They were supposed to be going at 9 this morning but departures were put off till 3. However they are safely away now and I don't suppose we shall ever see any of them again now that our ways have diverged like this. If it hadn't been for this sudden thunderbolt I would have been out of home today, having the day off. Everything had been arranged and I had quite made up my mind for the change of work, and then I was told in the evening that I must go on a day or two longer till Matron could make arrangements and get things settled up a bit. So, I find myself back at my old job again, just same as ever. Not really very sorry and still have whole day off in prospect.

I expect Bownes and I will soon have to be inoculated, as we are the only ones, along with M. de Roebeck, who haven't been done.* Sister Barton put me down for last Tuesday along with two others who had already been done. So as it was not worth being done alone I got a reprieve for a week or so. Certainly wasn't sorry about that.

---

* Dorothea fails to mention what she was being inoculated against, but it was probably typhoid and tetanus.

THURSDAY, 31ST AUGUST, 6 P.M.

After the awful storm and rain of yesterday it has been lovely today up till now, but it is clouding over for more wet weather methinks. Seems such a feeling of change and novelty in the air. The new Matron is so different from Miss Drage. Such surprise caused by her departure with Miss Barton to Eu on a shopping expedition this afternoon, leaving the hospital headless. Sister Hannah is being put in charge. They only just came back and meanwhile the whole of the Sisters' quarters might have been burnt down.

Just after second lunch a great flutter and excitement was caused by the combustion of one of the tents pitched between the huts. I rushed out to see the show, but all was over when I got there. Buckets of water were being emptied on smouldering remnants. Nearly all the staff of MOs were assisting, armed with fire buckets. Orderlies running armed likewise. The Major was in a great stew, careering over from an office in the distance, violently blowing a whistle all the way and summoning more orderlies from all directions. The hose was fixed under Mr Kinsella's directions, and that long after every spark had been extinguished. VADs and Sisters gathered round, looking out from every door and window to see what was going on. No such excitement has happened for many a long day and the audience and participators seemed quite loath to depart from the scene of action. All the same, it might have been pretty serious if not discovered and dealt with promptly, for the tents are so close to the huts that the blaze might easily have caught one side or the other.

Matron has been making some extensive suggestions in the matter of feeding the staff. She seems intent on launching out to the full extent of the Mess money, but I don't know how she will manage it! The poor cooks are tearing their hair, thinking this place will soon develop into a sort of hotel and rest cure for tired workers. Our two new French helpers seem getting on all right – they are nice girls, quite young and willing. They come from Armentières and have been through some awful times and witnessed some shocking sights. The eldest of them was telling me all about it yesterday. She has been gassed once or twice slightly and had some very narrow escapes from shellfire and evidently experienced much of the horror of warfare.

SUNDAY, 3RD SEPTEMBER, 6.30 P.M.

Church bell is ringing (or rather the bit of old railway line is being clanged) proclaiming the evening service and here I am sitting here wickedly and neglecting the means of Grace. I have great intentions of reformation when I come out of this 'ere home, which will be very soon now. Just a matter of a few hours will see me at the end of this strenuous job, and tomorrow I shall go to the wards again, to take Johnnie's place in the black surgical huts, under Sister Grayson. I am really sorry to be going for the sake of the work, which I truly enjoy, but think perhaps I have had long enough and a change will be a good thing. Yesterday Mrs Ward came to take Bownes' place and since she arrived I have been piloting her round. She seems very anxious and nervous – which I suppose I was too at first – but she appears quite unhappily anxious, and how she is going to pilot Johnnie tomorrow, I don't know. Complaining of her feet so very much and certainly it is the last job for anyone with bad feet, with so much running about to do. Don't know how she will stand it if she is suffering as much as she makes out.

Miss McCarthy paid a state visit yesterday to Matron and the hospital and was taken through the Mess and kitchen. She saw us all at work and expressed herself immensely pleased. She said she was going to get all hospital Messes worked in same way by Misses, so I forsee some sweeping reforms taking place shortly.

Was up to tea today, waiting on Matron and I had a little talk to her. Must try and see her again soon. Am afraid my inoculation is looming early in the future and that I will have no day off, except the wretched one recovering from the effects. Great sell, I call it, when I was so near to one last Wednesday. Bownes will probably be sufferer too, so we shall moan together. Miss Ram is continuing to be very amicable but keeping a fairly stern hand on us nevertheless and I can see she will allow no nonsense. Think she shall have a good many changes in the rules and regulations, though a good many surprises in store.

THURSDAY, 7TH SEPTEMBER, 6.30 P.M.

A very strenuous time we have been having since I last wrote. Just got back to the wards in time to be plunged full tilt into it. Tuesday and Wednesday no off duty and only one and half hours yesterday. On Monday I took my way to Sister Grayson's line 19 to 14 and reported to her. Things were fairly easy then, one blue-pus in 18 and two empty huts and a few patients in 14, 16 and 19. Only Sister Grayson, Sister Gower and Campbell and self were on line, so there was plenty to do even then. On Monday night the rush began and convoys came in heavy and thick and fast. There was great fighting up the line and advances made, but apparently at desperate cost.* The men were not altogether cheerful, though they were satisfied with results obtained. The wards filled up on Tuesday afternoon when empty huts were opened and yesterday was rather a day of pandemonium for patients were being continually transferred from one ward to another, for some reason. White huts sent over a lot of stretcher cases and walkers to empty some of their beds and other patients were transferred from our hut to another along the line, so things were pretty chaotic. However today, there being no fresh influx, all is calm again and the next evacuation will bring great thinning out.

Latest innovation is opening of Hut 20 as dressing station for walkers. Some of the staff have been posted there to do dressings, superintended by Major in great dominion. All our walking cases go up there to be attended to, which is really a help and leaves us free to deal with the ones in bed. As a matter of fact, yesterday and today I have practically only dealt with a little boy of eighteen, having been appointed to special him and to do his dressing, which prevents me doing any others for fear of contagion. Feel it rather a responsibility to be left in charge as the dressings are quite big, though his wounds are evidently much better. He has huge holes in both his

---

* The Battle of the Somme continued to rage, bringing more casualties. See Chronology, p. 351.

thighs – most painful. Burling, the orderly, helps with dressing and this morning Sister Grayson superintended, so I got various hints and advice. M. de Roebeck is now established at 19 and Sister G does 14, which has the worst and heaviest cases, and Campbell helps her. In my non-blue-pussing moments I scrimmage round 15, 16 and 17 tidying and 'sorting' – a hopeless job when there are so many up patients. The beds look like nothing on earth and one could make a continual round straightening beds alone from morning till night. I was pretty tired last night after three such hard days and coming out of home. No rest cure either.

Prospects of days off are very remote at present but I expect things will be quieter now as the rush seems pretty well over. Matron is here, there and everywhere. She must be pretty busy as Sister Barton is still away at Boulogne which makes her single-handed. She evidently approves of working full pitch when there is work to be done and discourages any off-duty time, but when we are slack we shall probably fare better with her than under Miss Drage's stern rule. The latter has written us such nice letters and so affectionate. Feel more drawn to her than ever.

MONDAY, 11TH SEPTEMBER, 7.30 P.M.

This evening the VAD course of lectures begins, the first of a series dealing with physiology, otherwise 'skillets'. There will be lectures twice a week after this, convoys permitting, so we should be well instructed by the end of the time!

Feeling more brisk today, refreshed by a delightful whole day off yesterday. Sister Grayson arranged it on Saturday and Rind secured a half-day, Jobbie and Fletcher getting theirs too. A delightful little party and very well attuned. Rind and I ordered a motor from Mers overnight and a most extraordinary old relic appeared very late to take us for joyride. It was manned by two boys – the recognized driver being slightly older than the other. The younger of the two is a little smitchet, apparently just out for the fun of the thing. I thought we should never get safely to our journey's end or ever reach the point we had in view, i.e. St Martin Église.

A small gathering of staff speeded our departure and amused themselves at our expense, but we were all out for a jaunt regardless. The car behaved very well, though grinding ominously when it was ascending any kind of hill. Neither of the crew in front had the slightest bump of locality and when we turned off the Dieppe road, they were fairly flummoxed. They had to ask several times and be taken in tow by a cyclist. That hardly saved us from going into a village pond and we took a most roundabout and dangerous way.

However, we reached St Martin Église safely and after ordering a huge meal at the fashionable Hôtel Jardins we drove on to Arques, a most fascinating old world place, with an ancient-looking house and fine old church. But the chief object of interest was the castle, standing up on the ridge above – a big, imposing pile of ruins. Betook ourselves up to see it, leaving the car down in the village. Not very much of the castle remains intact but our youthful guide laid off to us about the interest of the place and showed us the 'donjon', the fortifications etc. Finest part was the view and situation overlooking the valley, and there was something very nice about being in an atmosphere of antiquity after fifteen months of a very modern hospital. Down again, we went afterwards to see the church, clean and whitewashed and quite old-looking but with no special feature of interest. It was more interesting outside really than in. Looked as though the building was rather a mixture of periods.

Our old boneshaker conveyed us back to St Martin where we got our sumptuous meal in the hotel orchard, under apple trees laden with little hard cyder apples and by the side of a trout stream, one of special attractions of the place. Very crowded and Sundayish, the most amusing part of the entertainment being the company assembled, smart French bourgeois and smart English officers out from Dieppe. Galettes are a specialty of the place so we demolished one and it was very good indeed as were the eggs, bacon, bread, jam, fruit and coffee which completed our repast. Really felt very satisfied when we took our departure. Found our vehicle ready and waiting and packed in again. We decided to go by a new way so took the road further inland running parallel with the Dieppe Road, but the picturesque villages were swarming with French soldiery, a whole division quartered in the neighbourhood and every house seemed to have its complement.

TUESDAY, 12TH SEPTEMBER, 6.15 P.M.

Just been inoculated and now, before retiring to bed, am snatching a few moments to write more diary. After hovering for some time, I feel that fate in the shape of this operation has descended on me and M. de Roebeck and that Sister Fowles and I are victims of Capt. Paulley's machinations. Sister Burrell was assisting with iodine and swabs. We each went in turn into small operating room and Capt. Paulley punctured me with his needle. Now am awaiting results. Feel all right so far but am expecting not too restful a night and rather a so-so day tomorrow. Bownes has had a let off. No word of her being done though she is due for it as much as I am. Sister Mary Jane has just been in to say that I am to come to supper, so just having begun to get ready for bed, I must now get ready for supper, which is a bore.

The days off are falling thick and fast again and several members of staff are having a holiday tomorrow. Doesn't look too well in the matter of weather but I hope the rain will keep off. Would like to be going to St Martin again and repeating Sunday's expedition, but preferably with another car and not conducted by two such immature little boys. The little 'gamin', the smaller of the two, actually changed places with the other one en route and began driving us, but our nerves couldn't stand that, having survived some other shocks, so very soon we made a protest and he had to give up his place to the other one, with evident displeasure.

Hospital is getting very slack again and the wards are emptying rapidly. Evacuation today and several of our stretcher cases went. Some of them were very nice men. Some happy walkers went too. Now 15 and 16 are closed and all the up-patients are concentrated in 17, which makes the ward look like nothing on earth. Two blue-pusses inhabit 18, side by side and a new man who was transferred on Sunday from the white huts with an amputated arm and a very dirty-looking wound. Has continual irrigation which requires much paraphernalia and setting up. Suppose it does good, though it seems a very uncomfortable process.

Last night we had the first in our series of instructive lectures given by TT dealing with bones and skillets, joints and muscles. It was rather a preliminary preamble to the lectures following and very much going over old ground to some of us. But he made it as interesting as it could be and told us lots of little things that were new. Quite a crowd of VADs present, all seated on benches like a model school. Sister Barton was present to chaperone. All armed with notebooks and pencils and mostly very busy taking notes. TT wrote up names and diagrams on his blackboard and instructed us in a most able manner. Culmination of the lecture was his production of a most gruesome relic in the shape of an amputated hand. It had been part of a living person little more than a week ago. Had been well pickled but only made it look more horrible. Of course our lecturer never gave this point of view one moment's consideration as he was too used to the sight of such things. Invited us all to gather round while he demonstrated to us various things he had spoken of in his lecture. He prodded about at the tendons, muscle and joints in his ghastly relic for the different positions he was expounding. I thought some of us would be dreaming about it but no one apparently did, so perhaps are all growing callous too.

There seems to be serious outbreak of dysentery just now. Enterics are almost full and bursting with cases. Hear from all accounts that the epidemic is rife in various places. Hope it not serious. Anyway, the cold weather will not be long coming and that will make conditions rather better.

WEDNESDAY, 13TH SEPTEMBER, 7.15 P.M.

Inoculation proceeding today, but with strangely little effect. I have a stiff arm, not much redness but a feeling of slight nausea, a headache and a disinclination to do much seem to be the worst symptoms. Think I must have come off very lightly. C took my temperature last night and this morning and it was as dull as ditch water, disgustingly normal. However I had breakfast in bed and remained there reading and snoozing till 11.30 when I got up for first lunch. Had many visitors during the morning, kindly enquiring after my state of health and Madame racketing in with her brushes and pails and bemoaning the war with upturned eyes. C, Bownes and I have all spent a very peaceful afternoon, B being the most energetic for she got up from her couch and went for a walk before tea. The hospital is emptying again, orders having come to the Colonel to clear for another rush. Believe there is to be evacuation tonight but there can't really be very many to go. Hut 1 has one patient or it had, for Bownes says he has been transferred to a side ward of No. 2.

SATURDAY, 16TH SEPTEMBER, 8.30 P.M.

Night before last had second lecture of our VAD course – Mr Villandré on radiography. Only eighteen 'students' were able to go as the room too small to accommodate more. Matron put up a list of the chosen eighteen – nearly all the older stagers and the rest night birds. Sister Jocke was sent over to chaperone and shepherd a little flock together. The lecturer was quite a professional character, though inclining to be frivolous at times. I think him a silly little man, with rather a wee head. Still, he lectured fairly well and showed us some very interesting X-ray* plates of hand and foot and ribs etc., discanting meanwhile upon bones and joints and rather the same ground that TT went over last time. He finished up with a demonstration of his apparatus. Most thrilling part of all, I, standing near, was called upon to give my hand for a demonstration and it really was the queerest feeling to stand there and see one's hand just a skeleton represented on the plate, every bone showing, knowing it was a portion of one's own anatomy all alive and sensitive. Brought my arm in front of the rays next and showed the radius and ulnar plainly and then my elbow joint and, working it up and down, showed movement quite plainly. Rather rapid demonstration for precautionary reasons, these queer X-rays not being very safe.

---

* The use of X-rays (which had only been discovered in 1897) in obtaining precise information about damaged limbs and broken bones was widespread during the war, as a result of pioneering work which had been done during the South African War.

Next Taylor, the orderly assisting with the lecture, was called to offer himself as a demonstration of internal organs. He stood in front of the camera and the plate held against his body showed his heart beating and pulsating very plainly, a shadow of lungs in the ribs and then, lower down, his tummy very shadowy and diaphragm rising and falling quite distinctly. It was most interesting and educational.

Nowadays I have a terrible programme of late nights and outings, cinema, twice weekly choir practice, lectures two nights, musical evenings at home and now choral starting again to make another frivolity. This is all right when times are slack as they are now, but simply impossible if we were busy.

Hospital still clearing and clearing out and is very empty now everywhere. Rumours of a tremendous rush coming, but doesn't seem to be descending on us yet. The news is very good today, the British advancing very considerably and got important positions. Martinpuich seems to be great vantage point.*

MONDAY, 18TH SEPTEMBER, 9.30 P.M.

Early into bed after a busy day. We took in a large convoy yesterday evening. It was expected all day and everyone was ready and on tenterhooks by 10 a.m. when it was first rumoured to be arriving. Apparently a train went astray and it never turned up and another one came in at about 8 p.m. Went to early supper and came back on duty. Wasn't in bed till nearly 12 and didn't leave the wards till about 11.30. Every ward is full, except 14, not counting blue-pus. Stretcher cases are in 14 and 19 and all the others are so-called walking cases, though several of them were carried or supported along from arrivals hut. Convoy of nearly 700 altogether, so quite a big one. The dressing station was very busy all day today dealing with walking cases. C has been here assisting, as well as some of the other unemployed medical staff. We have been rushing up and down the line all day trying to bring order out of unutterable disorder. Added to our trials, the weather has been appalling.

---

* With several successes on the Somme, 15 September was proclaimed as the greatest day of the British Army's victory of the war so far. See Chronology, p. 351.

The up-patients' wards were just terrible, especially 16, till Sealy and I assaulted it and got the beds into something like order and respectability. Patients meanwhile were sitting around and gaping dumbly at us, thinking we were daft to be struggling away so heatedly at such minor details as beds. Seems quite a nice lot of men and from very mixed regiments. A good many New Zealanders among them and Canadians. They were all very tired and dirty when they came in last night. Had been practically a day and night en route, so were very thankful to reach a haven of peace and quiet at last. Things seem to be going very well for us still and the men speak cheerfully, but the casualties will be pretty heavy in the last fighting.

WEDNESDAY, 20TH SEPTEMBER

Another wild, stormy night with the wind whistling and sighing round the huts ominously presaging winter, which seems to have come ever so much nearer these last few days. Poor Blighty-ites we despatched today will have a tossing going over, but I suppose they will not mind with such a destination in prospect.

More work today. Convoy came in early this morning and practically every ward is full. Very heavy one for the white huts. Particularly severe cases and ops theatre going full swing. Am afraid there will be some poor dears going west and many maimed for life. Bad weather will put an end to fighting for present and doubtful whether there will be much more now before winter sets in. Men are all very cheerful but rumour has it that this fighting has been partly to secure better winter positions with no intention of making great advance, such as we all hoped for. Truly this war is a ghastly depressing business and I always have Little A at the back of my thoughts, beginning his soldiering and all the horrors to face.

Sent away three stretcher cases to Blighty, two being fairly bad dressings, so I expect things will gradually get slacker again. Several walkers who were struck off the list at the last minute today will be going tomorrow, if an evacuation takes place, and after that we shall be less rushed. Had a French, or rather Belgian, Canadian transferred to my hut today, a nice little man. Can only speak a word or two of English and understands practically nothing. Men have had some fun out of him but can't get on very well with conversing.

FRIDAY, 22ND SEPTEMBER

Am quite enjoying myself on the line now. Most of the men are dears and some especially so among the ones I know in 14 and 15. Other wards don't interest me so much. Helped Sister Gower in 18 with Newman this afternoon. Rather an unnerving proceeding for the poor little thing is quite uncontrollable now over his dressings. He lifts up his voice and howls and cries or else scolds and gibbers incoherently the whole time.

Rumour has it the CO is leaving to go to a camp at Havre and that the Major is going to carry on instead. Don't know what will become of the camp eventually as it is evidently taking a second place now. It no longer enjoys its former importance.

C has been moved from medicals to Hut 2 and is very busy there now, assisting with a ward nearly full of exceptionally bad cases. Last convoy was such a heavy one.

Had a letter from Schermuly last night, very anxious to come to a definite understanding. Quite thought he had dropped that talk, so got rather a surprise. Must write and suppress the notion as I don't quite fancy the idea of becoming Mrs Schermuly. Suppertime now, so no more tonight.

SUNDAY, 24TH SEPTEMBER, 9.30 P.M.

Our lights have failed again and I am writing in bed by candle-light. Wonder whether Zepps* are about – quite a night for them,

---

* Air raids on England by the giant airships known as Zeppelins, after their inventor Count von Zeppelin, began in January 1915 and continued for the next two and a half years. London was of course the principal target, but their long range enabled them to reach cities all across England. More than half the total fleet of 115 airships were destroyed by fighter aircraft and anti-aircraft gunfire.

cloudless dark and still. Afraid they will be troubling Blighty some-where even if they don't visit this neighbourhood. Been a lovely day and yesterday was the same. Ideal autumn days, warm and yet fresh. Have been on both afternoons so missed really best part of the day, but quite enjoyed the evening.

Another important change imminent is the departure of the Colonel to be DDMS* at Havre. Don't quite know who will take his place but rumour has it that the Major will fill the gap. If so we may expect some strong hurricanes whenever there is any sort of a rush. The camp will be very strange without either Matron or Colonel of the old times. We have entered upon a new era altogether and I don't think it will be a bit the same thing or so nice. Am moved now up into 18. Two new blue-pusses came in yesterday and Sister Gower petitioned to have me to help her instead of Sealy as she is so slow. I think she will find a good many flaws in me too, but at present we are very thick and fit in well together. 15 and 16 emptied into 17 and the line is quite slack again. Clearance made so quickly, these rushes never last long.

WEDNESDAY, 27TH SEPTEMBER, 9.10 P.M.

Camp still without light and water which is a serious drawback to it at present. Would have been having busy time just now but for the failure of important supplies. Fighting up the line is very severe but news splendid. Capture of Comples and Thiepval announced today. That is a great triumph.

THURSDAY, 28TH SEPTEMBER, 7.30 P.M.

A Gala Night tonight. Concert and entertainment in the Cinema at 8.30 in honour of dinner given by Officers' Mess to a whole collec-tion of French Generals and worthies. All the military dignitaries for the district in command of troops are here. Had a most entertaining time watching arrival of the guests for dinner at 6.30. They came in motorcars of all descriptions, military and civil. There are two

* Deputy Director of Medical Services,

ladies among guests, one is the wife of one of the officers, the other, I think, must have been Mayoress of Tréport – a stout gentleman in civilian clothes accompanied her. There was such a gathering of MOs and guests just outside the officers' quarters until dinner was announced. Then the party proceeded in with great pomp and state, a motley collection of MOs bringing up the rear, looking like a lot of schoolboys out on the spree. Our Mess was represented by all the red capes and one or two of the other Sisters and Rind and Johnnie. Both were very unwilling, proceeding to the party. I would rather like to have been at the function to see how everyone got on with the entente cordiale, how they all wrestled with a foreign language. Am thinking there could be some amusing moments. Now the convalescent camp band is giving selections at intervals by the light of an acetylene flare. I can see the dinner at full swing, everyone hard at it, talking and eating, through the windows of Officers' Mess. One of the Generals is quite an important personage – just done some great stroke on the front, taking some important position. All seemed to be bedecked with medals.

SUNDAY, 1ST OCTOBER, EN ROUTE TO WIMEREUX

A long to be remembered date! The occasion of our first move after nearly sixteen months at dear old No. 16. Can hardly realize it at all yet, but here we are – Fletcher, Jobbie, Bownes, C and I – in the train, off to 32 Stationary, said to be at Wimereux, and to new work and new surroundings. We are beginning all over again, on active service life. And dear Rind, left behind, which is the saddest of all. Malet and Johnnie and she will have to cling together, a very reduced little family party, gradually dwindling and dwindling away. Oh dear, it's a miserable world and the war is a miserable war that seems to take a delight in breaking up friendships.

The thunderbolt fell yesterday afternoon. I was working away in 18 with blue-pusses, being the only one on duty at our end of line, when Matron came through looking so gloomy that I thought something I had done wrong must have displeased her and I prepared myself to receive a scolding. But it was to launch the bombshell at me.

'Miss Crewdson, you are off tomorrow to Boulogne, you will pack your things tonight.'

I simply stared at her, speechless. Think my face must have grown a yard long and I couldn't express myself except by a series of 'Matron's.

She didn't stay long but bustled off to break the news to one of the other victims, leaving me in a state of severe effort at self-control. Went down as soon as poss. to see Rind and we nearly wept together over the dire news. C is having half-day and Bownes has a day off for inoculation, so they got the agitating message over in the quarters. We all assembled in time, bewailing our fate with the ones left behind.

Our next fearful undertaking was the packing, and the three of us in one room meant a fearful upheaval. However, it had to be done, so we got to work and made a beginning, but were then interrupted by a general adjournment into town of all the old nine, with exception of Bownes who, having been racketing about all afternoon, was feeling pretty seedy with the effects of inoculation. The rest of us all assembled at Hôtel des Bains for our farewell meal, a table d'hôte dinner and champagne to drink each other's health! We were all rather under the weight of things, but bearing up to make the occasion as festive as possible. The rest of the evening was spent in desperate packing and were pretty well completed when we got into bed about 11.30. Being the last day of September, the Daylight Saving Bill came into force and all the clocks were put back an hour.* So this gave us an extra hour's sleep. We came to second breakfast this morning having heard by that time that we were not off till 2, or thereabouts, so we had a whole morning to spend as we liked, mostly in packing and repacking, being visited by and visiting friends.

At 2.30 p.m. an ambulance came to take us, and our rather voluminous pile of luggage, down to the station. Colonel came over to say goodbye, and MOs, Sisters and VADs gathered round to speed the departing ones. Rind, Malet and Johnnie came to see us off at the

---

* The ritual of changing the clocks has become so much a part of the calendar that few people remember that it was a First World War innovation designed to save fuel. 1916 was the first year that it was introduced.

station. Capt. Horsburgh was a prop and mainstay in the matter of our luggage. The train was very late in coming and kept us waiting about ages, but at last we were off and here we are.

Must be nearing Étaples now and won't be so much longer after that before we make our destination. 'Quel changement!'

PART TWO

No. 32 Stationary, Wimereux

OCTOBER 1916 – JANUARY 1918

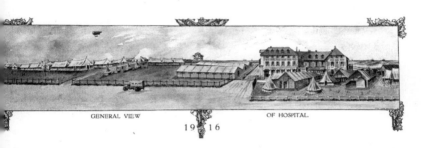

GENERAL VIEW   OF HOSPITAL.

19   16

GENERAL VIEW   OF HOSPITAL.

19   17

So much to write I don't know where to begin, so best to give rapid summary of events from the time when I last wrote, sitting in the train on my way here.

Not a very successful arrival at Boulogne. There was nothing to meet us – no instructions, no assistance. We were in a great fix, our piles of luggage there to be looked after. Eventually Fletcher and Jobbie stayed with the booty, C, Bownes and I hired a little fiacre and drove down to Hôtel Christof. A kind of plainclothes detective, the only English official on St Eloi Station, advised us to go there and enquire for Miss Crowdy. She wasn't in, so we were advised to go to a rest station in the station yard and enquire for Miss Woodforde. We found her successfully and got the necessary instructions. We were to stay the night at Louvre, that bustling poky little place, as we were to go to our destinations the following morning. So, having kept the fiacre, we drove back to the station, picked up the other two, left our luggage in the care of officials till the morning and presently were back at Louvre and being shown our rooms, very strongly resembling our apartments of nearly sixteen months earlier. Bownes, C and I slept in one room, Jobbie and Fletcher in other. Got a somewhat sparse dinner curtailed by all the lights going out, probably for a Zepp raid, and got off to bed quite sharp.

Next morning a big ambulance came at 9.30, took our little party on board as well as two more VADs who had come from No. 3 the day before and had also landed at Louvre for the night. We set off very full of qualms about our unknown future and really much alarmed. We seemed to go a long way out, though it was quite a goodish ride. When we got to Wimereux at No. 14 Stationary we dropped off our two fellow travellers, their hospital being an isolation one all in huts and tents. I could see lots of camps dotted about and kept wondering where we were going to be planted. On again, right beyond a train terminus and then in front of us, right down by the sea, I perceived a little group of tents and a businesslike-looking hotel behind.* We pulled up in front of this and very quakingly dismounted.

We sat in the hall till the Matron could see us and then she appeared down stairs. Seemed very nice and pleasant and quite welcoming. Conducted us all into her office and there had our interviews and got our particulars etc. She then took us over to our quarters, a nice seaside residence, partly villa and partly laboratory for students of Paris University, probably to do special research work under the most congenial circumstances. She then introduced us to Home Sister. Looked very nice indeed, a sweet face and very pleasant manner, so different from old Mary Jane.†

Presently were taken to the rooms allotted to us, C and I in a very nice little apartment, palatial compared to our hut dwellings, the only drawback being its extreme dampness. Fletcher and Jobbie are just upstairs, overhead. They have quite a nice room too, with a lovely view over sea from their window, but not quite so much elbow room. We seem to be considered lucky to get these rooms, so it is quite possible we may not stay here long. Bownes has got a little space in a big hall or library used by students, which provides accommodation for eight VADs and goes by the name of 'Zoo'. Not nearly such a nice situation as this, but still cheery if she likes her neighbours.

We were given time off and told to report at the office at 5 p.m. So we spent the rest of the morning and afternoon getting things unpacked and put straight, making our rooms habitable. Our luggage came on from Boulogne quite soon after us, so arrangements in the

---

* This hotel, like Le Trianon on the cliff at Le Tréport, had been taken over as a military hospital in 1914. It was then the Australian Voluntary Hospital, which had been set up and financed by Lady Dudley, the wife of a former Governor-General of Australia. It was developed with marquees and outbuildings until July 1916 when it became a British hospital, No. 32 Stationary, twenty-three of the Australian nurses staying on, and an English Matron, Miss Jessie Congleton, taking charge. Miss Congleton was Matron throughout D's stay at No. 32. Lady Dudley continued to take a special interest in the hospital.
† Sister Jones at Le Tréport.

end worked very well. At 4.30 we went along to the Mess for tea and afterwards we were despatched to various destinations.

9.15 p.m.

Still clinging together in the midst of strange surroundings. Still feel very like fish out of water, but getting a bit better now. C, F and J are all in surgical wards, acute ones with really bad cases and lots of amputations. Bownes has gone into home, her old job running round Mess, waiting at table etc. But she says it is cushy compared with the same work at 16. The Mess is much smaller and there are only two long tables, instead of eight.

I am up in the medical wards, under canvas. Just a long tent dwelling with anything up to 72 beds that are practically all full just now. Have been mostly in one of the tents, the busiest of the line. Some of the camp's men are hard at work putting up huts to replace tents for the winter months. The work seems much more like active service. Convoys and evacuations occur in very rapid succession, almost every day and night just now. There are very good orderlies in all the wards. They seem to expect to do work and don't shirk it whenever possible. Really seems as though we are still rather extra and we haven't quite got a position yet in the hospital.

It used to be Australian-run till July, when it was taken over by the Military Authorities. So it hasn't been going on present lines very long. Matron seems as though she doesn't quite know the ropes yet. I fancy it is her first hospital in charge but must say so far she has been very nice. The Sisters all seem very nice too and not at all ill disposed towards us. Some of them are Australian and have been here since the hospital was started and are staying on under a new regime. The VADs, I think, will improve on acquaintance.

For the last two days, I have had the afternoon off and the evening on alone, relieving for half-days. Really kept quite busy running round, but nothing very deadly. It is very windy today and the waves are lovely. The sea washes nearly up to the house. Must come uncommonly close in winter storms. The constant noise of surf just outside is rather pleasant really. Certainly couldn't be closer by the sea if we tried every hospital in France.

THURSDAY, 5TH OCTOBER, 6.10 P.M.

Just been having very pleasant little chat and – ahem! smoke – with Judge, one of the VADs here. Discovered her to have been at Bagthorpe and acquainted with Sisters Banham and Simms. She seems to have been as surprised at the antics of the former as we were and apparently didn't love her dearly. Have quite taken to Miss Judge after our little tête-à-tête and must try and see more of her.

I am the only one of our little party off tonight, so am sitting solitary now in our rather damp bedroom. Has one great disadvantage, its being too near in proximity to a certain apartment built in the best French style and pervading atmosphere of this place, with an odour of drainage. Shouldn't be surprised if C and I both got sore throats. Am sure it must be very insanitary. Still very rough and unsettled looking outside, the sea rolling and surging in with its unceasing noise.

This establishment seems partly to be a temporary laundry and keeps a number of French girls and women very busy rubbing and scrubbing. Rather a noisy party, they seem to enjoy themselves thoroughly and carry on with the English Tommies who are at work putting up huts just outside. There is also a little fat, rotund Monsieur who appears to live on the premises and helps with heavy work as well as two or three girls to do the chambermaiding. I am not sure about having so many people about. Think they must pay a good many visits to our room and probably everything is examined most intently.

SATURDAY, 7TH OCTOBER, 2.30 P.M.

Off alone this afternoon, which is dull and the weather is too uproarious to do much walking about. Would like to go down on the shore for a bit and watch the waves, but don't know whether I can face the gale. The wind was violent last night and is again so today. Don't know how our medical tents are going to stand the buffeting. Feeling very flappy and untidy already.

This makes two afternoons running for off duty. Yesterday by good luck, C and Fletcher were both off too. We went for a walk along the front towards Ambleteuse but couldn't get into the village because a river barred our way, so we turned back by road through weird countryside of sand dunes and grey sparse vegetation.

Have heard nothing yet from any of our dear friends at 16. Letters long in reaching us.

TUESDAY, 10TH OCTOBER, 5.45 P.M.

On the whole, have had nice day today. Quite enjoyed myself, rather busier for one thing and this p.m. have been in F Ward helping Levack with afternoon work and incidentally gossiping a good deal. Levack is a very nice girl, not always very judicious I should think, but very sporting. Hardly any one of the VADs already here that I dislike, and though I feel I shall not make lifelong friends with any of them, I still think they will be very pleasant companions.

Apparently the Sunday afternoon tea fight and concert in sitting room here – which I missed – was really quite nice and unstiff. Lots of MOs came and several of the staff contributed songs. C, of course, was one of the star performers and much appreciated. Can see her being very much in request at all the musical dos, just as she was at No. 16 General.

THURSDAY, 12TH OCTOBER, 6 P.M.

Have seen the far, distant cliffs of Blighty this evening. Oh! Beloved place, how I long to be there. Just a dark line on the horizon under a stormy orange sunset but must have been the coast and chalk cliffs rearing up above the grey sea. Made me feel quite sad and lonely and homesick, craving to cross that narrow strip of water.

Just after I got in to tea this evening, a Sergeant from the office brought a message across to say someone wanted me on the telephone. Got rather a spasm of anxiety at first but then remembered Charles at Boulogne.* Sure enough it was his voice and very pleasant

---

* Charles was an old Nottingham friend of the family who had joined the Royal Engineers and had landed up in Boulogne after being invalided from front-line duties.

and friendly to hear. Must try to get off on Saturday afternoon to see him in Wimereux. He seemed very anxious to arrange a meeting.

Seem to be expectations of a very busy time to come, a big attack said to be starting tonight and hope seems to be held that the Germans in our part of line will have to break and fall back, with no one knows what results. But oh dear! The poor wounded and the maimed and the suffering that will come drifting down here. Always hate the thought of these attacks.*

SUNDAY, 15TH OCTOBER, 11.30 A.M.

First morning I have had off since coming here. Sitting in sitting room and writing letters. Ought really to be out as the weather is really bright and lovely for the first time after a long interval of wind and cloud and a tendency to rain. Can see Blighty cliffs again, hazy and dreamlike in the sunshine, but still there quite visible and lovely to look upon.

Had a very pleasant, if short, rencontre with Charles yesterday p.m. Mildred wrote to tell him that I was here and he immediately responded by ringing me up and arranging a meeting. He is RTO at Gare Centrale in Boulogne, and from what he said he doesn't find the work at all congenial and much harder than the trenches. It was interesting at times when he had to go on business errands up the line and he said the desolation at the Somme and Ypres was inconceivable. He is looking rather thin and worn but is still bearing up and we had a very nice time together. Hope I shall have a chance of seeing him again. Perhaps a convenient half day will assist matters.

The sea is looking lovely this morning, so bright and sparkling and white-crested. Minesweepers were very busy just off the coast yesterday, the reason being that a ship said to be transport was sunk the night before. Everyone was saved, so rumour goes. Can see masts sticking up out of water so must have been quite near us when she went down. We certainly see much more at sea than at Tréport, a great deal of trafficking up and down Channel.

---

* The Battle of the Somme was in its closing weeks. See Chronology, p. 351.

WEDNESDAY, 18TH OCTOBER, 9.39 P.M.

Have got additional VAD now, so I am full time in G marquee with Lloyd Jones, one of newest VADs come to join our merry party. She seems a very nice quiet sort of girl and very capable. Two of the new ones are very competent-looking – not to say bossy – rather older and having the appearance of very experienced workers. Still, they all seem very pleasant and not at all overbearing in off-duty time.

Was rather amused when on duty the evening before last. I was just finishing medicines and turning my back on the ward, throwing dirty medicine glass water into a pail, when I heard Sister's voice behind me. I turned round and was amazed to behold her in company with Dr Scott. Great Scottie!* Knew he was in Boulogne because Mums had told me so, but didn't expect to see him turning up so soon. Sister was very nice and encouraged me to have a little talk with my visitor, so we strolled out and round the tents and up and down the road conversing very affably in the dark. He didn't stay very long as I had to get back on duty, but he was very anxious to fix up another meeting so promised I would try to see what could be done and he then departed back to Boulogne.

For the last day or two minesweepers have been very busy and one mine was discovered quite close in shore, opposite quarters here. Exciting if it had blown up! They were busy yesterday securing it and today C says it must have been brought ashore, for she saw it – helpless and harmless – being carted off by French sailors. It must have broken loose with the gales lately.

SUNDAY, 22ND OCTOBER, 8.30 P.M.

Feeling quite pleased with myself tonight. Have had an entirely enjoyable, and in every way successful, whole 'day off' today. Quite a stroke of unexpected good luck getting the holiday, but apparently every member of staff, whether newcomer or not, is having them.

* Another family friend from Nottingham, on the staff of No. 8 Stationary Hospital in Boulogne.

The five latest arrivals have been included too, so it was no matter of favouritism. C and Bownes have theirs tomorrow and Jobbie and Fletcher had theirs yesterday and the day before. Sad that I had none of the four friends to go out with, but foregathered with Lindberg, also whole-daying, and she made a delightful companion.

Had breakfast in bed rather late, a little scrambly dumped down on the table by Louise or Virginie, not sure which, tray swimming with spilt tea. But still enjoyed the stay in bed and not having to scramble away up to Mess for the meal. Got up soon after and about 10.30 went up to the Zoo dorm. Sought out Lindberg and presently off we went together in very holiday mood, both bent on pretty much the same ploys. Went straight into Boulogne and our first directed steps were to St Nicholas Church in market place where a service was going on. Too crowded to get in by the main door but found a way up into the gallery by a side entrance and after a minute or two the service ended and the entire congregation streamed out. We stayed on for a few minutes listening to a splendid voluntary on the organ, one of the finest I had heard for long time. It really was a treat to listen to such music pouring out so splendid and grand.

I was sorry when it was ended but as there was nothing more to stay for, we came away and next wandered down towards the station feeling very frivolous and keeping a sharp lookout for chance meetings with friends. There were so many officers about parading up and down so I cast an eye around for Charles in his RTO capacity. As good luck would have it, there he was, just inside the station talking to an officer and he welcomed us with smiles. We stood talking for a bit and then he took us both up to see an ambulance train just ready to go out and the very latest one running in France, the No. 31. It was beautifully fitted up with all the newest accessories. Had just come down loaded so it was in rather a campaigning state, but we could see it would look very nice when cleaned up.

After this we bid adieu to Charles, as he had to go on with his duties and we wended our way then into town again and sought a place for lunch. After some perambulating, we decided on the principal bun shop and got a very nice little feed there of omelette and buns and coffee. I had a nice walk to the cathedral on top of a hill and then round the ramparts and was very pleased with the old houses, all clustered round the cathedral and ramparts. Came back to market place to encounter Lindberg again at a bookshop, having practically followed me round on my peregrinations. We only met for a few minutes then I drifted down towards the quay, taking a walk round to fill the time and arriving at the bridge a few minutes after 4, Dr Scott was there waiting for me. Felt more frivolous than ever marching away with him in face of all the military conventions.* Seemed anxious not to incur disfavour by this meeting but we decided to put bold face on the matter and marched into the principal bun shop, which was very crowded and lively, and then we weren't so noticeable in a crowd. Saw Urquart there for second time sitting with an officer friend. Another time I saw her she was going into a hotel for lunch with two officer friends! She is evidently a hardened sinner and a bold-faced Miss.

Scottie and I had much to talk about and discuss and we sat for a long time over our tea, then finally emerged and, after taking a walk up the hill towards the cathedral again, we turned back deciding to stretch our legs over the road to Wimereux and No. 32, which we accordingly did, my cavalier and escort seeing me all the way safely home along a very dark road – except when a motor threw a detecting eye upon us and brought us into full glare of its flaming lamps.

Enjoyed the walk and pleasant converse very much and it made a nice ending to a nice holiday. Now I must settle into work again but don't quite know what is going to happen as the tents are not taking any more patients and lots of changes of staff are taking place. Weather was so glorious yesterday and the day before, and Blighty showed up wonderfully clearly across the water. Could even see something that looked like Dover Castle on top of a hill and the white chalk cliffs gleamed like a cloud where they stood up highest.

Landed another mine from the sea yesterday p.m. Saw a party of

---

* Social relations between nurses and the military were subject to the strictest rules and regulations, but there was just too much going on in Boulogne for these to be actively enforced.

marines down on the shore dealing with it. We seem to be in very dangerous spot here. Minesweepers pay great attention to this section of coast.

MONDAY, 23RD OCTOBER, 7.15 P.M.

Searchlights are very busy over the English coast tonight and certainly it's a very likely night for a Zepp raid – fine, hazy, no moon and no wind. Much warmer too. Quite expect the baby murderers will be out tonight. I was quite thrilled this p.m. by first experience of anti-aircraft guns in action. I was on duty in the tents when a great firing began sounding fairly near. Patients and staff ran out to see the cause. I ran too and right out over the sea could see little puffs of smoke from bursting shrapnel. Several of onlookers said they could see the aircraft. Some said it was an airship and some a Taube. Think it's more probable it was latter. Tried to imagine I saw it too but am not quite sure. Anyway, I saw the puffs of smoke and that was highly exciting. Didn't last more than few minutes and evidently the raider was then out of range and all was peace once more. Seems probability of seeing more excitements like these, especially as this is season for them.

THURSDAY, 26TH OCTOBER, 9.10 P.M.

Had half-day yesterday and was just getting ready to go to Boulogne and meet C there when Bownes came dashing in to say Matron (Miss Drage) had come to see us and was then having a rather belated lunch in the Mess. I was, of course, very thrilled at the thought of seeing her again. Hurried off and found her being entertained by Matron, lunching along with her chauffeur, a gentleman Red Cross man who was also fortifying himself. Matron looked just the same as ever, seemed very pleased indeed to see us and was full of smiles and gossip. Didn't stay long as she had to be off back to 23 again. She had come over to bring one of her VADs with scarlet fever and dysentery to the isolation hospital and induced the driver to take her on a bit further to 32. C was very regretful at having missed seeing her.

SUNDAY, 29TH OCTOBER, 9.45 P.M.

Been here nearly a month now, but seems much, much longer. We have had more wild stormy weather after a lovely lull at the beginning of the week. This part of the coast is said to be the windiest in the whole of France and I can well believe it. We are just at a bend which seems to be the draughtiest spot and a few miles inland the wind has carried the sand, piling it into dunes. Looking down from a height, one can quite distinctly see the hollow stretching up from the shore, filled in with these dunes and covering quite a wide area. The marquees are not at all attractive in the wind. I was on this evening in G and only two electric lights were working. The rest of the ward was dimly lit by hurricane lamps and we had to grope about among beds finding the right patients for medicine and treatment etc.

Last night there was great dissipation in the shape of a grand 'do' at the Officers' Mess, a celebration of the hospital's anniversary, and to do this properly we were all invited en masse up to the Golf House where the MOs are quartered. We were entertained with bridge, roulette and music, and refreshments came in the shape of wine and coffee and cakes etc. We were received cordially by the Colonel and staff and the party soon broke up, some to play bridge in one of fine large rooms, while others went off to play roulette and gamble with nothing more serious than counters. Another little party kept round piano and discussed music at intervals. C sang and Sister Wellstead played. When the music failed, Wyatt, Sister Wellstead, C and I and two padres played absurd games such as animal grab, much to the disturbance of the sedate-looking bridge players. At about 11.30 Matron made a move to go and after one or two more songs and then God Save the King, we all got on our wraps again and set forth over the links on our journey home, having had quite a lively evening.

There was a tea party again today and a lot of MOs turned up to that. We were only there the first part of the time but our little sitting room seemed quite full of company and more came later for singing. It is raining again now in torrents and blowing too. The sea is very rough in this weather but every day little minesweepers are out backwards and forwards up and down the Channel and today destroyers were very active indeed. A mail boat – the *Queen* – sank a day or two ago on her way back to Boulogne and there is a story also of some sort of scrap between German and our destroyers and two of them sunk, but I don't know whether this is true. Anyway *Queen* went down during the night, but with only loss of one life. Made our watchdogs very active and alert indeed.

TUESDAY, 31ST OCTOBER, 6.30 P.M.

A fearful night of wind made our marquee almost uninhabitable and this morning an order came through to the Colonel that all patients were to be moved into huts and the long-contemplated, long-discussed move took place this afternoon amidst awful confusion.

We packed up things all afternoon in our tent – and the same was done next door – and after tea all the walking patients marched down to the still unfinished hut and beds were made ready for them. All pretty well packed up together – 85 beds where there ought to be 70 – and Matron was directing things in the hut personally, the Colonel there also, superintending. I went back after tea to help with making up rest of beds and when patients came in I was dismissed by Matron, along with several other volunteer workers. Don't know how things will settle down. Seemed to be far too many patients coming for the number of beds. Stretcher cases were all going to the hospital and were being carried down the road to their new quarters. F, G and H patients all seemed to be muddled up together so I don't know how things will get on at all.

Yesterday evening, in off duty, went into Wimereux with Cook and Cran and had quite a sportive expedition with two pleasant companions. Cran and I are quite chummy at present, she seems such a nice gentle person with dolly face and large brown eyes, but quite attractive and has plenty of vim. Cook is a very nice girl too. She and Cran and Levack are my favourites so far. C doesn't seem to have picked up with anyone yet. She still pines for her friends at No. 16. I miss my dear Rind very much.

SATURDAY, 4TH NOVEMBER

Just ready for bed and sitting up enjoying a hot water bottle prepared by Madeleine and hearing sound of pouring, drenching rain outside. Dreadfully bad weather and state of the battlefields must be inconceivable, just a sea of mud. I have a bad cold in the head, so nearly wrote 'bud'. Snuffly all day and woolly-brained. Yesterday, I felt quite done up and thought it must be flu. However, already recovering today, so I expect it is only a cold, which I haven't had severely for some time.

Still installed in huts but now one end is shut up and it is only ours that has patients in it. Most of the men are clearing out too. Meanwhile, staff all kept on and tumbling over each other absolutely. Some have been helping with packing up in empty tents and some are in the empty ward. The rest find what they can to do in J, our inhabited end. It really was ludicrous one morning – I counted thirteen or so orderlies all in the ward at the same time, as well as Sisters and VADs besides – about fifteen of staff all at one go for not so very many more patients. Don't know what will happen for, as things are at present, other wards won't be opened and apparently staff will be kept on as before. Have two good stoves going and another one was put into the bunk yesterday, which heats the place up like a furnace. Makes one positively gasp for air after cold draughts of tents.

TUESDAY, 6TH NOVEMBER, 9.45 P.M.

Another day ended and another night's sleep in prospect. More wind and now rain. Thunderstorms too and hail at intervals. Just 'peastly' weather, but very lovely effect this evening when the moon was shining in a clear piece of sky and the lightning was flashing from a pitch-black cloud over the sea. The contrast of moonlight and dark cloud was very lovely.

Great thrill yesterday. Johnnie and Malet arrived in Boulogne to go on leave and being too late for boat had to stay an extra day, so were able to come out to see us. I was on duty in the afternoon but Jobbie, Fletcher, Bownes and C all set off in violent gales and rain to meet the dear ones and greet them. Apparently, they sighted them from afar on mutual recognition and immediately started running toward each other in a frenzy of joy. Whole happy party then came back to the hospital and I saw them at teatime. Heard they had come down to Mess at 4.30 and, having greeted them, I went back on duty till nearly 5 when I could come off with an easy conscience and see some more of the dear friends. They didn't stay very long though.

I went to Boulogne this afternoon and saw a ship that was wrecked last night in the gale. A large sailing barge, it was lying on the shore, landed high and dry, and crowds of people were looking at the wreck with great interest. I believe there were three ships wrecked quite close together, two at this place. The other one's crew was all lost at Audresselles. Must have been fearful at sea. Certainly the wind was worse than it has been ever before. Met Mr Clayton who used to be padre at 16, while shopping in Boulogne. He was waiting for the leave boat too, having come down from the line to get a holiday.

WEDNESDAY, 22ND NOVEMBER

The first three weeks of November had been relatively uneventful. Towards the end of the month the VADs' thoughts were turning towards Christmas and leave.

VADs are all off this evening to go to the first of a course of lectures, on a syllabus drawn up by Military Authority and subject to the supervision of Matron. Sister Reay gave a lecture in the small theatre in the hut next to D. We all assembled at 6.45 or thereabouts – the night birds, looking rather sleepy and sodden, had to get up to attend, poor things. All of us a bit jaded but we quite enjoyed the lecture all the same. Was a good deal on the subject of bed-making which, of course, we all knew something about, having been at it for months and months. Rest of the lecture dealt with medicines and some points on the care of patients. Lasted till 7.30 so that those who had been off this evening were able to go to first supper. The others went back on duty till 8 and had half an hour's scrummaging.

Yesterday I was not off duty at all, so had a very busy time. A convoy came in during the morning and whole of the other end of the ward filled up with stretcher cases. Everyone was occupied in there, blanket-bathing and settling up newcomers, so I had K1 pretty much to myself with Jefferson's occasional help, and got on well with work, which was quite straightforward.

SATURDAY, 25TH NOVEMBER, 7.30 P.M.

Just a month to Xmas. Nearly another year of VAD-ing abroad has swept by. Have been realizing tonight the inevitableness of things and the sad fate that keeps us out here when I should like, and feel I ought, to be home. Have wept a few weeps on the situation and felt very lonely and far away from dear ones, and the prospect of another long six months is not at all prepossessing. Have been very undecided what to do about signing, but a letter from Mums helped me to a final decision and I shall peg on a bit longer and hope another year will bring a more hopeful outlook and be more encouraging as far as success of the war goes. After encouragement of autumn successes, comes news now of Germans advancing steadily into Rumania gaining immense assistance from such a rich country and nothing seems to stem the tide of their advance.* Everyone seems to think this will prolong the war very much and there seems no reason why it might not last for years and years. Not an encouraging outlook certainly. Anyway have made the decision to stick on another six months and C is staying on too, so we shall peg away together in the same old style and face the rigours of campaigning life.

C and Cook have been practising all evening for the great Pierrot performance to be given by the VADs at Xmas. Judge, Mitchell and Wyatt are leading lights in the organization and were conducting a rigorous practice yesterday evening in the sitting room. It is quite an elaborate affair but they have some quite good ideas – if only we can carry them out neatly and in a smart theatrical style. The idea of us all being inside our kitbags, lying in a row, as curtain goes up is quite a good one. We shall be bacilli, labelled with various diseases. The opening chorus will be compered by the leading lights who

* See Chronology, p. 352.

shall explain them quite cleverly. Don't yet know what sort of audience we shall have, but hope we shan't create a scandal by our antics. There are only twelve in the troupe, so I am one of chosen few. I have got to produce some sort of item, but don't know yet what it will be. Am not much in the line of theatricals, but must do my best for credit of troupe.

Have had the second of the lectures for the instruction of VADs, delivered by Sister Reay according to strict orders to Matron from Military Headquarters. They evidently think we are still so ignorant and require coaching up in the art of nursing.

SUNDAY, 26TH NOVEMBER

Have quite a busy evening to look forward to being the only one on duty, with Sister Buckham to superintend. She doesn't seem at all well just now, poor dear. Think it must be worry and over-tiredness that is upsetting her. She is very impatient and irritable at times, which puts the wind up among the staff. Tomorrow she has to open a new hut, the third of the row, and I am going to try – if possible – to get a shift into that when it has patients. Feel I should like it better for many things. I don't at all want another addition, but it would relieve Sister Starbuck a good deal as she seems to feel the strain of responsibility considerably. Have no one very bad in the ward but one boy is pretty seedy today and paratyphoid suspected.

WEDNESDAY, 29TH NOVEMBER, 9.45 P.M.

9.45 pm by correct time, but my watch says 5 past and Mess time is about 20 past, so time just now is a rather uncertain quantity.

Have been to another lecture tonight, the fourth of series, and it was quite interesting though not quite so much as the last one. All the VADs are assiduously attending now. I hear there are to be twenty-two lectures altogether, so our brains will burst at the end of it all with an exam to finish too. Feel so much like going to school and can't believe I am the age I am.

Still pretty busy in our ward for Judge and I. Hadow came yesterday having arrived back from sick leave. She was put in temporarily but removed this morning to go and make up beds in the next hut, which is opening at the other end to receive patients. Sister Buckham very bucked at prospect of opening other ward with Major Patterson as the MO as it is to be used for nothing but PUOs to be watched and specialized in. A rather interesting ward and I am trying to induce her to let me accompany her as one of her staff, but haven't heard of any result yet.

Was on alone this p.m. with seventy patients. One new one was admitted while I was there which made the whole ward full up. No very bad ones. The new MO is not much good at marking men out either to Blighty or convalescent camp. Will have to get rid of them somehow though as our beds will be wanted soon.

SUNDAY, 3RD DECEMBER, 3.15 P.M.

A great event occurred last Thursday: three VADs and a Sister received their moving orders and departed at quite short notice to No. 18 General at Étaples. Worst of it was that two of them were members of the troupe, Wyatt being especially useful for organiza-tion etc. The preparations proceed slowly, however, even after the sending away of one of the leading lights. Have had some practices at the choruses and the next question concerns getting the costumes made, which does seem rather a problem.

Ward still full up, though there are now two empty beds as two patients went to convalescent camp this afternoon. Judge is having half day and Hadow, who is back again to help us, is off this morn-ing. Feel rather a pig these days for I appear to be very much the favoured one and at all times put up as the senior pro. Judge and Hadow having been longer in hospital must feel rather ousted sometimes, but I'm hoping that I don't appear too bossy. Certainly don't intend or wish to be.

THURSDAY, 7TH DECEMBER, 6.15 P.M.

News is dreadfully depressing just now. We are going through a black time again after the encouragements of the summer months. Things appear worse now than they ever did. The Government is

changing – Mr Asquith is out of office and a new Cabinet is forming.* Germans are installed in Bucharest and Greece is in a state
of ferment. Nothing doing on this side much at all. All eyes are
directed to the East again. Bad news and several other things have
made me feel very unsettled again after having made up my mind to
sign on in January. Now am inclining the other way but don't know
how to make a final decision and feel all the while the day is drawing
near when we will be asked definitely to make up our minds one way
or t'other. My threats are unsettling C too and she is in an agitated
frame of mind. It is very difficult indeed to know what to do in these
extraordinary times.

Still very busy with the grand Christmas entertainment, practising away at choruses. Hope all arrangements will go well as there
still seems a lot to do in only a shortish time.

SATURDAY, 9TH DECEMBER, 7.10 P.M.

Just in from a walk into Wimereux on this damp, unsettled evening.
I went partly to take a note to No. 8 Stationary in answer to one Dr
Scott wrote me, but we met in person instead and I asked him all
about his leave which seemed to have been not very exhilarating. In
fact he has come back in very pessimistic mood with nothing cheering to impart.

Still feel in state of uncertainty and indecision about signing on,
but got an opportunity to speak to Matron this afternoon and she
had, of course, many good reasons to put before me as to why I
shouldn't resign. She told me that I was useful and that we shouldn't
think at all of our personal inclinations at a time like this. Everyone
has to give up something, we must be prepared for sacrifice and it
was best to keep on with the work we could do most usefully. Every
one of these sentiments I quite agreed with, but am withholding
my decision for further consideration. She also said that C and I
would get leave as soon as she could get it through after Christmas.

* The Secretary of State for War, David Lloyd George, formally replaced H.H. Asquith as
  Prime Minister on 7 December, and formed a coalition with the Conservatives.

We were due for it then and from that point of view everything would be all right. But I think it very difficult to know what is right thing to do.

Had a very active rehearsal for our performance last night and really feel we are getting to know the choruses pretty well – quite a lot of go about them.

TUESDAY, 12TH DECEMBER, 7.15 P.M.

Have taken the plunge again! Another six months looms before me. Not actually signed papers yet but Matron has asked us all as the War Office people want to know the particulars. All our party is signing on but a good many of the originals are leaving when their time is up in January. Some of them have to go home, while others do not wish to stay on here. Suppose we shall have a whole lot of new VADs thrust upon us to take the place of departing ones and things will change very much with the New Year.

I made up my mind a day or two ago and C is very relieved thereat. She has thankfully settled down to another half year abroad. Leave is a treat in store and not so far off after all. Xmas intervening will make time seem shorter. We shall all be so busy till that is over with no time to think much about anything. Feel very kindly disposed to Matron since my talk in her office. She was so human and understanding then. Think she was pleased I was signing on, no doubt would lessen, to a small degree, her worry with all the changes impending.

Ronald is still away at Mauritien* with her bad abscess and won't be back for Xmas. Jax is the latest member of staff to be on sick leave and ill at home, so I don't suppose she will be back for a little while and we will have to get someone else to take her place in the troupe. Rehearsal tonight and the show is really getting on a bit. Had our kit bags yesterday evening and we practised getting in and out of them in time to the music as well as all our other manouvrings.

* The local hospital and convalescent home for Sick Sisters.

SATURDAY, 16TH DECEMBER (AFTER SUPPER)

These are strenuous times. Now Xmas is getting so near we are kept very hard at work rehearsing for our entertainment. By special permission and arrangement, all the troupe were off duty this evening so we had a real set to in the sitting room. Steele nobly got up to attend, so we had a complete party there. Murray, who is very shy and unassertive, had been called to take Jax's place and now we have Rheeder back to be the stage manager and look after our properties etc. It's a great thing to have someone capable of managing all the tiresome part of the business.

News of a big French advance* cheered us all up again after our dreadful depression a few days ago, but things seem still pretty black. Hope when Xmas is over and New Year comes, this will bring a more hopeful aspect to the face of affairs.

FRIDAY, 22ND DECEMBER, 10.45 P.M.

Too late to write much and besides so sleepy and tired, only too anxious to get off to byby – but don't know when I should get another opportunity of adding a word. So busy just now what with decorations in the ward and rehearsals in off-duty time. Had our first and only dress rehearsal tonight in the empty hut where the acting and entertainments shall be held. The stage is rigged up and has quite a hopeful appearance. Feel we shall keep up our reputation somehow, only hope show will go down well with the Tommies. It is to be held on Xmas Day from 5.30 to 8 or so, consisting of two short plays and the rest our Pierrot troupe. Rest of day is to be spent merrymaking in the ward, all normal work going to the winds to celebrate occasion.

Have heard no more about leave but am hoping so much it won't be long in coming. Would be such a nice following up of Xmas.

---

* This almost certainly refers to the relief and end of the siege of Verdun. See Chronology, p. 352.

SUNDAY, 24TH DECEMBER, XMAS EVE

One can hardly realize it at all. Weather changed again after the awful gale of yesterday. Today has been lovely and I do hope tomorrow will be so too. We are singing carols this evening after supper, a whole troop of Sisters and VADs will be wandering about the hospital through wards and buildings, warbling melodiously (perhaps!). So many have coughs and colds so don't think there will be any great volume of sound. Now Hadow has been reported sick with a very bad and painful finger again. Poor dear, she looked wretched today and is really suffering. It is bad luck. Lindberg and Bownes are also on the sick list. Former is really very poorly and that knocks one of the plays on the head if she isn't better. Really don't know how our performance tomorrow is going to carry on. And the sad thing is the MO considered it necessary, under orders, to send off twenty of our best up-patients and one or two bed ones not fit to go out. Really too pathetic. Could almost have wept. One man, called Skinner, has neuritis and is hardly able to walk, crawling away with a stick, and another one, hasn't been out of bed at all. We all feel very outraged. Think the MO could have managed better than that. He seems a hopeless person. Anyway, the ward is pretty cheery still and we hope to have merry Xmas in spite of these blows.

There is a great push on apparently and beds are wanted. Shall probably have a convoy in tonight which means tomorrow will be tremendously busy, in surgical wards anyway. I can't imagine how we shall manage everything. Must go now to supper and then to sing carols round the hospital.

THURSDAY, 28TH DECEMBER, 9.45 P.M.

Xmas – and all attendant festivities – over. Don't know where to begin with account of all the doings.

Xmas Eve – with all its preparations and arrangings for the next day and its rather clouded pleasure by the departure of all the convalescents except the rather tottery ones. The poor men could have stayed quite well as far as any rush was concerned and joined in all the festivities, as we hoped they were going to do. After supper we carolled as arranged, Friend leading on violin, Ellis in forefront with her fine voice and the rest of us tailing out behind.

We started our tour through J and K huts and made a bold beginning, but the violinist made a very brisk pace and we stepped along through the wards, in at one door and out at t'other, singing rather breathlessly, before the patients had hardly realized our presence. Not till we had whirled through E hut and done a good part of the tour, did word come that we were to go slower. Had repertoire of six. Some of the party having no music, no light, no voice and a good many lacking one or other. However, all are willing and so the procession wound up and down the stairs in the building, along corridors and into wards, and several male singers tacked themselves on at the end and added quite a lot to the volume of sound. Sometimes there was a good deal of diversity of opinion as to the speed of a carol on the ends of the procession but on the whole I think the general effect was quite good and seemed to gratify the patients. Colonel hovered around all the time and most of the MOs lent their silent support, and after the singing ended, all the waits hastened into Mess to imbibe hot wine and refreshments. The visitors drifted in too. Quite a nice time, though I missed the nice well-practised choral singing we had last year at Tréport with Chant as conductor.

Monsieur tapped on our bedroom door the next morning at 5.45 to call us by request for the early service and C and I unwillingly scrambled out of bed, dressed and went up to the hospital to attend Holy Communion. We climbed up to the little cramped chapel in one of the small rooms at the very top of the house. Quite a lot of people came to the service conducted by C of E padre and it was a very nice way to begin the day. On duty in the same old way and cheery greetings to all the men from the door. Really are all dear things, not one discordant spirit in our ward and all the remaining up-patients are such good workers. At 8 o'clock the Sisters arrived and we gave up any attempt to do ward work. We only took a very few temps and gave out no medicines or lunches. Just applied ourselves to setting out the ward tidily and getting things ready for dinner. Men were all wearing their smart paper hats crowned with little string of orchids hanging down, and they were all adorned with a paper flower rosette and badge of the ward to wear pinned to their coat. We spent part of time going next door to see what sort of merrymaking they were having there. Turned out they had a little party of convalescents all dressed up, parading about carrying on some sort of pantomime at the bedside. One of them represented a parson and part of his costume consisted of my old uniform hat. Don't know how he had got it as I had lent it to someone in the sergeants' plays as a theatrical property.

FRIDAY, 29TH DECEMBER, 3.10 P.M.

The wind has returned to wreak vengeance on us and is blowing hard today. Great waves tossing and splashing up over the sea walls. Just high tide now, so they are at their most turbulent. Had a sore throat at Xmas time, which was a nuisance and has pulled me down a bit but think I shall pick up all right, till I go on leave. Have that lovely treat in prospect as C and I both signed for the great event yesterday morning. Might be off any time now. We can't go by Boulogne I'm sad to say, because of a ship going down just at the mouth of the harbour, blocking the entrance absolutely. Can't be used at all as a harbour till the salvage corps comes from Liverpool to put matters right.

Had very pleasant half-day on Wednesday, very glad of it after the rush and bustle of the last few days. Our show on Xmas Day went off very successfully judging from the very complimentary remarks we had showered on us, and the congratulations of friends. Felt very nervous about it at first and had cold, sinking feelings before it began. There was a short play to begin the performance – Jobbie, Hall, Blake and Lindberg were all taking part. Believe it was quite good, but of course I was too busy getting ready at the back and making up to hear or see anything. Jobbie and Hall were both feeling pretty poorly, so were not at the best of their powers. Then we got through the first half of the programme. We managed pretty well and without any breakdown and some of the songs sounded very well indeed. Finished the first half by '10 Little VADs' poem – given to us by Sister Barrow, made up by someone at Mauritien – they disappeared one by one till only Franklin Smith was left to sing the last verse and then she disappeared too, amid much applause. We made a bad start at the next act but pulled ourselves together all right once we got going. 'Mechanical' Jane came on next acted by Fletcher, who was most excellent and Bayley and Bownes were both splendid as 'Jane'. I was able to see this sitting down in the front with all the other bacilli, waiting till our next turn came. The concert lasted till 8 and we had to cut out the Plantation songs at the end. Got through the last chorus successfully and with great aplomb, getting into our kit bags more or less in time but cheerfully anyway, to the tune of 'Pack up your Troubles in your old Kitbag'. My item came nearly at the end of the first half and I managed to render it with some dramatic effect, all the lights being out except for a candle. I was holding a flash lamp and others were waving at the back. Hut was absolutely crowded and I think everyone must have been there. Matron and Colonel and all the bigwigs were in the front. Very glad indeed that it was so well received as I really had great qualms and we had had so little rehearsing.

The show was followed by very hilarious Xmas dinner in the Mess. Everyone, especially the VADs, was in great spirits. Matron proposed toasts and we drank to the health of King and Country and then several other healths, absent friends etc. always in our thoughts. Delightful evening altogether – an end to a delightful day of competitions in the wards after dinner and in the afternoon. Great sport. The patients came in from all the other divisions to compete and we had quite a lively time with prize-givings and a very interested audience.

WEDNESDAY, 3RD JANUARY 1917

Entered the New Year and left the old year with all its varied associations behind, fading into a multitude of memories. I am facing this New Year with the prospect of another six months' VAD-ing here or elsewhere and then who knows if it might not be nearly over. Anyway, the war is showing some definite signs of conclusion. I signed on a day or two ago, really burning my boats. Bownes, who is away sick and now suffering from jaundice, poor dear, has refused to sign, occasioning some disturbance among the authorities.

Miss McCarthy paid us a formal visit yesterday, parading through the wards attended by Matron and Colonel. She said a word or two to me – gave me a searching look and a smile – and passed on. Wonder if she knows of our gay doings lately. Two parties up at Officers' Mess, one on Boxing Day and the other on New Year's Night. Both fancy dress do's. The chief frivolity, dancing, was a forbidden indulgence, but it was judiciously interspersed with games. At the first party all the Sisters were dressed up, quite elaborately. We went in our pierrette costumes, which saved a lot of trouble and looked quite nice. Some of the other costumes were very entertaining. Jobbie looked the nicest in her very prettily made shepherdess costume and got first prize, but the others were very pretty too and clever. We all turned up at different times. The party was in full swing when I arrived along with some other belated guests. One of the MOs was dressed up as a Sister, a very fat and rotund gentleman who could only just get the very fattest Sister's clothes to meet – and she is certainly not slim! Major Paterson created a furor by arriving in middle of some uproariousness as Miss McCarthy, in cloak and bonnet, looking a sight for the Gods, so solemn too and portentous about it all. Matron kept away and Sister Barrow chaperoned us all and the dancing went on merrily in spite of all authorities. Colonel evidently enjoys this sort of frivol, and quite in his element entertaining his guests.*

I wasn't feeling very well myself, had a sore throat and was very tired, so I didn't really enjoy the party quite so much as last year's one. Rather disapproved too of dancing in wartime and so I danced mostly at first with C rather protestingly, but I'm afraid my principles

---

* Miss McCarthy did not know *all* that had been going on. She wrote in her notebook: 'after lunch, went to 32 Stationary Hospital – went round the hospital and saw all the new improvements ... everywhere in Boulogne they seem to have had a most excellent Christmas with entertainments for the patients got up by the Sisters and the officers, and in each unit the officers had asked some of the Nursing Sisters to dine with them on Christmas night or New Year's night.'

went more to the wind at the second party and I had two or three dances with MOs – quite enjoyed a little mild flirtation. Was exactly same sort of thing, games etc. It was all arranged that we should just wear sheets as dominoes and go masked for a change, but I don't think the men liked it much. They were too puzzled at our indistinguishable appearance. They had dressed up much more elaborately and some were very smart. One MO was dressed as Bacchus or something of the sort – very marvellous and his costume was really very pretty. Another looked very good as a baby in long clothes and Maj. Paterson was very good again as a flapper, so tall and thin and angular in a bonnet and very short skirt that showed his lovely black legs and big feet. We all screamed with laughter when we saw him. I had a nice dance with a Colonel Fullerton, one of big wigs of the district, though I didn't know that when I was dancing with him. He seemed to quite enjoy himself too, though his dancing was not quite up to par. He has a wife and family in Ireland, so very safe from flirtation point of view. He seemed very nice and pleasant to talk to.

Our next excitement is leave. Looking forward so much to Sunday. Plaskett, C and I are really going home for a blissful fourteen days. The hospital is very slack still as the port remains closed. All our patients were moved into ward 1 today. Sister Starbuck has departed permanently to new huts and Sister Southworth is now in charge. She is very sweet indeed, but not the same person as S. Starbuck.

Our show comes again on Saturday and we are all trembling in our shoes. I believe there are to be lots of guests and that there is a vague possibility of Sir Douglas Haig being present, but probably this is all a myth.

Saw Dr Scott again too yesterday. He seemed to have survived all the Xmas festivities. They had dancing and frivol at No. 8 Station too, so this breaking of the rules was not confined to No. 32. Sergeants and orderlies gave their show on 1st January, at 5.30. I saw half of it and thought it quite good, but a bit heavy. Everyone implied that ours was far and away the best and put them in the shade altogether.

7TH–21ST JANUARY, ON LEAVE

*Dorothea wrote only a few entries while on leave. The ambulance
taking her and Christie to Calais broke down, and they were picked
up by another going the same way, where they found their old
Matron, Miss Drage, sitting in the front seat, also going on leave.
Rapturous greetings ensued ('clung to one another').*

*Dorothea returned from leave on 21 January to find the
hospital mainly occupied with medical cases, many suffering from
nephritis. 1917 was the most deeply depressing year of the war. The
French and British armies both experienced disasters, the French
in April in the Nivelle Offensive, named after the General in
command, and the British at Passchendaele.*

*For most of the year the weather was atrocious, a bitterly cold
winter followed by the second wettest summer of the twentieth
century. On 5 February, Dorothea took a walk on the shore and
was fascinated to see the icicles on the cliff 'cascading out of the
rocks and hanging like great curtains all different pale shades and
reaching down to the shore, spreading out in a great sheet of ice'.*

*After six very cold and relatively uneventful weeks Dorothea was
expecting to be put on night duty again.*

FRIDAY, 16TH MARCH

Days go by very quickly – here we are nearly at the end of another
week and well on in March. Am wondering and wondering whether
night duty will be my sad fate before long. I really wouldn't so much
mind now that Jefferson is a night orderly as he is a real rock of
support. Only distress of parting with C and general uprooting.

Had rather a frivol yesterday in the evening when I was off. Went
to Ambleteuse with Dr Scott and had a very substantial dinner there
at the Grand Hotel, returning by starlight to the hospital. I cut supper
for the first time since I came here, and no one noticed my absence.
I really quite enjoyed the jaunt. Dr Scott was entirely brotherly and
no hint of sentimentalism, which is not like the experiences I seem

to have had lately. Have received two letters addressing me by my Christian name, one being from Hardie that arrived tonight and very friendly and 'pally'. I was quite taken aback with this empressment.

SATURDAY, 17TH MARCH

St Patrick's Day. So, I was decorated with a little bit of shamrock, presented to me by Sister Robson, and I wore it all day though am not quite sure that my championing of the Emerald Isle was very sincere. I don't feel very drawn to our neighbours really. Both our orderlies, Keble and Kegan, very much appreciated a bit of their native emblem but I had no Irish patients in the ward so 'no bon' to them. One of new patients who came in last night recognized me as I passed up the ward this morning and told Mrs Lefroy and I went to see him but couldn't remember having had him under my care before. He had been at No. 16 in 15 ward last September, one of black huts, and was one of many patients who passed through our hands just then.

Great do this evening in the Dining Hall. A Grand Concert, arranged by Lady Dudley, to celebrate St Patrick's Day. Crowds of members of staff from other hospitals visited and the hall was terribly crowded. Entertainment was provided by some officers out of various crack cavalry regiments who were really good performers. The jokes were bordering at times, as was the rather broad humour, but it was still an excellent show and two of officers had delightful singing voices. Lord St Germans was one of the performers and gave a sort of dress performance of an old woman discanting with another crony on the war and it was a fine effort and produced much laughter. The arranger of the entertainment was Lady Dudley's brother and he recited very well indeed – quite thrillingly – so that one felt quite carried away with the excitement of the story. The whole show didn't last too long, which was a comfort. It was over at 7.45 and all the guests departed in crowds of motor ambulances and returned to their various hospitals after the little outing.

SUNDAY, 18TH MARCH

My fate is sealed. Heard today that I am going on night duty tomorrow. Bownes also, but not dear C and so we are separated indefinitely now after our 22 months of peace and happiness, living together. Very sad indeed and although I almost thought it would happen, I had hoped for the best that it wouldn't. I will have nice boys to look after though and there is Jefferson, a great prop and stay, to aid and support me. Sister Starbuck and Sister Robson were really quite put about when I told them this afternoon. Sister Robson has been so nice and I was just getting to like her very much indeed. I think that the liking is mutual and it would have been so pleasant working together, but alas and alack such is life and the happy time was too good to last.

Going on night duty

A new Staff Sister turned up in our ward this morning. She is a very pretty and attractive damsel, but rather too much so, on first acquaintance anyway, and it looks as though she intended to make a clean sweep of the men's hearts with her fascinations.

WEDNESDAY, 21ST MARCH, 1 A.M.

Night duty again and back amid the darkness, the whisperings and prowlings, the anxious alertness, listening for any sound of life from the prostrate forms wrapped in slumber. The wards are very quiet tonight. Nothin' doin' at all, but a convoy is expected in any time so it will probably be busy before night is out. Such a black, wild night of wind and rain and last night's gale was furious. Murray and Rheeder boldly ventured into one of the bell tents pitched at the back of the new hut to accommodate surplus staff. And these two bold spirits took up their abode in the tent yesterday, the same day this violent gale sprang, and had some lively doing. Every tent except theirs was blown down, though theirs very nearly went. Don't know how they will be getting on tonight in this tempest and wet.

Heard gunfire a short time ago and think there must have been some sort of scuffle at sea, though I wonder what ships would venture out to fight in such a storm. Bownes and I are established in our nice room but I long for my twin to be sleeping beside me. I feel quite homesick and lonely and think she feels the same.

Have such a lovely view from our two windows in the Zoo looking right along to Ambleteuse and Blightywards and the sea this morning was just wonderful, white breakers rolling in one after another. I didn't go anywhere, as the wind was too rough. Managed to go up to the canteen with Bownes, Blake and Bayley and then by degrees to bed. I slept pretty well and enjoyed my nice comfy bed. We lead a very exclusive existence in these wards, with Jefferson as our orderly. Sister McClaren pays occasional visits and Sister Harrison makes her regular rounds. We sometimes see Fletcher, generally concerning supper, but otherwise I just have to put up with my own company. I now have a very lonely supper, which I prepare on the stove here and, naturally, is not a very prolonged elaborate meal.

I was so dreadfully sorry to come off day duty as I was quite getting to love the ward and the Sisters and was enjoying work so much. This is not the same thing at all. All my dear friends in F ward snore and snoozle the whole night long and are not a bit of good to laugh and chaff with. We have Hazel back as a patient. He is not very grand, poor little man, and rather depressed at having broken down in the Mess. We got four new patients in last night, or rather, this morning, at about 5 a.m. Was just getting on full tilt with the morning work when the convoy arrived and upset the apple cart. Had a dreadful scrimmage after that to get work done in time and didn't feel it was quite as satisfactorily accomplished as it might have been.

SUNDAY, 25TH MARCH, 9.15 P.M.

Such a cushy night so far. Hardly any patients and those that we have are all sleeping peacefully. Just been gossiping in stage whispers with Lewis, our invaluable kitchen controller, a nice boy with many fondly admiring young lady friends. He has been here now for nearly seven weeks, so he seems quite part of the staff and considers himself as such. There was a large evacuation from G ward this morning. All the nicest people went away, including old Blandford, Cpl Godden and several more. Seems quite funny without them and the ward is so empty. A convoy is expected in tonight any time after 10, so we may get a few more in to keep us going.

Had the excitement last night of putting our clocks and watches on one hour from 12 to 1 for the Daylight Savings Bill. So pleased to skip an hour's watching in the darkness, but the men were all much aggrieved at losing an hour's sleep when they were woken up and found it only 5.30 by their pieces. Caused great confusion in the Mess too. Monsieur had been told to call everyone earlier but never explained why, and lots of staff that hadn't been warned the night before never took the bell seriously and stayed in bed another hour, so consequently came on duty long after time. Several had breakfast with us as they had come in thinking it was 7 a.m. instead of 8.

Quite nice this evening getting up in daylight and it certainly makes the days longer. There is more time to do things. C had a day off today. I paid call and took her breakfast in her altered apartment. She has Lax for a sleeping companion. Not at all enthusiastic and is trying to get Cook instead, as a more congenial room-mate.

THURSDAY, 29TH MARCH, 1.30 A.M.

Nothin' doin' yet, although a convoy is expected in some time tonight. They have been coming in very late and long after they were expected over the last few nights. Anyway, I don't expect we shall get much if it does come. All the patients seem to be poured into J, K and L. Poor Mitchell is on night duty now and very depressed and miserable. She doesn't like it although she is bearing up as well as possible. After feeling very chirpy for the first few nights, I am now developing the old familiar n.d. sensations. Heaviness, dullness and inclination to indigestion and headaches, but really nothing to complain about and the horrible sleepiness has so far left me more or less in peace.

The wards are still very empty – some went out of F ward to convalescent camp yesterday, including Hazel who, after being so useful to us, was invalided back again from there, spent several days in bed far from well and has now been packed off to go before a medical board. He will probably be sent to Blighty as unfit for active service and perhaps get some cushier job at home. He is a nice little man, but far from strong. Jefferson and I still jog along together very amicably through the watching hours. Long may this state of peace last, though I should really like some more work to wake me up a bit. Sister McClaren has just been in having a crack, telling me about Australia which she loves to do. Quite enjoy her little visits, makes a break in the monotony of night watches.

Yesterday morning was so lovely. After a night of sharp frost and clear starlit sky, there was a lovely spring look about everything. Everyone was otherwise occupied, so I went out for a little walk through the sand dunes towards Ambleteuse and enjoyed clear crisp air and glimpses of blue sea, so refreshing after the darkness and closeness of the night.

New staff keeps arriving. Three new VADs came the other day and now a new Staff Sister has turned up. Can't think what Matron will do with everyone. There seems to be such a congestion of forces combined with a lack of patients. A great rush still hangs fire, and at present things are going so well without it that I don't at all wish for the bloodier battles to begin. I must make a start on a pneumonia jacket* now. We are being set down to make these nightly so that we shall be employed and not spend our nights in idle uselessness.

MONDAY, 2ND APRIL, 1.45 A.M.

Had a large convoy of six last night and quite busy after 3.15 when they arrived, two in G and four in F. No one bad at all, but still something to keep us going. Numbers were getting so small I began to be afraid they might dwindle away altogether. Yesterday, being April 1st, there were greats schemes for April Fools. The men laid several traps for me and I fell into one absolutely. Lewis told me one of the G ward patients wanted me. It was old Rye. So I hurried to ask with motherly solicitude what he was wanting and he only stared

---

* Usually a muslin jacket lined with wool.

amicably at me. Whereupon it immediately dawned upon me that I had been 'had' and I ran out and scolded the 'have' well for his impertinence.

I feel wonderfully wide awake these nights – no tendencies to drop off to sleep with that deadly, leaden-eyed feeling that used to come over me at 16. Feel pretty lively here all night, due probably to having less to do and also to going to bed in good time and getting long and good sound sleep. Saw C tonight at supper and exchanged a word or two with her. We seem very remotely separated now and I am always hopeful that when I come on day duty again, things will be put right once more.

MONDAY, 9TH APRIL, 10.45 A.M.

Just a week since last writing – nothing very eventful except for the coming and going of Easter and also the beginning of a big rush of work. The last four nights have been really busy and yesterday morning we had a frantic push round to get anything like finished in time. The men were coming in all the time, having to be bathed and settled in and looked after. Now G ward is quite full up and one man is sleeping on a stretcher by one of the stoves. F ward fills up and empties more or less daily. Last night was so bad that we now have an extra orderly who is going to look after H ward when that is being used. It was occupied once and then emptied again on the same day, all the inmates being sent to the marquees, which are in full swing. It seems we are at the beginning of the great push, at last.* The poor things – wounded and sick and suffering – that will come to us in course of the next few days.

Easter Day. So very unlike an Easter. I only got to part of the 7.30 celebration just before breakfast. Rather a scramble to get away from the ward in time and then I went to bed instead of going to the 11 o'clock service and sought bodily strength instead of spiritual support in sleep. Not quite so busy last night. We only took in one man but a convoy was coming in just when we came off duty. One

---

* The Battle of Arras. See Chronology, p. 352.

of patients in our ward F haemorrhaged twice, once last night and again in the morning. Jefferson called me to him the first time and I had to bustle in and apply a tourniquet and send for Sister. First time I had ever had to deal with anything of the sort on my own, though I often expected it in the white huts. I got everything done as I should, so feel I could cope with an eventuality of the sort if it occurred again any time.

Am ready for sleep now so mustn't write more. Was lazy and didn't go out at all this morning. Normally I go for a walk somewhere up to the canteen or along the shore or to Wimereux. I visited Hopper the other day at 14 Stationary. She is warded there, suffering from paratyphoid and really very poorly with a temp. that won't come down. Still, she seemed quite cheery and just the same dear Hopper of 16 General days. I was so pleased to see her again. Bownes, Fletcher and I went, think C is going to try and see her soon.

THURSDAY, 13TH APRIL, 11.30 A.M.

In the thick of it now. Just my luck to be on night duty for a rush. For the last four days or so, the convoys have been pouring in night and day and every available bed and space is occupied with wounded warriors. We have taken Vimy Ridge with great success they say and made other advances. Nearly all the soldiers are Canadians and in spite of their wounds they seem elated, poor things. Fletcher was in H last night coping with a full ward and Bownes coped the night before. I had my hands full with F and G. Really couldn't do H as well. Poor Sister McClaren was nearly driven crazy with her five huts all needing attention. Last night started fairly calmly and then at about 3, stretcher and walking cases poured into F, already full up so the wounded all had to be accommodated in odd corners on the floor and down the centre.

Really an awful business. I couldn't get on with the morning's work and I couldn't cope with the new patients at all. Just had to get them settled on stretchers and leave them for the day staff to fix up. The ward looked chaotic this morning when I left. Don't know what will happen tonight. The poor men are all in their muddy khaki, the walking cases are as bad as the stretcher cases, staggering in, tired out, with sore feet. It really seemed like a nightmare. Add to this, the lights all went out just as convoy was arriving and we had to work by fitful beams of two hurricane lamps. Fearful gale of wind blowing too and raining as well. I don't think we are ever going to get any spring. Lots of new VADs have just arrived. Four came yesterday and two went straight on night duty in the marquees. They must have had a terrible first night's experience.

C is very busy now in theatre. She takes ops herself with Col. Fullerton and the various other swells who operate. Great responsibility but she seems to be getting on quite well. I don't know how we will manage if this keeps up long. I hope it won't though and yet must be some more big advancing before the Germans can be said to be on the run.

SUNDAY, 15TH APRIL, 11 P.M.

Still having 'some' busy time all over the hospital. We had well over 100 patients – stretchers every one – in our division alone last night. There are patients in every bed except for a few emptied by an evacuation held a short time before I came on. We are all surviving it somehow. I saw C this morning and had a little conversation with her. Now she is in sole charge of the VJ Theatre with Botham the orderly who is a boon in himself, but C has to take the ops working in both theatres till quite late and Bownes spends all her nights just now clearing up in the big theatre when ops are over at about 12. The rush is really frantic sometimes.

The night before last, someone gave in a return of beds for Hut G as 22 instead of 2 and the orderly officer, knowing no better, sent in 22 patients. Of course we had nowhere to put them. Despair seized us all as the stretchers were trundled in one after another and lined the floor and filled up every available corner. Sister Harrison was horrified when she came and went away to see the Orderly Officer who arranged to have ten taken away, so the poor weary stretcher bearers came in and bore off the ten and left us rather more breathing space. But I never saw such a ward, even as it is now still, with half the patients on stretchers both in F and G. It was never as bad as that at 16. We always had beds for everyone and thought it a bad case if any one single patient had to go for a night without a bed.

Convoys in and evacuations out follow each other as closely as possible. I don't think there were quite so many in last night. At least we didn't get them, but several trains are expected which means some cases from every train.

A convoy was just coming in when we got on duty the night before last and began an exciting night by one of the patients haemorrhaging from his arm. We had to have the Orderly Officer and several people in to look at him, amid much consultation. Fortunately Staff Sister Robson and Sister McInnes hadn't gone and assisted to settle things and once the haemorrhage had stopped, the patient had morphia and went off to sleep and gave no cause for alarm through the night.

We have had one or two rather bad cases. One dear boy, with the head of his femur smashed, was really very ill. He was so patient and good and uncomplaining. Nearly all the patients we had in a few days ago were Canadian after taking of Vimy Ridge, but now we are getting other regiments and they say one division has been very badly cut up and had fearful casualties. It certainly looks like it, with so many wounded coming in. Am pretty much left on my own nowadays, Sister having her hands full with the bad cases in all the other huts and not having much time to pay any lengthy visits. I'm supposed to keep an eye on H too which has some bad cases in it, but I really haven't time to go in except very occasionally. So it is left very much to the tender mercies of Paling the orderly, who is a very smart boy and quite capable really of looking after the patients and supplying their ordinary needs. There are rows of stretchers there too, but it is same everywhere. Every bed in the marquees – even the new ones that have just opened – are filled, and there are some quite bad surgical cases in these too. Hope against hope that all the fighting is bringing us nearer peace and not throwing away lives absolutely uselessly, as has been the case several times already. The brutes of Germans sunk two of our hospital ships and evacuations are already pretty difficult and will be more so now.

SUNDAY, 22ND APRIL, 2.20 A.M.

This is a sad, sad war indeed. If only it would show some signs of ending, but it goes on and on bringing so much destruction and misery with it. Had a letter tonight forwarded from the Schermuly homestead with a sealed enclosure from my old friend W.L.S., and the dear man has been killed in action. My faithful admirer – funny, rough, honest, sailorman – unswervingly devoted in spite of all my unresponsiveness. Nice little note from his father and mother with the sealed letter. They must be very decent people and I must try to see them sometime. These things grip one's heart somehow and bring one up with a shock to the realization of the actualness of the war.

There is a stirring in the air again and rumours of more big fight-ing and I think we shall soon be as busy as ever and the poor maimed and wounded will be streaming in. At present great peace prevails in the ward. We have some bad cases, four amputations in H and one in F, a dear Scotchman called Macfarlane and in G there is a little Scotch Canadian called Munro who has a bad fractured femur. He is such a delightful patient, so quiet and long suffering. Sister Fuller has been in charge here now for nearly a week and she seems very fed up with night duty and this place altogether. Nothing is right at all, but she isn't bad really. My time of freedom is over though and I am very much superintended now. Feel rather resentful at times but suppose it must be put up with and I can quietly take my own way in a good many things.

One very nice thing has happened in the last day or two. C has come on night duty to be the theatre sister during the night. She will take ops if there are any, or be there in case of emergency. Matron decided she couldn't have the theatre staff kept up till all hours during the busy times, so C is to relieve the pressure and take on all work after 8 p.m. with Bownes to assist. We haven't had busy nights so far, but one or two emergency ops so C has been able to justify her presence. She was very despairing at being put on night and separated from Sister Reay, but I think she is a little more recon-ciled now. By the kindness of Mitchie moving out of her room, I have been able to get with C again and M has gone with Bownes. C took Lax's place and she went into a tent with Tomlinson, so there has been general post to get things fixed up. Now all happily settled. Long may it last.

Great excitement last night – very heavy firing heard quite close, once earlier and once later in the night. The sound of it was really appalling and it seemed to vibrate through one and shake the very ground. Has proved to be an enemy raid on Calais and an action at sea, said to involve three cruisers or destroyers of the enemy sunk and one of ours disabled, but I expect we shall hear truth from the papers soon.*

Really am liking night duty here better than at 16. For one thing I am less sleepy, don't have that dead feeling I had every night trying to keep awake and not knowing how to manage it. Am really very well too and sleeping and eating like a trooper. Went to Boulogne a day or two ago, but thought it rather an expedition and only to be taken if absolutely necessary.

WEDNESDAY, 25TH APRIL, 11 A.M.

Rush is beginning again. Supposed to be a frantically big convoy in last night but not so many came in as were expected. Got about ten or eleven in F and G and several in H. There are some quite bad cases. Sister Fuller is settling down a bit more now, not quite so desperately fed up as she was at first. She has by degrees confided some of her past history to me, which from the little she has told me must have been rather an eventful one. Born in South Africa, she married when she was seventeen. Her husband was murdered by natives in Matabeleland and she never heard anything for three months after. She took up nursing though she hated anything to do with illness, but stuck to it determinedly and has had various Matron's posts before coming out to join His Majesty's forces. I get on quite well with her and try to make night duty as congenial as poss. under the apparently very unfavourable conditions.

---

* This was the Second Battle of Dover Strait. See Chronology, p. 353.

THURSDAY, 3RD MAY, 11.30 A.M.

Such a lovely day. Cloudless and warm and tempered with a fresh breeze. C and I have been out for a short walk along towards Ambleteuse, then a bask on the dunes – and, incidentally, a snooze – and back again very sodden after lying out in the open. All the last few days have been so lovely and beautiful and the nights clear and cloudless. C has heard a nightingale several times but I haven't been lucky yet, though I went out to listen last night in the early morning.

Have taken a great step and the more I think of it, the more alarming it appears – with its possibilities and uncertainties. I have signed a paper to say I will serve for the duration of the war and as long after as required in my VAD capacity. Sister Harrison brought the paper round one night and asked for all of us to make up our minds and C and I agreed that we couldn't possibly pledge ourselves to anything so desperate. Jobbie came up the next morning to collect answers and put us both down for 'no', which I felt quite sure was the right thing to say. But the morning after, when it came to actual signing and everyone seemed to be falling into line and many excellent reasons were put before us to shake our decision, we began to feel rather doubtful and decided to go to Matron and make enquiries and see if that would decide the right course. So C and I bearded Matron in her den and were received with her usual funny abrupt manners and then with the understanding kindness that Matron always shows when any difficulties are put before her. She saw our point of view but at the same time advised us to give ourselves up, unreservedly, to the service of our country and to share the severing of home ties with the men who had given up everything. After some discussing I announced that I would sign and the wretched yellow paper was produced and my signature appended and C then followed suit, so we came away having lost all loopholes for regaining our liberty unless anything unforeseen occurs. I don't know what will happen now and wonder very much whether we shall sometime be rejoicing in the day we made our pledge, or else deeply regretting it.

Night duty proceeds on its strenuous way. Sister gets very fed up with hard work and the roughness of this active service. She finds life here about as different from the comfort and ease of hospital ships as anything one could imagine. We have a lot of heavy dressings to keep us busy. Little Munro in G still hangs on and there is a very bad chest case in F ward and several more who have to be dressed every night, which all takes a lot of time. I have hardly had time to sit down for some nights now except for supper. Rest of the twelve hours is spent flying to and fro trying to get all the necessary work accomplished. Jefferson finds it very hard but pegs away, trotting about from ward to ward trying to take things as calmly as possible.

There was great deal of firing of anti-aircraft guns early the other morning. I went out to see what was happening and saw shrapnel bursting in little shining white puffs up in the sky, somewhere over Boulogne direction. It was very pretty in the early morning light. No sign of the Taubes, but one of the men said he could see one – hidden behind thin veils of cloud – but that shrapnel was peppering them hotly. They must have been closely pursued.

TUESDAY, 8TH MAY, 2 A.M.

'Pleine Lune', as the little French calendar tells me. But the sky is overcast tonight and there is no pleine lune to be seen. Last night was gorgeous and everything showed up like weird daylight. A sea of new marquees is going up, pertaining to No. 54 General, planted on the lower end of the golf links and No. 55 General is getting on splendidly beyond our camp on the way to Wimereux.*

My time on night duty is getting quite short now, less than a fortnight. Wonder where I shall go when I make the change. Sister McInnes has gone on night duty in place of Sister Donaldson who is coming here I believe. The other Day Sister is an Assistant Matron belonging to No. 55 General who is only here temporarily. I think

---

* The two new hospitals were being set up one on either side of No. 32, No. 54 in the direction of Ambleteuse, and No. 55 towards Wimereux.

Sister Starbuck is a little in awe of her and rather flummoxed at having her here.

THURSDAY, 10TH MAY, 11 A.M.

This hospital and neighbourhood seethes with novelty now. Besides two large general hospitals growing up on our borders, a big Rest Camp has been planted down at Ambleteuse and hundreds of troops have been marching out to it lately, a dismal procession, pegging along poor things, fully equipped and rather fagged. No wonder too because this stands for their leave. No going to Blighty now, they have to holiday-make at Ambleteuse where they are held in by rule and discipline. There was a great outcry, almost a riot among the men, because when the camp was not quite ready and the first contingent arrived, they were put on fatigues, which caused great wrath and indignation, this being the men's holiday.

This is another lovely day of shine and warmth. Went to Wimereux yesterday with C and Smitch. We stayed eating and drinking at the Club* for some time, so got back rather late and felt somewhat the worse for the hot, tiring walk back but today's rest should do good.

MONDAY, 14TH MAY, 9 A.M.

The Rest Camp over at Ambleteuse is very active and every morning lately the shore down in front of the village has been thick with far-distant, active, ant-like figures exercising strenuously, running about or bathing in hordes of pink scuddies. I haven't heard so much about rioting and discontent so I suppose things are settling down a bit but plenty of riotous men go past the hospital after 7.30 on their homeward way. They are allowed out to Wimereux at 6 and have to be in by 8.30, so there is not much time for indulging but they seem to manage all the same and go reeling back very disgracefully up to all hours of the night. French people must be rather appalled by the goings on of the British Tommy, but I daresay they are

---

* Clubs were a feature of social life in most British military bases in France. Dorothea mentions another one in Le Touquet in February 1918. One assumes that there was segregation of the sexes, though this is not stated explicitly in the diary.

accustomed to it by now. The little road past our quarters has been put out of bounds now as so many over-hilarious warriors chose to retrace their wavering footsteps by that route and got mixed up in the Sisters' tents once or twice, not altogether pleasantly. All the cafés in Ambleteuse have been put out of bounds so there can be no rioting there, but the men think it worth their while to tramp into Wimereux to get refreshment, regardless of rules and restrictions.

No. 55 General is now open for patients and we have sent along a selection of minor cases, cast-offs from various wards. I don't know how soon they will be ready for the convoys. We have plenty of empty beds at present and there seems no likelihood of a great rush.

Jefferson comes off night duty today and goes into F and G on day duty. I am very sorry that he is going as we have worked together very well and had some good times through all sorts of emergencies. Harris comes on instead, which isn't so bad as I know Harris too, but it won't be the same till Harris gets to know the routine of work which always takes some getting into.

THURSDAY, 17TH MAY, 10 A.M.

I haven't heard anything yet about coming off nights but time is getting very short now. Jefferson has given place to Harris as night orderly and I am finding the latter much more expeditious though not quite so absolutely reliable or so careful as Jeff. Still, he is very good and certainly quick and kind to the patients too. Langley, still in F, is such a quaint old bird and an absolute terror to the staff, fussing about something or other all night long except during intervals of sleep. For the last few nights he has been having a treat, with me taking him up a little snack after our supper, something left over in the way of sardines or toasted cheese. Last night there he was lying awake at 1 a.m. fussing away about his arms and one thing and another. I took him a fried sausage and a bit of bread and 10 gr of aspirin and, very soon after having consumed the comestibles, he was fast asleep and slept till morning so the light refreshment has a very sedative affect.

C has gone with Sister Reay up to the Château, so goodness knows what time she will be back. Sister Reay has an entire day off so she is at C's disposal. The grande passion continues and seems to be mutual. If anything happened and one or other of us was moved away to new place, I don't know what would happen. There would be a weeping and gnashing of teeth.

WEDNESDAY, 23RD MAY, 8 A.M.

Here I am at last, after over nine weeks of existence amid the shadows of night. Having my day off today and the weather is glorious and inviting. I was sorry when the time came for the change. I didn't like leaving the ward at all and feel very vague about where I shall be sent tomorrow. No place appears open or very inviting and wards F, G and H are a full house at present.

[later] This is a lovely spot – Hardelot – of old associations. Fancy being seated in the garden of Pré Catelan amid most gorgeous woods and young greenery on this lovely day. I am waiting for lunch, which is gradually preparing. Such a good opportunity of coming here that I really couldn't miss it, so I set off alone, got a lift into Boulogne in a Ford with the Colonel and took the train to Pont de Briques after some delays. Much interested in the movements of a large body of troops, either new reinforcements going up to the front or men returning from leave. They are all gathering and forming up just round the train terminus. A large number of them are Canadians and there are many little companies from other regiments. Most interesting watching them, but everything seems teeming with interest on a day like this and I am enjoying this outing enormously, so far.

SATURDAY, 26TH MAY, 9 P.M.

This spring evening is cool and refreshing after a roasting day. Enjoyed the luxury of a delightful bathe this morning.

Am working up in the marquees now under Sister Buckham's regime. Seems very like old times, quite reminiscent of last October, only without the everlasting flapping and tearing of canvas in the boisterous breezes. Bakingly hot these last few days – it becomes too warm at midday and makes one feel disinclined to work. Have another VAD to work with, one of an Irish trio and she is quite nice, very smart at her work. There are 70 beds in the marquees, as before, and nearly all are occupied. Quite lively times we have here. Really glad to be off night duty now I have made the change. I get more amusement out of life and a healthier existence altogether.

Had a very pleasant day off and the weather was gorgeous. After writing the last entry in the garden of Pré Catelan at lunchtime, I sauntered into the woods and explored there for a bit. It was blazingly hot, but after taking a climb up a sand dune I was rewarded with a most perfect and wonderful view of the country round. I shall never forget the beauty of the scene in such shimmering heat. Then I pottered down to Hardelot Plage, just to look at the place and to ascertain how much it had grown. Very hot and shadeless, so after drinking a citron and soda at the little corner café, or one near to it, I took the train back to Pont de Briques. I got into conversation with a lonely RAMC captain wiling away a leisure afternoon, and he has haunted me ever since. He came out to call the day after and pursued me into my ward on duty. Today, I have had a letter with a further request to see me. Quite a romantic affair altogether, but I rather guess he is dull and wants someone or something to amuse him and I seem to have filled the niche conveniently.*

Heard yesterday from little Al. He has come abroad. Was crossing probably on Thursday and now will be somewhere in this disastrous country, facing the fortunes of war.† This is too lovely an evening to think of war, but it hangs over us, a dark threatening cloud all the same.

WEDNESDAY, 30TH MAY, 6.45 P.M.

My Hardelot friend Captain Milne was to have met me this evening but he didn't turn up. Perhaps has found other attractions. I was amused at his persistent writing and then calling on two occasions. I

---

* The 'lonely RAMC captain' was Captain Milne, who reappears frequently during the coming weeks.
† Brother Alastair had now completed his training at the Guards Depot, Windsor, and had been posted as a Second Lieutenant or 'ensign' to the 2nd Battalion, Coldstream Guards.

took him to tea in the Mess on Sunday, after going for a walk, and he made himself quite pleasant to the ladies, though he was very nervous.

Matron informed me this morning that C had been mentioned in Despatches. Very pleased indeed to hear her efforts have been recognized and so they might be. She had some very strenuous times during the rush, working in the theatre up to all hours.

Sisters have been seen arriving in shoals waiting to be called up for the three hospitals near. The one upon the top of the hill is progressing rapidly and spreading itself out over the nice open space where our little short cut to Wimereux used to go.* Now we have to go by the rubbish tip and a sentry warns us off hospital territory if we dare trespass. The road is thronged with orderlies and Tommies, the latter from the Rest Camp at Ambleteuse where there must be thousands and thousands of them.

The big push hasn't been resumed yet, but is said to be very imminent now and to be directed chiefly from Ypres, which will affect us even more than the last fighting.†

SATURDAY, 9TH JUNE, 10 P.M.

Ages since I wrote my diary. How time does go by, simply amazing the way days slip by. Have been fairly busy over the last day or two. Things were a bit hectic in the marquees yesterday with convoys and evacuations and Sister Buckham on the rampage. We have extra stretcher beds in now and all were filled last night. Rush caused by the recent advance from Ypres and capture of Messines. Nearly all patients we had were Anzacs, New Zealanders and Irish. They must have borne the brunt of the fighting.

Have been relieving a good deal lately in Z, the TB ward. I go up there when McConnell is off duty and now quite like this funny little ward and the select company of patients, now that I know them a bit. Still feel X marquee is my home and am quite pleased to get back there again. Some of the staff from 55 who were temporarily

---

* This was No. 54 General.
† 'The big push' is not something that Dorothea should have known about on 30 May. Security must have been rather lax! See Chronology, p. 353.

here have been called back to their own hospital which has quite a number of patients now but is much handicapped by having no water. All the new hospitals are in the same difficulty and rumour is that two of them will have to move and take up quarters elsewhere. Just like the army, after all the trouble and expense of putting up all the marquees and appurtenances.

Still receiving attention from my friend Captain Milne and I spent a delightful half day in his company last week. It was not so much his company that made it delightful as the glorious weather and feeling of freedom and a lovely walk in the country to Souverain Moulin. We had a very peaceful, pleasant tea there, then a little walk and repose under some shady trees and then made tramp homewards in the cool of the evening. The Captain is a great talker and I don't have to bother much. Found out he had been a medical missionary in Palestine for four years. He has a great deal to say about the manners and customs of the East.

TUESDAY, 12TH JUNE, 10 P.M.

The frogs are having such a chorus again tonight. They croak away in the ponds and marshes among the sand dunes and are quite audible down here and strangely weird to hear. Levack, Cran and I have had one or two delightful after-supper promenades in the waning summer light, down along the path to Slack. Everything looked enchanted – owls and night birds flitted to and fro like ghosts and waterfowl splashed away from us among the reeds. It was both delightful and dreamlike. Must go again sometime soon, while the nice weather lasts.

Had a wonderful bathe this afternoon. Quite a gathering of bathers attracted over by warm afternoon. Some of the Sisters look a sad sight. Hardly decent really. VADs are rather better because their figures as a rule seem more presentable. A bevy of patients watched us from the shore, much interested in our proceedings. Things are so slack now up in the marquees, nothing doing whatsoever.

Fletcher and Michie are back from leave and Jobbie and Rheeder are away now. I suppose we shall be nearly the next to go and our time may not be so very far off now. C is still on night duty but due to come off soon. Problem then will be if we can get together again or how it is to be done.

THURSDAY, 14TH JUNE, 10 P.M.

Seem to have been shoved away somehow now into the TB ward and away from X marquee, which I regret very much. Have felt it coming for a little while since I began to do so much relieving up there. Seemed rather ominous and now that McConnell has gone on night duty it has become more obvious than ever, and my morning and evening today were spent there dealing with the little party of remarkably cheery patients. Two very gay Canadian boys came in last night and have had great daffings with them. I can't say the work is very arduous but still have all the responsibility if I am left in charge up there and there is the possibility of some bad cases.

Had a very pleasant afternoon out with my friend the Captain, again. A short walk and then a good rest in a shady little dell. Most romantic surroundings, utterly remote, and then we had tea at Wimereux and afterwards a bustle home as I had to be on duty at 5. Really hot weather again after a short break of unsettled conditions, and this afternoon the country looked wonderful.

THURSDAY, 21ST JUNE, 10 P.M.

The longest day! and Midsummer. Too sad to look forward to the days closing in after this but suppose it must be faced, however unpalatable, and the black cold winter is still a good way off. Another week has gone by and nothing out of the ordinary to record. It is still peaceful in the wards, slack everywhere. I have only seven in my little family now. They dwindle away one by one and I think it won't be long before ward is empty. Have got very fond of my own special department and having everything under my own control. Left so much to myself and that is always rather desirable, as I am reminded when the Sisters come fussing around. Matron was quite approving when she did her round this morning, so I felt satisfied that my efforts to make the ward look nice had not passed unnoticed.

I had quite a pleasant half-day last Sunday, spent in company with my friend Capt. Milne. A grillingly hot day and every movement made one sticky and moist. We went up the Vallée du Denacre to explore new ground, but being Sunday, the place was full of French trippers, picnicking and frolicking about. It is certainly a very pretty place with thick shady trees all the way up the valley. Would have been quite ideal if there hadn't been so much company.

C has been in tonight. She is now established temporarily in theatre again, on day duty just while Sister Andrews, the Assistant Theatre Sister, is away on leave. She is sleeping in the bell tent and had Sister MacDonald, who used to be at 16, for companion but she has gone now, so C is alone and the question is: shall I move in with her and give up my share of the grotto, which would be rather an effort.

THURSDAY, 28TH JUNE, 10.30 P.M.

Have twelve patients now in Z ward. Quite an extensive family but no one bad at all, and nothing to cause anxiety, for which I am thankful. One little boy with such a sweet face is diagnosed as positive TB and will go to England but the others are all queries and may not be lucky enough to get over the water.

Have seen Dr Scott again, after a long time of non-appearance. He is still at 8 Stationary and still at the same work and still as pessimistic as ever. My Scotch friend [Captain Milne] has gone to 5 Rest Camp at Ostrohove near Boulogne so I won't see so much of him. Thought he was going further away and rather a shock to find he was still within calling distance and I hadn't seen the last of him yet.

TUESDAY, 3RD JULY, 9.45 P.M.

Fine day again today, after some time of unsettled weather. Still very windy, a dry breathless east wind, not altogether pleasant. Was off duty this evening and enjoyed a walk when it was fresher. Still looking after my cherished little family of patients. After mounting up to thirteen, numbers have dropped to nine again and eight tomorrow, when one of my oldest friends is departing to convalescent camp. The latest addition to the party is a black man from the West Indian Contingent, an Indian by birth though his people came from Barbados. He seems very well educated and was going to study for the Bar, but when war broke out joined the army instead and has been doing his bit, till his health broke down. It is much more interesting to have only a few patients. Can get to know them so much better and they seem almost like personal friends.

Much commotion a morning or two ago when a large batch of German prisoners marched down the road with a band and their guard, and a little baggage train behind. Looked quite hale and hearty and very cheerful mostly. They were all going out to a prisoners' camp beyond Ambleteuse somewhere. They probably had been prisoners for a little while. Looked so well equipped and nearly all had extra luggage, boxes and bundles and parcels. A funny German brass band was playing them along in great style and quite added to the impressiveness of this march past. Wish the poor English troops had bands to accompany them to and from the Rest Camp. They look so weary tramping along that bare hard road backwards and forwards.

THURSDAY, 8TH JULY, 8.15 P.M.

Great excitement yesterday, over a possible visit from the Queen,* who is over in France for two days visiting hospitals in the neighbourhood. She came out to see the engineering works yesterday after dinner and her proximity to 32 gave rise to all the excitement. The

* Queen Mary, the Queen Consort, visited countless hospitals throughout the war in an attempt to boost morale.

hospital was all tidied up, the wards all decorated and the patients all smartened. Wind up everywhere. Then, of course, in the end she never came to see us. She spent a little while at the works opposite and one or two of the patients saw her. Lots of them went up to see what they could see and had a good view of Her Majesty coming out of the gate before she got into the car waiting for her.

Our new Mess is opened now and I have had two meals in it, quite lost in its comparatively vast expanses. Makes a very nice change from the cramped ménage we have been used to lately. There are four tables across the room, to accommodate all the staff – two for Sisters, two for VADs. Suppose they will never all be used though except at breakfast, the only meal we all sit down to together. The old Mess is to be turned into some sort of sitting room where it will be quite nice to while away a few spare minutes between off duty and mealtimes.

FRIDAY, 13TH JULY

Another week of the daily round and common task has flown by and we are appreciably nearer leave, having signed for it last Monday. When we shall actually get it, however, seems a very doubtful question.

Our latest interest is the opening of the antiquated bit of railway line running between here and Ambleteuse and joining into the main line above the golf course. There are two engines running up and down now, one light one and a big one that was brought down today. Quite a lot of traffic too, with the trucks and luggage vans. The big rumbling things pass in front of Z ward just down the road and right along in front of our quarters here, uncomfortably close to the hut opposite. There is nothing to prevent unsuspecting members of the nursing staff from walking out of the front door right onto the line to find one of these lightning expresses bearing down on them in a fiercely warlike manner. We are reminded of the Hun constantly just now because a large party of prisoners of war are at work on the line and they do the unloading of the trucks and any other odd jobs. Clad in rather dingy grey-green uniforms and little pork pie caps, they look a shoddy company. Some are very young, several are

Bosch out at work

bespectacled and all have very much the same type of face – a round head, high cheekbones, blue eyes and fair hair. They seem to have rather an inadequate guard with them, two or three Tommies armed with rifles and bayonets set, but I daresay the 'Gers' know it's no use trying to get away from here and probably haven't any ambitions to try anyway.

Had a half-day yesterday, such a hot baking day. Went into Boulogne to do some shopping and then met Capt. Milne. We went to tea at the Hôtel Maurice. Harry Mackie came walking in, having just returned from sick leave, so we exchanged a few words with him. It was quite nice to see a friendly face from home. I bathed this afternoon, which was very delightful. The sea was so lovely and bright and fresh and the weather very hot and sultry. So it was a most welcome plunge.

Quite suddenly at this point in the diary there is an unexplained void, lasting six weeks. Dorothea and Christie went on leave, having signed for it on 9 July, but we do not have the exact dates. They must have returned to Wimereux before the end of the month, just in time for the horrors of Passchendaele (or the Third Battle of Ypres). No. 32 Hospital would have been overrun with casualties, continuing right through August.*

* See Chronology, p. 353.

One can only speculate whether it was the horror of the battle and its consequences that deterred Dorothea from restarting her diary after her return from leave, or simply overwork and fatigue during those terrible weeks. It is worth noting that for the first time, when resuming her writing, she refers frequently to the 'shell shocks' or 'neurasthenics', patients with symptoms she had never experienced before.

TUESDAY, 28TH AUGUST

Phenomenal gale raged all last night and this morning. Scenes of great chaos and disturbance among the marquees and tents. The Sisters' bell tents suffered and several were blown down and the disconsolate inhabitants had to shift into other quarters wherever room could be found. This little homestead of ours is like a swamp. The door wouldn't shut tight and torrential rain swept in. I was up three times during the night, wading about in gumboots seeing what could be done. Had an influx of neurasthenics with shaking limbs and nodding heads into K ward from dismantled marquees. They filled up all our spare beds, so we were saved from having any more surgical cases.

TUESDAY, 30TH AUGUST

Many distraught people in the hospital tonight – two broken hearts anyway – the cause of the anguish being the arrival of Sister Reay's moving orders for tomorrow morning. Fletcher, all tear begrutten,* turned up at supper, and C was clinging to her beloved to the very bitter end. I am also somewhat distracted by Sister Searle's orders to move. But she is suffering from a nasty painful boil on the arm so almost certainly won't be able to go tomorrow. However, it seems like a choice between that and Mauritien, so it looks like we are losing her from the ward anyway and that is hard to bear considering what a happy time we've had together and how nice it has been working with her. She seems just tired out and hardly able to face questions at all. She had to go over for an interview with Matron but

* 'Swollen in the face by much weeping' (OED).

felt it a great trial and Matron's sharp remarks almost more than she could bear. Such are troubles of life at present. Matron is worried because of her staff going like this and none coming to replace them. It is all right so long as the marquees are away but if they go up again, the staff will be very scanty. I will miss Sister Reay's charming face from the throng of Sisters, she having been so nice to us always and a rather special champion of the VADs.

MONDAY, 3RD SEPTEMBER

There was real excitement last night over an air raid. We were just in bed at 10.30 when our attention was caught by unusual booming and banging sounds and the whir of machines. Then the dogs barked and voices began to speak in excited tones, so at that point we trundled out of bed and discovered the cause of all excitement was an air raid in our vicinity. It was a glorious night, cloudless sky and full moon, calm and clear. Saw searchlights and flashes over Boulogne-way and then later a lot of flashing in Calais direction. I got more fun and interest out of watching the odd apparitions that appeared out of the huts and tents to see what was going on than from the actual air raid, which was rather a washout as far as seeing any enemy aircraft was concerned. Matron arrived out in her night attire, a coat and her hair down and she, Sister Buckham, Bownes, the Corporal and I held a great conclave just outside the gate, watching the flashes and firing till after 11.

WEDNESDAY, 5TH SEPTEMBER

Another air raid over Boulogne last night, on a gorgeous clear moonlit night. Just asleep at 10.30 when the firing began. I woke up and found Bownes prowling out and followed in her wake. Camp was soon all in a hubbub. Members of nursing staff were all herded into the sitting room and passages to be out of harm's way, except for a few bold spirits who preferred to remain in their own huts and tents. The firing certainly was close and dud shells screamed down just past our quarters. Bits of shrapnel must have been coming down all round.

E.	Engineers Works
O.	Officers' Quarters. Golf Club House
M	Monument
C.	Cathedral
H.	Harbour
B.	Breakwater
SQ.	Sisters' Quarters
N.	Nissen Huts belonging to 55 General
P.	Prisoners & Chinese Camps
54.	General
R.	Road to Wimereux
S.	55 General
Ex.	Our marquee extension
AM.	Road to Ambleteuse
T.	Our tents
HO.	Hospital Building
CB.	Café Boutin
RA.	Railway to Club: past our quarters
8.	No. 8 Stationary Hospital

FRIDAY, 7TH SEPTEMBER

I was much startled and very anxious this morning when I received a communication from the office to say Al was at 14 General, wounded, and would I call and see him. My heart sank when I read the message. However it didn't sound very desperate, so having a morning off I set out as speedily as possible and arrived at 14 General about 10.30. Soon ushered into a nice large airy ward and there in the corner was our Al in a blue counterpaned bed, smiling a smile of welcome. I was delighted to see him of course and at once made enquiries on his state of health. It seems his injuries were not very severe, mostly bruising, a wound in shoulder and another in leg, apparently small pieces. Two bits had hit his face and something had given him a swollen lip and with his countenance adorned with some antiseptic, the whole effect was very impressive. We spent a little while talking then went out to buy him some necessaries for his toilet which he wanted. He had come without anything except his Private's uniform that he was wearing at time he was wounded,* so he hadn't much to pull along

* It had become the normal practice for officers to wear the same uniform as other ranks when in the front line so as not to attract the attention of snipers.

with, poor dear. The VAD in the ward entertained great hopes of his getting to Blighty and spoke cheerfully on the subject. Do hope he does and stays there for a little while. It was a whizz bang that caught him, bursting about two yards away, so no wonder he got hit. Very lucky to have come off so lightly as he did.*

This is a clear starlit night so I'm expecting momentarily to hear an air raid beginning and am not looking forward to prospect of alarms. All the poor shell shocks will be dancing about with fright if an enemy does begin his monkey tricks.† They were very much upset by the last raid and lots of them are as bad as ever again. Most pathetic, poor things. Their nerves seem to have absolutely gone to pieces.

Sister Reay and Sister Searle are still awaiting their moving orders. Very odd indeed that they haven't been sent to their destination.

SATURDAY, 22ND SEPTEMBER

Bownes has gone on leave and left me desolate. Not quite fully though, as Rheeder, one of mess VADs, has established herself in the vacant space during owner's absence.

Went to see Al yesterday, but not today. Seems very cheerful. He is still waiting for his medical board and then to get his Blighty leave. Hope he will get a good one.

Matron is away on leave and general atmosphere of calm prevails, though various changes of staff are taking place under Sister Harrison's regime. No more air raids, but the moon is waxing again and the nights are clear just now. Shouldn't be surprised if unwelcome visitors come down again soon.

---

* Alastair's battalion was holding an advanced position between Boesinghe and Lange-marck on the extreme left of the British line. He and his platoon were strengthening their 'trenches' (actually partly trench and partly parapet because of the mud) when he was hit by shrapnel from a shell-burst from a German 77mm field gun. The shell from this gun travelled faster than sound, so the 'whizz' of the trajectory came before the 'bang' from the gun, hence the slang term.

† The German air raids on British bases in France would become an increasingly serious problem over the next ten months, although not so much in the winter.

SUNDAY, 7TH OCTOBER

Since last writing things have been happening to me in that I have again been put on night duty in old K instead of Plaskett, who was due off. Very disgruntled indeed and not enjoying life in that respect at all. It has only been four months since I came off. Anyway, I had no say in the matter, so here I am back in the little room where I spent most of n.d. last time. Reeve has the other half of the room and is quite amiable, though she talks too much to my thinking. I came on the night before last, after a very curtailed sleep. Other VAD in the ward is Chapman, one of the new ones. She does K2. I do K1, and have plenty of work to get through and the morning push is hectic from 4 onwards. Have Walker for an orderly, he is quite good and takes life cheerfully, which is a great comfort. So here I am for two months at least, cut off from the outer world and living the miserable old nocturnal existence over again.

Last Monday night, there was a great excitement in the shape of an air raid. Beautiful weather – ideal for Fritz's machinations. Came over to prospect in the middle of the day and created quite a little commotion then, but didn't drop any bombs. Anti-aircraft were busy though and a dud shell dropped within a yard of the building wall just opposite our huts. Screamed overhead and gave us all a great start. But at night the band played and Fritz came up quite unawares. Bombardment and reply began at once and the whole place shook. Dwellers in the tents flocked over at once to building to take cover. Like last time, there were two distinct raids and the second one was worse than the first. Several bombs dropped no further away than 8 Stationary, just by the railway embankment, but did no damage beyond killing some horses in a field. Some dropped in Boulogne too, but with not much result. Anti-aircraft from French 75 guns gave the raiders a warm time. Finally, they retired, much to our relief and we were able to go to bed again. All the shell shocks in the hospital were absolutely off their heads and running about looking for shelter and collapsing altogether. The poor night staff on duty with them had a terrible time ... Now the weather has changed and I hope there will be no more excitements of that kind.

Al has at last departed home. I stayed up a bit longer on Friday afternoon to see him, before he went. Am going along sometime to call at 14 General to see the Sister, who was very nice, and Mr Wood, the poor fellow patient with the bad arm.

MONDAY, 15TH OCTOBER, 2.30 A.M.

On the whole, I have had a fairly peaceful time up to now. The ward is pretty heavy, but not many new convoys in, which has been a mercy. Got a whole lot of patients from E transferred to make room for the Portuguese who are filling up the hospital rapidly.* I have been on since last Thursday week and see a vista of many weeks before me, till the beginning of December when I am due off. We are all wondering whether we are to be given over to the Portuguese for their exclusive use – and to the shell shocks – which seems to be our fate just now.

* Portuguese soldiers had been on the front line since May 1917. An Army division of two brigades had been sent to France when Portugal joined in the war on the side of the Allies. Unfortunately their contribution to the fighting strength, with a few exceptions, was negligible. Dorothea's experiences with them over the next few months tell their own story, though by the end she 'liked them very much really'.

Bownes came back from leave surprised to find me spirited away to n.d. and Rheeder in possession of my half of the apartment. I have an end of the Zoo. I quite like my little cubicle, which has plenty of space and many shelves and a delightful outlook on sea and shore.

Went up to 14 General the other day to revisit old haunts and saw the pleasant, cheery Sister who enquired tenderly after Al. Mr Wood was looking better and more comfortable and seems to miss A. He had made a very good impression.

Smuts are falling thick like leaves in Vallombrosa in here just now. Fire has been stoked up and always has a good smoke at such times. We think we shall soon be kippered at this rate and I am quite sure I shall have to wear a gas helmet to prevent suffocation before long.

FRIDAY, 19TH OCTOBER, 2.30 A.M.

Night is wearing away and soon the morning push will begin. Have had very peaceful time. Patients all slept pretty well. Convoys just now are very few and far between owing to the small return of beds we make. So many now occupied by the Portuguese, or the 'Pork and Cheese' as the men call them, that the hospital is practically given over to them and shell shocks. They have their own medical officers who, everyone says, are quite good but pretty strict with the patients. They need to be, for really these people can't be trusted at all. There was great excitement last night because an Australian was stabbed in the leg just outside the huts here and taken to the theatre to be stitched up. He was brought in here after and has quite a bad wound and lost a lot of blood. Sister Beardsmore flew to the rescue tearing strips off her apron to tie on as a tourniquet and was quite on the spot with her assistance. There is a lot of ill feeling between Tommies and Portuguese and I shouldn't be surprised if serious troubles didn't break out before the matter is settled.

TUESDAY, 23RD OCTOBER, 1.15 A.M.

Still very, very slack and no indications of any more convoys. Can't quite understand why we are being kept so empty. Only the shell shocks and Portuguese keep arriving. Nobody likes the Pork and

Cheeses and they are a very poor type of men, consumptive and weakly and most of the injuries they come in with are suspiciously like self-inflicted wounds. They have a hospital out at Ambleteuse near the camp in the course of construction but it is not quite ready yet and meanwhile we get the casualties, which are many.

Spent the morning with Sister Garnett one of the old 16 Staff. It has been two years since she left there, but has not changed a bit. Seemed as cheery as ever. Had great recalling of old times and discussion of the people we knew in the old days. She is now on night duty at 14 Stationary, so I hope to see her again sometime.

THURSDAY, 1ST NOVEMBER, 12.30 A.M.

Great change in ward at my end. All the sick have come down here from marquees before moving into new Nissen huts, so the number of empty beds is much reduced and have all these Ports down pro tem. All the old friends from K1 moved into K2 which is full up and Chapman looks after them. I do my best with the FBs* but not too successfully. Fortunately none of them are bad except one TB, who isn't too bad either really but the worst of the patients. Some seem quite getatable, but others very stupid. Too many of them have poor physique and nearly all have TB, in some form or other. Have great struggles getting them up in the morning. They don't like washing in cold water.

I don't know what is going to happen to this hospital. There are all sorts of mad rumours about but probably nothing much will happen. Maybe this winter it will simply be made a base for the shell shocks and Portuguese.

2.30 a.m.

Lights still out and have had a new excitement about an hour ago. Short and sharp but very noisy while it lasted. Apparently Fritz swooped down out of the clouds just over here – seemed from the sound to be right on top – and fired his machine gun several times, alarmingly loudly. Meanwhile, AA batteries were banging away with

---

* Foreign bodies?

tremendous vigour and shaking the whole hut with their vibrations. Tremendous din while it lasted but fortunately with no ill effects. Poor shell shocks went scuttling off, like a lot of rabbits, from the marquees to the building. These night raids put the wind up and their shattered nerves won't stand the shock at all. Little Ports stood the racket splendidly. They nearly all woke, but didn't seem to get at all excited, making only whispered remarks about Bosch no bon and the noise.

All peaceful again now. Maybe we shall have a return visit later, though I am rather hoping the villainous Fritz won't come this way. Has been very busy tonight everywhere, guns banging away in Blighty for a long time.

SUNDAY, 4TH NOVEMBER, 1.15 A.M.

Very quiet again tonight, in my end anyway. Porks sleep like tops all night as a rule, but Chapman was kept rather busier at her end attending to the poor woundeds. I went to Wimereux yesterday morning, driving in part of the way with Bownes who was going on special leave for seven days to see her fiancé, before he goes back to New Zealand. I didn't even know she had a fiancé and this seems to have been a surprise to everyone. Anyway, she is away to see him and very anxious in case he should be gone before she arrives.

Have just raised a laugh with this drawing. Adventure last night when Chapman induced us to believe that the foghorn on a light-ship in the harbour was a cow that had wandered out of its way, mooing in our neighbourhood. Thought it unlikely, but still partly convinced by repeated assurances. Only when I went out to listen did I discover how absurd we were.

MONDAY, 12TH NOVEMBER, 1.45 A.M.

Our Portugooses are having rare old competition of coughing tonight. Got 31 new cases in last night and filled up both wards. Nearly all are slight medicals and lots of them with very little the matter.

English Tommies suffering from these complaints would get medicine and duty if they reported sick. But these Ps are a feeble lot with no stamina. Seem to go under very easily and all look more or less TB. Have had one or two British admitted this evening, all shell shocks. One in Chapman's ward is very nervous of going to sleep with Ps in the ward, having some tale of one up the line shooting three Canadians and stabbing another and he thought perhaps the same might happen to him.

One of the excitements lately is the dramatic departure of Bownes from our little 16 party. She went home on special leave to see her fiancé and the next thing we hear she is MARRIED. Fiancé turns out to be an old patient from A Div: wounded in the head and now invalided out of service. No one seems to remember what he is like. He is a New Zealander and Bownes will go out there to live probably, so that is goodbye to little Bownesey and I am really sorry for she was a nice little person in spite of her funny independent ways. So the original party is dwindling. Some go sick and this one resigns and that one gets married and so the numbers fade away and diminish. Next thing will be a moving of one or more of us and the 16-ers will be more reduced than ever.

FRIDAY, 15TH NOVEMBER, 1.45 A.M.

Very active last night, more so than any for a long time. Two convoys of shell shocks came in and we had to take most of them, there being no room in C Div and not many beds anywhere else. So Porks and SSs are all mixed up together now. Probably a good thing for the SSs anyway. Will cheer them up and distract them a bit. Got 24 in altogether and all our beds are full now. Chapman has deserted me and Mrs Giles has come in her place. Chapman has been sent off to A instead of Cunningham, who has proceeded on day duty again and left our diminishing little Zoo party. Only five left to keep things going in the slack times. Mrs G quite nice but don't like her yet as well as Chapman. She can speak Portuguese well though, which is a great advantage as she understands the needs of the poor little foreigners and doesn't stand gaping before their flow of conversation. A Portuguese officer went dotty in B Div this evening, shouting and throwing furniture about and very violent. Had quieted him down a bit when I went over a short time ago, but they are sending him off post haste somewhere where he could be looked after better. One of the little excitements of night duty to pass the time away.

There was a further thinning of our ranks yesterday. Fletcher and Murray got orders to proceed to 11 General, most likely en route for Italy. They only heard at 9 the night before and had to be packed and off by 6, so they had a terrible scramble and not much sleep. Nor did anyone in H Hut who all witnessed the preparations, some even assisting with the packing. So now only three of our 16 party are left, C, Jobson and self, and who will be next to flit off I wonder.

Hot water bottle parade

Shouldn't much like to go to Italy really – it seems too far away and too much an unknown land, but it would certainly be a venture.

Got up early this evening, met Capt. Milne and went out for a walk with him. C thinks his eyes look as though they are glass ones! But they can't be as he appeared to be gifted with very keen vision.

WEDNESDAY, 21ST NOVEMBER, 1.30 A.M.

Only got about a fortnight more of night duty to do now. Time soon goes and the discouraging array of weeks melts away in a marvellous manner. Still having very peaceful times and though the ward keeps almost full up, nobody is bad at all so we don't need to get unduly worried. The cough trouble is still the worst disturbance of the night's peace, and we have one or two raw old barkers in the wards just now. All the SSs transferred after a night or two to the next ward and I was really rather relieved as they were a source of anxiety, especially if there was any prospect of an air raid, which would have driven them completely off their dots.

Sister Reay was down for a night on her way on leave, staying at the hospital here, much to C's joy. She must have been having a terrible time with air raids practically every night and living in dugouts with no chance of getting much sleep.*

TUESDAY, 26TH NOVEMBER, 1.15 A.M.

Had a great to-do yesterday morning in the Zoo. Terribly windy day. Whole place was shaking with it and we were all just well off to sleep when I was roused by the ominous sound of cracking and a rush of wind. I lifted up the partition curtain to investigate and saw a window, about two cubicles down, just coming out of its frame, gently but firmly. So, I tripped out of bed and went to the rescue and was only just in time to save the whole big window from crashing in. Mrs Giles, the nearest to the scene, came to my assistance while I was struggling in the throes of holding the window in the teeth of an

---

* Dorothea does not say where Sister Reay had been sent, but it may have been St Omer, very near the front.

awful beast and we got it down on the floor safely and then I had to get the assistance of one of the maids who went round outside and shut the shutters. That would have been all right but they couldn't be fixed and the wind banged them and pulled and pushed them, in spite of my best efforts with string, so that our slumbers were disturbed to say the least of it for the rest of the afternoon. Then I had to get up early to go to a farewell walk with Capt. Milne who was going today, or yesterday rather, to Trouville, so I didn't get much rest anyhow.* The window has been replaced again now by two handy khaki workmen and we had a peaceful rest yesterday to make up for lost hours. Chapman has deserted our nightbird party now and Braithwaite is on in her place.

THURSDAY, 28TH NOVEMBER, 1 A.M.

Full moon, but hidden by scurrying clouds except when they clear away for a second or two and the shining orb gets a chance to look through. Mrs Giles 'maiesto occupato' with her patients who are all waking up and getting restless. She has one bad case in K2 but none of mine are ill at all and are getting on quite well. The Night Super will be making her round before long and enquiring tenderly after the health of our patients. She is very nice and uncritical, always quite cheery and not at all the stiff sort. I haven't much more than a week on nights now. Will be quite sorry in some ways to come off, and get back into the crowded day staff, but shan't be sorry to get the more restful night's sleep, instead of spending afternoons sleeping.

* Trouville was a long way away, south of Le Havre, so it must have felt like a final parting.

MONDAY, 3RD DECEMBER, 12.55 A.M.

Very sleepy tonight for no reason I can think of
except perhaps for the cold, which for a change is
pretty severe tonight. An icy wind is blowing
and the moonlit sky is clear and cloudless.
Am sure the poor little Ports must be feeling
cold, very much not being accustomed to the
rigours of this climate. They all complain that
France is 'no bon' and that they are 'muento
frio' which no doubt they are. They sit as close
to the little stove as poss. to make the most of its available warmth.

I don't think Gerry Bosch will venture out in his aeroplanes
tonight in the teeth of such a freezing gale. Night-duty time is
getting rather short now, but I don't know if I shall come off to the
day or not. Should be Thursday if so. Really not in any hurry for the
change, though I never care for n.d. Shall miss Blake's company very
much. She has been a very good friend and we have had delightful
time together, practically never apart in off-duty hours.

*Charlie Chaplin
à la Blake*

DC and Blake

MONDAY, 10TH DECEMBER, 9.45 P.M.

AND OFF NIGHT DUTY NOW. All the dark prowling things
of the past are once more living and moving in daylight, but all the
same I am finding it a little hard to settle down to the new conditions. Really had a very happy time indeed on n.d. thanks partly to
my friendship with Blake and to the easy work and lack of pressing
responsibility in the wards. Liked my little Portugueses very much

too and quite miss them now I am away from them. Funny little Gomez in 17 – and Machado in no. 12 – always so smiling and bright. I went in to see him a day or so ago to such greeting and welcomings.

Am working up on C floor among Blake's very own specials, the old, dithery shell shocks, all shaking and stammering and looking depressed and scared – but only at times. Otherwise, they are very cheery and willing. It is a very full house up there, like a rabbit warren as we run in and out of those little rooms with their attic roofs and small windows. I like it pretty well but it takes a little getting used to.*

THURSDAY, 27TH DECEMBER, 10 P.M.

Christmas is over and all its accompanying festivities, and on the whole it was a very happy time but decidedly exhausting. Quite a cheery Xmas up in C Div with the stammerers. The augmented staff were all present including the latest arrivals, Forrester and a Staff Nurse. Far too many of us for what there is to do, for really there is hardly enough to keep one occupied much less six. It is the same everywhere, though there is an awful state of overcrowding as we wait till the Nissen huts open, when we can expand again a bit.

The Ports gave a very good concert yesterday afternoon. I wasn't able to go to it though I should have liked to. I think they all thoroughly enjoyed a brightish Xmas and appreciated the festivities, the

---

* It would seem that the shell shocks had been segregated and put into top-floor rooms in the old hotel.

officers certainly. There was great entertaining in the Mess after carol singing on Xmas Eve. Nearly all the MOs were present and there was much speechifying and drinking of healths in strong Portuguese wine, a gift from our allies. It was really very good but it went to the head a bit, not seriously certainly but I felt a bit nervous of the consequences. A lot of us were affected that way, but it certainly made a gay evening. Disgraceful though to be indulging in these hard times when people at home are economizing in every way.

SATURDAY, 5TH JANUARY 1918

The New Year has begun and what will it bring forth for all of us? A peaceful homecoming or a continuance of this strange, half-monotonous, half-unsettled existence here and the shadows of war always on our minds. The New Year is bringing me a change of work for tomorrow I am going to B floor – leaving the old doddering shell shocks and coughing TBs – to wait on the British and Pork and Beans officers. Don't somehow fancy the idea and am sorry to be leaving C floor and its queer rabbit warren of long corridors and little rooms.

Latest excitement is another batch of RRCs.* C is a recipient, Jobson another, as are two Sisters. Great congratulations going on this evening when the thrilling news was circulated. They appeared at dinner this evening with little bit of ribbon already pinned on by Matron who is quite proud of their exertions. The next event will be the receiving of the medal. Suppose that will take place while the honoured ones are on leave, unless they get a special holiday granted in order to appear before the King. A list of names was published in the papers today, so it was only when the papers came in that discovery was made. Three VADs here have got the decoration now. Wonder what the Sisters think of it all. I don't think they love Jobbie, by any means. Her manner aggravates them, but I think C's is received with approbation.

---

* The Royal Red Cross Award (nothing to do with the BRCS) was instituted by Queen Victoria in 1883, for exceptional services in military nursing. There were two categories: Member and Associate. The Associate Award was given to Dorothea posthumously.

Was out last night till 11.15, frivoling at a very excellent performance given by the officers of 14 Stationary and Sisters from the
Anglo-American Hospital. It was a sort of skit on *Chuchinchow*,[*]
with some of the music from the play and the same sort of plot.
Really pretty and well carried out. The dresses were very artistic and
eastern and quite becoming to the wearers. The performance was
held in Wimereux canteen (not nearly big enough hall for size of
audience anxious to be admitted) and Mitchie, Eden and I got there
very early, determined not to lose the chance of a place – we had
passes to admit us but those didn't ensure us places. Two other VADs
came presently and we were all just inside the door wondering what
to do next, when Capt. Lyall and five other 32 officers came pushing
in. We fell in with their procession and marched into excellent seats
in the centre of the room and sat tight not meaning to be moved,
if possible. And no one made any demur, so we saw beautifully
and considered ourselves very well off. Nearly a mob among the
Tommies outside – hundreds couldn't get in and had to be turned
away. They were quite indignant and nearly burst in the doors, but
burly military police came to rescue and thrust out the invaders. We
came back in the darkness, well-escorted with our attendant MOs,
and felt we had had a great evening's frivolity in wartime.

FRIDAY, 11TH JANUARY, 7 P.M.

Nearing the end of a 'perfect half-day' and bed is well in view, after
an early supper. Quite an executive afternoon – succeeded in visiting
Sister Hobbs of 14 General who looked after Al, and Sisters Garrett
and Gower at 14 Stationary. Had tea with the latter, my second tea,
having already had a meal at the Club with C. Am now quite ready
for bed and rather tired after the frivolity of Wednesday night when
a reception was given by the new recipients of RRC to the nursing and medical staff of hospital. All foregathered in our Mess and
entertainment was provided in the shape of 'book titles'. We all went

---

[*] *Chuchinchow*, based on the Ali Baba story, was the smash hit musical in London that ran for
five years after its premiere on 3 August 1916. It was a favourite show for troops on leave.

representing a book – medical officers as well, as several of them appeared in disguise. Mr Lammar, the Portuguese, came dressed as a Jock. Capt. Lindsay made up wonderfully well as Capt. Kettle. Some of the whatnots were present in costume (a few of the VADs dressed up for the occasion too). We had quite a good time but no dancing was allowed by Matron-in-Chief's orders. So we had to manage with music and singing, except for the little interlude when C, Eden and M. Castro-Lammar danced the Vida – the Portuguese national dance – with great effect.

Blake etc. came back from leave last night and are installed in the new huts, as they are at last opened and accommodating most of the occupants of H – but not all, much to their disgust. Three masseuses arrived today. What on earth they are going to do I can't imagine, but rumour has it that we are soon to be busy again – and with British too – so maybe they are sent for a purpose.

Leave is happily in sight. Haven't so very long to wait for it now and then! Once more for Blighty and here endeth this vol. of my diary.

PART THREE

No. 46 Stationary, Étaples

JANUARY 1918 – MARCH 1919

Dorothea is sitting on the ground, second from the right.

SATURDAY, 19TH JANUARY, 8.15 P.M.

A suitable occasion to open a new vol. of diary, to celebrate our arrival in a new and strange abode. New faces, new work, new surroundings, another phase in this active service life of ours. After fifteen months of 32 Stationary with all its varied activities, its changes, its pleasures and its trials, we have been whisked away and planted down now in this queer place – an isolation hospital for measles, mumps, scarlet fever etc., all sorts of things we have never had to do with before. Never in my wildest flights of imagination did I picture ourselves being landed in a place like this.*

The dire news came to us on Monday morning just about 11 o'clock when we – that is C, Reeve and I – were all peacefully employed in our various stations, carrying on with our appointed duties. Matron being away on special leave, Sister Harrison broke the news to us, though I at least first heard from Sister Slingsby, who had gleaned the news from the Colonel. Anyway, we were told to go off at once and set to pack with all speed, as we had to catch an afternoon train and an ambulance was coming for us at 12.30! There followed a hectic hour when we struggled with the packing, manfully assisted by friends who did wonders in the way of stowing our goods. I never imagined I could have got away in such a short time considering all the things I had. We all had to leave a good deal behind, but not such a vast amount all things considering. Just a hurried lunch before we went, a very few speedy goodbyes and then the three of us were off

* Étaples became a huge British military encampment during the war, and shared with Boulogne and Rouen the distinction of having nine British military hospitals, the highest number anywhere in France. No. 46 had always been an 'isolation' hospital, catering for patients with infectious diseases. It had been the Isolation Block of No. 24 General, the next-door hospital, from July 1915 to March 1917, before it became independent as No. 46 Stationary. It continued only to have medical, not surgical, wards.

to our new sphere of action, sent away ruthlessly from friends and pleasantly familiar surroundings

Not a very long journey to Étaples, our destination. We were turned out there on to the dreary, strange platform and the clerk at the RTO's office rang up for an ambulance to convey us to 46. After a little delay we were whisked away up here and planted down, bag and baggage, in our new home. The quarters are quite nice, though possibly very cold in parky weather. Haven't tested them yet in a frosty spell. The House VAD took us to Matron's office and we were all interviewed in turn by Miss McCord.* She is not a regular and used to be in charge of Croydon, where Giles Chapman worked. A rather hard-looking little woman and dried up, but not very alarming to talk to. C and I have been given a room together and Reeve is next door and we settled in as well as we could to the new abode. We ate our second breakfast of the morning and then had another interview with Matron, the result of which is that C and Reeve went to the wards and I came into the Mess to run round with plates and dishes and minister to the needs of the staff. I am very lucky in having two extremely friendly VADs to work with – one being quite a possible friend, when I get to know her better.

Since Tuesday I have been gradually settling down to this new life and am not finding it too bad, but certainly it feels a bit strange still. C has gone on night duty tonight which is sad as we have to part again so soon, but I am getting Williams – my co-worker in the Mess – in her place, so I won't be so badly off after all. C is in seventh heaven, having Sister Reay† so near on night duty. She sees her every day and worships more and more at her shrine.

The hospital is not so very large and not at all busy just now. Ours is the busiest job of any, I should think. I went to Étaples one day and found it a bigger place than I expected and with some quite possible shops in it. Paris-Plage, which we went to yesterday, is quite a metropolis. This place is one vast camp and just round here the

---

* Miss M. F. McCord was Matron at No. 46 throughout Dorothea's time there.
† The Australian Theatre Sister with whom C worked closely at Wimereux.

hospitals and camps are crowded thickly. All the various bases are in the vicinity and everywhere is seething with khaki and representatives of an expeditionary force, in every shape and kind. It is very interesting in a way to be at such a big base, but I miss old 32 all the same and above all I miss the sea, which is a good way from here and can only be reached by a tram-ride to Paris Plage. Wonder how long we shall be here before we get our next push on. Perhaps we shall see the end of the war here – who knows!

TUESDAY, 22ND JANUARY

Am writing on duty, a shocking thing to do, but really there seems nothing to keep me employed just now. Sister is having half-day so I am left to my own devices for afternoon and evening. Have had a move into the wards, temporarily probably, as the Mess is short-handed now, but while so many changes are in progress Matron has seen fit to put me here to fill a gap, so I am back with the 'bhoys' again.

I had a half-day yesterday and Sister was off in the morning. There are only the two of us for the ward and we shall just alternate with our off duty. It was a nice afternoon yesterday and I went up to play hockey, having promised one of VADs that I would go and try my legs at a match got up by officers and MOs from our hospital and some other energetic young women from the neighbourhood. Was quite enjoying the game, which was held on a fine open ground just at the back of this place in the convalescent camp. And then a sudden twist and my knee gave, in the old tiresome manner, landing me on the ground, precluding me from the rest of the game. Very stiff today but hopeful it will be better tomorrow. No more hockey though for me, if this is to be the result of my efforts.

Must go now and take temps. Some of the patients are not malade at all and very uproarious, particularly three Canadian boys, who are always in a state of immense energy.

TUESDAY, 29TH JANUARY

Another week gone by and the strangeness and novelty of this place is wearing off a bit. I am beginning to feel rather more at home, but am still longing for the old days at 32, though I fear they are never to come again. One's life out here seems to have such distinct phases. A move brings such an absolute change of scene and surroundings and one never seems to get the chance of ever taking one glimpse back into the past stages. Tréport seems a sort of dream now and soon 32 will drift back to the same haze of recollections. Have seen very little of C since she went on night duty. She is out every available moment with Sister Reay, basking in her presence and her smiles. Williams makes a very nice 'sleeping partner' and we fit in quite well or have done so far. Still down in my dips ward* and getting to know the men better now. There are some quite nice ones among them, but they are rather a rowdy company as so many are up-patients.

Had one great excitement this past week in the shape of a visit from 'wee man' [brother Alastair]. So delighted when Assistant Matron came down to tell me he had come and I was to see him at 5, when I came off duty. He is just on his way home for leave, lucky boy – the leave I was mulcted of by coming here. Rumour has it that all leave will be stopped at the end of February for two months, so what chance of getting home before summer, what what! Al and I had a delightful little dinner together in the town at a café, then came back here again after a little stroll down the road beyond. We parted, he to go back to the station and I to return to this strange work-a-day life. Have been having glorious nights of moonshine lately, alas too glorious, for news has come of very bad air raids in London and some more innocent victims of this ferocity.

Williams and I went for a long and very pleasant walk a day or two ago inland and got to a most wonderful viewpoint, where we looked down on the country for miles around spreading into the dim distance and rolling hills. It must be very pretty in the spring and I am quite looking forward to coming of better weather so as to be able to explore the neighbourhood.

Williams tells me tonight that Sister Reay has got her moving orders, so there will be some weeping and gnashing of teeth at that fell blow!

* The diphtheria ward.

SUNDAY, 3RD FEBRUARY

Nice long evening in bed and four letters written, which causes me untold joy. Only as fast as I write them, more come and I always have umpteen on my mind waiting to be answered. It is not so cold tonight, which is a blessing. The last few days have been freezing and we dropped right back into winter after the lovely warm weather of last week. Really everything was looking very pretty in the country round here and there was an anticipation of spring, which was very cheery and pleasant.

Last Friday, I went with Williams to one of the camp orchestra's performances, an evening entertainment at 8.45 and a programme consisting entirely of Gilbert and Sullivan. It was an excellent show and there were first-rate soloists – three men singers and a VAD from the St John's A, looking very nice in her clean uniform and she sang very well indeed. I really thoroughly enjoyed the concert and the nice fresh pretty music, all so familiar and well known. The hall was crowded to the door with officers and nursing staff. Yesterday afternoon, Williams introduced me to the local Club corresponding to the Wimereux one and I became a member at the cost of fr 2. Quite a nice place and will be lovely in the summer for a haven of refuge in tiring weather.

THURSDAY, 7TH FEBRUARY

Williams and I just completed a hearty bedroom meal of Maggi soup, concocted by self on the little Beatrice stove,* and bread and butter abducted from the Mess. Café au lait followed our soup, biscuits, honey and jam. We also prepared dessert of two apples, but felt too compleat to partake of them. I meant to do a lot of writing tonight, but the supper preparations have taken up such a lot of time that it is getting fairly late now and I shan't get much writing done, after all.

Had a very lazy evening off, my only exercise a little trip to Murray Hut to get tickets for tomorrow night's concert (Lena Ashwell) and to

---

* A portable paraffin stove.

the Post Office to pay for a sketch skilfully pressed upon me by one of the post officials – who is by way of being an artist and really sketches very nicely – and then to large and sumptuous canteen, full to overflowing with all sorts of things we never could get at Wimereux, biscuits and cigarettes, chiefly. There were oceans of jam, tinned fruit, sausages and even camp furniture, boots, shoes and stockings, which our canteens never aspired to in the same abundant manner. Came back armed with two tins of cigs. Straightaway had a glorious hot bath, then settled in for the evening at home and supper chez soi.

Had rather a busy afternoon on duty, one patient, little Kelly, is very ill indeed. I thought, during the early afternoon, that he wasn't long for this world, but he pulled up a bit later and I left him a little more comfortable. He came in apparently with bad tonsillitis but it seems as though he must have had some other complications. Has failed so suddenly when he really seemed to be getting on well. The other patients are difficult to keep in order and are getting too lively to abide their enforced recumbent posture. Also their appetites are much too keen for the very light diet and food – their cruel treatment in being denied something solid is a favourite subject of ardent discussion. Our end of the ward is pretty full up with bed cases now, which keeps us busier, running round looking after them and also keeping them in order.

TUESDAY, 12TH FEBRUARY

Shrove Tuesday, but no pancakes, at least not so far. Maybe they will turn up for lunch or dinner. Winter seems well on its way when Lent begins and really we have had very little cold weather so far, which is lucky. Nothing like last year. Yesterday I was enjoying Al's company. He came here on his way back from leave on Sunday evening. I got off at 5 and spent a delightful time with him. We had dinner in town, as before at our little restaurant, and then he went to the Officers' Club for the night. I persuaded him to go by a later train yesterday morning, so saw him again till 12 when he departed by the leave train for Arras and I was able to speed him away from the station. It was delightful seeing him and I hope to get another glimpse of him, if he can manage to come down here from the battalion, which he thinks is quite possible. I never saw such an awful ramshackle old thing as the leave train, made up of all the oldest French coaches imaginable. Most of the windows were broken and replaced by boards just roughly wedged in. All the doors looked as though they were never meant to shut and would burst open at any moment. However, this seems usual condition of these trains, and the travellers were taking it all very calmly.

Had rather a strenuous week and Kelly, the little boy who was so ill, died on Saturday afternoon. He was requiring a great deal of attention before a Sister came to special him and was with him when he died. Sister London was off duty. His people never came and it seems doubtful now whether they were sufficiently notified, but he was ill so short a time it was possible they wouldn't have reacted in time anyway. Eleven patients – all the rowdy and hard-working up-patients – went to Blighty this morning, so we are left with 23 mostly in bed and some of them are very rowdy too. They don't know what to do with themselves and the exuberance of their energy requires a good deal of squashing to keep them in order.

FRIDAY, 22ND FEBRUARY

Have been half-daying and I cut supper again which is now against all rules and regulations, unless with special permission from Matron which I haven't got. However, Williams, being in the Mess, had excused me and promised not to give me away to the higher authorities. The inhabitants of the next room are telling ghost stories, trying to make their blood curdle. We can hear every sound in the next cubicles with their scrim partitions. Rather a disadvantage sometimes, when the next-door neighbours are of this talkative, sociable, entertaining sort, up to all hours of the night.

Our wounded boy in the ward is still hanging on in a marvellous manner and really seems better – certainly his diphtheria is much improved. We still have an extra Sister in to help and we are all kept quite busy, especially when the dressing has to be done which takes a long time and seems to me is always a bit fuddled. Collins, our big

Guardsman – 6ft 6ins – and Jordan, our bantam, are both getting up now in the afternoons. Haven't been in blues* yet but I am looking forward to seeing them together when they are both up and dressed.

MONDAY, 25TH FEBRUARY

This is night of full moon and consequently it is brilliant, fine and clear. After a blustery, squally February day with a soupçon of the coming spring in it, the clouds have all blown away and the moon and stars are shining out serenely. There will be some dirty work on both sides tonight for sure. Nothing came this way yet, but one never knows. There was an alert on Friday night. All lights went out at about 8.45 for twenty minutes or so, but nothing happened and we got our night's sleep undisturbed.

Have very much enjoyed a weekend visit from the 'wee man' who slipped away from his soldiering duties to come and look me up. It is not so long since he came back from leave, but it seems much more than just a week or so. He turned up on Saturday afternoon, close on the heels of Capt. Milne, who was going on leave and took the opportunity to break his journey and also pay us a visit. He could only stay a very short time but I entertained him to tea. He on one side, and Al on the other, and I felt very elated with my two visitors. Unwisely I went to Matron and got a refusal from her to go out at all with either of my visitors, it being a very strict rule in the camp that one shouldn't be seen out with an officer – even a brother – nor somebody else's brother. So we had to stay in the sitting room circumspectly, but yesterday I met Al outside and we slipped down to the town and had our usual very pleasant little meal at the small café and were entertained by the charming host and hostess. This morning again, having begged a morning off duty, I went down to the same shop with C and Al. We had a cup of coffee together in great amity. Al was going back by the leave train at 12, the same rackety arrangement that he went in last time.

---

* Convalescent soldiers who were still on the sick list wore a pale blue uniform.

Our poor boy, who was so ill in the ward, died on Saturday at 10.30 after a week's terrible misery and he had suffered a lot before that too. Tonight we got our two new arrivals, but neither are very bad. Sister Aitken is still helping us, but expects to go on leave quite soon.

MONDAY, 4TH MARCH

Had a busy evening on duty in the ward now that we have so many bad patients. They make a lot of work and bed-making is a large item too. Sister Aitken departed again to take charge of two Sister-less wards – three more of the staff having had moving orders – so 'Bunty' and I are on our own again. We have all had days off this past week, Sister L first, then Sister A and then me on Saturday. Unfortunately, my morning was rather spoilt by my getting a head-ache through lazifying at the usual energetic hour, and feeling very so-so and squeamish till I had had a good walk with Williams in the biting wind and snow to a little village called Frencq a short distance away. This bucked me up again and I felt quite restored in the evening, especially after an early retiring to bed and a nice little supper chez soi.

Last Thursday night I went to an excellent orchestral concert, with solos interspersed. It really was one of the best I have been to and I thoroughly enjoyed it. Went with two of the Sisters and Williams joined us later, when she could get away from the Mess. C and I signed for our leave on Saturday. What hopes now I wonder? Two VADs went away on Friday, so perhaps we shall go when they come back from their holiday. Anyway, it is something to have signed and we feel more cheered about our prospects.

THURSDAY, 14TH MARCH

More than a week has slipped by since last writing, not a very inci-dental interval of time, except this last day or two. Yesterday brought the reappearance of Alastair and consequent delight on my part. He has turned up now for a course of Lewis Gunnery at the school down at Le Touquet. It is just a week's course but anyway, a joy to have him here and away from the line, even that space of time. He is very cheerful and pleased to have been sent here and certainly is a stroke of luck, as there was a chance of him being despatched to the trench mortar school near Arras which wouldn't have given me a chance to see him. He had lunch here and we met again in the evening and look forward to several meetings, if I don't get leave before he goes. C is getting agitated about leave and there seems no further prospect of it, but we are rather hoping to get away this next week when two other VADs come back. Capt. Milne called on Monday on his way back from leave and I got a morning off to spend renewing our acquaintance and wandering about the woods by the chateau. It was a glorious morning, hot as summer, so we had quite a nice time.

Have an extra VAD in my ward now, one newly come to the hospital, with three others, straight from Brighton. Two are Assistant Nurses but haven't quite focused their position yet – something between VADs and Staff Nurses. The ward is still pretty full and there are crowds of up patients, which isn't altogether a joy when the ward has to be kept tidy – but they are a hard-working lot, which is a comfort.

TUESDAY, 19TH MARCH

The rain is pattering down on the frail roof overhead tonight. Quite an unfamiliar sound after almost weeks of fine weather. Has been a real wet day but warm, no wind. I am still enjoying Al's occasional visits and had a lovely half-day with him on Sunday. We drove to Paris-Plage and spent an afternoon on the sands, enjoying the delightful fresh air and the sea and the lights and shades over the sand dunes. Really a very pretty afternoon for colouring and I think we both enjoyed our jaunt to the full. We had dinner in a restaurant at PP seated in a little private sitting room, overlooking the street

in case the DDMS should happen to fancy the same resort for his dinner. Then we came back to the camp in a taxi, most frivolously. Proper square pushing and wild extravagance in wartime. I should have seen A this evening too, but Sister elected to have a half-day so I had to be content as possible with the morning off.

The question of leave is still concerning us, C and I. C went about it yesterday and again today and elicited no more cheering an answer than that we were next due to go – which of course we knew very well – and that Matron couldn't let us go just now because some of her staff were being taken away and she couldn't see how she could spare us. We feel quite discouraged because we did hope to depart when the other two came back and now leave looks as far off as ever – perhaps we shall have to wait till Greenwell comes back. It is quite sickening. C is expecting to come off night duty soon, but has heard nothing definite about that either. I bought some chevrons for her and some for myself to swank about with at home – three blue ones for our long service out here. Next June we shall be due for another, which will make quite a brave show, but we don't want any more thank you. Would rather go home and enjoy the comforts of peace.

Had a concert yesterday in the convalescent end of our ward. The harmonium was again requisitioned and a VAD named Robinson came down and played and did her very best to keep things going. She really worked nobly and played and sang with great zest. The men seemed quite to enjoy the sing-song, even with the wheezy little hurdy-gurdy groaning out its accompaniment. Ferguson, another VAD, came in for a short time and sang some songs and Sister reappeared in her off duty, so we had quite a gathering. The night before there was a whist drive in the wards so the prize-giving for that preceded the concert. Ferguson was whisked away to the tanks for duty there on Monday, so I am left alone in my glory. There seems plenty to do with so many patients. Have been quite busy all day today.

SUNDAY, 24TH MARCH, 10 P.M.

We had a sad disappointment, C and I, this morning. We were to have been swabbed preparatory to departing on leave and then the order came through that all leave was stopped. C has just come off night duty and I came away at 8.45 from the ward after bidding a tender farewell. Now, after a day off to console us a bit, we have to go back on duty. Since Thursday when the horrible German attack started, there has been nothing but the wildest rumours flying around. What we have lost and what we have held, huge casualties and awful carnage. It's all so ghastly to think of. There is some truth in the rumours but also a great deal of exaggeration and one cannot believe half one hears. Anyway, though we have been driven back a bit, the case is not desperate by today's account and the Huns may give up the attack as hopeless.* C is worrying about Sister Reay, the fighting is all down in the part where she is, not far from La Fère, and I am anxious about Al who went back up there again last Thursday morning. The Guards will probably be in the fray somewhere, but I hope they will be kept at Arras further north.†

We had the wind up last night at about 9 p.m. Lights out and almost immediately the Archies‡ began, the enemy machine or machines were plainly heard coming from the direction of Camiers. They were flying low, so there was not much anti-aircraft after them. In a minute or two there were some terrific bangs, which we all knew were bombs dropping somewhere. After this, the planes seemed to do a tour round or were driven off by our machines and gradually the hum dwindled away and the excitement subsided, although the staff were all wandering to and fro in various stages of attire. We had a little concourse in the passage and sat on the steps till everything was over. C and Sister Searle and some stray wanderers kept each other company.

---

* The Second Battle of the Somme began on 21 March when the Germans launched their Spring Offensive. See Chronology, p. 354.
† This was precisely where they were, desperately holding the line in the area of Hénin, about four miles south of Arras.
‡ Anti-aircraft guns.

C and I went across the fields by the railway this afternoon to see the damage where the bombs had been dropped. One was nearly on the railway track. They only just missed by a hair'sbreadth and the other two holes were further back and had done no damage except to the marshy field. The Bosch was probably trying for the railway bridge over the river and he wasn't far off either. These are the first bombs that have been dropped over Étaples, but probably not the last by a long way.

Latest rumour has it that we will have to go through a gas test as Fritz has taken to dropping gas shells. That will be a nuisance, but I suppose it has to be included in the hazards of war. Bunty is on night duty now. Sister Searle,* who to my intense pleasure turned up here for duty on Wednesday, was sent to G to take her place by a wonderful stroke of luck, so I am very happy in that way. It is delightful having her here at the hospital to befriend me. The question now is *when* shall we get our leave? But I mustn't think about it too much. Suppose it will all come right some day.

FRIDAY, 29TH MARCH

Good Friday and a time of dust and ashes. Certainly the past week has been an anxious one, and for the first few days, one's hearts sank pretty low. There was an atmosphere of unrest and alarm perhaps created partly by a lot of fussy women, as sometimes we seem to be, but the bad news came from outside sources – from the crowds of men coming in wounded, the tales of Sisters down from evacuated CCSs and numbers of other people who had some woeful tale to tell. Anyway, the Germans were advancing quickly and fiercely and the fighting was terrific. We heard of first one place and then another being taken and everyone was beseeching for news and when it was told it only made our hearts sink deeper. Amiens had fallen several times according to rumour and Abbeville was hourly expecting a complete and rapid evacuation. We all felt very heavy-hearted – at least not all, for there were some optimistic ones – as our two chiefs

---

* One of Dorothea's favourite Sisters from No. 16.

were more depressed than any. Matron had quite made up her mind we should have to pack up and fly – unless the Germans were too quick for us and we were all taken prisoner.*

The news is slightly more hopeful now, but no one has received news from any relations in the fearful fighting. I suppose there has been no time or chance to send any sort of message. I don't believe the people at home realize what the state of affairs are, they don't see the men straight from the line or know of the panic that comes with the steady advance of the enemy. It certainly has not all been plain sailing for us. I went with Williams to the 6.30 service and was pleased to see such a large gathering of men and the three-hour devotional service was well attended. I believe the camp just now seems packed with soldiers. There is just a solid stream up and down the main camp road, of all conceivable regiments and departments.

WEDNESDAY, 10TH APRIL

A time of suspense and waiting, while the [German] offensive pauses, to be renewed anon with fresh vigour. Easter has come and gone since last writing. It was a quiet, rather sad Easter with thoughts of the appalling losses – on both sides – that the awful fighting was causing. Several of us went at 6 to the early service at the big military church. Quite a nice simple service and a smallish congregation – mostly Tommies from the neighbouring camps. I spent the evening off duty in the woods with Williams, getting wild flowers, which just now are lovely and so abundant – anemones chiefly and periwinkles, like patches of blue carpet, violets and cowslips and now the wild hyacinths are beginning to come out and the woods will soon be full of them.

All this week past the weather has been very unsettled and really only last Sunday has been fine the whole day through. I suppose we are paying now for the lovely March, but it doesn't matter as the wet must be baulking to the Germans, and certainly soon after Easter the first big push fizzled out and things began to quieten down. But

---

* Matron's readiness to 'pack up and fly' would have been quite appropriate if the Germans had been successful in their offensive. See Chronology, p. 354.

since the offensive began the camps have been a real beehive for business, crowded with troops coming, going, concentrating, drilling and recuperating, and new tents and huts seem to have shot up like mushrooms everywhere there are clear spaces. One positively has to elbow one's way down the road into the town now, all the men being given free pass in and out of the camp. It is too dangerous I suppose to try and keep such numbers within bounds after the mobs last year.*

Have seen a few Coldstreamers, not very many and I haven't spoken to any of them yet, but I intend to one day to see if I can find out how the regiment is faring. This is now the Headquarters of the Life Guards – such big, fine-looking men and such a contrast to the misshapen undersized little creatures one sees so many of, rigged up in khaki fighting for King and Country. I was struck today, going into town, by the youth of the troops. We really can't say anything about the boys in the Bosch army when we have such children in our own.† I expect a good many are new drafts just come out from England, but it seems sad to have to depend on such a lot of boys to fight our battles for us.

Yesterday and today I have met old patients from 32, which rather pleased me. I came across a man called Jones who used to be in K ward and then was in the convalescent section for a long time. This evening I met a boy, a New Zealander, who used to assist at the bathing parties last summer, rowing the boat and giving instruction on swimming. Had quite a little gossip with him about old times. We have a Yankee in the ward now, one of a few new admittances since last writing, a quaint, talkative creature with very scholarly aspect wearing large horn-rimmed round goggles and doing much studying of some deep works. He is an orderly at the American Hospital at Camiers and evidently considers himself a good deal.

---

* This was the notorious mutiny of September 1917, which began when a soldier was arrested and jailed for visiting Le Touquet, then out of bounds to troops. Vera Brittain, who was serving as a VAD in Étaples at the time, refers to it in her memoir *Testament of Youth*.
† The official minimum age was eighteen, but there were many boys in the Army who had lied about their age.

TUESDAY, 15TH APRIL

Afternoon visitations – one to Sister Searle and one to C next door. Have now come to bed, glad to get that refuge from the cold which is prevailing at present. For the last day or two – in fact since Friday – the weather has been very bad. Cold and damp, and yesterday and the day before there was a violent gale blowing, raising up clouds of dust to the intense discomfort of everyone passing up and down the camp road.

Williams and I had a half day together on Thursday and spent a gorgeous afternoon going out to Camiers, walking all the way there because the chance of a lift failed us but getting a good deal of interest out of the movements of troops on either side of the road. Since the push began the camp has developed considerably – the old 'bull ring'* training ground is now occupied by a GSC camp with lines of horses and mules tethered to their ropes and rows of wagons and carts stretching up the hill. Another part is occupied by the trained messenger dogs, each with its separate kennel, a little enclosure and its rations in a sack on the roof of the house. There are all sorts and kinds of dogs – mongrels and curs, but mostly of the sort of Airedale and Collie description with some Retriever thrown in. As they are fed they are bombed vigorously to accustom them to the noise, the bombs presumably being harmless ones, or there wouldn't be much left of the dogs of war.

Williams and I pursued our way into Camiers Camp and I left a note with Sister Reay from Ellis and saw her very busy at work in the theatre as a case was brought in. Then, we had tea at the Club and lay out in the garden, basking in the lovely sunshine. Afterwards we went home, getting a lift in a most lovely open car driven by an official of the motor ambulances, with another official seated beside her who kindly offered us the lift.

We went on Saturday evening to an entertainment at the Mt Lebanon Cinema given by the Sunshine Party in aid of the Serbian

* The troops gave this name to the vast stretch of land beyond the hospitals, which was used as a training ground throughout the war.

Fund that Sgt Major Flora Sandes* was collecting for. She herself appeared in the interval, attired in her Serbian uniform, a fine handsome grey-haired woman with such a nice face, so round and cheery and sensible, and she spoke a few words, getting quite an ovation. She has been with the army throughout the campaign and is going back to it after a short leave. She must have been through a good deal for she was wounded very badly once and saved at the greatest risk by some Serbian soldiers when she had nearly been made prisoner; so she has done her bit. The place was packed and the audience very appreciative.

The feeling was very tense that evening as the Germans were then in the height of their second push and making strides towards Calais, rather too successfully. We were all feeling rather depressed but the fun of the show did us all good and certainly there seemed no great tendency to depression in the spirits of the audience. Things seem to have quietened down again now – at least there is a comparative lull up the line in the fighting – but this is probably only temporary. We are anxiously awaiting the next move but the feeling everywhere is very optimistic, probably a reaction from the dark days we have been through lately. The camp seems emptier now – great drafts of men go away every day – but there always seem more to go, so our army has some reserves yet.

SATURDAY, APRIL 20TH

After a bitter cold morning of heavy frost and then later a blizzard for a short time, this evening is lovely and just like spring again.

---

* It was appropriate that, just at the tensest moment in the German offensive, one of the most remarkable women of the First World War should turn up in Étaples. Sergeant Major Flora Sandes of the Serbian Army was the personification of the English tomboy. Before the war she had been brought up in Suffolk, where she learnt to ride, shoot and drive her old racing car. She volunteered to be a nurse when war broke out but was turned down due to lack of qualifications. Instead she joined a St John Ambulance unit and went to Serbia, but with the medical services in disarray as the Serbian Army retreated, she joined a military unit instead, serving as a fighting soldier with the rank of Corporal and later Sergeant Major. She was seriously wounded in hand-to-hand combat, but was given the highest Serbian military decoration for gallantry. Wearing her Serbian uniform and the decoration, she toured Great Britain and the British hospitals in France, raising money for the Serbian Army.

Truly we do go through some changes of atmospheric conditions these days. War news seems no better but today it is no worse or at least it wasn't yesterday. Everyone thinks we are in a parlous condition and certainly things look very black indeed, but are we downhearted? No! After those first few days of panic when the Bosch pushed forward nearly to Amiens, we seem to have settled down very gravely, but still gatheredly, to await events and hope for the best. The Germans are only 46 miles away from here – not so very much after all when one considers that they nearly covered that distance in that first offensive. Well, if we have to go packing to Blighty we shall have to make the best of a bad job and retire to the safety of our own shores in as dignified a manner as possible.*

A hospital has just arrived today from St Omer – No. 9 Stationary (Canadian) – and I went along to the 'bull ring' training ground nearby to see what it was doing with itself and how the preparations were getting on. All the hospital equipment and stuff was dumped at the side of the road in a confused mass looking pretty hopeless, but the orderlies waiting there seemed happy enough in spite of the hard work before them. There is said to be another hospital setting up just beyond the 'cemetery',† a very cheerful neighbourhood. All the hospitals except CCSs are moving from St Omer and soon it will be another of these poor, stricken towns deserted by its inhabitants, as rats desert a sinking ship. The cemetery is a pathetic sight these days, especially in the early days of the offensive. There are literally thousands of new graves. No one can guess how the men have been dying like flies in these base hospitals, and this is only one base. Our losses must have been terrible.

My little friend L/Cpl Docker came down here wounded and landed at 56 General. He wrote to me and the letter took two days to reach me, so I only had one day to see him before he went to Blighty, but I managed to spend a very nice afternoon sitting with him sharing a great 'crack'. He had a broken leg, painful but not a very bad

---

* The Battle of the Lys was not yet over. See Chronology, p. 354.
† The military cemetery was just to the north of the hospitals area, and nowhere near the post-war Imperial War Graves site which is 1.5 kilometres north of the town.

wound fortunately. He was hurried back with the Div. he was in from Italy and plunged straight into the fighting. There seemed to be no organization. Contradictory orders were given continually, they had no food before they were sent forward and just pretty well had to fend for themselves and then he was wounded quite soon after they got into the fight. The stories one hears of the continual bungling and mismanagement of the troops are not very encouraging certainly. Mr Poole, our MO, asserts that the leadership of our army is rotten, and that is why we are doing so badly, and maybe he is right. Certainly we don't seem to have very gifted strategists in practice anyway.

After a long, rather anxious interval of waiting for news of Al, I was much relieved to receive a letter from him and find he was quite safe and out of the line when he wrote and that he had got his second 'pip' and was now a full Lieutenant. I wonder what part of line his division will be sent to next. Right into the thick of it somewhere, I expect.

This hospital is still very slack. Our ward has never been so light, but we have a nice set of men and manage to enjoy ourselves, notwithstanding the absence of work. C has moved into the next room here and we can carry on a conversation through the thin partition. It's almost as good as being in the same room but not quite.

SATURDAY, 27TH APRIL

Finds me back on the creeping, crawling night duty again, a very unwilling victim. I was sent for yesterday morning and beamingly told by Matron that I was to go on n.d. However, the news was not at all beamingly received – in fact I pulled a face – but of course it had to be. I was so much distressed by the change that I didn't take proper notice of what she told me and failed to take in the fact that I was to report at the office at 8 p.m … So, this evening I gaily went down to 9 ward, fully equipped, planted myself down there, went gossiping with the patients, took a report from a VAD in 15 about the patients there and generally made myself at home. The next thing was that the Night Super came in to send me up to the office and I went there at once to find a fuming Matron, furiously angry because neither I nor Read, who has also come on n.d., had appeared and she was very late for dinner in consequence. I just stood dumb before her outburst and the next I knew was that I had been ordered off to the tanks* to begin work there in an absolutely unknown field of operation with strange patients. Felt 'fed to the teeth'! Read got her wigging soon after mine, having to pursue the irate Matron to the dining room, and she has taken my place in the dip. wards. We are both very sick about it, feeling we could do so much better the other way round. But there it is; one must put up with these caprices and make the best of it, only it doesn't tend to make the first night much more agreeable or easy.

I have four wards of 21 beds to look after and nearly all are full. No one is bad, so it has been a cushy job so far. There is one orderly for three wards and another ward under the surveillance of an orderly at the top of the line. There are no bunks† here, so I sit in one of the wards by the stove and listen to the snores of the sleepers. I go over to the Office for supper, our one excitement for the night – otherwise no one seems to bother their heads about one down here. I feel werry lonely, separated from all my dearest friends and sent away just when everything was so nice. I don't know what Sister Searle will say in the morning. She will expect to find me on duty and we promised to see each other as soon as possible. She will find Reeve ministering there, so all our little plans have been frustrated and my nice boys, that I was so sorry to leave after nearly three months in that ward, will be rather grieving too I hope, but not so much as I am. Feel no very friendly feeling towards all these strangers round about here, but perhaps I will feel differently after a night or two, when I get to know them better.

I'm a bit stiff still from the result of yesterday's exertions at NZ Sports. I went with Sisters Porteous and Beesly and VAD Riley. The two former departed at teatime, leaving us two half-dayers to

* An undefined term in this context, but in January 1918 Miss McCarthy had visited No. 46, and noted that a new division of 200 beds had recently been added, and that these were in Nissen huts. 'Tanks' must have been a colloquial term for these huts.
† A separate nurse's cubicle.

disport ourselves as we liked. Three more of our staff were there, so we joined up later and enjoyed ourselves muchly, chiefly over the tug of war in which we competed against WAACs.* We had three great pulls, the third one to decide the winner and we came off victorious, after a most strenuous tussle. It really was great sport and the audience – all Tommies and officers – gave us a most enthusiastic backing, getting thoroughly worked up over the event. We were given tea afterwards at the Officers' Mess and then seen home by two nice NZ padres – respectable company for the young and frivolous.

FRIDAY, 3RD MAY, EARLY MORNING

In the small hours and getting rapidly to that disagreeable stage of somnolence, which is so much associated with this night duty. Of all detestable things about this existence, these sensations are the most acutely disagreeable. You try to prop your eyelids open again and again and they are closing again the next minute. Your brain begins to feel dizzy. You lose your grip on the surroundings and the immediate situation. Your head nods and you come to life with a violent start and tingling of nerves to your very fingertips. You make another desperate effort to shake off the somnolence. You sit bolt upright and take up your book firmly and set to work to read with great intentness only to find that in another minute the same thing happens again and you pass through the same disagreeable routine of sensations. Finally, you either give in and have a short snooze which gives you only very modified satisfaction or you get up and stagger round the ward wondering if you've got a large squidgy wad of cotton wool for a head or if you'll ever feel wide awake again. I am rapidly approaching these stages now, but am trying hard to stave off the evil hour when sleep overcomes me.

* The Women's Auxiliary Army Corps, a forerunner of the ATS in the Second World War and later the WRAC.

Didn't have an extra good day's rest. Went latish to bed and then woke at 5 or a little before and lay most of the rest of the evening. My sleeping companion, in an excess of energy, got up and went [repeated] … for a walk and got back just at dinnertime… It would too hot to sleep … we were suffering very much from the heat of day. Tonight is still … !!!

At least a dozen lines of nonsense, whereat I smile and smile. Have been out to shake off the incursions of sleep and feel slightly recovered. Will go over soon and have a cup of tea with Morris over the way in her happy house and then the morning won't be long in coming and another long night ended. So the time goes on. One thing we don't get here are convoys either going out or coming in which makes things very quiet. On every other night duty the comings and goings have been the great excitement at times when we got flooded out with new cases as sometimes happened.

WEDNESDAY, 8TH MAY, 12.45 A.M.

Just over the border and into the next day and the creepy hour of midnight has nearly gone. Very yawny and sleepy tonight – perhaps slept too soundly today, I mean yesterday. Went in the morning to Paris-Plage on an unsuccessful errand to get my hair washed. Found the coiffing establishment couldn't take me till 11 a.m., which of course was too late, so I had to return discomfited and to get air and exercise I walked back through the woods and also got wet, for the rain came down in sheets before I got back into Étaples. However fresh air seemed to have made me sleep, for I had a better day's sleep than I have had for a little while past. Poor Riley was awake most of the day and found the noises outside very disturbing. Building operations were just by the Sick Sisters' ward and the aeroplanes are crossing overhead, which they do frequently now during the day, and all afternoon there were people playing tennis and disporting themselves outside. Not much rest for the wicked, with all that going on.

WEDNESDAY, 15TH MAY

Just settled down for a short time, after doing the preliminary rounds. Hardly expect the patients to settle down very soon this warm, still evening and it seems to be taking some of the men a little while to get off. Have no acute invalids in my four wards, only PUOs and trench fevers, and the erysipelas boy in this ward, who has been pretty bad but is now getting better. Had a busy time for a night or two with a pneumonia case – such a nice little boy, only nineteen and very ill indeed. Then he was transferred to one of the other wards with two other pneumonia cases, so that relieved the pressure of work considerably. I was sorry to see him go because he was a nice wee boy and a good patient. Then there was another boy with a very bad throat and dip case, who was transferred to No. 9 ward, so there is really nothing bad at all and no one needing great attention. After being established for a night or two in ward 20, I have now come back to 22, my old home where I feel the surroundings are more familiar.

I am wondering what will transpire about leave. C came to bring me another application for leave to fill in, the last one being out of date. Matron had permission to send a few of the staff who were due, if they were tired and required a rest. She told C she would be sending her, but hummed and hawed over rumbustious, so maybe I shall have to stick on a bit longer. However, she was putting in my application and was going to interview Miss Stronach* about it.

Levack came yesterday afternoon to call, bursting in with C at about 5 p.m., and I woke up to find them laughing at my bedside. She was very full of affection and talk as usual, but didn't stay very long. She is at Camiers and had got over here on a half-day.

---

* Miss Stronach was the Principal Matron with overall responsibility for all the hospitals in Étaples.

MONDAY, 20TH MAY

And into bed after the events of last night. Oh what a night it was! I just can't keep my thoughts off the happenings! It's all been so terrible. An air raid began at about 10.30 and lasted till after 2 and it was ghastly all the time. Our poor boys tragically suffered heavy casualties, especially in the lower tank, where a bomb dropped right in front of them and inflicted heavy penalty. I don't know exactly how many were killed – at least fourteen or fifteen anyway. The machine came straight up the hill and dropped four bombs. One of them fell just opposite my tanks and oh, the noise and light, the crash, choking dust and smoke, and then the calls of the wounded. It was pitiful to hear them. When the atmosphere had cleared I got up from my crouching position to see what damage had been done and went to the assistance of a man with a nasty wound in the face, and then another who had been wounded in the buttock. It was heart-rending to see them. A good many of the wounded were taken over into 29 ward and it was like a shambles, all in very subdued lantern light. The end of the hut next to the one I was in was blown in too, and a great deal of damage done to it.

I found afterwards I had got a little splinter of something in my shoulder. A very tiny place, but still it is going to get me a gold stripe. Oh I don't want to see a gold stripe or any other sort of stripe if I have to go through such horrors to win one. I ought to be trying to sleep, but can't help thinking and thinking about it all – hearing again the noise of the falling bomb and then that awful crash – and I know the demons will be over again tonight. The sky is absolutely cloudless and the moon waxing and brightening every night.*

WEDNESDAY, 22ND MAY

Now that the first shock of the raid is over, I will try and put down a more detailed account for future reading. We all certainly had the

---

* After the German High Command launched its largest and last raid on London on 19 May, the British bases in northern France became a new target for the Gotha bombers. See Chronology, p. 355.

wind up in a greater or lesser degree that night and the effects are still evident with a good many of us, but we managed to keep pretty cool last night when Jerry began his evil tricks again. He delayed his coming for a bit and hovered in the neighbourhood and then we heard the uneven hum of his machine and presently our barrage opened up and my! What a barrage it was. Since Monday night the defences must have been very much strengthened for the firing was practically continuous, right overhead, and presently the huts began to be peppered with shrapnel falling down on the iron roofs with a sharp thud. Evidently, Jerry found very soon that things were too hot for him, for after one attempt to get over the centre of the camp he went off in disgust, depositing his evil load at various places in the neighbourhood. From the looks of things Boulogne must have got it very hot last night and the shrapnel was bursting well over in our direction, but once Jerry had departed he didn't choose to return to run more risks, so, though one was kept on the qui vive for some time, nothing more happened.

Apparently, the raid the other night caused something like 1,000 casualties and many deaths. No. 7 Canadian caught it the worst and No. 2 Canadian had a good many casualties too. 20 General was damaged, and of course we got our share and a pretty heavy one too. Then there were two tanks blown in like ours at the top of the hill and the bomb did some damage to our orderlies' quarters. The bomb that dropped in front of my tank caused the most casualties among the orderlies though, for they were all drawn up on parade by the reception hut and the ones nearest the bomb went to swell the list of dead and wounded. On the next page, I have made a plan of the position of four bombs that dropped so near us.

Poor Brampton* must have had a dreadful time and now is suffering from definite shell shock and over in Sick Sisters being looked after. Her two front tanks looked simply terrible the next morning. The floor was smeared with pools of gore and nearly every bed had its gruesome horrible mark – the mattresses all torn and

* The nurse on night duty in the next block of 'tanks'.

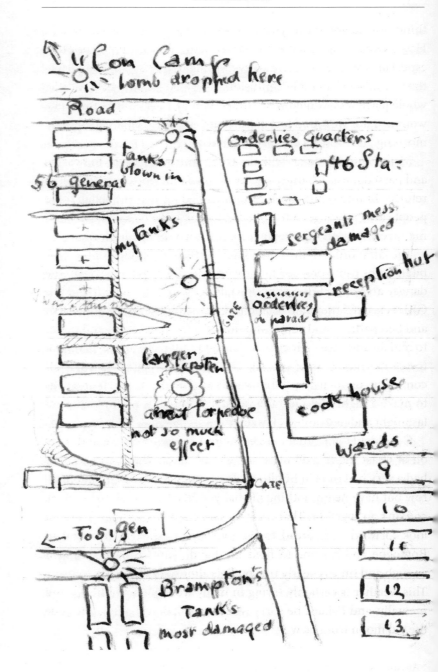

things tossed about everywhere – the whole place a perfect wreck. How anyone escaped alive is a marvel. My tanks were pretty bad too, especially the one I was in and everything in that end of course was thrown into unutterable confusion. Every bottle smashed and the whole place was riddled with shrapnel. It's a marvel not more were wounded, for we found lots of little bits of shrapnel in the beds next morning just roosting among the blankets.

Major Duncan came with Matron in the afternoon to see me and passed me as a battle casualty, so my name goes onto the list of returns. Brampton has been recommended for the M. Medal; some people say I might get it too but don't think it likely. There will be so many really deserving people recommended for the decoration.

The latest order of the DDMS now, is that all day staff of the hospitals in the camp proceed to the woods for the night to be out of the danger area and all the convalescent camp is marched off and the GBD* cleared. The camp is practically deserted except for night staff and bed patients and some who don't bother to clear off and prefer to remain and take their chance. It is quite a scream now every night to see the members of the nursing staff from the lower hospitals coming up on their way to the woods armed with blankets and rugs to make a night of it until the worst is over. Some of our staff went last night and had quite a cheerful time.

C suddenly got orders yesterday to proceed on leave and went off at 9 last night. I do hope she will be all right – she must have had a very bad time in Boulogne. I am supposed to be going tomorrow but have heard nothing official yet. Very disappointed that we couldn't go together. That really is very hard to bear, and I almost look forward with dread to the journey home with the night in Boulogne and no one to hold my hand. Think I have scribbled enough and time is nearly 11.15 but it is almost too hot again to sleep. This weather is certainly trying in many ways, both physically and mentally, and I shan't be sorry when some clouds come up to hide the old moon from view.

---

* An Army Service Corps abbreviation for General Base Depot.

SUNDAY, 2ND JUNE

And a safe, long distance away from the scene of recent horrors. In fact, I'm enjoying a long looked-for leave. This is the first peaceful Sunday at home for ten whole months. The only fly in the ointment is the way in which the time is flying, but that subject doesn't bear thinking about. Sufficient unto the day is the evil thereof.

I only got word of my impending holiday from Miss Porteous* on Monday morning. Didn't expect to be going so soon, as last thing I heard was that I shouldn't get away till the end of this last week. However, the authorities saw fit to push me off on Tuesday [28 May] and I was no unwilling victim of the pushing. Miss P found she had to keep me on duty on Monday night, owing to shortness of staff – Solly the orderly having proved a broken reed again and gone to bed with lumbago – so I didn't have a great deal of rest before departing. We had no more excursions and alarms after Tuesday night, though guns could be heard once or twice in the distance. The full-moon night was cloudy, as was the one before, which saved us from considerable anxiety and after that the waning moon didn't provide so many opportunities for assault. But ever since the raid, the fatigue parties from the camps have been working feverishly making trenches and dugouts and sand-bagging up the huts all along the two medical lines. Every precaution has been taken now the mischief is done, but of course some of it should have been done long ago. I am doubtful, though, even if it would have saved us greatly. We feel sure the Huns meant to make their brutal attack and no amount of white crosses showing up would have kept them away.

I spent a morning shopping in Paris-Plage before leaving and a good deal of time packing and slept from 1 till 5. Then after second dinner at about 9, the ambulance came to take us to the station. I had two companions – two officers from the sick officers' ward going home on sick leave. Nice boys and they were given charge of me and I must say they looked after me like brothers. Sister Searle came with me to the station and then walked up again.

* Senior Staff Nurse.

We got away by the rather belated train about 10 and arrived in Boulogne shortly before 12 – not a very rapid journey. Just as we were making our way from the station, out went the lights and off went the four warning guns – rather a palpitating sound, especially with the nerves rather on the stretch anyway. However we got across to the Hôtel Louvre and there, one of the officers, Capt. Spargle, investigated the matter of getting rooms. All the proprietors and staff of the establishment had retired to the basement and he had to pursue them down there, eventually securing rooms from the old lady who was established in one of the underground bathrooms. He returned, armed with his numbers, and then we got some coffee served in the lounge by candlelight and before long we wended our way up to bed on the top floor. Nothing had followed the alert and at about 1 a.m, just as I was getting into bed, the 'all clear' was sounded and I was able to get to sleep peacefully. I spent the next morning partly in shopping and partly in making an expedition out to 32 with Lt. Upton, one of my escorts, who wanted to visit 55 General. I was so pleased to see dear old 32 again, looking much the same and very attractive – so fresh and breezy – down by the sea. I saw various of the old friends, including Mitchell and Batten, and some of the medical officers and Matron and the Colonel. The latter took me back into Boulogne with him in the car, for which I was very grateful.

The two other travellers both turned up at different times for lunch, so we sat at different tables but joined forces afterwards, and before long we were journeying over the Channel to beloved Blighty and home. Didn't get up to town till about 7.30 so I spent the night with [sister] Jean and we had a great evening of talk and reunion after the ten-month separation. Next afternoon saw me down here and greeting Mums rapturously, and here I have been since, enjoying life to the full and making the most of my precious spare time.

TUESDAY, 19TH JUNE

Back at 46 Stationary again and carrying on as before. Passed through some doubts and fears, before landing back here again. A most delightful and dreamlike and all-too-short leave ended on

Tuesday 11th June, after a weekend in London on a grand finale. Was in great doubts as to my future when I left England, as from various rumours and letters I had gathered that there were great changes in progress in the camp and possibilities of the whole of the hospitals – ours included – packing up and departing en masse. There had been two more bad raids after the Sunday night and great destruction wrought on St John's H and 51 General and one or two others, so the wind was up in the camp more than ever. I felt very much in doubt and rather forlorn at the prospect of perhaps being separated from everyone I knew and pushed into a strange locality with no one to support me. Christie had got a month's extension of leave, so I knew I couldn't depend on her joining me.

Miss Woodford* met the members of the nursing staff arriving by the train and boat and also I had a friend and escort in the shape of Dr Scott, who was standing on the quay looking out for me. Miss Woodford gathered all her flock together and pushed them off either to their destinations or to the hostel for the night. She seemed to infer at once that I shouldn't be coming back here, which rather depressed me. However she discovered later there were no orders for me, so told me to report at this place next morning to find out what was happening.

Meanwhile, I spent quite a nice evening with Dr Scott who dined with me at the hostel – rather nervously under the eyes of so many ladies. I wasn't allowed to go out anywhere with him and we parted company soon after a little stroll along the front. I came early to bed to prepare for an early rise the next day. The Canadian Hotel Hostel was much nicer than any of the other places in Boulogne and I had a good night, undisturbed by alarms, though it was glorious starlight.

Got up in good time next morning and was soon en route for 'Etapps' again, with one or two more travellers in this direction. Duly arrived at the familiar station and then, as there was nothing to meet me, walked up feeling hot and dusty and, rather to my surprise, found the hospital looking precisely as I had left it and carrying on exactly

---

* Miss Woodford held the important post of 'Embarkation Sister' at Boulogne.

as before. Greeted very welcomely by everyone I saw and Matron was almost effusive greeting me with a long hand clasp, though I suspect she was relieved to see me as she was short of staff, so many having gone on leave, and she was having difficulty in finding enough people to do the work.

I was told to go on duty at once and did so rather leisurely, having a lot to unpack and all my things to collect and bestow in my room – also a lot of friends to interview and stories of the raids to hear. Apparently there is no prospect of 46 departing and the other hospitals are keeping more or less open too, except of course St John's and Liverpool Merchants which had evacuated. For the first day or two, I gave my services to Sister Archer in 7 and 8 wards, but since then have been chopping and changing about all the time and sometimes relieving which I don't like.

On the first night, I had my first experience of life in the woods. We were all packed off in a big charabanc with two ambulances at about 8 p.m. We were carefully roll-called and ticked off to see that we were all present. It was like a joyride, only everyone was rather bored with having had so many of these expeditions. We all carried bundles of rugs and pillows and some of us were provided with provisions, refreshments for the morning. Sister Searle took me under her wing and we made up our couches of twigs side-by-side, under a tree. I felt a great feeling of hilarity over the whole proceeding. There was something so quaint and unusual about it all. Two MOs came with us to keep guard and Matron's pet batman, Montmorency, came to look after her, spreading out her bedding in the little arbour.

We drove about 11 kilometres, out beyond Frencq, to a remote little wood – except for a USA camp not far off. There, the staff disposed themselves among various piles of cut brushwood and made themselves as comfortable as possible. I must say I managed to make a very cosy corner with the pillows and rugs, softer really than a camp bed, and if it hadn't been for the feeling of having all one's things on and no opportunity of toilette either in the night or morning, the sleeping-out business would be quite attractive and I'm sure very healthy.

FRIDAY, 21ST JUNE

The longest day. Will another 21st June see us out here? I have a feeling it won't. Something will have turned up by then. Well, our nights have been very peaceful lately. The weather has turned very unsettled – blowing hard all day and raining at night, which is all we ask for.

Meanwhile, the rather unwilling fatigue parties from the camp proceed with our dugout, which is in under the bank at the back of the quarters. It is eventually to have a connected passage with three openings. At present it has the two openings without passage. The orderlies are making one for themselves further down and the Sergeants and NCOs another. We shall all be like rabbits soon, popping in and out of our burrows at the least alarm.

Had two on successive nights a short time ago, the first night in fact after the woods regime was finished. We had all settled down to enjoy a good rest in bed when the dinner bell (our air raid signal) went loud and long. I woke up with a violent start, scrambled into some things, snatched up my pillow and eiderdown, joined a wretched hurrying throng in the corridor and skidaddled down the hill, with some stumbling over pitfalls, to our shelter – just a sandbag affair, not the new dugout. Seven of us gathered there, the pre-arranged party all waiting palpitatingly for the first guns and sound of planes. The lights had gone out and that was taken as warning. Anyway, we sat there for nearly a solid hour till 12.30, getting very tired and sleepy and really in the end dozing, and then were told we might go to bed, so we trailed up again very fed up with life and got back to bed. The same thing happened the next night, only at nearly 1 a.m. The bell went, we leapt feverishly out of bed and bolted to the dugouts. This time there were certainly planes overhead, but no other warning sound. They proved to be our own machines, but everyone had the wind up. The orderlies, MOs, patients – everyone – was hiding in the shelters. We weren't kept up long this time, but anyway it was a disturbed night's rest and a shock to the system.

Rather funny too, when looked at from its humorous side, for then the Bosch would have laughed if he had known.

People are beginning now to arrive back from leave and soon the staff will be complete. The hospital is filling up too, still mostly with this strange new epidemic. I'm glad to say it hasn't reached any of us yet and hope it won't, as it may lay us all low if it starts.* The WAACs have got it and there are a lot in hospital now. The ward I am in is beginning to get lively. A lot of the fifty patients are up now, and consequently there is a hopeless untidiness everywhere. Most are just boys of eighteen and ready for any uproariousness.

Rumour has it – apparently, officially – that the three MMs [Military Medals] have been awarded to Sister Monroe, Brampton and self, as well as lots from the other hospitals as well, so I can't consider it a very high honour, though of course I can't deny being pleased to have won it. Not been told officially yet, though. Perhaps I will hear tomorrow.

FRIDAY, 28TH JUNE

Hope we shall have a peaceful night tonight. Last night at 10 to 1, the guns began and we all woke up with the sound of them and began dressing into our things and then, after we were all well under way preparing, the bell rang furiously. Jerry had been over the day before in the daytime, so we rather expected him at night but it was very overcast and not at all a suitable night for a raid. However, there was some alarm and anyway half a dozen shots were fired – enough to wake us all up – so off we went to the dugout, clutching garments and belongings, in all stages of attire. The

---

* Some pathologists believe this to have been a preliminary outbreak of the major Spanish flu epidemic which spread worldwide later that year.

new passage is ready now and two openings have been connected, so everyone from long corridor – 26 of us – took refuge there.

Great excitement among some members of the party – too much so for my liking. There is no need to grow rampageous about small items, such as lights showing in the bottom of the tunnel. There is accommodation for everyone and, finally, we all settled in. There was nothing further outside. No excitement or sound of any kind, so after sitting down there in the clammy chalky burrow, the all-clear was given and we climbed out again and so back to bed to resume a disturbed night's rest. Shouldn't wonder at all if we were hailed out again tonight, even though there are clouds about, but that does not seem to make very much difference for false alarms.

Have been wearing my little bit of ribbon pinned in my coat and on my apron. Feel very proud of it, though still regretful I couldn't feel I have deserved it more. Had a congrats card – with the little bit of ribbon fastened in a corner – from Miss McCarthy, which seems to make it more official.*

Am still in 10 ward and fairly established for the present. Not very busy, but just enough to do. Sister Yarnell is quite nice – a little excitable, but pleasantly so. Had a very bad pneumonia case in a few days ago. He died – very sad because he was such a nice boy (Hancock) and so uncomplaining. Since then, have not had anyone very ill, mostly patients who are on the mend. Much hoping to see Al this weekend. He has written to say there is a chance he may be able to come, perhaps on Sunday if he has any luck. Time for bed now and a long sleep if poss.

FRIDAY, 5TH JULY

Have been through various episodes since last writing, including three air raids – but nothing like the first one. After those false alarms we were allowed to sleep peacefully for a night or two and then came the first real visitation. The bell rang loud and long about 11.30 and we were all summoned, post-haste, out of our comfortable beds.

---

* Dorothea's citation for the Military Medal, which also appeared in *The Times* on 31 July, read: 'For gallantry and devotion to duty during an enemy air raid. Although herself wounded, this lady remained at duty and assisted in dressing the wounded patients.'

My preparations didn't take long, having got everything pretty well prepared beforehand – coat and jersey put out ready and my shoes just beside the bed. I seized up my eiderdown and fled off through the sitting room and dining room and out to the dugout. All the staff was assembled, crowded in tightly, and the guns were going hard by this time. They began in fact as soon as the bell rang. After that, there was nothing to do but to wait as calmly as possible till it was all over, so we sat for about two hours hearing Jerry's engine distinctly every now and then and the barrage opening up on him whenever it could and then at intervals the bombs dropping. Three were planted quite near the lower tanks again, two of them on 51 tennis court, where they left big dints. The tanks were riddled with shrapnel but only one civilian workman was hurt. The wards are being used just now by English labourers working for McAlpine. The other bombs were dropped in the town and by the bridge. The all-clear sounded at last at about 1.35 and we all got to bed to finish our broken slumbers.

To my great joy, Al turned up the next day and I had a most delightful, peaceful time with him. I was anxious about him though, because, finding no room anywhere to be housed for the night, he had to go to the Rest Camp – which only provided him with a bed in a bell tent – and the weather being gorgeous I felt sure Jerry would visit us again. However, I had to chance it, so we parted with some anxiety on my part. At 11.10. I was lying awake still when the take-cover whistle went and before long, while we were getting up, the bell was rung loud and long and we made the same hurried exit to our underground refuge. It was a worse raid than the one before and lasted longer: the bombs all seemed to drop about the same place and all down just above the Rest Camp. Then, before long, some distraught men came up and spread the rumour that the Rest Camp had been blotted out. Imagine my feeling of horror and despair, wondering what could have become of poor Al. However, we heard nothing more and things quietened down. Soon the all-clear went and we returned to our rooms. Hardly had we got there when the bells and whistles went again and we had to fly back, helter-skelter. For another half-hour we endured more suspense and heard another load of horrible engines of death tipped out on the camp, with their ominous thundering crash resounding far more underground than they would do on the surface. After that we were allowed to creep out rather shaken by a double ordeal and I felt especially so with all the anxiety about Al added. However, I got an hour or two's sleep and then up to work again.

Matron heard about my anxieties and said I might go down to the Rest Camp. She was being very nice about it, so I hurried off with Williams and after some enquiries found the dear boy was quite safe and he presently appeared himself – deshabillé – to reassure us. The bombs were not far away at all though, much too near to be pleasant, and I was truly thankful he was safe. After that we went round to survey the damage but nothing very vital had been done. The officers' baggage stores went up in one big flare and everything in it was destroyed, the whole place burnt out of existence. The bakery was much damaged as were some other wooded buildings nearby and one or two bombs were very near the bridge. The rest were dropped further over the river way.

It was another sweltering day and Al and I had the afternoon together and went to Paris-Plage and sat on the shore, basking in the sunshine and delicious air. Much to my relief he had taken a room for two nights out at PP in a hotel. I could hardly have him staying in camp again.

The evening was glorious and, as we quite expected, the third warning came. We had plenty of time to get into the dugout comfortably before the guns began, but he came all right, with his noisome load of death-dealers, and for over an hour kept us on tenterhooks. He was trying again for the railway and bridges, but kept more over the town, except he managed to knock out the WAACs' Mess and canteen and do some mischief in that direction. The poor old town got it again and more houses were destroyed. We went next day to see the damage and inspected a huge hole in some of the back gardens where three large bombs had dropped.

We were beginning to feel pretty jaded after three nights' disturbance and consequent lack of sleep. All the patients who could be moved were, of course, put into trenches and dugouts, so their rest was disturbed as well. This made the night staff anxious and we were thankful to be left in peace the next night and in fact have been so since then, which has been pleasantly restful.

Al and I had a half-day on Tuesday to enjoy each other. We went to Paris-Plage again and among other entertainments got our photographs taken, but I haven't much hope of the portraits being great successes.* Anyway, we had a lovely time and it was sad indeed when after supper and a short walk we had to part, not to meet again till goodness knows when.

THURSDAY, 11TH JULY

No more air raids since last writing, but the next might come any time if the weather clears. Meanwhile, there is great activity in the camp in the matter of digging and sandbagging and preparing of dugouts and trenches. The huts are all pretty well sandbagged up now and in the smaller ones there are even barriers of sandbags inside the ward across the door – to the ruination of the look of the ward, of course. We are threatened with a row of them down the middle of our wards, but sincerely hope the threat won't be carried out, as it would be disastrous to the ward if it were. We only have twenty patients in now. After the influenza epidemic abated, we have not taken many more in. It is the same everywhere.

Many rumours continue to float about, but I think the hospital is staying whatever is happening to the others. The latest innovation is that we are allowed to frank our own letters. Had to sign a book first to promise not to infringe the rules of censorship and now we can close our letters and don't have to have them read here which is a mercy. Think the Colonel will be pleased too. He must have been fed up at times wading through our correspondence.

---

* One of these photographs is reproduced on p. xx.

SUNDAY, 21ST JULY

Just teatime but feel called upon after such a long pause in the diary to begin an entry, even if interrupted by the mundane process of eating. Life proceeds pretty much as usual with small incidental happenings and minor excitements. Have been very lucky in not enduring a single Fritzy night for nearly the whole of this month. The weather has been too changeable and unsettled lately. Just when it seemed inclined to turn lovely and give us anxious nights, a thunderstorm came up and brought rain and change with it, easing our minds and giving us a good restful sleep. Yesterday was very stormy and thundery and has developed today into a tremendous gale of wind with bright sun and fresh air. Just a lovely day, except for its boisterousness.

Christie turned up safely on Thursday, very pleased to be back but not so pleased to be put at once on night duty pro tem, and still less pleased – in fact quite desolée – to have a hurried visit from Sister Reay with the news that her moving orders had come and she was departing the next day. Not a very happy greeting for poor C, but she is bearing the loss bravely in her odd phlegmatic way. The term of night duty is over now and she comes back to day work tomorrow, so I hope to see more of her than I have done up to the present.

9 p.m.

Just had a little tour round with C after supper. We explored the dugout again to see what progress had been made with it since we were last there, some little time ago now. We shall perhaps be visiting there tonight but it is very windy still and that may keep Jerry away. Has been blustery all day but also clear and fine, a storm wind following on the thunder. I have become quite a fair expert on weather signs by dint of critically studying the heavens, especially in view of raids and suitable nights. I look specially for the direction of the wind and as long as it is west feel fairly safe. East and N.E. are very ominous winds and generally mean trouble in store.

Rumours of moving and leaving this place still continue to circulate, but tonight Matron said that 46 was remaining here, even if all the others moved. Not quite sure if I'm sorry or otherwise. Rather sorry really, as I don't much care for this place and still less when it becomes a sort of garrison and headquarters, full of red tape and army rules and regulations. All the hospital is very empty now, hardly any patients coming in and wards are closing down.

FRIDAY, 26TH JULY

To our relief the weather has turned very unsettled and stormy this evening and up till now the rain has been coming down in sheets. We were enlivened by a very severe raid the night before last and it has left us all rather strung up and over-tired. The first guns went at 10 to 12. I nipped out of bed as per usual and urged C to be as speedy as possible. Of course I was ready first, as my preparations don't take long nowadays. Was off down the corridor without much delay, leaving C to come on as soon as she could. The staff all gathered in the dugout, which is now a long tunnel with three entrances, so there is ample room for everyone. We disposed ourselves as comfortably as we could, but it was very cold and damp and I wished I had a good warm rug with me.

The barrage was going almost immediately and Jerry was cruising about overhead in his usual evil manner. There seemed to be several relays of planes. The barrage kept dying away and then springing up again as a fresh lot of planes came over. A good many bombs were dropped but we only really noticed a half-dozen or so. One was fairly nearby at the Scouts Hut a little way down the road; another was the most enormous horror one can imagine. It fell in the centre of the Medical Board depot not far away down the hill and swept it almost clean away. It reduced huts to matchwood and blew away tents wholesale. A lot of men were buried in their trenches and dugouts and others were killed with the shock. The casualties there were about 80, I believe, but every account differs.* The bomb, according

---

* The actual number of casualties (excluding civilians) was 39 killed and 91 wounded.

to some, weighed something like half a ton, and the plane carried only one, so it took some time to manoeuvre to get it in the right place. We felt the concussion quite distinctly in our dugout and it 'put the wind up' us as the saying is. Other bombs fell in the town again and destroyed some more houses in a street we are constantly passing through and it killed a lot of people taking shelter in a cellar. Really it's a dreadful war and a few more nights like that would reduce us to a rather pulpy state.

WEDNESDAY, 1ST AUGUST

A baking hot day, but with an easterly breeze bringing up the usual cloudy haze. Williams and I are sitting out under the trees just below our hospital, a very nice, shady little wood only lately opened up to the public and encircling the big old farmhouse at the bottom of the hill here, which looks incongruous in the middle of the busy camp. All its fields and spaces of land have been built over now with huts and sheds and stores – very different from the old peacetime surroundings. This part of the wood smells deliciously of pine trees. I could almost fancy myself in Scotland, as in any haven of refuge and rest where there are fir woods and the smell of pine needles and moss, as there is here. On the other hand, to bring one to the grim realities of life, we have just had a visit from one of Jerry's scout planes. At just about 2 p.m. the big guns started to bang. These new archies make a tremendous noise. They are French 75s I believe and their explosions are almost as loud as the bombs dropping. We could hear the shells whistling up overhead, but the bursts of course were very high. Jerry kept well up in the clouds out of harm's way. Before very long he was away altogether but not alas before he had amused himself with several photographs of our domicile, which he intends to do away with one of these days or nights.

Last night, the conditions being perfect – except that there was no moon till 1 a.m. – he appeared on the scene. Fortunately, we got good warning and were all well established in the dugout before he came, but we had the usual scrimmagy departure and sudden awakening which I think is almost the worst part of the proceeding.

I couldn't find my way into the sleeves of my coat and jersey at all and wasn't ready with my usual despatch, but still it wasn't long before C and I were on our way down the corridor, together this time, and found a little tidy corner where we ensconced ourselves and sat waiting for the worst. Not nearly so bad this time though as the raid a week ago. Over much sooner and the planes just hurried up, dropped their bombs and were away without any manoeuvring around at all. No bombs dropped very near to us and some were said to be duds, but rumour has it that the town was damaged again and that some Canadians and Australians were killed. One of the planes came down very low, low enough to be fired at by a Lewis gun on the ground, which popped away with quite a dramatic sound. The barrage was poor but that might have been due to the fact that for the first time the electrified wire system of defence was being used – wires very highly charged with electricity hung between two captive balloons guarding the most vital places. Don't quite know how the defence works, but I don't think Jerry likes it much. Anyway he didn't stay long. We were nicely back to bed about 12 and getting to sleep again when some more shots were fired and everyone stampeded out to cover, bugles and whistles were blown and the whole camp was back underground or as near to it as possible, and there we remained for quite a while awaiting the next attack which never came. It proved to be a false alarm – someone getting rid of extra cartridges by firing them, instead of extracting them silently. So we finally got to bed at 1 a.m. and slept well the rest of the night. Shouldn't be surprised if Jerry paid us a visit tonight after his midday call. It usually means violent attacks in the near future.

My name has at last appeared in the paper for the MM and another photograph, which I am not pleased about as everyone remarks on it, and it is silly to appear twice within such a short interval. A little account of my doings in very embroidered language appears too in *The Times*. I wonder when the Presentation will take place. Suppose not for some time yet. About 34 got the medal altogether as an outcome of that raid and the two following ones, when St John's Hospital was so knocked about.

The hospital is still very slack and empty, and rumour is rife. Meanwhile Matron, in great generosity of soul, continues to deal out days off and half-days galore and we are quite enjoying ourselves. C and I got a day off together last Monday and spent a lovely time bicycling to Berck, taking a day to it and lunching out. It was very nice indeed just pottering along and I enjoyed the expedition thoroughly.

SUNDAY, 12TH AUGUST

The end of a long hot day and it looks like the beginning of a fine clear night. Night duty is impending I fear though – from the rumours I heard, I should be going on tonight. Nothing further transpired, but I fear it is imminent, perhaps tomorrow if another ward fills up. Three days ago the dysentery push started. Empty wards were opened and ours was pressed into service. We have only one empty bed now, alas, for its smart appearance and its lovely floor. It may wear a very different aspect with practically every bed full. Most of the patients we have are not bad at all but two or three of them are very poorly and with so many in, there is a great deal to do. Really have been very busy indeed since the ward filled up.

The last few days, in fact just the weekend, have been so hot and fine, almost too much of a good thing when we are so busy. Also, after more than a week's peace, we had an unwelcome visit from Jerry on Saturday night. His last visit was on Thursday the week before, the night of the same day that his scout plane was over taking photographs. This was not a bad raid and fairly soon over and most of the damage done was over in the Le Touquet woods I believe. The last raid was much worse, though there were not many casualties. One or two of the bombs were much too near to be pleasant, just over on the other side of the bank of trees at the bottom of our compound. It was the Medical Board Depot that got these again and it was there that some officers and men were killed and wounded taking refuge in a trench. Some more of the town has gone west. A big house just out of the market place was smashed to bits and its owner, who, unluckily, was at home, got killed in his bed.

Other houses at the back were wrecked too. The poor little town is gradually going to rack and ruin and it looks very war-worn now.

The war news is good just now, which is encouraging. We needed something to buck us up a bit. It seems certain now anyway that the Germans can't make another offensive this year. Meanwhile, more Americans are arriving, which is always hopeful, and the Germans must be feeling rather uncomfortable at the prospect of all these fresh reserves coming in.*

MONDAY, 27TH AUGUST

Another long pause in my entries. There have been plenty of incidents to record, but no time or inclination for the recording of them. The dysentery rush continues fairly rampantly, chiefly among the WAACs and officers whose wards are full up pretty well and the staff kept very busy.

Since last writing, Christie and I have received promotion! We are now both ANs – otherwise Assistant Nurses – and privileged to wear 'AN' on our shoulder and to be called upon to bear more responsibility.† Orders for our promotion came through from headquarters, so it was independent of Matron or any of our Matrons. I suppose it was really a matter of the length of time of our service. I was threatened with night duty some time ago, but whether for the reason of the 'leg up' or for some other reason, Matron has kept me off and now she has seen fit to give C and me the added responsibility we are judged capable of and we are both in charge of wards – C of 3 and 4 and I superintend 7 and 8. I have no one to help, the VAD who was there before having been sent on night duty, so yesterday and today I ran the place practically alone and an orderly was removed for night duty at 5 yesterday, so that further shortened

* The Allied armies had launched a major offensive on 8 August. See Chronology, p. 355.
† Miss McCarthy's notes on the subject of Assistant Nurses suggest a good deal of confusion about this rank. It had previously applied to professional nurses who had had two years' experience in a 'fever' hospital. Then, without any preliminary discussion, on 2 August 1918, she reported that authority had been received 'for promotion to Assistant Nurse of 92 VADs who had been recommended for promotion'. Dorothea and Christie must have been on the recommended list.

my staff. However, a new one was sent this morning, a great long boy newly transferred to RAMC from infantry and knowing nothing whatsoever of ward work, but I dare say a little instruction is all he wants. We have twenty patients in both wards – that is all beds full up. Quite nice boys, most of them, but as always there are a few grumblers among them. C and I, having neither of us any assistants, interchange in our off-duty times and we both have four wards to look after during either the evening or afternoon, so our AN-ship does seem to have produced a very decided result in a very short space of time.

Another event to chronicle is the succession of moves taking place just now. All the original VADs who were here last year – the survivors of the old staff – are gradually being wafted away and new ones are coming in their place, some from Blighty and others from base hospitals, none of them very promising-looking. Maybe they will improve on acquaintance. Meanwhile, Matron is really rather short-staffed and several people are away on leave and others are due to go immediately. If we got a rush of really bad cases it would be really difficult to manage.

And what of Jerry? Well, we have been summoned out of our beds three times I think, since I last wrote, but all efforts have been abortive. I am convinced Jerry has some other schemes and one, most certainly, is to concentrate his principal efforts on the aerodromes and leave bases and more dangerous places like this alone. He was certainly there on the first of the three alarms. We could hear his machines, but he dropped nothing in our neighbourhood. The second time – a brilliant moonlit night – he was supposed to have got as far as Frencq and then to have turned aside and gone elsewhere to deposit his evil burden. The last time, which was Saturday night, he was nowhere very near but he searched the neighbourhood for aerodromes and got one, fairly wiping out the whole squadron and dropping one bomb directly on the dugout where everyone was sheltering, killing the whole lot, including twenty staunch young pilots.

We heard all this on our way out to some sports at the big aerodrome about nine miles inland from here behind Berck, on Sunday afternoon. We had a great afternoon driving there and being brought back the same easy fashion, in an RAF tender. It was a lovely day, the last of the fine weather as it happens. A thunderstorm at night changed its aspect and now it is wet and stormy. The sports were held on the flying ground with the hangars in the distance. Crowds of RAF were an audience. It was a great event and we quite enjoyed the little while we had there. The tug of war was not a great success as far as we were concerned, the opposing team being much too strong. I merely spectated all the other events, though some of the others took part in potato race and so forth. Williams and I went together and supported each other.

Got back to duty a little after 5 and when I arrived, found that Alastair was awaiting me. He had turned up on his way to rejoin his battalion after being at the Trench Mortar Battery School, and just had the evening in Étaples. He came down to the ward with me for little while and then came back after dinner and stayed till nearly 10. I was very loath to part from him. So delightful to get such a surprise visit and see him looking well and happy too.

Have been busy today dashing from 7 to 8, getting things straightened up a bit, and looking in on 3 and 4 this evening during C's absence. I am enjoying the business but it's rather wearing and fatiguing and I shall not be sorry to get additional help to relieve things a bit.

SUNDAY, 9TH SEPTEMBER

A pouring wet night, the first really hopeless spell of weather we have had for months almost. We are all getting quite out of practice in the matter of raids. Nothing has happened in that line for ages, partly owing to the unsuitability of weather conditions and also maybe to the rapid retirement of the Germans to their old line again. They have just reached it now – after severe fighting and desperate retirement – and have been harassed and plagued all the time. I expect this bad weather will put a damper on the fighting and hamper our advance, but a good deal has been done already and the Germans can't feel too happy about it all.

Have been getting some correspondence accomplished and there is a great deal more that is calling for attention, but I have no strength of mind to set to work with it. Am really very hard-worked these days, still having the two wards, 7 and 8, to look after. Both are full up again, after a short respite the week before last, when they emptied a bit and there are some quite poorly patients among them. One little black boy is on the DI list and is very sick indeed. Probably TB in advanced stages, so in that case there will be no hope for him at all. He looks so pathetic, poor little thing. He is just twenty, and looks quite a boy, with his big eyes in his very black face.

We have had many changes, such comings and goings among the MOs, nurses and orderlies, but in the end I am left alone with three orderlies and Capt. Hewitt, from the laboratory, is the MO. Lieut. Birkett, who was in charge originally, got dysentery himself in its worst form and was removed on a stretcher from his quarters to Sick Officers, feeling about as bad as he could feel, so we shall not see him any more for some time. The MOs are all very hard-worked just now owing to the rush of patients and shortness of staff and the nursing staff are pretty strenuously employed too, despite the arrival of several new VADs, a great many of whom have gone on night duty. C is still busy in 3 and 4 opposite to my wards.

TUESDAY, 18TH SEPTEMBER

My poor neglected diary takes another little advance tonight. Nine days' lapse of time. Not much of great excitement has happened during the interval. No air raids or visits from Jerry of any kind, except prisoners, which is a satisfactory visitation, and no speedy sorties to the dugout – which will soon seem quite a strange and unfamiliar spot. The newcomers haven't even had a chance of experiencing the throes and excitement of this particular form of nocturnal adventure yet. A new Sister was added to the staff today, but three have got moving orders, so we shall still be short. Three of the nicest of our few remaining 'stripies' are leaving us, with only two or three rather mediocre ones left to carry on. Still, we manage fairly well though we are a bit pushed at times. I felt very pushed this evening, everything happening at once and heaps of work to do. Have two very valued patients, one in each ward, who nobly supported me as far as they could. Oakly, my No. 7 bunkman, is invaluable and does all sorts of odd jobs most usefully.

Another change of MO today – a Capt. Ward, bespectacled and very much of the army doctor type, but I don't know whether he is a regular or not. Have been having Major Wood, who was very nice, so this is rather a change and not altogether a welcome one. Anyway, he marked two boys for Blighty so I have nothing very much to complain of.

The war news is good still, but the weather just now is not – very unsettled and tonight much inclined to rain. Nearly all the staff are out at a concert in the men's Mess and soon will come tramping back, kicking up a fearful shindie. Been to very little in the way of entertainment lately, having not much inclination for frivolities and generally a good deal of shopping to do. The camp is still very full of khaki, but not nearly so much so as a little while ago – especially in the early days of the German offensive, when the camp road was a real sight.

SATURDAY, 5TH OCTOBER

This is the night for putting our clocks back one hour. Therefore we get an extra hour's sleep, not at all unwelcome. It isn't a Jerry night either, as the wind is blowing pretty hard and stormily and it is pitchy dark. All last month and so far through October, we have had very unsettled and stormy weather and consequently no disturbances at all of the old-time sort, except for a very brief one which didn't last long and was more of a reconnaissance than a raid so far as bomb-dropping was concerned. One or two nights have been quite fine and still we have rather awaited the summons, but nothing has happened, so am beginning to think that Jerry is getting rather discouraged about his raiding expeditions since he had so many setbacks. The news is still wonderfully good and encouraging. How soon shall we see the end of it all, we wonder? Will it come suddenly or gradually? And what happens to us all here on the day that peace is declared? Well, time will prove – meanwhile, we plod along here in the same old way.*

Other hospitals, everywhere, are beside themselves with work and have been for some time. The fighting must be terrific, especially up round Cambrai, which the Huns are still holding on to. 24 General is practically all given up to the Bosches now – there are hundreds of them in with wounds and lots of bad cases too. We got a convoy of dysenters† in the other day who had been turned out of 24 to make room for the Bosch. I got eight of the transfers into my wards, none of them were very bad. Both wards are nearly full up now, all but one bed in each.

Jones (Assistant Nurse) was sent to assist me some days ago and I am finding things very difficult with her there. She hates being under me, having had more or less regular training and being more a professional nurse than I am. She resents having to take orders from me very much and I hate being above her, but Matron refuses to sanction her having one of the wards, so things continue very strained. I leave her to her own devices in 8 pretty well, but do the round with the MO which incenses her beyond measure. Have had the present MO, Capt. Ward, quite a little while now. He is an odd sort of man. Very clever – almost too much so for these slight cases – but quite nice to work for and with, though he is very unprofessional at times, rather tiresomely so, and I don't quite approve of his carryings on, considering he is married. He ought to know better.

SATURDAY, 11TH OCTOBER, 10.15 P.M.

This volume of my diary begins at a late hour and only a few words can be added. There is nothing very epoch-making to put down anyway, as far as hospital doings are concerned. All our attention is fixed on the course of the war which really begins to show signs of finishing. Le Catelet is ours now, according to today's news, and we must be pushing on fast. The question is, will the Germans hold

---

* The Allied forces had by now successfully taken the Hindenburg Line. See Chronology, p. 355.
† Dysentery patients.

out through the winter and if not, shall we be home for Xmas? I suppose, as usual, we must wait and see, and it won't be long I expect before events prove what is going to happen to us. Rumours today are specially active. The Kaiser has either been assassinated or has abdicated, the Crown Prince has been taken prisoner at Cambrai and the Turks have thrown up the sponge etc. etc., all of which wild tales are awaiting official confirmation. Meanwhile, we proceed with our work calmly. The hospital is not at all busy and the staff rather numerous, which is troubling some of them very much as leave is held up for the present and they can't get home when they could well be spared from here. The surgical hospitals are all so full and so frantically busy that Miss Stronach, the Matron-in-Chief of this district, has refused any leave and we have to be counted with the other hospitals, though the rush is affecting us so little.

Jones has gone from ward 8 where she was anything but happy, feeling it an insult to work under me when she was my equal in length of training and was properly trained at that. It was hard lines certainly, to expect her to settle down to such an arrangement. I don't wonder she felt it. Anyway, now she has gone and Greenwell has taken her place and I have practically parted with ward 8, which I feel rather sad about as I was fond of it and had mothered it for a long time while I was single-handed. However, I buzz round there while Greenwell is off duty. Otherwise, I stay in my own little department and look after the boys in 7.

SATURDAY, 19TH OCTOBER, 7 P.M.

Have been half-daying and employing the holiday hours by bicycling to Paris-Plage, with Williams & co. It was such a lovely morning and promised so well for a fine afternoon but the clouds gathered up and the rain was threatening almost before we started off. However it never came on seriously, so we were able to potter about PP and get our shopping done and then ride leisurely through the woods, which are getting very autumny now. We got some red leaves en route for ward decoration and then went to the Club at Trépied, which none of us had been to before but had heard a good deal about. It turned out to be a dear old-fashioned rambling little cottage, nicely fitted up for the accommodation of members and guests. We got quite a good tea and Williams had to pay a sub and join, so that she might be the member inviting C and me as guests. Then we cycled home in the dusk. It gets so quickly dark nowadays; sadly so, as winter seems very imminent when the days draw in like this.

Yesterday was lovely and fresh and fine – the nicest day we had had for a long time – and the night was wonderful and cloudless, with brilliant moonlight. In the old days of not so long ago, it would have been a sure Jerry night, but we hope now that the days of those desperate events are pretty well over. It won't be easy to fly over nowadays anyway, with such a much longer distance to cover. The news is still good. Evidently the evacuation of Belgium is beginning and we are now established in Ostend, which seems wonderful to think of. After all this long time in German hands, that little seaport has gone back to its rightful owners amid great rejoicings. The houses in PP still had some of their bunting displayed. I believe there were great signs of rejoicing there yesterday.

Unfortunately, all this advancing still means casualties, and the hospitals here and everywhere seem to be very busy. Leave hasn't opened yet for this area and we are rather over-staffed just now. Some of the VADs are helping at 26 General, where the work is very heavy. I suppose Matron was ordered to let them go, otherwise she would have clung to them under the pretext that we needed every available member of the staff here. She is a veritable miser in the matter of parting with her staff and can hardly bear the thought of  their being taken from under her vigilant eye. She is in very cheerful mood just now and always very beaming when she comes into my ward. Too much so altogether, as she will spend such length of time in talking and arguing with the men, preventing me meanwhile from getting on with my work. Then Capt. Ward saunters in and stays gossiping, wasting more of my precious moments, so that I am generally finishing my time on duty in a fearful rush.

Poor little Jimmie does not seem so well now. His little black face looks woefully thin and pathetic and he is dreadfully weak, which is disappointing when he really seemed to be making fairly good progress. Both wards are still full up which keeps Greenwell and me fairly busy, really. She jealously guards her department in No. 8 and I keep in mine, and No. 7 is my particular domain. What will happen when Greenwell goes on leave, I don't know. She expects to go some time soon.

One of the boys in my ward got news that he had been awarded the French Médaille Militaire and, to celebrate this great event, we had a 'do' in the ward in the evening. I provided some extra food and smokes and bought a bottle of wine at the canteen in which the patients all drank his health and gave him three cheers, much to his confusion – he being a very bashful, very nice youth, a Welshman too, but by no means of the Cambrian type. We also had some singing and then the gramophone to end up with, so we had quite a cheery evening, apparently enjoyed by all. It is nice to have little outbursts of this kind, now and then. It helps to keep the men cheery and their spirits have a lot to do with their general health.

SUNDAY, 27TH OCTOBER

Have just finished scribbling three letters and now for a few lines of diary – poor neglected little record – a party in full swing next door, rather distracting my thoughts. Much talk and converse on all manner of subjects, chiefly tittle-tattle about the hospital, which is a never-failing source of interest and amusement and gossip. It's a queer little world of its own – everything that happens is common property in less than no time, especially the intercourse between the nursing staff and MOs, which is watched by many pairs of interested eyes. Captain Ward escorted C and me to a concert the other night and no doubt everyone had much to say on that topic, though I haven't heard any rumours of it yet.

There is the party taking its departure next door, with many goodnights and much cheerfulness. Someone has stayed behind to wash up, so the conversation is as strenuous as before.

My ward is now an influenza department and I have thirteen 'fluers' filling the atmosphere with germs. I am wondering if I can escape by any means myself. I felt sure the complaint was attacking me this afternoon, but now I feel better again and there is still hope. Some of the patients are quite poorly, but others are recovering. One is our own Mess cook – the Mess is very hard put to it without him, and hoping, I think, to get him back as soon as possible. And there is Sgt. Gardener, one of Major Wood's minions. He has been quite bad, but is slowly recovering now. Maj. Wood trots in and out in his comfortable, fatherly manner and takes blood cultures and advises about the patients. It's all very interesting and I'm glad to be in charge. It makes a change from the everlasting dysentery, which we are getting very tired of. However, the season for that is passing by and influenza will be gaining in numbers I expect. There seems every prospect of a bad epidemic shortly and the other hospitals are taking in numbers of cases. There are strong rumours that the complaint is very rife in the camps, and knowing how infectious it is, one shouldn't be at all surprised at its sweeping through everywhere. Two of the staff have already been laid low by it and I expect more will shortly follow suit. The WAACs have it in their camp and quite a lot have come in, some fairly bad. Well, I must sleep now and prepare for more work tomorrow and probably more admissions – perhaps a ward-full.

TUESDAY, 6TH NOVEMBER

This morning finds me lazifying in bed, when all the rest of the hospital world is at its busiest. Yesterday I had a slight, but decided, touch of the flu with a small temp. and the symptomatic aches and pains and general feeling of squeamishness and, having had a sick headache the day before, I pleaded for a half day in bed to recuperate and this is the result. Here I am still and it's doubtful I shall be allowed on duty today. Very annoying, as I am afraid of losing my wards. C was stricken down the day before yesterday and has gone to Sick Sisters. She had the tiresome complaint quite decidedly, with a temp. of 101.6, so was wafted off to the home of the invalids very speedily. Being on duty during the afternoon and evening, while Lang my assistant had a half-day, I knew nothing of C's departure till Capt. Ward launched the information at me in the evening, much to my surprise and rather consternation. Seems quaint we should both be invalids at the same time and it's only just a day or two ago that we were laughing and saying whoever went sick, it wouldn't be us, as we appeared to be immune to all manner of diseases.

Am sorry to be away from the wards and wondering today how they are getting on and who is relieving there. Have three Sergeants in 7 just now, two of them on the hospital staff and another from the convalescent camp, so we should be well kept in order – or they will be, as the case may be. The rush of influenza, however, seems to be abating slightly and we haven't had to open out the whole hospital for it, so far at any rate, as we did in the summer. On the other hand, there seems to be a larger percentage of pneumonia among the invalids and one or two have died of the dreaded complications. Two Lovat Scout men – hardy Scotsmen – were admitted some time ago, both with pneumonia, and one died only a few days ago. Such a nice man, I believe.

The camp here doesn't seem nearly as full as it was, though there are still plenty of troops about. The last time I was down on Tipperary Road, the men (Highland Infantry Brigade) were all very busy, taking up every tent and lifting the floorboards, digging up the sand underneath and I suppose disinfecting it to try to combat the flu germs, which seem to almost be causing a panic among the authorities. The weather is wretched again, two whole days of almost incessant rain, which will help the Hun, I'm afraid, to hold out a bit longer. We were all excited over the Turkish and Austrian surrenders, but not unduly so.* I think the men are too fed up with the war to enthuse about anything.

* The Turks surrendered on 30 October, the Austrians on 3 November.

MONDAY, 11TH NOVEMBER

A momentous day, the occasion of the signing of the Armistice and the cessation of hostilities and possibly the harbinger of that peace we have all waited for so long. Can this really be the end of the war? Can the desperate, horrible fighting and struggling really all be over? One can't realize it one bit, and it all seems so vast and inconceivable. Germany seems to have absolutely gone to pieces. The Kaiser and Crown Prince fled to Holland and new ministers are in power. It remains to be seen now how she extricates herself from the hopeless situation she has put herself into, and also how we set about disentangling our affairs and straightening out all that the war has brought about.

There is no very evident sign of rejoicing about the camp here, but rumour has it that Paris-Plage is being made lovely tonight and I can imagine Aussies and Canadians painting the place red. We suspected something of import when this morning, at about 7.30, just before we went on duty we heard cheer upon cheer in the distance from one of the camps and all through the day, spasmodically, there has been distant cheering. The rumours soon leaked through and were officially confirmed by the CO later on. It came through in a communiqué during the morning and when written down in black and white could hardly be disputed. Still, there does not seem any great spirit of elation, perhaps because no one quite realizes the event yet, and also of course there are still very sick men in the hospital who are fighting for their lives and that always brings one face-to-face with serious things and the realities of life. It is real enough though, that the murder up the line has ceased, and that is something to give heartfelt thanks for.

Poor Alastair – he is in bad luck this time, with his wound; a few days more and he would have been quite safe.* Christie is still in

---

* Alastair received a second wound in the very last week of the war. It was more serious than the first one, and while in hospital in Nottingham a few weeks later there was talk of his having to have an arm amputated. Fortunately a second opinion saved him from that. He was fairly sure that he was the victim of 'friendly fire', the British artillery failing to keep up with the rapid advance of the infantry.

dock, recovering slowly and still looking very white and pulled down. I was not kept long. After two days I was turned out, back to duty again, partly by my own doing as I couldn't be bothered being in hospital any longer, and as I knew Matron was wanting more staff, I preferred to turn to again and not act the invalid any longer. So, having been transferred to Sick Sisters on Wednesday after two days in bed here, I went back on duty on Sunday morning. After bobbing about in various wards and tanks, including doing extra and relief, I have now landed in ward 11 pro tem to take Sister Clough's place, as she is moving to 24 General tomorrow. The patients are all flu and some are very bad, so it is a bit of a responsibility and one I don't relish much. Capt. Ward is the MO while Capt. Bloom is invalided. He was amused to see me turning up again, but he is too busy just now to think about much besides his work. Four of the MOs are sick, so the ones that are left of course have double the work to do.

It's late now, so I must go to bed. All the corridors are celebrating peace with great merrymaking and parties and the MOs over the way are having a grand dinner with much singing and festivity. They won't feel very festive tomorrow I'm afraid, after such a jovial and racketing time.

WEDNESDAY, 20TH NOVEMBER

We are still trying to acclimatize ourselves to the altered order of things and the coming of peace. Not quite peace yet, but still very nearly, and every day brings news of some further step towards the final day of the war. Of course rumours are flying around in great numbers, but it seems fairly certain that this base is to be used as a large demobilizing centre and that, whatever become of the others, our hospital and 24 are to remain for some little time to deal with accidents and the local sick. So, if we are left here there might be some months of active service still ahead of us.

At present the hospital is fairly busy filling up with the epidemic of flu and also with the aforesaid local sick. I have fifty patients in the ward, but no one is very bad. The severe cases are transferred up to ward 6 and taken off our hands, which is rather a blessed relief. One can't look after a full ward and special the very sick men at the same time. Two orderlies, who were in our ward and were sent up to the pneumonia ward, have both died, casting rather a gloom over the staff, as they are the first of the orderlies to die from sickness in the camp since the hospital was established. One of them died of TB, so it was not altogether to be wondered that he succumbed so suddenly to the flu. The TB must have been working its wicked way with him for a long time without his noticing it particularly. I have several of the staff in now but they are all mending nicely, and I don't want any more at death's door, like those two. Christie is still away sick and does not seem to throw off the complaint easily. She now has a bad relaxed throat and looks thin and pulled down.

The last few days have been so cold, a real sharp snap of winter. There is ice in the basin and jug and my sponge is frozen stiff – all the horrid accompaniments of the cold weather. It is cold again tonight and damp as well. I expect the frost will set in again after a short break.

I went to such an excellent concert last night, really the best I'm sure I ever have been to since coming out to France. It was held at the Red Cross Hut. Capt. Ward escorted me there. He went on leave this morning at 4 a.m. – an unearthly hour to set forth. We didn't get back from the concert till after 11.30, so it was a very lengthy affair – but I really enjoyed it all, every minute of it. There was a first-rate violinist who played most beautifully. I could have listened to him for hours. There were two very good singers and also a VAD from 56, who sang very well indeed. The orchestra formed the backbone of the performance and gave us several excellent selections. I haven't enjoyed a concert so much for a very long time and wish we could have some more like it.

A few nights ago, we celebrated the signing of the Armistice by a fancy dress party among ourselves. The Mess provided refreshments and we had whist and dancing and entertainments. Some of the costumes were most ingenious and very pretty. Sanderson and

Sister McMahon got first prizes, the former in very cleverly devised picture garb and the latter in early Victorian costume, equally cleverly put together. I went in a Blighty bag – I think it was quite an effective costume – and nearly everybody turned up in something quite creditable.

Leave has opened again and no one has gone yet, though expecting we shall be able to go very shortly. Barker is due first. I wonder when I shall get mine. Not before Christmas anyway and perhaps not for some time after.

WEDNESDAY, 27TH NOVEMBER

Another week has gone by and Christmas – and all its doings – doesn't seem so far off now. From all appearances we shall all be here for the festive season. There are no signs or symptoms of the hospital or staff taking flight, not even any signs of movement orders among the VADs. I don't really think I want to be moved just now. This seems as interesting a place as any to be at this time of change and variation. If it is to be a chief centre of demobilization there will be plenty doing and we shall probably be kept quite busy. Of course, all sorts and kinds of rumours are afloat anent the future. We have heard, several times, that we are packing up, but as many times that we are staying here and perhaps going to be the most permanent of all the base hospitals. Other rumours have it that all the nursing staff everywhere are very shortly going to have the option of resigning, but nothing is certain about this at present. No doubt it will come though, as the authorities will want to get rid of most of us as quickly as possible.

One still can't realize that the war is ended. Everything seems to go on so much the same here and the troops come and go as before, only with a more cheerful appearance and full of hopes of returning to Blighty before long. A good part of the Army seems to be already establishing itself in Germany, carrying out the terms of the Armistice, and one hears of a good many people being up in the Rhine towns. I wonder how they are liking the visitation into enemy country.

The flu is still raging apparently, and certainly doesn't seem in any way scotched out here or at home yet. We are still taking in a lot of cases, some bad ones among them and pneumonia is claiming a good many victims. It seems a weird complaint too, for the virulent forms are so rapid and complications develop before you know where you are. The ordinary straightforward cases are just very flu-like. I wonder if the experts will really discover what the complaint is. The latest theory, I believe, is that it is a form of swine fever and post-mortems have revealed various interesting signs and symptoms.

At present my ward is fairly light. Most of the patients are convalescent and as hungry as wolves and the constant trouble is to feed them. They grumble incessantly about the shortage of food, which is very discouraging when one does one's best to supply their needs, extending the rather meagre rations as far as possible and supplementing it from one's own resources. There were a few men who would always grumble at anything and they upset everyone else and bring a bad spirit into the ward. One or two were discharged today, so I hope things will calm down a bit now.

Christie is back again in the room here and it is very comforting to have her companionship. I missed her while she was away. She is on light duty in Sick Sisters and will take Barker's place when she goes on leave, which will be quite soon now. Matron expects to be departing on leave in a few days' time. Her holiday will be only just due. Mine is due on 11th December, but I don't see any prospect of getting it then. There are too many waiting to go before me.

Glad to think of Alastair being safely over in Blighty again, even though he has a wounded arm. It is comforting to think that he is out of the country and nearer home, even if the fighting is over and the danger gone. One never knows what might happen though. Sickness is rampant, even if the horrors of shot and shell are things of the past.

Dorothea was home on leave from 10 to 27 December

TUESDAY, 31ST DECEMBER

The last day of the year – a momentous year too, with all its anxieties and stress and surprises. Am back, once more, in the old hole in my little wooden hut, and back at work in the wards. I am in No. 8 this time – a familiar haunt – but now looking after measly cases, not flu, as they were when I was last there. I was sent down to the ward yesterday and arrived to find it nearly full, a good many of the patients being quite convalescent but my appearance must have been such that in a very short time the order came that all the patients, en masse, were to be transferred to another ward, so in the afternoon the whole of the flock took flight and there was I left in an empty ward, with a good deal of clearing up and spring cleaning to do. However, the orderly went and summoned the assistance of a fatigue party of Bosches and after having done all the transferring of the patients – carrying the stretchers and so on – they helped all afternoon to get the ward straight and worked quite fairly hard, as hard as one expects these prisoners to work. I have two orderlies, a very tall and rather spotty-faced youth, but not so bad as orderlies go, and the other, very small, who apparently rejoices in the nickname of 'Tich'. He seems quite a good little worker, though of rather the rough and ready sort. Today, five more measles have turned up from another ward, so we have not been left patient-less for long. These are real measles we have got in, and the patients sent out were German measles, so as the ward has not been fumigated I am wondering whether these poor things are expected to have a double dose. Really, the ways of this hospital are beyond imagination.

Poor Christie is suffering very much from a septic thumb. She has practically not slept at all these last two nights, and of course, is off duty and can't do anything except attend to the ill-behaving member, soaking it and having it fomented. Really very tiresome for her and will pull her down.

Christmas seems to have been well celebrated in the hospital, with concerts and feasts and dances. I took part in the final outburst last night when the staff were the guests of the Officers' Mess at a dance in the Red Cross Hut along the road, not very far from here. We had a delightful evening and I renewed all my youth, dancing on the light (questionably so) fantastic toe. There were a lot of extraneous people present, guests from the neighbourhood. I got several introductions and one or two were really good partners, but on the whole there was not much of a show of dancing. Two or three of the couples, who seemed to keep themselves to themselves – very much convoy girls and their favourite swains I think – were doing wonderful things, quite beyond my powers. Must have been the Fox Trot à la mode,* not very becoming but very neatly done. We had the convalescent camp orchestra and they played very well, though some thought a little slowly. We kept up the giddy whirl till nearly 1, so were not in bed till the early hours and consequently today I feel a trifle chewed-paperish. These frivolities couldn't be repeated very often.

I have a morning off and have paddled down into town but found nothing much to buy. Very wet weather, but not cold. I suppose that will come before long and we shall be shivering and shaking in the icy blast. It is nearly lunchtime now and I will be back at work again for a whole long afternoon and evening. How boring!

SATURDAY, 4TH JANUARY

Another wet evening and the familiar sound of that pitter-patter of rain on the tarpaulin roof is the accompaniment to my scribblings. Well, I am alone again reigning solitary in this little compartment. C has gone to Tino† to have her thumb seen to. She was really in such pain and discomfort with it that she was anxious to get it properly treated and the little digs Major Duncan took at it with a scalpel were not doing any good. She went off two or three days ago, and I have not heard yet whether she had her thumb opened up and if so, how she got on. I meant to go today, but another ploy prevented me carrying out my intentions. This was to go to tea with the officer

---

* The Fox Trot was still a new dance, having originated in the USA in 1914.
† The Villa Tino was the nurses' convalescent home in Étaples.

staff at one of the prisoner-of-war camps along the Camiers road. The guests consisted of just Williams and me, and we were invited last night at another dance by Mr Duncalfe. I discovered, when I danced with him at the big dance in the Red Cross hut, that Mr D came from Cropwell Bishop near home, so we found a good deal in common and got on quite well together. Last night he came armed with this invitation and, as I had to have a chaperone, got Williams to accept too and accordingly at 3.30 this afternoon we turned up at the little camp and were entertained to tea and talk by the three officers who comprised the staff – Lieut. Duncalfe, an Irish Captain and a sub whose name I didn't hear. We had a very nice little party and I was quite sorry to come away. Williams had to be on duty at 5, so we had rather a rush but got a lift back in the trundling camp lorry with great speed for our benefit, so we could be ready to start as soon as possible – the Bosches being made to double like anything by a very fierce-voiced and -mannered Sergeant.

Now I am going to be early and cut supper, so as to have an extra hour or two of sleep to make up for what I lost last night. The dance was delightful and I really enjoyed it much more than the last one, though the floor wasn't so good, nor the band. But it seemed altogether less formal, or else I was more in the spirit of the thing. Anyway that's the last of the frivolities for the present, en tous cas. Our little fling is over and we must settle down to sober life again. Rather sad really, as these dances have been very great fun and one can get to know people that way when one doesn't as a rule get the chance of meeting them. I am still in 8 ward with the measly ones, but really rather bored with work at present. Only seven patients and none bad, I am glad to say. Not looking forward much to the day when the ward fills up and the real scramble begins.

MONDAY, 6TH JANUARY, 3 A.M.

A sudden change has occurred since I last wrote, for here I am on night duty again. Matron announced the startling fact of my fate yesterday morning and I was rather taken by surprise, even though I knew I was quite due for the nocturnal job. Don't really mind so very much, except for the disagreeableness of the actual night duty. I shall be very much deserted anyway presently when Williams goes home this week and C follows suit soon after, so I might as well be as friendless and forlorn in this new artificial life as I am on day duty, which I should have found decidedly dull. Have been shot off to wards 11 and 12 to take Morris's place and find a large crowd of unruly patients in each ward, a good many waiting for convoy and getting rather impatient at the delays. Only one man is bad and he has slept fairly well so far, so cannot say I have been exactly pushed. Night is wearing away to the sound of pitter-pattering rain. Feel very lost as to work, but suppose I shall find my way with things shortly – it's a beastly sort of existence and I cannot 'thole'* it at present.

THURSDAY, 9TH JANUARY

Yesterday morning Paul, Whalley and I went out to Merlimont to pay a chance visit to the Tank School† and see what we could see. Hardy and Scott tacked themselves on, as a lift was available for the whole lot of us, so we were quite a large party. I was rather hoping to see one of the officers who came to the dance here, but there was no one about except the Sergeant and Corporals in charge. We saw the big tanks, all lined up looking like huge antediluvian monsters, but well covered and all sleeping soundly – nothing doing there in the way of a ride. However, the Whippet Tanks‡ some little distance away were in action, so we and a large party of ASC§ Sergeants, also sightseeing, were conducted across the sandy and heathery ground to where, among the trees, these queer creatures were lying low.

After a time, one of the Tank Corps got his Whippet stirred up into action and brought it round with much fuss and noise and we all climbed in and on it. Not much room for sitting inside, but four or five of us packed in with the driver. The rest were ensconced on

---

* North Country word for 'put up with'.
† The British Tank Gunnery School had been established at Merlimont, just south of Le Touquet.
‡ The Whippet Tanks were the fast, light tanks with a revolving gun turret on top on which all the later tanks were modelled.
§ Army Service Corps.

the top and front, clinging on. We started off with terrific noise and much petrol fumes and trundled along over the rough ground at quite a fairish pace. There was a lot of water lying out in ponds every here and there and we steered gaily through these without bothering in the least. It was very jolly and bumpy and noisy and the heat got rather overpowering before long, but the experience was amusing. We took a long turn round and then came back to rejoin the other animals looking like a herd of queer-shaped elephants in the distance. Before finishing the trip the driver took us up a steep little sandbank at a tremendous angle and then down we dumped over the other side into a pool of water and the bump this time was so sharp that two of the Sergeants were shot off the top right into the pool and were left struggling in the shallow water. They picked themselves up – very dismal and soused through – much to the amusement of their friends. We didn't stay long after getting landed safely on terra firma again.

Three of us set out first and Hardy and Scott came behind. We had to walk a goodish distance before getting a lift and then a RAF tender came buzzing along and, much to our joy, picked us up and we were landed home again about 12.30. It was a lovely day, just like spring, so we didn't mind the long morning and we enjoyed the expedition tremendously.

There are no lights tonight which is a great nuisance and I am writing by the light of a candle, wondering what we shall do tomorrow morning. It will be a nuisance getting the ward roused in the dark.

C is getting on pretty well at the Tino. I went to see her one morning and found her still in bed with her hand much bandaged and besplinted, but very cheerful really and with some nice room companions to look after her and give her assistance.

Williams has departed home today, so I feel rather deserted, but I find Whalley and Paul both quite pleasant companions on night duty, so am not doing so badly. Miss Porteous goes on leave to the south of France tomorrow and when she comes back will probably straight away be sent to her new duties on an ambulance train. So that will be a change. Wonder what the next will be.

The wards are both considerably emptier than when I first came on, for a night or two ago eighteen went out from next door and thirteen from here. Some more are marked up, so at that rate the wards will soon be empty. Capt. Ward came and paid me a call this evening, the second one since I have been here on n.d.. He stayed quite a little while, gossiping until Capt. MacDonald turned up to enquire for his patient and bore him off to his bed.

SUNDAY, 12TH JANUARY

Just settled both my wards down for the night and especially the next-door unruly ones who are always apt to be a bit of a handful. The evacuation of stretcher cases goes on. Tomorrow a.m. at 5.30 two of the patients from here are going, so the little party will be more diminished than ever. Capt. Ward was in again last night, sitting a long time and drinking camp coffee which I prepared for him. He was telling me all about the very gay and giddy dinner at the RAF the night before. There were amazing doings in the matter of drinks it appeared, too much so for Capt. Ward's taste. It's a pity these young airmen are so wild. They are just boys, many of them. Capt. MacDonald was one of the party and at the end of the evening riot – about 2 a.m., just as the guests were departing – Capt. MacDonald fancied one of the parachute baskets the men hang on the aeroplanes as a souvenir. Capt. Ward, stirred up, also fancied one and they both removed the coveted property – big things, about the size of clothesbaskets – and bore them home in the tender. Capt. MacDonald discovered halfway that his basket contained all

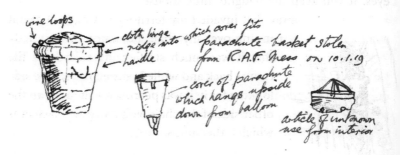

wire loops

cloth hinge which cover fits
ridge into which
handle

parachute basket stolen from R.A.F. Mess on 10.1.19

cover of parachute which hangs upside down from balloon

article & unknown use from interior

the table napkin rings belonging to the airmen's Mess. Capt. Ward found various odds and ends of equipment in his, but nothing so valuable. Anyway, the whole party was evidently very gay but not a dissipation to be indulged in too often.

I went to see C again yesterday, bicycling out to Tino and quite enjoying the ride. Found the invalid better, but still looking thin and tired. Hope she will not have to wait long before getting home. Williams has departed for home, so I am left lone and lorn, but at present find Whalley a pleasant companion. She will be going soon though and I shall be left in the lurch again.

WEDNESDAY, 15TH JANUARY, 10 P.M.

Such a night of rain and storm, but really very mild which is rather a comfort. Just got the families settled off to sleep, at least most of them. Must go presently over to 12 ward and see if all is peaceful there. Have only one orderly since old Davenport went sick, so Brown assists me in here nowadays and 12 is left to look after itself. All the patients are very convalescent, so it doesn't much matter if they are without oversight.

My bunk chair, at least one of them, is occupied tonight by a little furry black kitten stretched out comfortably sleeping having made itself very much at home and settled down here for the night. No – it is awake now and scratching the back of the chair and looking at me with its bright little eyes. It will keep the naughty little mouse away that invaded my territory last night. I saw it running over my chair, but came in so quietly that it was much startled. It ran behind the canvas back and while I peeped round one side looking for it, it was peering out at me from the other side of the chair with its beady black eyes which rather amused me.

MONDAY, 20TH JANUARY

Well, here is a thrilling adventure in prospect. Hardy (VAD) and I start off tomorrow, if nothing unforeseen occurs, in answer to a summons from the Matron-in-Chief to report at 32 Stationary armed with small baggage necessary for three or four days _and a cap_, specially emphasized, and then after probably a night at my old haunt we start on a trip up the line.* It's too amazing almost to be conceived of and somehow I never thought I should have such luck. It seems the choice falls on those with longest service, which of course made me a certain candidate as I have been out here longer than anyone else at this hospital. Hardy comes next but one or two more equal or run her very close. Well, it's a great adventure anyway, and I am full of speculations as to what form and in what direction the trip will take. Naturally we are objects of the greatest envy to all the other VADs but I expect they will all get their turn if these tours are being arranged now as a regular thing for everyone who has not yet had a chance of seeing the battlefields. It seems small selections of VADs are being called up from all the hospitals in this area. Some have already gone but nobody is back yet to say just what happened.

There are also day excursions being arranged locally. Big charabancs I think to take whole parties of staff up the line. Some are going from here tomorrow but don't know yet who are the lucky ones. Good opportunity to get all these trips in while the hospital is so slack. Quite a lot of the wards are standing empty now and the staff is kicking its heels wondering what to do to occupy itself with days off showering down and now these excursions will be a great godsend to the unemployed ones on a very interesting occupation.

Christie came back from Tino today looking better but still thin and white. She is to wait here until her leave is through which may not be for some little time. Meanwhile she is to do light work in the Mess as her finger not being properly healed up is not considered

---

* Miss McCarthy was approached by Major Lord Greville on 15 January with plans for three of these trips to the battlefields, which she clearly approved of, and the full details of the itineraries appear in her notes for that date.

in a fit state to allow her to do ward work. She is very sorry she is missing these trips but I hope she will get the chance of the day expedition so will see something before she goes home.

Wonder who is looking after my boys tonight and whether Capt. Ward will be dropping in for a chat only to find me absent from duty. He stayed a very long time the other night talking about prehistoric man and animals. Then Capt. MacDonald appeared and joined his voice to the discussion. It was really most interesting what they said and I listened with all my ear, drinking in their learned remarks. They stayed till after 12 so it was a late hour before they had stumped off to bed. Must compose myself for sleep now in this solitary room.

WEDNESDAY, 22ND JANUARY

And here we are at the end of the first day of this most wonderful tour. One can hardly face the all too difficult task of writing an adequate account of the proceedings.

Well – to start off. Hardie and I left 46 Stationary yesterday afternoon at 2.45 and were driven in an ambulance to the station. There, after not much delay, got on train to Boulogne and had a very conversational journey owing to the vivacious efforts of an Aussie officer who was really very anxious to be good company and seemed a nice cheery sort of creature. Two more of the touring party joined us at Camiers so the four of us were able to exchange notes about our prospects and information and quite fraternized on our dawdling way. At Boulogne we proceeded into the town to the Christol and there left our baggage. The other two tourists were met by a swain and wafted off to get to somewhere. Hardie and I set off on our own to report to Matron-in-Chief right up in the old town as we were told to do. It was a long walk up and we had quite a wait when we got there but eventually had our very brief interview and were despatched to find our way out to 32 Stationary as soon as we could.

We made it convenient to have tea first at the Club and fortified ourselves for our long journey out to Wimereux. Just succeeded in catching a train by the skin of our teeth and after stopping to do some shopping in good old Wimereux proceeded out to 32. Hoping to get a lift but no luck at all and we had to walk all the way bearing our weighty luggage, and felt very glad indeed when our haven of refuge appeared in sight. We reported at the Mess and were given a cheerful welcome and then we went up to interview Matron and had quite a friendly little chat though she was rather concerned about the non-arrival of the other two who had showed no sign since we parted from them at the Hotel Christol. However they turned up in time for first dinner so Matron's mind was relieved.

It was very pleasant to be back at the old place again and to exchange greetings with quite a lot of the old friends, more of them than I realized were left of the old staff. I was allotted a bed in my old room down the little stair, sharing it with Maconochie, one of the original pair, Kay and Maconochie, who used to be there in the old days. I spent an active evening visiting friends including M. and Mme Cappin* in their little haunt. Found Maconochie a very talkative companion and eventually she went off to call on someone and I proceeded to bed. Slept fairly peacefully but found the pillow rather hard and uncongenial. However, didn't mind with such thrills in prospect on the next day.

Up this morning in time for the first breakfast with the rest of the party who had slept three together in a room upstairs, Sisters Reay and Gabriel's old room. Drifted across to the Mess armed with bag and baggage ready for the road. I renewed acquaintance with friends, some that I hadn't seen the evening before, and felt quite a centre of interest.

Not much after 7.45 we started off on the great trip. Matron Congleton was in charge of the whole party as it happened, so she escorted her little band of us four and one VAD from her own staff up to 83 General, conveyed thither in an ambulance. There we joined all the rest of the company, a motley collection of Sisters and VADs all ready and eager for the road. We had to wait rather a long time till our conveyances arrived. Meanwhile I ran across Philp and Sister Mary Jones, the latter rather to my surprise as I didn't know

---

* M. Cappin was presumably the old sailor man who knew all about the weather.

she was on the staff at 83. At last about 10 to 10 the cars turned up and the whole party of fourteen with a sigh of relief set out on their journey. There were five open touring cars, very comfortable and luxurious, and the party fitted in excellently. Our two friends from Camiers and Hardie and I packed ourselves into one of the cars, the others disposed themselves according to taste. The officer-in-charge, a rather fat, florid person, went with Matron and her VAD.

Well, the cavalcade set off in glorious weather, freezingly cold but beautifully bright. Swished through Boulogne and out along the road to Montreuil. Before long one of the cars began to give trouble but after a short pause we went ahead and our car shot on right away, leaving everyone else some way in the rear. Everything went without an 'itch as far as we were concerned. The ride was lovely though a bit cold certainly.

After Montreuil we went out into new country and then through numbers of small villages all carefully named with enormous signboards with such familiar appellations as Conchy, Ligny, Aubin St Vaast etc. Everything getting more exciting and interesting as we proceeded. However there was no sign of war on this part of the run except for the multifarious notices and signboards directing troops to their ways and means. Finally we reached Doullens, quite a flourishing little market town through which we shot like an arrow from a bow and away out on the other side up and over a steep hill and down to Gézaincourt, our first real stop. Here we pulled up in front of a fine old chateau, a sort of wayfarers' hostel providing board and lodging for sightseers such as we are and for any other travelling parties on the road.* We are here now staying the night and all tucked up ready for sleep, the same party of four all gathered in one room and quite ready for the rest. We had to wait when we first arrived here for the rest of the party to turn up. Meanwhile we had our very light lunch of tea and sandwiches but welcomed it very much to warm us up a bit. Other cars were waiting to take us on the

---

* The château at Gézaincourt had been turned into no fewer than four Casualty Clearing Stations during the 1918 German offensive.

afternoon tour, the really interesting part of the trip. The four cars of our morning convoy were not long in turning up and disgorging their load of passengers. Everyone was allotted bedrooms and deposited their luggage then, and then after all had rested and lunched without waste of time we set out again – the five new cars were exactly the same model as the last ones and our little quartette kept together as before, packed in warm and tight.

Away we went back, nearly to Doullens then out eastwards hurling along the road in fine style. Before long reached the first of the lines of chalky trenches zigzagging across the hills, then gradually we began to get into the battle zone proper, more trenches and now and then damaged cottages and then the dugouts and shelters began along the road and along the hillsides and in woods and very soon little crosses dotted the countryside; but there was nothing very obvious till we dropped into the first really ruined village, a little place which had evidently suffered severely from shellfire. The country round about was all wide open, rolling hills and dales and all scored and marked with trenches, dugouts and shell holes. All so wonderfully interesting after all one had heard. Not long after, we reached Albert, and there we stopped in front of the famous cathedral. Oh, the ruin and the wreckage and the wanton destruction. Certainly not a house round about left intact and the great building wholly, utterly devastated. We went inside climbing over heaps of rubbish and picked up a few souvenirs but didn't stay very long as time pressed and we had to be proceeding. But we had long enough to realize what the bombardment must have been like and how much destruction the shells can bring.

We presently all embarked again and then away on and out into more battlefields, the country growing more and more desolate as we proceeded. Torn and wrecked trees stood up everywhere, devastated woods showed in the distance and everywhere shell holes and remains of trenches and bits of wreckage of war. It was a wild but fearfully impressive scene viewed in the clear cold winter's day, not a living soul anywhere around, just shattered dugouts and rent and torn ground and little crosses singly and in groups here and there.

SATURDAY, 25TH JANUARY

At this point I had to break off to get my much needed night's sleep. Now the great trip is over and I am back again in my little bed but will resume the narrative from the point where I left off.

A few miles out of Albert our little convoy pulled up alongside the road and we all dismounted to see the biggest mine crater ever made. This was at a place called La Boiselle. A village had been near but now there was nothing to mark it but a few stones. The crater of the mine was certainly enormous, 1,000 feet across and 600 feet deep I believe, all blown out of the white chalk hillside. When this mine went up in summer 1916 it was the signal for the great Somme push to begin and there was a general advance then all along the line. Harry Lauder's son's grave was somewhere near, and the little man himself when he came out to see the grave had sung to assembled troops from the centre of the crater with his audience lining the sides and top all the way round.*

After leaving this place we shot away into wild, wild country, up hill and down dale, seeing great stretches of torn and broken forests and then open hillsides churned up with shell holes and trenches all overgrown yet clearly visible. We passed many German notices stuck up as evidence of their occupation and many of our own to show how we had superseded and triumphed over them. All the well-known places were labelled, villages that once were quite presentable little hamlets but now nothing remaining of them but heaps of rubble, sometimes not even that. Mametz and Contalmaison were some of the familiar-sounding names and one shuddered to think what these names meant to our troops when the fighting there was at its worst.

Our ultimate objective was Trones Wood and we pulled up there in the most desolate spot imaginable close beside a salvage dump, a collection of all sorts and kinds of trophies of war and a happy

* Sir Harry Lauder (1870–1950) was one of the greatest of all Music Hall entertainers, the absolute Scot in dress and voice. In memory of his son, he wrote what was perhaps his most famous song, 'Keep right on to the end of the road'.

hunting ground for souvenir hunters. We all turned our thoughts from contemplating the horrors of war to the important matter of collecting souvenirs when we saw so many at hand, but having gathered some selection together we followed our guide over rough ground pitted with shell holes towards the wood. It looked battered and war-worn, the trees standing there broken and dead seemed as though they were mutely protesting against the cruel machines that had brought them to that pitiable state. Not far away we came upon a most pathetic sight. Just the leg with boot and sock of one of our own boys sticking up out of a shell hole where he had been hastily buried. No name and no identification, only his rifle stuck into the ground beside him, a grim emblem to mark his lonely grave. A short distance away three dead Germans in a low dugout were partially buried, and all the men mourned by some loving one.

While we were making our little tour the drivers were very busy playing about with German hand grenades – things like a small oilcan fixed on the end of a fairly thick wooden handle. They threw them some distance away and then after a second or two the oilcan-head exploded with a great noise and a good deal of commotion but, the drivers seemed to think, with very little effect.

After collecting one or two more souvenirs at the salvage dump we climbed into our cars again. It was getting latish then, otherwise we would have gone on to the Butte de Warlencourt* which was not far away, but we had to get back to Gézaincourt before dark as there were no headlights on the cars. So we just hastened back the way we came, over hill and dale, through the devastated lonely country, never passing a soul till we got nearer our destination. It was getting dusk and very cold. When we finally turned into the gate of Gézaincourt Château again and pulled up in front of the wide steps there we all disentangled ourselves and got out the piles of trophies and afterwards went up to our respective bedrooms. Another party crossing with ours, one from Calais, was also staying there the night so there was a large gathering for the WAAC staff to cope with.

---

* An ancient burial mound dominating the Somme Valley which marked the limit of the British advance in the Battle of the Somme.

We had sandwiches and tea when we arrived, for which we were all very grateful. By that time the weather had turned ever so much colder and we were really all perished and didn't know what to do to keep warm. Dinner at 7.30 helped somewhat and we sought our beds fairly early. The other party had a very conversational and cheerful guide who was giving them quite a lecture on what they had seen during the day. Our fat old stick-in-the-mud was not nearly so forthcoming.

The hot water arrangements were rather so-so and we had to boil a kettle for our hot bottles, which wasn't altogether satisfactory as it filled so few each time it boiled up and the Sisters belonging to the other party we thought were being pushing and mean about the hot water. We all got our bottles filled in the end and went to bed fairly comfortably though the room was like an ice-house and the beds rather hard and insufficiently blanketed. But the trip was well worth any small discomfort of that sort and we had enjoyed every minute of the day.

MONDAY, 27TH JANUARY

Am back on night duty again, in ward 16 this time, with a new lot of patients to get used to, but as no one seems very ill and in fact most are fairly convalescent can set to on my diary again and scribble some more about the great tour.

The next day of the trip was spent at Arras and the battlefields beyond and was the longest and most interesting of the exped-ition. After a rather cold night at Gézaincourt on very moderately comfortable beds and in dubious bedclothes we woke up to a grey, chilly morning and proceeded to dress and then to breakfast feel-ing anything but warm and cosy. However the hustle of preparations for departure warmed us up a bit and presently the cars being all ready we got ourselves sorted out and packed in – Sweet, one of the two girls from Camiers, having selected a nice-looking driver – and without much delay we were off on the long run. The other party were still preparing when we left but no doubt it would not be long before they were under way too. Without passing through Doullens we turned away north up along a straight switchback road for some miles which eventually brought us to Arras, the first stage of our journey. As soon as we got into the town and even beyond in the outskirts we began to see the damage done by the shelling and as we passed through the narrow picturesque old streets many of the houses seemed to be toppling on to us, or rather their ruins, which looked sometimes as though the merest tremor would bring down great showers of bricks and stones. Others were mere shells, all the interior blown out and perhaps the frontage bulging out with the force of the explosion. Then there were streets with quite a lot of the buildings wiped out altogether. A church we passed was absolutely ruined and hardly recognizable for what it had once been.

We drew up in one of the main streets and in a small square in front of a fairly important-looking building, the town mayor's office, and here our guide got down to secure the necessary permits for us to do our sightseeing. The weather was still grey and cold and threatening to snow which was anything but pleasant and we had a very cold ride along the exposed high road that brought us up to Arras, so that really we were quite glad to get a little exercise to restore warmth and circulation and clambered out of our rugs and wrappings as quickly as possible when we stopped again in the Grande Place to view the damage there. We had taken a local guide on board, a Corporal from the office, and he proceeded to take the party in tow. The big square was a most impressive sight. At one side stood the great ruins of what must have been the Town Hall, utterly reduced to piles of bricks and rubble with only here and there bits of wall left standing. The rest of the square was formed by Flemish-looking houses, all alike with an arcade, pillared and very attractive. One felt the wickedness of the Germans in destroying a beautiful old place, but that certainly wouldn't preserve it from their worst efforts. There was a large notice put up by the French to the effect that nothing was to be touched as the ruins were to be preserved as a national memorial, a continual accusation against the Hun. This notice was also stuck up in the ruined cathedral, which evidently was not to be restored in any way.

Our guide took us down some steps into the basement cellar of one of the houses in the square and there began his tale. I didn't manage to take it all in, but it was very interesting about the old Spanish buildings and their innumerable cellars which the Sappers during the occupation of Arras had joined up together and made a continuous underground passage, with the long tunnel to Cambrai of 45 kilometres, our guide said, used for bringing reinforcements up without exposing them.* He took us through these connected cellars for quite a long distance, showing us a very old crypt of a chapel on the way and various other items of interest. He finally brought us into the light of day again under the walls of the huge ruined building which I took to be the Town Hall.

Our next visitation was made to the German dugout tunnel on the outside of Arras and we drove there in the motors as it was some little distance away across the railway. There were wonderful places certainly made by the Germans, a shelter for their troops and also a field dressing station. After they were driven out and we took possession we made use of it for the same purpose, and one side of the narrow entrance passage which runs a long way straight underground is lined with two tiers of stretchers on which the wounded were laid when brought in to have their wounds dressed. Gas-tight doors closed the passage at intervals and further on we came to a perfect labyrinth of caves and passages all labelled for their distinctive uses: operating theatre, surgeons' room and so on, and another was a cookhouse, and finally the system ended in a high cave where our guide showed us the place where British and German sappers met each other tunnelling vigorously to get the mastery. The Bosch, needless to say, got the worst of the fight that followed and we thereupon occupied his caves and he never got them back again.

Our whole party as we paraded through these underground vaults looked weird in the extreme. We were still muffled up for our drive and each of us carried a candle. We looked like some queer

---

* This must have been a misunderstanding. The total length of the tunnels under Arras was 22 kilometres, but there was no tunnel to Cambrai. Perhaps the guide meant that the length would be equivalent to that of a tunnel to Cambrai.

procession of inquisitors or heavily disguised brigands in their subterranean lair. At last we appeared above ground again and gave up our candles, returned to the waiting cars and off again into the town. Back to the town mayor's office where we left our guide and then away out into the open country again. We were right among the battlefields then and everything was teeming with interest. We followed another straight bare high road lined with gun emplacements and dugouts and with desert shell-holed hillsides stretching away on either hand. Clumps of trees here and there, and the inevitable, all too pathetic little white crosses dotted about.

Before long we were on one side of the famous Vimy Ridge. Here we pulled up and got out and our guide pointed out to us Mt St Éloi in the distance crowned with a few ruins of the village. Near to where we stopped was a little cemetery which we went to see, mostly Canadians buried there and some of the British killed in the push this last year. A large solid-looking memorial Cross had been erected to the Canadian officers and men who fell in the famous attack when the ridge was captured. This stood at a fork of the road in a very outstanding position. Following our guide we walked on along the road right over the famous ridge past Thélus, a well-known name, and down the valley on the far side. All was weird and a desolate camouflage along the road falling to bits, dugouts long since deserted. Everything silent as the grave as though nothing had survived the terrible storm of war that had passed over there.

Our cars had gone on ahead and we rejoined them some little way down the hill and then got our rather simple sandwich lunch with cold water to wash the sandwiches down. The drivers meanwhile had gathered round a little fire in a sheltered place near a dugout and were quite enjoying the respite from the very cold job of driving. At one side of the road here the land sloped very sharply away down to a small valley. This was said to be the toughest part of the ridge to capture and many lives were lost on this bit of the ground.

Impossible to describe it all adequately. The sights one saw will leave an undying impression, but almost oppressively sad, chiefly because of the utter loneliness and desolation of the scene.

Unexploded ammunition lay about and in fact everywhere we went we saw plenty of this besides many untouched dumps and stores.

Under way again once more and proceeding along the road leading from the foot of Vimy away towards Lens. Very soon we began to come into the region of the coal mines and saw in the distance huge black slag heaps towering into the air and the pithead machinery a mass of twisted scrap iron lying in the neighbourhood. Small villages dotted about were no better than rubbish heaps and when we got to Lens itself it was beyond imagination. In the whole of that small town not a house left standing, all reduced to rubble and matchwood. The streets practically wiped out except the main road we were on. We passed through too fast to take it all in but my impressions are of lines and lines of ruins. Some Chinese and German prisoners working away among the hopeless debris, and a few French people poking in the crumbling remains of their old homes to see what they could possibly recover.

Beyond shattered Lens we sailed out into open country again dotted with other smaller groups of ruins and battered stumps of trees, one of these seen in the distance being the famous village of Loos. Hulluch too was quite close, all suggestive of the fearful fighting in 1915. Hill 70* must have been plainly visible, but I wasn't aware of its being so near. A short run brought us to Vermelles where we turned off towards La Bassée and along a rather bumpy road with marks of old shell holes here and there through the same war-wasted country to the centre of so much fighting. The village itself was much like the other places utterly laid waste and ruined streets lined with rubble heaps and bits of roofs and splinters of wood. At one place we stopped and all got out and our guide showed us a German observation post, a big concrete shaft built up inside a house with two storeys to observe from. The house had since been shot away except for a bit of the roof which remained hanging on the top of the concrete erection. We climbed onto the pile of debris

---

* The scene of much fighting and considerable losses in August 1917, when the Canadian Corps attempted to draw the German troops away from the Third Battle of Ypres. See Chronology, p. 353.

to investigate the place nearer but didn't attempt to climb up into it as the ascent looked too difficult. Having rejoined the cars we set off again back to Béthune leaving the worst of the battle area behind us. But a good deal of damage was done to Béthune too this last year, when the Bosch shelled the place heavily. They aimed specially for the centre of the town and entirely destroyed the big buildings there and a good many houses as well. Others were badly knocked about and nearly every street we passed through showed traces of the bombardment.

Being by this time very weary and rather cold some of the party suggested a cup of tea somewhere and, having seen a YMCA as we passed through, whenever we got an opportunity we all pushed off to find it, Matron Congleton in the forefront. The place was a good way on but we came to it at last and threw ourselves on the mercy of the rather stern-looking gentleman in charge. He didn't look too pleased to see us, but invited us in to a seat at one of the bare tables. The YMCA itself, being established in the ground floor of a great big factory, was lit only by dim gas jets and very bare and draughty. It was a rest anyway and we drank up the rather tasteless cocoa provided and ate biscuits with great relish. It seemed a queer sort of place to land in but the town didn't evidently lay itself out for catering for tourists and we didn't see any other hopeful-looking restaurant, though our guide seemed to be able to find his way to one with two members of the party.

From Béthune we went right away coastwards again, soon leaving behind all the battle area and the signs and symptoms of the dreadful contest. We had had one or two punctures en route during the day but otherwise the drive had been without contretemps and now we sped along as fast as possible, the evening and darkness speeding almost as fast as we did.

TUESDAY, 28TH FEBRUARY

Seated once more in ward 16 bunk for another night's labours. If one had energy what a lot could be accomplished in these long idle hours, but I always feel more or less atrophied on n.d. and can't set seriously to work on anything, so time slips away and I get nothing done. However, intend to finish the history of the great trip, so here goes …

The second night of the expedition was spent at Blendecques just outside St Omer. Another large cold chateau much like the last one in general appearance and nearly as cold.* Our quarters this time were in huts outside in the grounds, quite nice places but the beds were nothing to boast about, the blankets a bit fusty. However one had to put up with these trifles as these hostels were not set out in Carlton and Ritz style. A very nice WAAC officer had charge of Blendecques, almost nicer than the one at Gézaincourt, very cheery and welcoming. We were fairly late in arriving as we had two punctures en route, one of the sufferers being our car.

Quite near our lodging place we passed the chateau where Lord Roberts had died.† The driver pointed it out as we skimmed by in the dark. Sad to say I was rather the worse for wear all evening after getting overcome with one of my usual headaches so my recollections of the evening are not too happy. Just managed to stick it through dinner but went to bed directly afterwards and slept off the overtiredness quite successfully. Matron very solicitous and came to see me but I wasn't worrying, knowing the old complaint too well. Woke up next a.m. feeling fresher but very cold. Was rather cold all night, really the getting up was a horrible job, the frost was so biting. But I was soon ready and adjourned to the dining room where we were served with a nice hot breakfast, waited on by WAACs looking the very soul of propriety. Ours was the only party staying there and also the last of the touring parties, before long the place was going to be closed and the WAAC dispersed in various directions.

It was not very long after breakfast before we were en route again being established now in a fresh set of cars, our fourth change since the trip began, and presently we were skimming along the road towards St Omer. There were only three of us in the car this time, Croysdale having established herself in one of the vehicles where

---

* This also had been a Casualty Clearing Station in 1918.
† Field Marshal Frederick Roberts, one of the most celebrated Army commanders of the nineteenth century, died of pneumonia while visiting troops at St Omer in November 1914.

there were only two passengers. So Sweet and I had the back seat to ourselves and were able to settle in very comfortably getting right in under the rugs and coverings. Hardie sat upfront with the driver. Her eyes had been dreadfully bad with the run of the day before and she did look rather a sight in the morning first thing with two bung eyes and hardly able to see out of one. However, this improved as the day went on and she found the best and most sheltered place was behind the windscreen in the front seat.

We had only quite a short run to St Omer and were soon threading our way among the very narrow, picturesque, old-looking streets up to the cathedral. Here we disembarked again and our guide conducted us into the fine old edifice. There did not seem to be anything of very special interest to see, but as none of us had any guidebooks or any idea what to look for and our CO seemed only anxious to get round and out as soon as possible, being I should think a *most* unecclesiastical person, I daresay we missed anything that we should have specially noticed. I was more interested in the quaint little funeral ceremony that began soon after we got into the cathedral and stayed behind to watch the catafalque proceeding up the aisle, preceded by the fat priests and acolytes and followed by a long procession of mourners dressed in deepest black. Our curiosity cut us off from the rest of the party, who followed the guide down to the big square, and when we came out they were nowhere to be seen. We began to feel rather lost and had to do some questioning and wasted some time wandering about searching for our friends. At last we got directed to the Grande Place and there we found the cars drawn up in line waiting for us and everyone established in their places wondering where we could have got to.

Passing through St Omer we saw several houses that had been wiped out by air raids and a great many more damaged. Last summer must have been a dreadful time there but it was always rather a 'windy' place for air raids. We were soon out on the high road again and had a clear run to Calais. Very cold and very dusty but plenty of good fresh air.

First though, I was forgetting we visited a big ammunition dump at Audruicq several miles down from St Omer. Our guide had to get the necessary special permits and someone to take us over and then we were admitted to the sacred enclosure. We shed the gallant Captain at the office orderly room and were escorted thereafter by quite a nice enthusiastic little officer who seemed immensely interested in everything and gave us a lot of information on the subject of bombs and shells. He explained first of all the workings and methods of shells and bombs and showed us examples of them, and then took us round the dump or at least part of it and showed us the huge howitzer shells stacked in their hangar, shells waiting idly for the employment which I hope will never come and all kinds of other shells, 18-pounders, shrapnel and stacks of high explosive etc. Stacks and stacks of them there were in long sheds protected by sandbags over the roof, and everywhere the whole place was well prepared for air raids. The Bosch was always over trying to blow it up but never succeeded except when he first paid a visit in 1916 at the time of the Somme push when a whole army's ammunition was stored there and in consequence of its disappearance the 'push' had to stop, so the Germans must have congratulated themselves greatly on that piece of work.

There were still the remains of the old explosion to be seen – twisted girders from the old sheds and the scars in the ground where the dump had stood and scattered about over quite a large place remains of a whole store of cartridges, small ammunition rounds and rounds of it which popped off merrily in the midst of the inferno. The extraordinary part about it was that no one was killed except one old man in a neighbouring hamlet, this hamlet being laid out absolutely by the blast of the explosion. We passed it on our way round past the camp afterwards and certainly the poor little cottages had suffered severely. There was not enough of one of them to call a dwelling.

Our talkative, anxious little guide had only an hour at his disposal to take us round so he just showed us the most important things and then brought us back to the main entrance again where the cars were duly awaiting us and our CO Capt. Ogilvie. In we climbed again and snuggled down among our rugs and blankets. Then after many adieus and politeness sailed off on our way once more.

After this we made all speed towards Calais and were getting on famously when the front car in which 'Mamma' and 'Papa' were established broke down. A damaged axle was the trouble and quite incurable, so after a short consultation it was decided to carry on with the four cars and leave the damaged one behind to be brought in later. So we had a rather more crowded journey from this point onwards. However it wasn't very far to go and presently we pulled up in Beaumaris Camp outside the WAAC Headquarters. There we had lunch in a big fresh-looking hut with the WAAC officer-in-charge presiding at the head of the table.

A visit to Calais was to have been part of the programme and a night spent there, but Matron Congleton wanted to get back to 32 as soon as possible so it was decided to cut out Calais altogether and finish our trip this same day. So after waiting a bit and getting a photograph taken of the assembled party we were ready to start off again, this time alas not in our beautiful smooth-running highly distinguished touring cars but in a rattling shaking old charabanc, which trundled along very unceremoniously through the streets of Calais. We had a very bumpy journey along the coast road, which, although very pretty especially in the clear winter sunlight, was not exactly a finished high road and full of terrible holes which made our going rather slow. We went by Wissant and then along to Andreselles and Ambleteuse and so back to the old camp again. It was rather nice being on the old familiar road again that I had walked along so often as far as Andreselles and more often to Ambleteuse. Still we were not sorry when the journey was ended as the last part was not a paragon of comfort and we were quite ready for a good cup of hot tea in the Mess and the greetings of the friends again.

Everyone else but the 32-ites went on in the charabanc to be dropped gradually at their various destinations with all their trophies and much loot. We had our fair share too, especially Sweet, who had a whole armoury of weapons and shell cases. I spent the evening with Mitchell gossiping and after supper sat with her and Jobbie for a while talking before going to bed. The other three members of our party slept in their room upstairs and had rather a cold night but I was quite comfortable in my bed in Maconochie's room. I was glad of the night's rest and repose next day. We got a train back to Étaples in the morning and arrived without further contretemps, leaving Sweet and Croysdale at Camiers standing on the platform rather forlorn beside all their belongings. So ended a very happy three days, and it being the very last of these tours, Hardie and I considered ourselves very lucky indeed to be chosen to take part in it. It was just a chance of chances.

One of the most interesting things I saw up at the battlefields was the camouflage one has so often heard about. Some of the ruined houses were covered over with nets to which small tags of stuff were fastened of grey and red exactly matching the walls and slates remaining on the broken roof. The gun-pits of course in places were heavily camouflaged in the same way but with green. Another thing I saw was a sniper's post in an imitation tree. This was set in a row of tree stumps and looked exactly like one of them but it was made of iron and couldn't have been a very comfort-able spot judging from the way it was riddled with shrapnel holes. A house in a village we passed through had a screen right across the front of it towards the enemy lines painted in imitation of ruined doors and windows. It was a very dilapidated cottage with a large hole blown right out of both walls and the screen was to prevent the enemy seeing troops passing down the road at the back of it where otherwise they would have been plainly visible through the gap.

We saw several observation posts built high up in trees, one very cleverly hidden among thick ivy. Also we saw along the high road from Arras several of the German reinforced concrete blockhouses and pill boxes, one quite the real old sort made of iron and shaped rather like a pillar box. The reinforced concrete erections were all smashed to bits. The bombardments must have been terrific to reduce them to that state as one could see they had been built tremendously strongly. We also passed, quite close to Doullens, the Canadian Stationary Hospital in a splendid old moated build-ing which was bombed so badly in the summer and the theatre wiped out while an operation was in progress.* It was still open as a hospital and looked a wonderful old place with a deep moat and high wall all round.

One will often think of all these things again and recall them all to mind and many more which I haven't put down in this account.

WEDNESDAY, 28TH JANUARY

Embarked upon another night and hoping that the patients have all settled down quietly to their many hours' rest. One goes to Blighty at 2.15, that is our only excitement apparently for the rest of the night. Went into town with Whalley this morning and shopped. Shall be sorry when she goes. She is a very nice girl though difficult to know at first, but one gets to like her better on further acquaintance. She has only five patients to look after in her ward so cannot be called exactly hard-worked. Yesterday I was very frivolous and went out with the Reid who was my chaperone(!) to tea with Mr Duncalfe at his new prisoner-of-war camp down opposite headquarters. We arrived soon after 5 and had a very pleasant hour or two in the funny little Mess room with the four officers to entertain us. Afterwards Mr Duncalfe and one other officer escorted us home up through the camp. Was only just in time to change and get in to supper without being disgracefully late. As it was I ran into the arms of Matron when I came in at the door and got a mild reprimand but nothing more serious than that.

I seem to have seen a good deal of the Bosch lately with my day and a half in the tanks looking after the prisoners, some of whom were very sick men. I thought I was going to stay there altogether but Matron changed her mind and put me into the shadows of night again at which I was not altogether surprised. I must say in a way I rather liked the Bosch wards. They were quite interesting for a change and I aired my small knowledge of German with some success though I found my vocabulary was decidedly limited. There

---

* This air raid on the night of 29 May 1918 caused the death of 25 staff and patients and was unquestionably a deliberate attack on a hospital.

was no difficulty getting things done anyway. One had but to say the word and the commands were carried out instantly and there was never a sound of grumbling. The men were all too glad to be in hospital instead of down in their camp working and having rather a hard time of it really. Some of the patients are brought in in a really disgraceful state of neglect, but it's said they come to the camp in a bad state of health and their stamina is very poor after being in the German lines. Some of the dysentery cases were just skin and bone, wasted away altogether and in a fearful state of bedsores and general unhealthiness. The tanks are the busiest part of the hospital now. There is nothing really over this side at all and a lot of the wards are closed down partly owing to coal shortage. Oil is very short too and in this cold weather it doesn't make life any more congenial. We are hoping and praying for warmer weather to come soon but I'm afraid it's too soon to expect any very lasting change.

One of our night Sisters got herself into fearful trouble the day before yesterday by going lorry-jumping to Arras and then getting stuck somewhere on the way down so that she didn't arrive back till 9.30, a VAD from 26 General was also missing and it turned out that the two culprits had gone out together. Everything was soon discovered by the Matron of 26 telegraphing to our Matron and the latter immediately proceeding to make enquiries. There were fearful to-dos when Sister Berger arrived back and the wind blew a gale for some minutes. Miss Stronach was up yesterday consulting about the matter but I haven't heard what the sequel to the story is. These are the little excitements of life that crop up now and then to give us something to think about.

SATURDAY, 1ST FEBRUARY

Nothing very exciting happened since last writing. The stillness of night wraps me around at present, the ward being in profound peace. Was up early this afternoon at 4.30 to go with Reid to our second tea party at the POW. Quite enjoyed the little excitement as before, though none of the company present wildly exciting and Mr Duncalfe a little under the weight of a bad cold which was making him feel a bit so and so. He goes home for demobilization this next week, he thinks, so there will be no more paddings out after this evening's sortie. Am not caring very much as the quiet and sober life is always recommendable for night duty. Any undue dissipation makes me feel very tired and so-and-so-ish.

C seems at last to have got home. Heard this evening of her departure from the Tino at 4 a.m. this morning by convoy. Feel a bit lonesome, deserted by all my friends. Whalley goes probably on Monday if not tomorrow. She is off night duty and Paul, who is back from south of France leave, is taking her place. Paul, is now sharing my room instead of the masterful Sister Miller, rather a welcome change in some ways. Weather still desperately cold and one gets really frozen going out of these fairly well-warmed-up wards into the freezing night air. Hoping every day a change will come but nothing appears 'to be doing' yet.

Still no word of the looked-for demobilization. Meanwhile the staff increases and the work lessens except for the influx of Bosch sick who are still being kept over in the tanks, though these are speedily filling up.

THURSDAY, 6TH FEBRUARY

Just after the midnight hour so I can alter the date with an easy conscience. There is a constant drip drip outside tonight from the melting snow. It must have snowed very heavily during the day as the ground was thickly covered when I woke up and there were only a few flakes when I went to bed. Paul and I took a short walk over the sand dunes to get a breather after a night spent in these stuffy wards and it was quite fair though the wind was cold. A little more to do tonight owing to influx of eight Jerries admitted last night about 11.30. We were told to expect sixteen and got everything ready for a big invasion, however only these eight turned up and here they are still. Sisters Monroe and Gracie had a rude shock when they came on this morning and found this addition to the family, not having bargained for Bosches being planted into the newly cleaned end of the ward, made nice and tidy for the next comers.

These prisoners are poor-looking specimens, one especially is nothing but skin and bone and looks fain to 'shuffle off this mortal coil' without much delay. Most of the others are feeble and under-fed creatures. One is running a high temperature and is a possible typhoid: he came in as a walking case and hardly able to stand with weakness and exhaustion. They have all come from some Stationary or CCS Hospital up the line and have been in a day or two I think, but they must have been in a poor state before they were received as patients. It's rather disgraceful that our prisoners should be allowed to get so dreadfully ill, and whether it is the result of underfeeding or overworking or sheer neglect something ought to be done to improve matters. We can't say much about our men being neglected if we allow these Bosches to get into a state like that. Of course it's likely enough that many of them were in a very poor condition when they were taken prisoner and a great number of them are the latest called-up recruits, probably poor and weedy specimens to begin with, but still they do come in covered with sores and many of these dysentery cases have been left days without attention, with the result that they get too far gone to do anything for. One man died twenty minutes after admission to the hospital the other night. He really should never have been moved at all being much too ill, but when the patients are Bosch that doesn't seem to be considered so much.

I am struggling along with my German such as I can remember and make myself pretty well understood, though I get very tied up at times and bits of French and Portuguese worm their way into my linguistic efforts sometimes. However a smattering of the language serves its purpose and one can't talk to these Germans like one can to our own men so there is nothing needed really but the bare necessaries of conversation.

Our own patients at the other end of the ward were very resentful at this intrusion and had many suggestions to make this morning as to how to get rid of the whole lot of the Jerries, but I haven't heard so much tonight about them. I think they are rather impressed with the miserableness of the creatures, and the two kitchen men and I dare-say others as well have been waiting on their foes and ministering to them during the day very goodheartedly. It's always our way to make a great fuss and show of resentment and antagonism and then to behave in just the opposite way when there is any actual opportunity, much to the surprise of the enemy who can't make our attitude out at all.

At present everything in the ward is peaceful and quiet. Soon it will be my suppertime and I shall hie away through the snow up to the little Mess truck where we partake of our nocturnal feast. Life seems very dull just now, no concerts for us night birds to go to and no attractions out of doors these bitter cold days. Most days I get out for some exercise and fresh air, as it is a bad plan to go to bed straight away without any 'breather' at all. I find my room companion quite pleasant though talkative. She and I go about a good deal together, neither having any other friend to fly to.

FRIDAY, 15TH FEBRUARY

What with one thing and another the days have slipped away and the nights too, so fast that the poor old diary is many days behind. Tonight finds me in the Sick Sisters ward where I have been since Tuesday. Took Jones's place at Matron's command, and she went down to Lamb's ward, and Lamb came to my ward, so there was a general post for no apparent reason except that Matron wanted to give Jones a shift from this ward and send her to an easier one as she seemed to feel it a job. It has been a job too and I very well know it.

There were only four patients when I came but one, Miss McArthur, was very ill indeed with flu developing later into pneumonia and I spent three nights of practically constant waiting on her. She was one of the YMCA workers and such a nice girl, or seemed to be, but of course when I first saw her she was very ill then and not quite normal, too feverish to be bothered much. Her aunt is working here at the same YMCA, rather a fussy lady but very well meaning and kindly. She and a friend were looking after the girl most anxiously, and well they might for she got steadily worse and the second night I was here she was already on the SI list and had developed pneumonia with the worst of symptoms. Her aunt and friend stayed all night, sleeping in one of the rooms in this ward and looking very fussed and anxious. Sister Smith the night super and I watched over the invalid, at least I did most of the watching. Sister relieved me once or twice when she had the opportunity. Miss McArthur's parents had been sent for by this time and next day she was so ill that it seemed doubtful whether her people would come in time. However, she lived on till 5 in the morning and her father and mother arrived at 7 p.m. and were able to be with her all night. She wasn't really conscious and not able to speak to them but sometimes seemed dimly aware of their presence. Poor little thing and poor parents. It was dreadfully pathetic. I practically never left the room all night except for short intervals. It was a bit of a strain to one's nerves and a very harrowing time. I felt quite overwrought in the morning. Sister and I had to lay the body out, which took a good while, and then had to scramble my morning's work as well as I could, so it was a great rush altogether.

There is plenty to do always in the mornings here with all the little odds and ends of jobs and no orderly to assist one. The stoking of the fires alone is quite a business through the night. These last two nights I have had to do the WAACs as well as Sick Sisters, Matron evidently considering we are not sufficiently employed with only two convalescent patients here to look after. I was looking forward to a nice restful time after the three strenuous nights and so was much disappointed to have this extra charge foisted upon me. However it just has to be done, so one must carry on and make the best of it, although it keeps me pretty well on the go most of the night for there are extra fires to be looked after and sixteen patients in the two wards who need attention. All flu cases in various stages and they seem nice girls but I have had very little opportunity to speak to them.

I went this morning to Miss McArthur's funeral, joining forces with Sister McGregor and Sister Strike who were deputed by Matron to represent her at the funeral. It was a big affair, very well attended by all the YMCA workers in the neighbourhood and some rather sad-looking Tommies who must have been in her classes. She used to lecture and teach the men. She was an educational worker and doing very good and clever work apparently, only twenty-five too, so she was quite young. It was a very sad thing altogether, the poor parents looked broken down with grief. I spoke to them just to say goodbye after the funeral. The aunt was there too, supporting and staying the bereaved parents and looking very broken down herself. The ceremony was quite simple but conducted with all the military honours as befitted the girl's work among the soldiers.

It has seemed queer these two nights to have no one in that room at the end of the corridor, the scene of so much bustle and coming and going. It almost gives me the creeps for the very quietness and loneliness of it. This is a very quiet ward altogether, different from the men's wards where there is always some sound to break the monotony. Before I left 16 there was plenty doing as we entirely filled up one end with Bosches who couldn't be accommodated elsewhere. One was so ill that he died only a day or two after being admitted. He was just skin and bone and the MOs said from the first that there was no hope for him. Anyway, he gave us some busy nights, and then the two convoys in kept us fully occupied during two nights too. So altogether we were having rather a strenuous time. Then I was suddenly switched away, and not much more rest for the wicked to be found here.

The frost seems to have gone tonight, whether temporarily or permanently remains to be seen, but the ground is in a fearful state with the thaw and one walks in oceans of mud over these soft paths. I had two days of strenuous tobogganing which I quite enjoyed though it was hard work, but the weather was simply glorious with bright hot sun and shining white snow. The nonconformist padre took us out and was loaned the sledges from the officers. They were first-rate ones and I only wished the run had been longer. It seemed such a short distance to fly down and such a long tramp back again.

Now I am getting very sleepy and tired so must make another round of my wards to wake me up again. Whalley went home yesterday for good. Sister Searle goes quite soon and very soon I shall be quite deserted by all my friends and must hurry up and get home too.

WEDNESDAY, 20TH FEBRUARY

Am disgracefully sleepy but that's simply with having so little to do. The ward is still very slack – only four convalescent patients under my care and three WAACs over in Observation all suffering mildly from scabies, which is not a very exciting complaint. The little French girl whose fiancé comes from Rothesay of all places seems to be getting on well but looks rather dull, having no one to speak to all day. She has not had her tonsils out yet and apparently can't do so until her throat clears up a bit which it doesn't seem in a hurry to do. I practise my French on her in great style and love to hear her speaking so prettily.

Went out to a concert yesterday afternoon at 5.30 getting up at 4.15 from my comfortable and beloved bed to attend the function. Paul went too and two others of the night staff and we enjoyed the entertainment very much. It was really very good and made me laugh very much, parts of it anyway. It is quite a long time since I went to a really good concert, or in fact any concert at all. I have generally been too lazy to get up but this one was supposed to be exceptionally good and I made a great effort and went.

MONDAY, 24TH FEBRUARY

I was too sleepy to be very coherent the last time I wrote the diary and had to leave off abruptly when somnolence completely overcame me. There was no time for snoozing last night. I have been fearing a move for the last few nights as I was so slack in Sick Sisters and nearly all the wards in the compound were rampant with flu cases. However, I was spared till last night when Matron gave me orders to spend the night in 15 ward, where Sister Wales is already established and coping with several very bad pneumonia cases. There must be quite eight of them and six on the DI list and three on the SI list, a very heavy percentage in a ward of 48 or so patients, according to our usual reckoning. This wretched epidemic seems quite as bad out here as the last and likely to carry off numbers now of our people's precious lives. The three of us – Sister, the orderly and self – were kept going the whole night, hurrying from one to the other of the worst invalids and administering cough medicines to noisy coughers, of which there are a great many.

The night before I relieved in 17 ward, while Lamb was away at supper and I thought I had never heard such a variety of coughs in that short time in the whole of my nursing experience. Loud, short, hoarse, wet, dry, barking, bronchitic and sepulchral. Sometimes one at a time, sometimes all together in concert or else duet and twosome, in a variation to the concert. I wondered really how anyone could stand being in the ward the whole night with such a racket. The coughers in 15 last night were not nearly so persistent, though noisy enough at times. Some of these men make no effort at all to suppress their cough, they just put their heads out from under the bedclothes where they have usually retired into invisibility and just make as much noise as they possibly can. Then if you go up to them with a dose of cough mixture, they either subside utterly and appear to be sound asleep, or else the paroxysm grows ten times worse and you have to stand there glass in hand till the worst is over and you can deliver the dose and a word in season all the same. One could write a whole book on coughs and coughers. Another peculiarity is the way a man will cough and cough while you are out of the ward and the moment you get inside the door with the medicine and try to detect the sinner, there is the silence of the grave throughout the ward. No one stirs. Everyone sleeps soundly. You go back into the bunk and put away the medicine and sit down comfortably again and begin reading or writing, when off starts the cough again and you have to repeat the process of investigation. I have been three or four times into the ward like that with increasing degrees of rage and finally when I have found the villainous patient he is probably coughing in his sleep and is much insulted at being woken up to take some medicine.

One of the men's relatives, a very poorly dressed and grimy mother, came late last night to see her son. She seemed calm and tired with the journey and spent most of the night sleeping on a bed behind a screen at the end of the ward. Her boy is very ill though not quite one of the worst, but she was saddened by the sight of him this morning in daylight. He certainly looked rather far through then.

I have just completed the operation of washing my hair and am sitting up in bed now and hope soon to be peacefully slumbering. Paul is already 'well away'. She has had a hard night too and seems very tired.

SUNDAY, 2ND MARCH, 2.20 A.M.

Have had yet another move since last writing. This time, back to my old haunts – 16 ward and also to 10, which is diphtherias but fairly convalescent. Both Sisters Mackenzie and Shields, who had charge of these two wards respectively, are too busy now with bad flu cases to carry on their oversight, so Matron has given them over to my care and much to my regret removed me from the sheltering precincts of Sick Sisters. Had just got settled in there and was enjoying life very much. Not too strenuous, yet a fair amount to do, and I enjoyed the company of the Sick Sisters for a change. But still here I am, back with the Tommies again and have to make the best of it and settle down to the new conditions again. No one in either ward requires much special care, so I have quite peaceful nights. A small evacuation of three walking cases goes out this morning from this ward – the dips. Otherwise, there are no excitements before me.

Flu is still rampant and nearly every flu ward has one or more bad cases, which, sad to say, nearly all end fatally. There have been four deaths in 15 ward in a sadly short space of time and one or two more of the cases there are very serious. Nothing seems to be of any use in these pneumonia cases. No amount of careful nursing attention can check it and the MOs are getting really rather depressed by the hopelessness of the disease, they feel so helpless in the face of its virulence.

The Bosch are everywhere, all over the hospital now. There are some in this ward – cheerful mortals too they seem – and of course in 16 ward, half of it is entirely Bosches. They are the same old lot that I admitted when I was last there before, all convalescent now and all up except for old Borak, the typhoid case, who needs more careful nursing. Capt. Ward was saying this evening, when he was in calling, that a most vigorous investigation of the POW camps up the line is being carried out owing to the condition some of these prisoners arrive here in, and in one case the whole staff of a camp has been put under arrest, so evidently things were not as they should be. The prisoners seem to be literally starved when they come down from some of these up-the-line camps, and though one doesn't cherish any feelings of great tenderness towards the Hun, it is still only fair to treat them with decency and some degree of humanity. Down at the bases here they do very well. Almost sometimes one is inclined to think they really get a bit spoilt, especially in hospital where they are treated of course just like our own men and are not allowed to want for anything. It is astonishing to see how little the average Bosch realizes the defeat of his country. It almost seems sometimes as though they believed themselves to be the conquerors or at least to have divided the honours equally, and consequently to be able to be on perfectly friendly and brotherly terms with their quondam foes. Our men rather encourage them too, certainly in hospital, to let bygones be bygones, treating them rather as amusing pets and sometimes making quite a fuss of them. We are queer creatures, and it's no wonder foreigners can never understand us.

I feel rather forlorn having now lost Paul, my last hope and stay in the matter of companionship. She has got her moving orders for Boulogne to go as a cook to Miss McCarthy's office and went off rather in a hurry, being wanted at short notice. Not altogether relishing the prospect of the new work, especially the cooking which rather alarmed her. So now I have to have one of the new Sisters in my room, a poor exchange, though she seems a harmless sort of little person. I miss the nice sociable intercourse with a VAD.

THURSDAY, 6TH MARCH, 3.30 A.M.

Only just time for a few lines before preparing the morning repast. These nights seem to go so fast that there is no time to spare for any dawdling. I have nine patients in now. One of the new Sisters was admitted yesterday with flu(?) and general upset. She was on night duty and a most queer little person who appears to have come from 47 General, Le Tréport, accompanied with the soubriquet 'Susie'! She had great ideas of setting us all right and teaching us the way we should go at mealtimes. When she presided we were hardly allowed to open our mouths to make a remark. All 'shop' was utterly forbidden. I was rather concerned when I heard she had been admitted here, wondering whether I should be kept on the trot all night. However, she has been very quiet and not made a murmur since the light was put out.

I am plagued just now by imagining that the various invalids are ringing their bells. It is difficult to hear them always, and just now especially, as the rain is pattering down heavily, drowning all other sounds, one can quite well imagine that one hears the sound of a distant bell through the noise of the rain. I must say though, all the patients have been very good and quiet tonight and made no stir at all. Last night I was kept much more on the go, as some of them were quite seedy and needed attention from time to time. I am quite happy back in my old home again and even though the mornings are rather hectic, I like them better really for a change than the men's wards, which are more restless and more difficult to look after. I only had a very few nights down in the other wards before Matron recalled me here again. Sister Shields had come in then with bad flu, along with one or two other new ones, so Sister Rusk who was running both officers and this ward found it too much to do to look after so many patients and give them adequate attention.

I have done a good deal of night duty and am thinking my time must be getting rather short. Matron said yesterday that this hospital would probably be closing in a month's time and if that's so, Étaples – that muddy old place – won't see us much longer. I wonder where we shall go to then. Not home certainly, if one knows the Army ways and anyway, general demobilization won't begin before peace is signed which doesn't seem likely to happen before April.

Feel now as though I shouldn't mind when I get to go home. Sister Searle went yesterday afternoon so that is the last of my friends gone, and I have no one now that I am in the least interested in or care to take up with. Certainly there is no one on night duty who presents the least attractions to my fastidious spirit. There is a sort of feeling everywhere of just carrying on, with everyone rather stale and tired of work and tired of the state of things. But matters are not too bright at home, with the flu and strikes and one thing and another. Let's hope that the country pulls itself together soon and emerges better and stronger in every way.

That poor girl who went on the trip up the line died at the Tino a day or two ago, so she paid dearly for three days of pleasure. She couldn't have been very strong or else she must have got very chilled indeed with the travelling and certainly the weather was dreadfully cold.

I meant to go to the woods this morning to pick daffodils, which I believe are all out now or coming out fast. Last year they were lovely, and close on their heels followed the wild hyacinths and primroses and periwinkles. I wonder if we shall be here to see those again. It seems queer to see the seasons round year after year, in these foreign lands.

This finishes my volume. Next will come the 'peace' number of the diary and will see me home again I expect.

Dorothea Mary Lynette Crewdson
died on 12 March 1919 of peritonitis.

A memorial service was held at
Holy Trinity Church, Lenton (Nottingham)
on 21 March 1919.

Dorothea in 1918: the four stripes on her uniform mark her four years of service.

Matron's letter to Mrs Crewdson:

13 March 1919
46 Stationary Hospital
BEF France

Dear Mrs Crewdson,

I am dreadfully grieved to have to write you of the death of your dear daughter. She was apparently in good health till the night of March 8th when she reported at 8 p.m. unfit to go on duty (she was on night duty) owing to a 'bilious attack'. Next morning – Sunday – the sickness had stopped though she had still a feeling of nausea. In the evening she felt well enough to have some tea and toast and said with the exception of a headache she was better, and was going to take some aspirins and would be alright after she had slept. Her temperature was 98.8 next morning though apparently later her temperature was 100 when I asked the Colonel (Doctor) to see her and she was taken to Sick Sisters quarters where she seemed to be going on satisfactorily till the morning of Wednesday at 2 a.m. when she had an attack of severe abdominal pain and began to vomit. She was then seen by Sir John Rose Bradford and Mr Beazly surgeons and they decided it was necessary to operate. The operation was not done here – her bed was placed on a wheeled stretcher and taken to 24 General Hospital where there is an operating theatre. The operation was done at 1.30 p.m. about and she died at 2.45 p.m. Just before leaving here she gave me her money and clock to keep for her and I told her I would write you and she said give them all my love. I had meant to see her later in the day when she had recovered from the operation and perhaps get other messages for you, but alas it was not to be.

It has been a dreadful shock to us all (as she was always apparently so well and healthy) and to you all what must it be. I know she was a devoted daughter and sister. Here she was loved by everyone – so thorough, thoughtful and reliable was she that any seriously ill patient who had her for a nurse was more than fortunate – and so honourable gentle and loyal, always working straight on out to help and helping with all her mind as well as her body. She is a serious loss.

We laid her to rest at half past nine o'clock this morning in the Military Cemetery which your son can describe to you. There were many beautiful wreaths from nursing staffs of the various hospitals, also officers and orderlies, but the one that touched me most was a large Maltese Cross of daffodils – 'with deep sympathy and loving gratitude from the patients of 46 Stationary Hospital'. The men made it all themselves sitting late into the night to do so and it was the most beautiful.

Dear Mrs Crewdson words are useless and sense of loss and heart-break are so acute at such a time – but I have sometimes wondered whether if the Choice was given it would not be the most glorious and happy death to go off in the midst of work. No long waiting and wasting illness, just laying down tools at the end of a happy day and walking into the light – and your dear girl was perfectly happy in her work. Forgive this long letter, but I wished you to know all I have written.

With my most sincere sympathy, believe me,

Yrs v sincerely,

M.F. McCord

Matron

22 APRIL–25 MAY 1915

The Second Battle of Ypres   One of the most horrific engagements of the war: the German forces preceded their offensive with their first use of poison gas, against which the French and Canadian forces had no defence and suffered terrible casualties. Having advanced about two miles the Germans were held by the British Second Army, and after that gained little extra ground, although the city of Ypres was now within artillery range of the German guns. Their offensive was called off on 24 May, but minor engagements continued during June, including the British attempt to recapture the château and small village of Hooge, with many casualties. Unlike Verdun, at the extreme opposite end of the Allied defence line, Ypres was not a specially constructed fortress, but it became the key point in the Flanders line of defence as it blocked German access to Calais and Boulogne, the Channel ports which were essential to the BEF in maintaining reinforcements and supplies, and for the evacuation of the wounded. Despite being flattened to the ground by shellfire by the end of the war, Ypres was never taken by the Germans. Dorothea and Christie arrived at Le Tréport about three weeks after the end of the battle.

25 APRIL 1915

Allied landing at Gallipoli   With stalemate on the Western Front, the Allied forces had mounted a joint naval attack on Gallipoli in February, on the western shore of the Dardanelles, with the object of taking Constantinople. The Gallipoli campaign was a catastrophic failure, with great loss of life. The decision was eventually taken to withdraw the troops at the end of the year.

JULY–AUGUST 1915

Fighting continued in the Ypres sector with very little ground gained on either side, but heavy casualties were suffered as the forces faced each other at such close quarters.

25 SEPTEMBER 1915

The Battle of Loos   The BEF's second major engagement of 1915 was planned as a combined offensive with the French Army, another attempt to break out of the fixed lines and hastily constructed trench system before the onset of winter. Before the offensive, the order came for all hospitals to be cleared in preparation for the inevitable casualties. The battle was a disaster: the British forces suffered more than 50,000 casualties with nothing to show for it. The principal blame fell on the Commander-in-Chief Sir John French, who was replaced by Sir Douglas Haig shortly afterwards.

13 OCTOBER 1915

The final stage of the Battle of Loos was the attempt to capture the strongest defensive position, known as the Hohenzollern Redoubt, created around an old mining dump. Despite gallant fighting for which two Victoria Crosses were awarded, the attack failed.

JANUARY 1916

The outlook for the Allied forces at the beginning of 1916 was particularly bleak. Their Russian allies were struggling on the Eastern Front; the campaign in the Dardanelles had ended in failure and crippling losses at Gallipoli; and on the Western Front, despite a steady stream of casualties, the stalemate could not be broken.

FEBRUARY–MARCH 1916

The Battle of The Bluff   The Germans attacked a strongpoint three miles south-east of Ypres, an artificial hill known as The Bluff. There were nearly 1,300 casualties. The British recaptured the hill on 2 March, but suffered more than 1,600 casualties. The German subsequent counter-attacks failed. British soldiers were issued with steel helmets for the first time.

24–28 APRIL 1916

Easter Rising   There were anxious moments before the British forces had the situation in Dublin under control, nipping a full-scale Irish rebellion in the bud.

APRIL 1916

German Offensive at Loos   Fighting continued in the Loos area. Dorothea refers to a gas attack which occurred at Hulluch, taking the Irish Brigade by surprise. The Germans fired non-poisonous gas shells first, so no precautions were taken, which they followed with poison gas.

1 JULY–18 NOVEMBER 1916

The Battle of the Somme   Planned by General Joffre and Field Marshal Haig as a massive attempt to break up the German line and restore some movement on the Western Front, and also to relieve some of the pressure on Verdun where huge numbers of French troops were still engaged. After months of preparation, the Germans were well aware that the attack was imminent. The first day of the battle has become notorious for the appalling record of casualties suffered by the British infantry, through faulty tactics and the artillery's failure to shatter the barbed-wire defences. What is less often remembered is that despite this terrible first day, the battle continued to rage for three months with varying degrees of success for the Allied armies. When it was finally over Field Marshal Hindenburg, the German supremo, decided to withdraw his armies to a stronger position between ten and thirty miles back from the original line.

SEPTEMBER 1916

The British Army in its southern sector, along with the French, made steady advances against fierce opposition in the Somme. The casualties arriving at No. 16 at this time were probably those wounded in the attack on Guillemont or in the capture of Delville Wood.

15 SEPTEMBER 1916

This day was claimed as 'the greatest British victory gained up to date in the war'. Some of the famous place names of the Somme battle were finally captured and secured on this day – Martinpuich, High Wood, Delville Wood and Flers.

OCTOBER 1916

The Battle of the Somme was in its closing weeks. Despite appalling casualties significant advances had been made and German self-confidence in its 'invincible' army badly dented. The British front line was now about seven miles east of its position at the start of the battle.

NOVEMBER–DECEMBER 1916

The end of the Somme Campaign on 18 November left a sort of grim vacuum. What would happen next? Were the terrible battles and the vast number of casualties justified? On the Eastern Front and in Greece the war was going badly, Romania had been crushed and was now subject to German occupation. It was a depressing prospect; with the onset of winter the end of the war appeared to be nowhere in sight.

18 DECEMBER 1916

The end of the siege of Verdun

The longest, costliest battle on the Western Front began when Verdun was attacked by powerful German forces in February 1916, and was fiercely defended in succession by every division in the French Army. The German objective was to weaken the French by a process of attrition. In the event their own casualties in the siege were just as severe.

1917

1917 turned out to be the most deeply depressing year of the war. The French and the British Armies both had disasters, the French in April in the so-called Nivelle Offensive, named after the General in command, and the British at Passchendaele; the only difference was that half the French infantry regiments mutinied after their battle, whereas the British ploughed grimly on. However, the Allied fortunes were transformed when America entered the war in April 1917.

9 APRIL–16 MAY 1917

The Battle of Arras Planned to coincide with the French Nivelle Offensive, a large British force had been preparing during the winter months to attack the Germans on a twelve-mile front stretching from Arras to Lens. As the German front line was almost in the eastern suburbs of Arras, a huge amount of tunnelling had secretly taken place under the city. On 9 April, using the tunnels, the assaulting troops achieved complete surprise. The battle continued with mixed results and inevitably very heavy casualties until the end of May. The most notable event on the first day of the battle was the brilliant capture by the Canadians of the high and very steep Vimy Ridge.

22 APRIL 1917

The Second Battle of Dover Strait   Two British destroyers engaged a superior force of two flotillas of German torpedo boats whose mission was to bombard Dover and Calais and the Dover Barrage, the linear minefield that blocked the Channel to German shipping. One of the British ships was heavily damaged; two German ships sank.

7 JUNE 1917

The Battle of Messines   This followed a massive detonation of mines which British tunnellers had set under the German front line, causing major dislocation. The attack was carried out by the British Second Army involving ten divisions and was completely successful in gaining its objective. Anzac, New Zealander and Irish soldiers (including a Southern Irish division) participated in the battle.

31 JULY 1917

'Passchendaele', or the Third Battle of Ypres   The impact of this battle was like no other, because the soldiers were fighting not just the Germans but also the weather. After the hot and sultry July weeks, it rained every single day of August, and the combination of the massive bombardment of the battlefield and the notorious Flanders mud made conditions not just impossible but horrific. Troops had to fight across what had become a giant, dark brown honeycomb. Unless immediately pulled out by comrades, anyone falling into a 'cell' would suffocate or drown. It is not always remembered that the 55,000 names recorded on the Menin Gate at Ypres are only those who 'went missing' and have no known graves, nor that 35,000 similar 'missing' casualties are recorded on the Tyne Cot Cemetery Memorial nearby because there was no room for their names on the Menin Gate. Haig's insistence that the battle must be continued through August despite the terrible weather was his worst mistake of the war. When the weather eventually improved in September the Allied advance petered out and the little village of Passchendaele was as far as they got. Later, in their March 1918 Lys Offensive, the Germans quickly recovered all the ground lost.

SEPTEMBER 1917

The German air raids on British bases in France would become an increasingly serious problem over the next ten months, although not so much in the winter.

21 MARCH 1918

The German Spring Offensive   After a very quiet winter 'up at the front', the collapse of Russia, which signed a peace treaty with Germany at Brest-Litovsk on 3 March, made a new German offensive on the Western Front, reinforced by all its Eastern divisions, almost inevitable. Using new tactics and successfully disguising their build-up, the German forces achieved total surprise and the British Fifth Army was in full retreat. The Germans advanced about twenty miles towards Amiens before they were halted on 5 April. If they had succeeded in capturing Amiens they would have effectively split the Allied armies (as indeed they did in 1940), and the French and British might well have decided to join their new American allies in peace negotiations, which had been under discussion by various intermediaries during the previous twelve months.

5–29 APRIL 1918

The Battle of the Lys   German forces were halted ten miles outside Amiens, but that was as far as they got. On 9 April the second German offensive, known as the Battle of the Lys, was launched against the British First and Second Armies further north in the Ypres sector. The objective was to break through the Allied lines and capture the Channel ports. Haig issued his famous Order of the Day on 11 April: 'With our backs to the wall ... each one of us must fight to the end.' The ruined city of Ypres remained in British hands and the German dash for the ports ended on 14 April. Although there were more offensives during the summer, the German grand design to smash the Allied armies before the Americans could engage in the war had failed. But the Germans attacked again, this time with the objective of capturing the hill south-west of Ypres known as Mount Kemmel which overlooked the whole country to the west. The hill was captured on 25 April and another close by, Scherpenberg, four days later, but German losses were very severe, and they lacked the reserves needed to continue the offensive. With the Germans having advanced altogether about ten miles, the battle ended. This was to be the last German offensive of the war in Flanders.

20 MAY 1918

The German Air Offensive   After the German High Command
had taken a strategic decision to call off their bombing campaign of
London and other major English cities, the big Gotha bombers were
assigned to new targets: the British bases in northern France were an
obvious choice. It was of course a breach of the Geneva Convention
to bomb hospitals, whose red crosses were clearly visible from
the air, but no doubt the Germans took the view that if the British
established hospitals in the middle of an Army base and alongside
a railway line it was just bad luck if they happened to be hit. The
air raids would continue intermittently (and almost nightly when
weather conditions were favourable) for nearly three months. They
were very unsettling and stretched some of the hospital personnel
almost to breaking point. The worst thing about working in hospitals
during air raids was that it was impossible for the bedridden patients
and the staff on duty looking after them to take cover. Three of the
Étaples hospitals were very seriously damaged and were closed down
as a result of this and subsequent air raids, the worst one on 31 May.

8 AUGUST 1918

The Final Allied Advance   After more than six weeks' intense
preparation carried on under the strictest security, the Allied armies,
British, French and American, launched their major offensive against
a German Army weakened and demoralized by the failure of the four
Ludendorff campaigns which had been fiercely fought since March
and which had so nearly broken through the Allied defences. It was
the beginning of the end, and would lead without interruption, despite
heavy casualties on both sides, to the end of the war and signing of the
Armistice in November.

27 SEPTEMBER 1918

The British Offensive on the Cambrai Front led to the storming of
the Hindenburg Line, which the Allied forces took and passed in
the following weeks. There was little now in the way of formidable
defensive positions to bar the entry into Germany.

11 NOVEMBER 1918

The Armistice was signed at 5 a.m. and came into effect at 11 a.m.

APPENDIX

Dame Maud McCarthy, GBE

If Florence Nightingale in the Crimean War was 'The Lady with the Lamp' then Maud McCarthy in the First World War was surely 'The Lady with the Notebook'. Working throughout the war in France from August 1914 until August 1919 she carried the ultimate responsibility for the British and Colonial Nursing Services on her shoulders, with a very small staff in a little office in Abbeville. The office was responsible for the deployment of all nursing staff, but she made all the important decisions. She also kept a detailed daily record of everything she had done or dealt with. This in its entirety can be accessed on the internet (www.scarletfinders.co.uk) and is an invaluable source of information about the First World War Nursing Services, and all its daily problems.

Miss McCarthy created her own job. She had been a Matron in military hospitals since the end of the South African War and Principal Matron at the War Office since 1910, but neither of these appointments would have prepared her for the enormous scope of her job as Matron-in-Chief of the BEF in France, a responsibility that only grew as more and more hospitals and clearing stations were required to deal with the hundreds of thousands of wounded and sick soldiers. With no deputy, she did everything herself, including the round of visits to hospitals and casualty clearing stations that she made almost every week.

Dorothea, like all VADs and nurses, was very much in awe of her, and in August 1916 indignantly recorded in the diary the cruel treatment which Miss Drage appeared to have experienced when interviewed by her on her way to her new hospital appointment. Miss McCarthy's notes indicate that this was almost certainly a misunderstanding. She had had to transfer Miss Drage as a matter of urgency from No. 16 to No. 23 General at Étaples because of the chaotic state of that hospital, which had been run up to that point very unsatisfactorily by an American team of nurses called the Chicago Unit. The unit was now leaving. Miss McCarthy commented in her notebook that 'the need of suitable people for the large units for Matrons becomes increasingly difficult daily'. So it is most likely that Miss Drage's shocked appearance when she emerged from the interview was due to her horror at what she had just been asked to undertake, to bring up to standard a very run-down hospital with virtually no nursing staff. It was not surprising that one of the first things she did after taking over as Matron was to ask for nine VADs to be sent from No. 16.

When Miss McCarthy made a visit of inspection at No. 16 a few weeks later she reported that 'everything in this unit is as usual in first-rate order'. She must therefore have regarded Miss Drage as one of her best Matrons, even if not always the easiest to deal with.

Dame Maud (as she became in 1919) finally retired on the fifth anniversary of the outbreak of the war, on 4 August 1919. She was given a grand dinner in Boulogne and a great send-off ceremony on the quay the next day, shaking hands with everyone, before she embarked for the cross-Channel voyage. By that time most of the British military hospitals in France had been closed. There were just nine still open; the last of them (at Abbeville) closed in January 1920.

Dame Maud McCarthy died in London at the age of 89 in 1949.

W&N

blog and newsletter

For exclusive short stories, poems, extracts, essays, articles, interviews, trailers, competitions and much more visit the Weidenfeld & Nicolson blog and sign up for the newsletter at:

www.wnblog.co.uk

Follow us on
 and **twitter**

Or scan the code to access the website*

... very ... I should feel much
... to quite good at work.
thorough & methodical but
... exact & hating being
... I sent home £6 of my pay
... yesterday, though it had
to go back to England anyway
... much good out here &
really robbery getting so much
worth ...

... and am still
... occasional visits
... self dry with her
P.P. ... an after...

... trying ... the ...
... sea & the,
... the sand de...
... afternoon ...

... etc. was
... alone, ha...
... settle down
... feels very dou...
morning. ...
all possession
... & daily's
removal of ...

... had to sup...
speedily afte...

Rooney.

settled down here for the